The Social Psychology of Music

The Social Psychology of Music

Edited by

DAVID J. HARGREAVES

Reader in Psychology, University of Leicester

and

ADRIAN C. NORTH

Lecturer in Psychology, University of Leicester

OXFORD

UNIVERSITY PRESS

OXFORD

UNIVERSITY PRESS

Great Clarendon Street, Oxford OX2 6DP

Oxford University Press is a department of the University of Oxford.
It furthers the University's objective of excellence in research, scholarship,
and education by publishing worldwide in

Oxford New York

Athens Auckland Bangkok Bogotá Buenos Aires Calcutta
Cape Town Chennai Dar es Salaam Delhi Florence Hong Kong Istanbul
Karachi Kuala Lumpur Madrid Melbourne Mexico City Mumbai
Nairobi Paris São Paulo Singapore Taipei Tokyo Toronto Warsaw
with associated companies in Berlin Ibadan

Oxford is a registered trade mark of Oxford University Press
in the UK and in certain other countries

Published in the United States
by Oxford University Press Inc., New York

A catalogue record for this book is available from the British Library

Library of Congress Cataloging in Publication Data
The social psychology of music / edited by David J. Hargreaves and
Adrian C. North.
Includes bibliographical references and indexes.
1. Music—Psychology. 2. Music and society.
I. Hargreaves, David J. (David John), 1948 -. II. North, Adrian C.
ML3830.S57 1997 781'.11—dc21 96-45586
ISBN 0 19 852383 1

Printed in Great Britain by Bookcraft (Bath) Ltd, Midsomer Norton, Avon

Preface

It goes almost without saying that music exists in a social context. The many and varied ways in which people create, perform, perceive, and react to musical sounds are vitally dependent on the particular situations in which they do so. This includes the specific places, times, and other people present in those situations, as well as the broader historical and cultural context of musical behaviour. Surprisingly little attention has been paid to this aspect of music psychology, and this book attempts to redress the balance.

One of us wrote about a decade ago that 'music psychology has probably never been in a healthier state than as at present: the explosion of research over the last decade or so has meant that specialized tributaries of the mainstream are beginning to emerge' (Hargreaves 1986). In the intervening years the health of the discipline has improved still further, such that the tributaries of cognitive and developmental music psychology are now well established and thriving in their own right. Our aim in this book is to identify and explore another tributary which might be called the social psychology of music. A book with this title was first published by Paul R. Farnsworth in 1954, and a second edition appeared 15 years later (Farnsworth 1969). Farnsworth was explicitly interested in the cultural determinants of musical behaviour as distinct from its biological and physical bases, although a sizeable proportion of the book's contents did in fact deal with the latter.

We have two main motives in compiling this book. The first arises from developments in other areas of psychology: there is a clearly-identifiable move towards the study of the social and cultural context as an integral and inextricable part of many aspects of behaviour and cognition, and this is long overdue in the psychology of music. The second motive arises from the technological changes which have occurred since Farnsworth first tried to delineate the field, of which one of the most prominent is the increasing availability and networking of personal computers. The growth and increasing popularity of the Internet in the mid-1990s is already pointing the way towards centrally-held music libraries which are stored digitally, and which are potentially available to all users of the worldwide computer network. Although the commercial and legal implications of these developments have yet to be worked out, their potential effects on people's use of music in the next century are diverse and far-reaching.

The development of digital technology has also had a direct impact on the creation, recording, and performance of music over the last 15 years or so. At the centre of this has been the development of MIDI (the Musical Instrument

Digital Interface), a digital language which enables musical sounds to be coded in such a way that they can be recognized, stored, and manipulated by computers. This development has already had a profound impact on the recording industry, revolutionizing the ways in which music is recorded, processed, and transferred between locations. Aside from the mechanics of recording and storage, it is already becoming apparent that these techno-logical developments are having a direct effect upon the working methods of composers in many musical genres; upon attitudes towards composition and performance; and upon the accessibility of these activities to sections of the population who would not hitherto have had the means, or perhaps even the interest, in taking part.

Another welcome effect is the general breakdown between musical style barriers, in particular the long-standing polarity between 'serious' music (usually synonymous with Western 'classical' styles, the province of the traditional 'composer') and other forms of 'popular' music, including jazz, folk, pop, and others too numerous to mention, in which oral and aural means of communication are often equally, if not more, appropriate than written notation. Such divisions are becoming a thing of the past in many contemporary educational and musical institutions in that all forms of world music are seen as having equal validity, relevance, and indeed, seriousness. Put simply, musical behaviour has become increasingly ubiquitous, diverse, and 'demystified', and this is having direct effects upon the role of music in many people's lives. These changes need to be at the centre of a con-temporary view of the social psychology of music, and indeed, of music psychology as a whole.

We should like to thank all our contributors for the enthusiasm with which they accepted our invitation to contribute, and for their cheerful forbearance in dealing with our frequent editorial interventions. We are particularly grateful to John Baily, Cary Cooper, James Kellaris, Vladimir Konečni, and John Sloboda for their invaluable comments on early drafts of some of the chapters, including our own. Finally, we should like to thank Vanessa Whitting and Martin Baum of OUP for their help, efficiency, and encourage-ment at all stages of the editorial process, and Jennifer McKendrick for help with indexing.

Leicester   D.J.H.
November 1996   A.C.N.

REFERENCES

Farnsworth, P. R. (1954/1969). *The social psychology of music.* Iowa State University Press, Ames, Iowa.

Hargreaves, D. J. (1986). *The developmental psychology of music.* Cambridge University Press, Cambridge.

Contents

PART IV DEVELOPMENTAL ISSUES

PART VI REAL WORLD APPLICATIONS

13. Clinical and therapeutic uses of music

Leslie Bunt

14. Music and consumer behaviour

Adrian C. North and David J. Hargreaves

Contributors

Leslie Bunt   Music Space Trust, The Southville Centre, Beauley Road, Bristol BS3 1QG, UK

W. Ray Crozier   University of Wales – Cardiff, School of Education Annexe, 42 Park Place, Cardiff CF1 3BB, UK

Jane W. Davidson   Department of Music, The University, Sheffield S10 2TN, UK

Su-lin Gan   Office for Graduate Studies, College of Communication, University of Alabama, Box 870172, Tuscaloosa, AL 35487-0172, USA

Andrew H. Gregory   Department of Psychology, University of Manchester, Oxford Road, Manchester M13 9PL, UK

David J. Hargreaves   Department of Psychology, The University, Leicester LE1 7RH, UK

Michael J. A. Howe   Department of Psychology, University of Exeter, Perry Road, Exeter EX4 4QG, UK

Anthony E. Kemp   Department of the Arts and Humanities in Education, University of Reading, Bulmershe Court, Earley, Reading RG6 1HY, UK

Adrian C. North   Department of Psychology, The University, Leicester LE1 7RH, UK

Bengt Olsson   School of Music and Musicology, University of Gothenburg, PO Box 4539, S-402 29 Gothenburg, Sweden

Susan A. O'Neill   Department of Psychology, The University, Keele, Staffs ST5 5BG, UK

Philip A. Russell   Department of Psychology, King's College, University of Aberdeen, Old Aberdeen AB9 2UB, UK

Dean Keith Simonton   Department of Psychology, University of California, Davis, CA 95616, USA

John A. Sloboda   Department of Psychology, The University, Keele, Staffs ST5 5BG, UK

Glenn D. Wilson   Department of Psychology, Institute of Psychiatry, University of London, Denmark Hill, London SE5 8AF, UK

Dolf Zillmann   Office for Graduate Studies, College of Communication, University of Alabama, Box 870172, Tuscaloosa, AL 35487-0172, USA

1 | *The social psychology of music*

David J. Hargreaves and Adrian C. North

Music has many different functions in human life, nearly all of which are essentially social. We use music to communicate with one another: it is possible for people from widely differing cultural backgrounds to establish contact through music even though the languages they speak may be quite incomprehensible to one another. Music can arouse deep and profound emotions within us, and these can be shared experiences between people from quite different backgrounds. From the physicist's point of view, music consists of a set of sounds with particular frequencies, amplitudes, and timbres which are organized by the composer and/or performer into highly organized and predictable patterns: what makes these sounds into music is the way in which people collectively imbue them with musical meaning, and a vital part of this process is the social and cultural context in which the sounds exist.

In other words, the psychology of music should deal with the effects of the physical properties of musical sounds themselves, with the ways in which individual listeners perceive and interpret those sounds, and with the social and interpersonal context in which musical meaning is constructed. Surprisingly little attention has been paid to the last of these, which might be described as the social psychology of music, and this book aims to redress the balance.

There are two main motives behind this enterprise. The first stems from the recent changes which have occurred in the role of music in society. As a result of the rapid technological developments which have occurred in recent years, the availability and ubiquity of music in all its forms is unprecedented in history. The growth of the mass media since the 1960s and increasing availability of relatively inexpensive records, CDs, tapes, and videos means that virtually any music can be heard by a considerable proportion of the world's population. These developments have been accompanied by advances in miniaturization and portability, which are epitomized by the ubiquitous Walkman. Such changes have also increased the range of uses that people make of music. Aside from its straightforward use as a source of intellectual and emotional pleasure, music might be used to achieve proficiency in a skilled task; to convey a particular self-image or personality; to accomplish particular aims in medicine, therapy, or education; to sell commercial products, just to name a few examples. Music takes up a larger proportion of the everyday lives of ordinary people than ever before.

The second motive relates to recent developments within psychology and social science more generally: the study of behaviour and cognition *in its social context* has become an important feature of various branches of psychology in recent years. The field of *social cognition*, or 'how people make sense of other people and themselves' (Fiske and Taylor, 1991, p. 14) has become an essential feature of contemporary social psychology, for example: the title and contents of a textbook like Eiser's (1980) *Cognitive social psychology* make this quite explicit. The same trend can clearly be seen in developmental psychology, in which an increasing amount of contemporary research emphasizes the integral role of the social context in the process of human development. Butterworth (1992), for example, writes that 'the contemporary view tends to be that cognition is *typically* situated in a social and physical context and is rarely, if ever, decontextualized' (p. 1). The old distinction between cognitive and social development is becoming increasingly unclear and irrelevant because of the inextricable link between contextual constraints and the acquisition of knowledge, and this orientation is spelt out very clearly in Durkin's (1995) recent authoritative textbook, *Developmental social psychology*.

As we said in the Preface, an important landmark is Paul R. Farnsworth's *The social psychology of music* (1954, 1969). The rationale for this book was that 'earlier workers tended to overstress the importance of the biological and physical bases of musical behavior almost to the point of ignoring its cultural determinants . . .' and therefore '. . . tried to bring the picture a little more in balance' (p. 4). Farnsworth felt that many psychomusicological investigations were severely limited in ignoring their cultural context, so that attempts to look for phenomena such as absolute standards in musical performance and taste were misguided.

Although this view coincides with our own, at least half of the chapters of Farnsworth's book deal with perceptual rather than intrinsically social pyschological topics (e.g. scales, intervals, melody, and musical ability testing), and he admits in the preface to 'a heavy emphasis on the so-called serious music of the West, with attention paid only here and there to the several varieties of jazz, to chance music, to folk music, and to other sorts of music in the Orient and the Occident' (p. xii). However, the book also includes chapters on 'Language aspects of music' and 'Applications of music to industry and therapy', and perhaps its most original and important features are the chapters on 'Nature of musical taste' and 'The measures of musical taste'. The latter contain a detailed account of Farnsworth's own pioneering research from between the 1930s and 60s on historical trends in musical taste and the eminence of composers.

The rest of this chapter falls into four main sections. In the first and second, we attempt to characterize the social psychology of music from the perspectives of music psychology and social psychology respectively. In the third, we provide a historical context for the book as a whole by describing Farnsworth's work on eminence and musical taste, and by outlining the other main areas of research as they existed in the 1950s and 60s, i.e. when the two editions of his book were published. These are sketched in the briefest detail in five subsections covering occupational studies; music education research; medical and therapeutic uses of music; research on musicianship and composition; and ethnomusicological studies respectively. In the fourth and final section, we preview the contents of the rest of the book.

PERSPECTIVES IN MUSIC PSYCHOLOGY

The rapid growth of research in music psychology has meant that several distinct tributaries of the mainstream are now clearly identifiable, the most prominent of which are those which focus on the cognitive, developmental, and social aspects of musical behaviour. These are of course closely interrelated, and indeed the interdisciplinary boundaries amongst the parent disciplines of music, musicology, psychology, education, sociology, anthropology, and cognitive science are in a constant state of change. In one sense 'music psychology' will always be an interdisciplinary area since musical behaviour itself is not functionally coherent. Unlike, say, developmental psychology, which deals with a set of functionally related behavioural phenomena (i.e. regular changes that occur with age), music cuts across a number of different psychological processes (perception, creation, cognition, skill, learning, and so on).

In a broader sense, however, it may well be fruitful to identify common concerns, and Sloboda (1986a) has made a bold attempt to establish a paradigm for the psychology of music. He suggests that 'there are five characteristics of a healthy paradigm: an agreed set of central problems; agreed methods for working on these problems; agreed theoretical frameworks in which to discuss them; techniques and theories which are specific to the paradigm; research which is appropriate to the whole range of phenomena in the domain being studied' (p. 199). Sloboda suggests that the psychology of music has reached this stage. He proposes that the central problem for music psychology is to explain *the structure and content of musical experience*, and that Lerdahl and Jackendoff's (1983) *Generative theory of tonal music* epitomizes the concerns of this paradigm, such that the psychology of music can be considered to have 'come of age'.

In making this proposal Sloboda is defining the main concerns of the discipline, with a particular focus upon cognitive psychology, and these concerns are indeed central to the other identifiable subdisciplines. They form the basis of a good deal of research in what has become known as the developmental psychology of music (see Hargreaves 1986a). Musical development continues throughout the life span, and specific theories of developmental processes and mechanisms in music have been proposed (see review by Hargreaves and Zimmerman 1992). Although this review shows that there are various different interpretations of the broad course and structure of musical and artistic development, a considerable body of detailed empirical research is emerging in this field (see Deliège and Sloboda 1996). Two other noticeable features of this subdiscipline are that it is closely related to music education, and this relationship deserves a good deal of attention (see Hargreaves 1986b). The second feature leads back to our main theme, since an increasingly prevalent trend in the developmental psychology of music is the recognition of the integral role of the social environment in explaining age-related changes.

This encourages us to pursue the social psychology of music, which of course overlaps with the cognitive and developmental subdisciplines. It is also worth considering how this newly emerging subdiscipline has antecedents and parallels in other parts of music and social science respectively. As far as music and musicology are concerned, many theorists have pointed out that musical meaning is defined essentially by reference to cultural norms. The essence of Meyer's (1956) well-known theory of musical meaning, for example, is that the communication of shared meaning via music can only take place in a cultural context. Lundin (1967) has also similarly argued that the perception of musical qualities like timbre, melody, tonality, dissonance and so on are also only possible within the rules of a given culture.

The broader perspective of social science might be represented by Nattiez (1990), who defines *musical semiology* as how a piece of music functions as an art work in society. This can be conceptualized on three levels. First, we can analyse the structural properties of the music, and this can be done at the level of the physical properties of the frequencies, timbres, etc. of the sounds involved, as well as at the level of musical structure, which is the province of music theorists and analysts. Second, it is possible to study the cultural background and context of different musical structures: historians and musicologists interpret them in relation to accepted norms and standards. The psychologist's particular perspective, which represents the third level, is to investigate the cognitive and perceptual processes which people use in forming these understandings: theorists such as Serafine (1988), for example, have proposed core cognitive processes which people use in constructing 'music' from the sounds they hear. The psychological study of music perception should take into account structural properties as well as the immediate and broader social context.

Our argument is that psychologists have neglected the social dimension, and that a social psychology of music ought to include the effects of the immediate social environment as well as the impact of broader-based cultural norms. The social psychologist's role is thus to investigate the effects of particular listening and performing/composing situations, as well as those of cultural standards and norms which the historian and the musicologist might investigate. Cross-cultural studies are one means by which the latter aim might be pursued, and the whole field of ethnomusicology, which has had little impact so far on music psychology, should be given more prominence (see Chapter 7). At the level of the immediate social situation, the growth of environmental psychology shows another promising way forward.

The characteristics of the different contexts in which music is produced and perceived have received little attention in music psychology, but some of the research to be described in this book is beginning to redress this balance. We adopt a very broad definition of social psychology, incorporating areas which display a clear social dimension (e.g. individual differences, developmental studies) alongside intrinsically social psychological phenomena such as small group and situational effects.

PERSPECTIVES IN SOCIAL PSYCHOLOGY

The field of social psychology itself is one with a complex history, and upon which many theorists have different perspectives: its very definition is by no means straightforward. Hewstone and Manstead (1995) define social psychology as 'the scientific study of the reciprocal influence of the individual and his or her social context' (p. 588): individuals have an effect upon their social environment just as this environment determines and constrains the individual's behaviour. Behind this apparently simple definition lie two distinctions in theoretical emphasis.

The first is that between what might be called psychological and sociological social psychology. The former 'seeks to understand the impact of social stimuli on individuals, and adopts a primarily experimental methodology . . .'; the latter '. . . concentrates on the reciprocity of society and the individual, sees its fundamental task as the explanation of social interaction, and relies methodologically on naturalistic observation and surveys' (Hewstone and Manstead 1995, p. 589). The dividing line between these two traditions is fairly clear, and is likely to remain entrenched. Most psychologists would regard the former as the mainstream of social psychology, and it reflects the approach taken by the majority of contributors to this volume. One important feature of it is a predominant emphasis upon cognitive forms of explanation, which has been apparent since the 1980s:

the reaction against this tendency by sociological social psychologists was regarded by some as a 'crisis' in the discipline in the 1980s (see, for example, Harré 1979).

Harré suggested that the traditional experimental approach to social psychology through laboratory studies was inadequate in two main respects. First, he suggested that the individual actions which are the focus of many traditional experiments are *decontextualized*. Since real life action sequences are embedded in their own settings, involving specific roles and actors, we should study *episodes* rather than *actions*. We should pay more attention to the *accounts* which people give of their actions in their social lives, which may of course be very different from the interpretations of the outside scientific observer. Although some theorists (notably discourse analysts) have taken this point to imply that traditional experimental approaches are fundamentally inadequate, a more widespread effect is an increased willingness on the part of psychological social psychologists to consider the ecological context of their experiments, and to investigate everyday behaviour rather than that in laboratories. This is shown in an increasing use of qualitative methods alongside quantitative ones, and an increased emphasis on real world issues and problems (see, for example, Argyle 1992).

The second distinction has some features in common with the first, although it is more difficult to pin down. It is that between the North American approach, which has a primary focus on the individual, and the European tradition, which places more emphasis on what Tajfel (1981) described as 'the social dimension', which he saw as involving 'a direct concern with the relationship between human psychological functioning and the large-scale social processes and events which shape this functioning and are shaped by it' (p. 7). Although both of these might be regarded as variants of psychological social psychology, the main difference between them is that the European approach looks at more macroscopic social influences such as national or cultural identity or intergroup relations in determining the individual's cognition and behaviour, whereas the North American tradition focuses more on specific social contexts.

It may be possible to bring together and to clarify both of these distinctions by referring to Doise's (1986) proposal that there are four distinct types of explanation or 'levels of analysis' in social psychological research. The first is the *intraindividual* level, at which we investigate the mechanisms (e.g. cognitive and perceptual) by which people appraise and organize the social environment. The second is the *interindividual* and *situational* level, which deals with the processes which occur between different individuals within a given situation, such as a small group, but which does not take into account the positions or roles that the participants occupy outside that situation. At the third, *social-positional* level, the emphasis moves beyond the immediate situation to differences in social position, such as different group memberships. The fourth *ideological* level deals with the broader cultural systems of beliefs, representations and norms that people take with them into experimental situations. Doise suggests that most research in psychological social psychology operates at the first and second of these levels, and that in sociological social psychology at the higher levels. He also proposes that European social psychology is more likely to operate at the higher levels than in the North American approach.

All this is rather overwhelming when we try to define the scope of the social psychology of music: for now our own approach can be summarized in terms of three key features which characterize the contributions to the present volume. The first is simply that we draw on all these perspectives, adopting an eclectic approach in applying them to musical behaviour. The book is organized into parts according to different levels of individual–social analysis which are directly related to Doise's analysis: all four of his levels of explanation are represented, though most operate on the first and second levels.

The second feature is encapsulated in the definition of social psychology given above, namely the *reciprocity* that exists between the individual and the social environment. This can be clearly seen, for example, in the development of children's singing: in the early pre-school years, many infants' songs contain elements of their own spontaneous vocalizations combined with phrases from songs they hear in the world around them (see Hargreaves 1986a). In formulating his view of developmental social psychology, Durkin (1995) explains that the importance of reciprocal influence in social life partly involves harmony between people: developmental advances can be produced by collaborative activities between children, their parents, and their peers. However, divergence and conflict can also lead to developmental change, and this second form of reciprocity should not be overlooked (e.g. in studying adolescents' musical preferences).

The third feature derives from the predominance of the cognitive approach in social psychology, and this characterizes several of the present chapters. *Social cognition*, which we mentioned earlier, involves applying the information processing analogy to social representation. Perceivers are seen as 'going beyond the information given' in their social encounters, and as using their previous knowledge and experience to interpret new information, thus changing their beliefs and judgements. There is also an affective component in the process, since social cognition is essentially evaluative in that social comparisons are continuously made with other individuals and reference groups. This cognitive emphasis has led to a research emphasis on cognitive structures such as schemas, stereotypes, attributions, expectations, and attitudes, and this will be apparent in the social psychological approach to music.

EARLY RESEARCH IN THE SOCIAL PSYCHOLOGY OF MUSIC

Many social and applied psychological studies of music were carried out before the publication of the first edition of Farnsworth's *The social psychology of music*, and these studies covered a great range of topics. For the present-day psychologist, it is difficult to know what to make of a body of research that is rather nebulous; occasionally bizarre; sometimes methodologically suspect; and often ideologically and ethically dubious and/or naïve, in terms of present-day values, when dealing with such issues as racial or gender differences. After reviewing the early research on eminence and musical taste, with a strong emphasis on Farnsworth's studies, we have done our best to discern some recognizable trends and general directions in five other main areas of early work.

Eminence and musical taste

Although some early studies of musical preference investigated the effects of different cultural, situational, and individual factors (e.g. Cattell and Saunders 1954; Erdelyi 1940; Fisher 1951; Geiger 1950; Mull 1957; Rigg 1948; Schuessler 1948; Suchman 1941; Wells 1929; Wheeler and Gaston 1941; Wiebe 1940; Williams 1942, 1943), Farnsworth's was probably the first programme of research to attempt to identify systematic regularities in the social psychological aspects of musical taste. His research dealt with evidence for consensus on the nature of musical taste, and with its historical evolution: this work is reviewed in some detail in his earlier book *Musical taste: its measurement and cultural nature* (1950).

Farnsworth's studies employed a series of measures derived from public polling and music archives. For the former, a typical method was to send a list of the names of between 100 and 200 classical music composers to members of bodies such as the American Musicological Society (AMS). The members were asked to 'mark those composers whose work deserve to be called to the attention of others and preserved as part of our musical heritage'. Farnsworth allocated the responses alternately to one of two subgroups on the basis of the order in which they were returned. By correlating the data from the two subgroups, he was able to establish the degree of consensus on musical taste within his sample.

Farnsworth also investigated the issue of consensus by drawing on the vast resources of data available in music archives. For example, he measured the amount of space allocated to the different composers in histories of music, music encyclopaedias, and general encyclopaedias; the frequency with which the composers' works were played by a symphony orchestra; the number of times the composers' works were played on the radio; and the frequency with which the composers' works were recorded. This rich data base enabled Farnsworth's conclusions to possess a much greater degree of ecological validity than many other empirical studies of musical taste.

By these means, Farnsworth established that there was general consensus on the relative eminence of composers, with the same small number of individuals (e.g. Beethoven, Brahms, and Mozart) continually receiving the highest measures in both split halves of given sets of data (e.g. encyclopaedia space allocations or AMS members' eminence selections). Furthermore, Farnsworth (1950) reports a high level of correspondence between the results from different ways of measuring musical eminence (e.g. between AMS members' ranking of composers for eminence and the frequency with which orchestras played the composers' works). This led him to conclude that 'We agree on the composers we call eminent' (1950, p. 7), and that 'We agree on what we enjoy' (1950, p. 10).

Four other studies seem to corroborate this view, two of which are outside the domain of music. Gordon (1923) presented two groups of subjects with pictures of oriental rugs, and found a close correspondence between the two groups' choices. Similarly, Clow (1946) demonstrated that professors of English agreed closely on the relative eminence of English authors, and that different encyclopaedias allocated similar amounts of space to these authors. In a more recent study, we have found that two subgroups agree closely on the most eminent exemplars from a list of 200 pop groups and musicians (North and Hargreaves 1996a), and a similar study found high agreement between two subgroups of the general public for pop and classical music, and also films, plays, paintings, and novels (North and Hargreaves 1996b).

In some related work, Farnsworth investigated historical trends in the eminence of classical music composers. For example, he tested the popular idea that taste in classical music is governed by some sort of 'reverence for the past', such that the most eminent composers are those that have been dead the longest. His data revealed a form of 'reverence for the intermediate past', in that those composers who had been dead for an intermediate period (approximately 150 years) were rated as more eminent than those in the more distant or more recent past. In a similar vein, Farnsworth looked at the correlation between musicologists' eminence rankings of composers obtained in 1938, 1944, 1951, and 1964. Whilst there were generally high correlations between the rankings from each of these years, the size of these correlations decreased as the temporal distance between the rankings became more extreme. There were also some interesting trends for specific composers with, for example, Palestrina's position in the ranking decreasing over the years, Haydn's increasing, and Brahms' increasing and then decreasing (Table 1.1).

This corresponds with some earlier research by Mueller and Hevner (1942) who investigated American orchestral programmes between 1876 and

Table 1.1 Eminence rankings by musicologists in four different years (adapted from Farnsworth 1969).

Rank	1938	Rank	1944	Rank	1951	Rank	1964
1	Bach	1	Bach	1	Beethoven	1	Bach
2	Beethoven	2	Beethoven	2	Bach	2	Beethoven
3	Wagner	3	Mozart	3	Brahms	3	Mozart
4	Mozart	4	Wagner	4	Haydn	4	Haydn
5	Palestrina	5	Haydn	5	Mozart	5	Brahms
6	Haydn	6.5	Brahms	6.5	Schubert	6	Handel
7	Brahms	6.5	Palestrina	6.5	Debussy	7	Debussy
8	Monteverdi	8	Schubert	8	Handel	8	Schubert
9	Debussy	9	Handel	9	Wagner	9	Wagner
10	Schubert	10	Debussy	10	Palestrina	10	Chopin
11	Handel	11	Chopin	11	Chopin	11	Monteverdi
12	Chopin	25	Monteverdi	15	Monteverdi	12	Palestrina

1941. One of their most interesting findings was that the frequency with which different composers' works were performed tended to demonstrate a gradual waxing and waning rather than continuous rises or continuous falls: 'Each composer has a life cycle' (p. 108). For example, over the period investigated, Wagner started high in popularity, declined in the late 1880s, rose to second place in 1910, and then declined again.

In explaining their results, Mueller and Hevner cite a number of social psychological factors that may mediate the nature of cyclical vogues. Contemporary events influenced the music performed by the orchestras: for example, the First World War produced a decrease in the number of German works performed, and a corresponding increase for French and American works. Similarly, the rate of turnover in the works performed reflected the amount of new music available: the declining frequency with which Beethoven's works were performed was 'practically equal' (p. 103) to the increase in the performance of modern composers' works. They also argue that the works performed by the orchestras reflected not only public taste but also that of the conductor, with the employment of a new conductor being associated with radical changes in orchestras' output. 'Such extraneous influences . . . reflected themselves repeatedly and convincingly' (p. 103).

Mueller and Hevner conclude that trends in musical taste 'can no longer be esoteric and mystical' (p. 109), and it is worth noting that these kinds of finding are similar to those of more recent research discussed by Simonton in Chapter 6, and two smaller-scale studies by Ortmann (1932) and Zipf (1946). However, the importance of Farnsworth's and Mueller and Hevner's research on taste is clearest when considered within its historical context: these were the first research programmes to demonstrate systematically that social psychological aspects of our responses to music are lawful, and as such amenable to study within a scientific framework.

Occupational studies

The Second World War gave rise to a growth of research on the effects of music on factory workers' productivity and morale. These effects were assessed by means of questionnaire measures in conjunction with un-obtrusive observations, and this work generally indicates that appropriate kinds of music could decrease boredom, conversation, and absenteeism whilst improving morale, particularly on repetitive tasks (see, for example, Kaplan and Nettel 1948; Kirkpatrick 1943; McGehee and Gardner 1949). The effects on productivity were much less clear, although Humes (1941) and Smith (1947) found that music could increase piecework production and decrease scrappage rates. However, as Soibelman (1948) notes in a review article, much of the early literature on these industrial uses of music tends to be characterized by supposition and discussion rather than empirical research. Nevertheless, these studies might be seen as the ante-cedents of research on the commercial uses of music which is reviewed in Chapter 14.

Music education research

The relationship between music psychology and music education is the subject of perennial discussion, and one of the main concerns has been the practical usefulness of psychological research for music teachers (see, for example, Sloboda 1986b). A number of suggestions have been made as to how this usefulness might be increased, including the proposal that 'viewing this issue from a developmental perspective may enable psychological researchers to organize their knowledge in a way which makes it more amenable to practical application' (Hargreaves 1986b, p. 84). Ten years later we might add that the same ought to be true of the social psychological perspective: although relatively few studies in music education research have explicitly adopted this approach, Bengt Olsson has made a pioneering attempt to draw them together in Chapter 15 of this volume.

Alongside these psychological aspects, a good deal of music education research naturally deals with issues involved in teaching methods, teacher training, and curriculum issues: several review articles provide good over-views of the early empirical literature. Leonhard (1955) reviews 71 articles which cover philosophy and aesthetics, the psychology of music, the history of music education, curriculum issues, and teaching methods. Similarly Freeman (1952) summarizes research trends in studies of musical interest and ability, the music curriculum, psychology of music, and musical behaviour, and there are also earlier reviews by Borchers (1938), and Mursell and Madison (1938).

One obvious characteristic of this early research is predominance of the psychometric approach, with its strong emphasis on the evaluation and assessment of musical ability. Many psychometric tests of musical aptitude, achievement, and attitude were developed for the selection and assessment of pupils in music education in the early part of this century, and these have been extensively reviewed elsewhere (e.g. Shuter-Dyson and Gabriel 1981). This emphasis gave rise to a number of early studies of the nature–nurture debate, and the question of the unitary and/or differentiated nature of musical ability (Gates 1946; Haecker and Ziehen 1931; Koch and Mjoen 1931; Mjoen 1925–26, 1928; Reser 1935; Schank 1936; Seashore 1939, 1940a; Terry 1929). Although standardized tests are still extensively used by music educators in certain countries, the theoretical dominance of the psychometric approach has declined considerably in recent years.

Medical and therapeutic uses of music

This area of research is fairly well represented in the early literature. For example, Schullian and Schoen's (1948) book *Music and medicine* contains several chapters on the medical uses of music in a variety of cultures and historical periods. Early empirical studies of music therapy tended to be characterized by a diversity of client populations, approaches to and forms of music, measurement techniques, and therapeutic methods. There is also a good deal of emphasis in this literature on individual case histories, and on the development of specific treatment programmes rather than general theoretical discussion.

For example, some interesting early studies investigated the relationships between music and alcoholism (Zanker and Glatt 1956*a,b*), schizophrenia (Wenger 1952), speech defects (Kaplan 1955), catatonia (Sacristan 1932), cerebral palsy (May 1956; Weigl 1954), epilepsy (Critchley 1937; Reese 1948), and brain damage (Fields 1954) (see reviews by Gaston 1951; and Soibelman 1948). Then, as now, there were calls for more music therapists in hospitals (e.g. Preston 1950), and concerns were voiced about the profession's need for an adequate theoretical rationale (e.g. Sherwin 1958).

The early literature also indicates that the historical development of music therapy varied widely between different countries, and that this was influenced by a diversity of theoretical approaches ranging from psychoanalysis and humanism to behaviourism. In the USA, the National Association for Music Therapy played an important role in the development of a scientific, research-oriented approach, involving systematic data collection and hypothesis testing. This approach is now an important feature of the field, and two recent British books (Bunt's (1994) *Music therapy: an art beyond words* and Wigram, Saperston, and West's (1995) *The art and science of music therapy*; see also Chapter 13 of this volume) give a comprehensive overview of the current state of the emerging profession of music therapy.

Musicianship and composition

Early research on musicianship tended to deal with the particular practical concerns of musicians rather than with musical performance itself. Studies were conducted on such diverse topics as performance anxiety (e.g. Bagley 1949; Moreno 1944); other occupational concerns such as associated health issues (Gutheil 1947; Schweisheimer 1949; Whittaker 1948); links between musicianship and other vocations (Lorge and Blau 1942); professional aggrievances (Becker 1951); the role perception of composers (Nash 1955); and career development processes (Becker 1953). It is only in the last two decades or so that musical performance has received systematic empirical investigation from a coherent theoretical viewpoint, and the social psychological aspects of this research are reviewed for the first time by Jane Davidson in the present volume (Chapter 11).

A number of early studies were carried out on the process of musical composition, and some of their results can be interpreted in the light of Wallas' (1926) well-known four-stage model of the creative process, which includes *preparation* (gathering of relevant information), *incubation* (unconsciously 'mulling over' the problem), *illumination* (derivation of a solution), and *verification* (formalization and adaptation of the solution). Bahle (1936), for example, presented 30 composers with texts as a source of inspiration for composition, and concluded from their reports that the texts and feelings they aroused were expressed in the structure of the composition: there were also very wide variations in the extent to which the compositions were based directly on the texts. Bahle (1949) argued that genius in composition involves a progression through three stages which draw first on innate unconscious sources, then on conscious effort, and finally on a merging of the two.

Apart from the process of composition itself, a discernible group of early studies attempted to identify the characteristics of successful composers, and their methods of working. For example, Gross and Seashore (1941) suggest that superior composition skills are associated with superiority in vocabulary, auditory discrimination, work methods in composing, and temperament. Nash (1957) argued that a successful composer must be able to work in the face of social non-support, assume other vocational roles, and pursue solitary activity. Seashore (1940*b*) considered the lack of pre-eminent female composers, and suggested that there are no sex differences in musical talent, musical intelligence, musical temperament, creative imagination, or musical precocity. Gender differences (which are reviewed at length in Chapter 3 of the present volume) were also considered by Farnsworth (1952), who found that some composers are perceived consistently as producing music with either masculine characteristics (e.g. Bach, Handel) or feminine ones (e.g. Chopin, Debussy).

Ethnomusicological studies

Some of the early studies in this area are often as fascinating for the light they throw on the prevailing *Zeitgeist* and ideology than as for their scientific content. For example, it is difficult to imagine a present-day researcher analysing the musical talent of Jewish people in terms of a compensation for a genetic tendency toward defective hearing (Rosenthal 1931), or arguing that jazz cannot develop into 'good' music because to be 'good' requires that it loses the characteristics that make it jazz (Ortmann 1931). Some of the early research in this area dealt with ethnic and racial differences, suggesting for example that white westerners possessed the highest levels of musical ability as measured by the psychometric tests (e.g. Allen 1942; Garth and Isbell 1929; Johnson 1931; Ross 1936; Sanderson 1933).

Not all of the early research suffered from such ethnocentrism and cultural bias, however, and other studies emphasize the importance of the broader social and cultural context of music. For example, Densmore (1934) describes the uses of music for magic and medicine in Native American culture, and Gundlach (1932) describes how different songs within Native American culture have different uses. For example, songs used in warfare were typically rapid and low-pitched, whereas love songs were higher and had less rhythmic regularity. There were also studies of the music of Eastern Europe (Molnar 1931), and the Slav countries (see Troj (1931), whose experimental study is untypical for its time), as well as calls for the greater utilization of Indian music in research (e.g. Ganguly 1952; Kamalesh 1944) which are still being made today (e.g. Gregory and Varney 1996). More recent research deriving from the ethnomusicological perspective is reviewed by Andrew Gregory in Chapter 7 of the present volume, and it seems clear that this should be an increasingly integral part of the future development of the social psychology of music.

PLAN OF THE BOOK

In organizing the fairly diverse subject matter of the book into six sections, we have drawn on Doise's (1986) different levels of explanation of social influence, outlined earlier. Thus, the two chapters in Part I work on the intraindividual level, dealing specifically with studies of individual difference factors in musical behaviour. This area of study is traditionally associated with psychometrics, and the factors of personality and gender are those which have received most attention with respect to music. In Chapter 2, Anthony Kemp investigates individual differences in musical behaviour, using the personality structure of the musician as his central focus. In Chapter 3, Susan O'Neill undertakes a broad-ranging review of the literature on gender and music, considering the evidence for gender differences in musical aptitude and achievement, and examining the role of gender stereotyping in perpetuating these differences.

In Part II, the focus moves from the individual to what Doise calls the interindividual and situational level of explanation, thereby looking at the effects of small social groups and situations on individual behaviour. This is a well-defined area of social psychology in which numerous well-established phenomena such as conformity, group polarization, prejudice, and stereotyping have been experimentally demonstrated. In Chapter 4, Ray Crozier looks at the process of social influence in music, considering the role of music in personal identity, and small group studies of the effects of music on mood. In Chapter 5, we review some of the major theories in experimental aesthetics, and evaluate their effectiveness in explaining musical preference and taste in everyday life.

In Part III, we move on to Doise's social-positional and ideological levels in taking a broader view of large-scale social and cultural influences on musical preference. Dean Keith Simonton reviews what has become known as the historiometric approach to music in Chapter 6, drawing extensively on his own pioneering research in the field on the relationship between broader sociocultural variables (e.g. warfare) and musical taste and creativity. Andrew Gregory adopts an ethnomusicological perspective in his review of the roles of music in society in Chapter 7, and in Chapter 8, Philip Russell undertakes a broad-ranging review of the effects of sociodemographic factors and other social influences on the cultural stereotyping of musical taste.

Parts IV to VI operate on one or more of these levels of social influence, and are characterized instead by their focus on specific areas of musical behaviour. Part IV deals with developmental aspects of musical behaviour, and contains two chapters which deal with the environmental background to the development of musical taste in adolescence, and the development of musical skill across the life span. In Chapter 9, Dolf Zillmann and Su-lin Gan review the social, individual, and situational variables that determine teenage music preferences, which are of course a crucial factor in many other aspects of their lifestyles and behaviour. In Chapter 10, Jane Davidson, Michael Howe, and John Sloboda investigate the environmental factors which shape the development of expert musical performance across the life span, drawing in particular on their own well-known research on talented young musicians.

The two chapters in Part V look specifically at the social psychology of musicianship. In Chapter 11, Jane Davidson undertakes a pioneering review of this field, considering the sociocultural influences which shape different aspects of performance largely in Western art music: her discussion includes audience effects, and the ways in which the presence of others affects the nature of performance in musical ensembles of different sizes. In Chapter 12, Glenn Wilson deals with the universal and debilitating phenomenon of performance anxiety, reviewing its prevalence and symptomatology; different theoretical explanations of its operation and effects; and the different ways in which it is managed by musical performers.

Finally, Part VI contains three chapters which deal with different aspects of what might be called the applied social psychology of music, each covering a specific area of application. In Chapter 13, Leslie Bunt reviews the main clinical applications of music in medicine and therapy, and discusses the different theoretical models which have been proposed to explain its beneficial effects. In Chapter 14, we review the many ways in which music mediates consumers' responses to advertising and shops, and then consider the music industry itself. In Chapter 15, Bengt Olsson delineates what might be called the social psychology of music education. He draws primarily upon attribution theory, social learning theory, and symbolic interactionism in explaining the results of empirical research on the attitudes and motivations of music students; teacher expectations and attributional styles; and on teacher training, drawing in the latter case on some of his own research in Swedish music education.

REFERENCES

Allen, M. E. (1942). A comparative study of negro and white children on melodic and harmonic sensitivity. *Journal of Negro Education*, **11**, 158–64.

Argyle, M. (1992). *The social psychology of everyday life*. Routledge, London.

Bagley, S. R. (1949). The singer and stage fright. *Etude*, **67**, 291–322.

Bahle, J. (1936). Die Gestaltubertragung im vokalen Schaffen zeitgenossischer Komponisten. *Archiv für die gesamte Psychologie*, **91**, 444–51.

Bahle, J. (1949). *Hans Pfitzner und der geniale Mensch: eine psychologische Kulturkritik*. Curt Weller, Konstanz.

Becker, H. S. (1951). The professional dance musician and his audience. *American Journal of Sociology*, **57**, 136–44.

Becker, H. S. (1953). Some contingencies of the professional dance musician's career. *Human Organization*, **12**, 22–6.

Borchers, O. J. (1938). The psychology of music in relation to music education. *1937 Proceedings of the Music Teachers' National Association*, 67–78.

Bunt, L. (1994). *Music therapy: An art beyond words*. Routledge, London.

Butterworth, G. (1992). Context and cognition in models of cognitive growth. In *Context and cognition* (ed. P. H. Light and G. Butterworth). Lawrence Erlbaum, Hillsdale, New Jersey.

Cameron, W. B. (1954). Sociological notes on the jam session. *Social Forces*, **33**, 177–82.

Cattell, R. B. and Saunders, D. R. (1954). Musical preferences and personality diagnosis: I. A factorization of one hundred and twenty themes. *Journal of Social Psychology*, **39**, 3–24.

Clow, R. M. (1946). *A study of the rated eminence of authors of the several periods of English literature*. Unpublished Ph.D. Dissertation, Stanford University.

Critchley, M. (1937). Musicogenic epilepsy. *Brain*, **60**, 14–27.

Deliège, I. and Sloboda, J. A. (ed.) (1996). *Musical beginnings: Origins and development of musical competence*. Oxford University Press, Oxford.

Densmore, F. (1934). A study of Indian music in the Gulf states. *American Anthropologist*, **36**, 386–8.

Doise, W. (1986). *Levels of explanation in social psychology*. Cambridge University Press, Cambridge.

Durkin, K. (1995). *Developmental social psychology*. Blackwell, Oxford.

Eiser, J. R. (1980). *Cognitive social psychology*. McGraw-Hill, Maidenhead.

Erdelyi, M. (1940). The relation between 'radio plugs' and sheet sales of popular music. *Journal of Applied Psychology*, **24**, 696–702.

Farnsworth, P. R. (1950). *Musical taste: Its measurement and cultural nature*. Stanford University Press, Stanford, California.

Farnsworth, P. R. (1952). The musical taste of an American musical elite. *Hinrichsen's Musical Yearbook*, **7**, 112–16.

Farnsworth, P. R. (1954/1969). *The social psychology of music*. Iowa State University Press, Ames, Iowa.

Fields, B. (1954). Music as an adjunct in the treatment of brain-damaged patients. *American Journal of Physical Medicine*, **33**, 273–83.

Fisher, R. L. (1951). Preference of different age and socio-economic groups in unstructured musical situations. *Journal of Social Psychology*, **33**, 147–52.

Fiske, S. T. and Taylor, S. E. (1991). *Social cognition* (2nd edn). McGraw-Hill, New York.

Freeman, W. S. (1952). Music education. *Review of Educational Research*, **22**, 136–40.

Ganguly, M. (1952). Suggestions for experimental study of Indian music. *Indian Journal of Psychology*, **27**, 127–30.

Garth, T. R. and Isbell, S. R. (1929). The musical talent of Indians. *Music Supervisors' Journal*, February.

Gaston, E. T. (1951). Music in therapy: a review of some recent research literature. *1949 Proceedings of the Music Teachers' National Association*, 118–25.

Gates, R. R. (1946). *Human genetics*. Macmillan, New York.

Geiger, T. (1950). A radio test of musical taste. *Public Opinion Quarterly*, **14**, 453–60.

Gordon, K. (1923). A study of aesthetic judgements. *Journal of Experimental Psychology*, **6**, 36–43.

Gregory, A. H. and Varney, N. (1996). Cross-cultural comparisons in the affective response to music. *Psychology of Music*, **24**, 47–52.

Gross, B. and Seashore, R. H. (1941). Psychological characteristics of student and professional musical composers. *Journal of Applied Psychology*, **25**, 159–70.

Gundlach, R. H. (1932). A quantitative analysis of Indian music. *American Journal of Psychology*, **44**, 133–45.

Gutheil, E. A. (1947). Occupational neurosis in a musician. *American Journal of Psychotherapy*, **1**, 448–67.

Haecker, V. and Ziehen, T. (1931). Beitrag zur Lehre von Vererbung und Analyse der zeichnerischen und mathematischen Begabung, insbesondere mit Bezug auf die Korrelation zur musikalischen Begabung. *Zeitschrift für Psychologie*, **120**, 1–45.

Hargreaves, D. J. (1986a). *The developmental psychology of music*. Cambridge University Press, Cambridge.

Hargreaves, D. J. (1986b). Developmental psychology and music education. *Psychology of Music*, **14**, 83–96.

Hargreaves, D. J. and Zimmerman, M. (1992). Developmental theories of music learning. In *Handbook for research in music teaching and learning* (ed. R. Colwell), pp. 377–91. Schirmer/Macmillan, New York.

Harré, R. (1979). *Social being*. Basil Blackwell, Oxford.

Hewstone, M. and Manstead, A. S. R. (1995). Social psychology. In *The Blackwell encyclopaedia of social psychology* (ed. M. Hewstone and A. S. R. Manstead). Blackwell, Oxford.

Humes, J. F. (1941). The effects of occupational music on scrappage in the manufacturing of radio tubes. *Journal of Applied Psychology*, **25**, 573–87.

Johnson, G. B. (1931). A summary of negro scores on the Seashore musical talent tests. *Journal of Comparative Psychology*, **11**, 383–93.

Kamalesh, R. (1944). Scientific study of music. *Indian Journal of Psychology*, **19**, 39–45.

Kaplan, M. (1955). Music therapy in the speech program. *Exceptional Children*, **22**, 112–17.

Kaplan, L. and Nettel, R. (1948). Music in industry. *Biology and Human Affairs*, **13**, 129–35.

Kirkpatrick, F. H. (1943). Music in industry. *Journal of Applied Psychology*, **27**, 268–74.

Koch, H. and Mjoen, F. (1931). Die Erblichkeit der Musikalitat. II. Geneostatistische untersuchungen. *Zeitschrift für Psychologie*, **121**, 104–36.

Lerdahl, F. and Jackendoff, R. (1983). *A generative theory of tonal music*. MIT Press, Cambridge, Mass.

Leonhard, C. (1955). Music. *Review of Educational Research*, **25**, 166–75.

Lorge, I. and Blau, R. D. (1942). Broad occupational groupings by estimated abilities. *Occupations*, **21**, 289–95.

Low, H. B. (1933). What is the field of school music? *Peabody Bulletin*, **30**, No. 1, 18–20.

Lundin, R. W. (1967). *An objective psychology of music* (2nd edn). Ronald, New York.

McGehee, W. and Gardner, J. E. (1949). Music in a complex industrial job. *Personnel Psychology*, **2**, 405–17.

May, E. (1956). Music for children with cerebral palsy. *American Journal of Physical Medicine*, **35**, 320–3.

Meyer, L. B. (1956). *Emotion and meaning in music*. University of Chicago Press, Chicago.

Mjoen, J. A. (1925–26). Zur erbanalyse der musikalischen Begabung. *Hereditas*, **7**, 109–28.

Mjoen, J. A. (1928). Inheritance of musical ability. *Child Studies*, **5**, 3–5.

Molnar, A. (1931). Die Bedeutung der neuen osteuropaischen Music. *Archiv für die gesamte Psychologie*, **81**, 166–78.

Moreno, J. L. (1944). Psychodramatic treatment of performance neurosis; case study of a musician. *Psychodrama Monographs*, No. 2, 1–31.

Mueller, J. H. and Hevner, K. (1942). *Trends in musical taste.* Indiana University Publishers, Bloomington, Indiana.

Mull, H. K. (1957). The effect of repetition upon the enjoyment of modern music. *Journal of Psychology*, **43**, 155–62.

Mursell, J. J. and Madison, T. (1938). Psychology and methods in the high school and college: music. *Review of Educational Research*, **8**, 58–9.

Nash, D. (1955). Challenge and response in the American composer's career. *Journal of Aesthetics*, **14**, 116–22.

Nash, D. J. (1957). The socialization of an artist: the American composer. *Social Forces*, **35**, 307–13.

Nattiez, J.-J. (1990). *Music and disclosure: Toward a semiology of music.* Princeton University Press, Princeton, New Jersey.

North, A. C. and Hargreaves, D. J. (1996a). Eminence in pop music. *Popular Music and Society*, **20**, 41–66.

North, A. C. and Hargreaves, D. J. (1996b). Affective and evaluative responses to the arts. *Empirical Studies of the Arts*, **14**, 207–22.

Ortmann, O. (1931). Notes on jazz. *Peabody Bulletin*, **28**, No. 1, 11–17.

Ortmann, O. (1932). In forty years. *Peabody Bulletin*, **29**, No. 1, 3–16.

Preston, M. J. (1950). The organization of a music program, as a rehabilitation measure for the mentally ill. *Psychiatric Quarterly Supplement*, **24**, 119–27.

Reese, H. H. (1948). The relation of music to diseases of the brain. *Occupational Therapist*, **27**, 12–18.

Reser, H. (1935). Student pedigree-studies. 44. Inheritance of musical ability. *Eugenical News*, **20**, 8–9.

Rigg, M. G. (1948). Favorable versus unfavorable propaganda in the enjoyment of music. *Journal of Experimental Psychology*, **38**, 78–81.

Rosenthal, H. (1931). Die Musikalitat der Juden. *Zeitschrift für Individualpsychologie*, **9**, 122–31.

Ross, V. R. (1936). Musical talents of Indian and Japanese children. *Journal of Juvenile Research*, **20**, 95–113.

Sacristan, J. M. (1932). Disposicion musical y alucinaciones acusticas en el circulo familar de un caso de esquizofrenis catatonica. *Archivos de Neurobiologia*, **12**, 40–9.

Sanderson, H. E. (1933). Differences in musical ability in children of different national and racial origin. *Journal of Genetic Psychology*, **42**, 100–19.

Schank, A. (1936). The inheritance through six generations of pronounced musical capacity. *Eugenical News*, **21**, 14–16.

Schneider, E. H. (ed.) (1959). *Music therapy.* National Association for Music Therapy, Lawrence, Kansas.

Schuessler, K. F. (1948). Social background and musical taste. *American Sociological Review*, **13**, 330–5.

Schullian, D. M. and Schoen, M. (ed.) (1948). *Music and medicine.* Henry Schuman, New York.

Schweisheimer, W. (1949). Do musicians live longer than others? *Etude*, **67**, 54–5.

Seashore, C. E. (1939). The psychology of music. XXIII. Validation of laws of musical inheritance. *Music Educators' Journal*, **26**, 23–4.

Seashore, C. E. (1940a). Musical inheritance. *Scientific Monthly*, **50**, 351–6.

Seashore, C. E. (1940*b*). Why no great women composers? *Music Educators' Journal*, **26**, 21; 88.

Serafine, M. L. (1988). *Music as cognition: The development of thought in sound*. Columbia University Press, New York.

Sherwin, A. C. (1958). A consideration of the therapeutic use of music in psychiatric illness. *Journal of Nervous and Mental Disorder*, **127**, 84–90.

Shuter-Dyson, R. and Gabriel, C. (1981). *The psychology of musical ability* (2nd edn). Methuen, London.

Sloboda, J. A. (1986*a*). Cognition and real music: the psychology of music comes of age. *Psychologica Belgica*, **26**, 199–219.

Sloboda, J. A. (1986*b*). Achieving our aims in music education research. *Psychology of Music*, **14**, 144–5.

Smith, H. C. (1947). Music in relation to employee attitudes, piece-work production, and industrial accidents. *Applied Psychology Monographs*, No. 14.

Soibelman, D. (1948). *Therapeutic and industrial uses of music: A review of the literature*. Columbia University Press, New York.

Suchman, E. A. (1941). Invitation to music: a study of the creation of new music listeners by the radio. In *Radio research* (ed. P. F. Lazarsfeld and F. Stanton). Duell, Sloan, and Pearce, New York.

Tajfel, H. (1981). *Human groups and social categories*. Cambridge University Press, Cambridge.

Terry, C. S. (1929). *The origin of the family of Bach musicians*. Oxford University Press, Oxford.

Troj, F. (1931). O muzickoj osetljivosti Juznosrbijanaca, Sumadinaca i Crnogoraca. *Contr. Phil. Ethnopsychol., Skoplje*, No. 1.

Wallas, G. (1926). *The art of thought*. Watts, London.

Weigl, V. (1954). Music as an adjunctive therapy in the training of children with cerebral palsy. *Cerebral Palsy Review*, **15**, 9–10.

Wells, F. L. (1929). Musical symbolism. *Journal of Abnormal and Social Psychology*, **24**, 74–6.

Wenger, P. (1952). The value of music in the successful psychotherapy of a schizophrenic patient. *Psychiatric Quarterly Supplement*, **26**, 202–9.

Wheeler, R. H. and Gaston, T. (1941). The history of music in relation to climatic and cultural fluctuations. *1940 Proceedings of the Music Teachers' National Association*, 432–8.

Whittaker, A. H. (1948). Occupational diseases of musicians. In *Music and medicine* (ed. D. M. Schullian and M. Schoen). Henry Schuman, New York.

Wiebe, G. (1940). The effect of radio plugging on students' opinions of popular songs. *Journal of Applied Psychology*, **24**, 721–7.

Wigram, A., Saperston, B., and West, R. (ed.) (1995). *The art and science of music therapy: A handbook*. Harwood Academic Publishers, Reading.

Williams, G. D. (1942). The effect of order of appearance on the appreciation of music selections. *Journal of General Psychology*, **27**, 295–310.

Williams, G. D. (1943). The effect of program notes on the enjoyment of musical selections. *Journal of General Psychology*, **29**, 261–79.

Zanker, A. and Glatt, M. M. (1956*a*). Individual reactions of alcoholic and neurotic patients to music. *Journal of Nervous and Mental Disorders*, **123**, 395–402.

Zanker, A. and Glatt, M. M. (1956*b*). The influence of music on groups of alcoholic and neurotic patients in a mental hospital. *Journal of Nervous and Mental Disorders*, **123**, 403–5.

Zipf, G. K. (1946). On the dynamic structure of concert-programs. *Journal of Abnormal and Social Psychology*, **41**, 25–36.

PART I

Individual differences

2 | *Individual differences in musical behaviour*

Anthony E. Kemp

INTRODUCTION

This chapter takes personality studies as its central focus. My reasons for this reflect the view that aspects of personality interrelate with, if not drive, most aspects of individual differences. Besides, this chapter might help redress the notorious neglect of personality psychology by most music psychologists. If one scans the range of published material which has mushroomed in recent years in the field, a fact that cannot be overlooked is its main preoccupation with music cognition and the virtual exclusion of dynamic psychology and concerns with people's less cognitive musical responses. Clearly musicians engage in highly cognitive processes and execute exceedingly complex skills, but the view developed here is that the development of these, in many respects, is dependent upon the existence or acquisition of unusual combinations of personality factors. By considering musicians' personality and temperament we may well open up new ways of understanding their motivational drives, their single-mindedness, and their investment of so much of their self-concepts in music.

No doubt, this neglect of personality research was largely caused by Mischel's (1968) devastating attack on personality trait theory in which he seriously questioned the stability of personality traits and their ability to predict behaviour across different kinds of situation. This resulted in a somewhat overpolarized debate concerning whether people display consistent patterns of behaviour regardless of differing situations or, alternatively, whether behaviour is powerfully determined by the different circumstances in which they find themselves.

More recently, these two views have been reconciled by the proposal that 'behaviour depends on an interaction between qualities of the person and qualities of the physical and social environment' (Deary and Matthews 1993, pp. 299–300). And clearly, the notion that aspects of personality (for example, anxiety) can be viewed as being states as well as traits (as in the work of Spielberger) has helped to clarify this issue. In this chapter and elsewhere (Kemp 1996) I have argued that musical development reflects the kind of person musicians tend to be as well as the environment in which they tend to be nurtured.

However, another debate continues. This involves disagreements between the trait theorists themselves and has also helped fuel the controversy mentioned above. Put at its simplest this concerns two main issues: first, whether the proponents of trait theory have identified the correct structure in their psychometric procedures; and secondly, whether primary traits, the smallest components of personality, are stable enough to be adopted as reliable and valid experimental variables. The first controversy stems from the adoption of different techniques of factor analysis (Eysenck's use of orthogonal rotation and Cattell's of oblique) and resulted in quite heated exchanges in the research journals of the 1970s. The second issue tends to stem from the first, namely that even if primary factors represent the simplest factor-analytical solution, disagreement exists as to whether it is more appropriate to adopt the 'second-order' clusters of these, namely dimensions such as neuroticism and extraversion. More recently it was hoped that the development of the 'big five' dimensions by Costa and McCrae (1992) would help calm the waters. These dimensions present a structure of five dimensions each with its own set of contributory primary traits. However, both Eysenck (1992) and Cattell (1995) remain unconvinced, the former maintaining that Costa and McCrae's conclusions are premature; the latter dismissing their work as 'a fallacy'.

Another, more fundamental issue separates the theoretical positions of Cattell and Eysenck and this relates to their respective attitudes towards Freudian psychology. Aspects of Cattell's personality theory are underpinned by psychoanalytic concepts. For example, Freud's *id*, *ego*, and *superego* typology has influenced his psychological interpretation of his primary factors of ergic tension, ego strength, and conscientiousness. Unlike Eysenck, Cattell considers that it is foolish to dismiss pyschoanalytic work on the grounds of methodology. He maintains that although more scientific approaches ensure accuracy, the clinical work of Freud and Jung may have revealed important insights through the accumulation of 'data' of a very different kind (see Cattell and Kline 1977). On the other hand, Eysenck eschews all aspects of pyschoanalytic theory although, curiously, he incorporated the Hippocratic personality typology (melancholic, choleric, phlegmatic, and sanguine), also largely derived through speculation.

A more general and fundamental point needs to be made at the outset. Personality dimensions do not exist in a vacuum within the study of any occupational or interest group. They interrelate and interact with the perceptual and ability factors which they help to explain and this is reflected in the approach of the present chapter; the central features of the musician's personality interrelate with and underpin several aspects of individual differences. It is for this very reason that both Cattell and Eysenck's research heavily reflects a preoccupation with integrating personality factors into general psychology. They believe that perceptual abilities, memorizing, learning and motor skills, and motivation, for example, reveal the influence of certain personality traits during formative development. Both deplore the tendency to subdivide psychology into its traditional and rigid structure which resists such research being undertaken and results in the isolation of personality work (Cattell 1971; Eysenck 1976).

INTROVERSION/EXTRAVERSION

One dimension which units all personality theorists is introversion/ extraversion. This is often ascribed to Jung, although, in fact, its appearance in eighteenth century dictionaries clearly predates him. However, whereas Jung's more psychoanalytic view of the dimension permeates Cattell's definition to some extent, as one might expect Eysenck eschews anything which bears such connotations. As a result, Eysenck focuses upon the social aspects of the dimension; extraverts are gregarious and impulsive, they like parties and need to be surrounded by people. In contrast, Jung maintained that introverts' minds were inwardly directed, and focused much more on the inner world of ideas and abstract inventions. Cattell's four contributory primary factors of introversion/extraversion attempt to capture both elements; extraverts certainly tend to be participating, enthusiastic, impulsive, and conventional, but introversion is seen to characterize a critical detachment, introspection, restraint, and yet revealing an inner resourcefulness. His use of the term 'invia' captures the essential ingredient of 'living inwards'.

It is well documented that musicians tend to be introverted, although within this generalization considerable variation amongst different types of musician has been found (Kemp 1981a; Martin 1976). This research shows that musicians' introversion takes a different form to that of the general population: whilst displaying the primary traits of detachment and self-sufficiency, musicians do not exhibit those traits related to seriousness and shyness. This tends to suggest that musicians are indeed self-contained people but that this is a self-imposed result of their work patterns which have been instilled from the earliest stages of music tuition. The extended period of isolation spent in practice rooms require the young musician to be comfortable in that kind of environment. In other words, music, and especially the playing of complex and demanding instruments, attracts self-sufficient and more socially aloof types; and frequent engagement in extended periods of solitary practice is likely to accentuate these traits.

What we might deduce from these results is that musicians are less characterized by timidity and shyness and more by their resourcefulness and self-sufficiency. Storr (1976) develops this notion of the 'schizoid' type whose detachment results in finding solace in things—painting, reading, and music. In this way they find their identity and a sense of mastery and autonomy, they communicate on their own terms and their art objects remain totally within their own control. In the light of this notion it will not come as a surprise to the reader to learn that, of all groups of musicians, it is the composer who emerges as the most introverted (Kemp 1981*b*). This of course leads us to develop the psychoanalytic notion a little further. An inherent aspect of creative thought, and of musical thought in particular, is the capacity to internalize musical sound, musical ideas, total pieces of music, and to operate freely in this internal world of aural and symbolic experience. The cognitive psychology of music has attempted to access this phenomenon through the study of musical memory and imaging. Researchers such as Gordon (1993) have coined the term 'audiation', and some pedagogues led by Jaques-Dalcroze (Bachmann 1991) maintain that the phenomenon has a strong kinaesthetic basis. All these approaches stress the essential nature of this feature of musicians' temperament which encapsulates the notion of their inner strength and resolve to master and bring order to their internal lives.

Seashore (1936) maintained that, by definition, the performing musician had to be an extravert, but this overlooks the form that the musician's introversion takes. Drevdahl and Cattell (1958) coined the term 'bold introvert' to describe the temperaments of creative types, and this appears to accord with Storr's (1989) more recent view that the capacity to be alone can be interpreted as emotional maturity rather than a manifestation of fear. In other words, most kinds of musician possess the capacity to be comfortable during long periods of practice but, at the same time, their rich, powerful, and symbolic internal life empowers them to display high degrees of autonomy on the concert platform. In other words, musicians take this power-base of their inner reality out onto the concert platform and perform on their own terms. It is often for this very reason that conservatoire students frequently have to be reminded that their job is to communicate to a listening audience and to learn appropriate behaviours.

Before moving on, an important aspect of introversion needs to be addressed briefly: this concerns arousal theory as expounded by Eysenck (1967). His theory relates to an information processing loop in the lower regions of the brain thought to be responsible for sending arousal messages to the cortex which then may, in turn, send messages back to the reticular formation to continue the state of arousal or, alternatively, to switch to inhibition. These two functions which can be seen as working in opposition, relate to the excitement seeking stance of the extravert, and to the inhibition of the higher levels of arousal in introverts. Put at its simplest, because of their higher resting states of arousal, introverts tend to be superior at tasks that require high levels of concentration (such as isolated and repetitive practice) whereas extraverts might perceive these tasks as being mono-tonous or boring. This appears to be the case during extended time periods in which extraverts' performance on such tasks deteriorates considerably earlier than that of introverts. The response patterns of extraverts and introverts to auditory stimulation were investigated by Stelmack and Campbell (1974) who successfully showed the effects of the inhibition mech-anism in the latter. Whilst introverts generally showed greater sensitivity to low auditory stimulation than extraverts, introverts demonstrated a pro-gressive lowering of sensitivity to higher levels. However, extraverts showed the opposite trend.

In musical terms a number of points can be made at this stage. Firstly, the Yerkes-Dodson Law suggests that performance levels on tasks is an inverted-U function of drive or motivation levels and that these are medi-ated by the level of difficulty of the task in hand. This suggests that intro-verts, who are characterized by higher levels of arousal than extraverts, will tend to complete a moderately difficult task more efficiently in a low stress situation. However, in a high stress situation, the performance of introverts will deteriorate more rapidly than in the case of extraverts. This clearly has important implications for any discussion of performance anxiety.

Stelmack (1990) used the Yerkes-Dodson Law in his work on the 'hedonic curve', suggesting that introverts will experience a pleasant level of arousal at lower levels of stimulation than extraverts. Weisen (1965), cited by Wilson (1977), made a similar observation, since extraverts worked hard to achieve a reward of loud jazz music under experimental conditions, whereas intro-verts actually made clear efforts to avoid it.

INDEPENDENCE

The concept of independence as a dimension of personality not only helps elaborate the notion of the 'bold introvert' referred to above, but also embraces a number of interconnecting concepts frequently seen as important aspects of individual psychology. We shall pursue these a little later. Firstly though, it has to be conceded that, for some personality theorists, there is a problem of finding a dividing line between independence and extraversion. For example, McCrae and Costa's (1989) 'big five' dimension of extra-version seems to encapsulate independence. Nevertheless, as we shall see here, studies of the musician suggest grounds for retaining the dividing line between the two factors seeing that they generally emerge as low on one and reasonably high on the other.

Fairly strong evidence suggests that in spite of their introverted tendencies mature and skilled musicians emerge as independent types (see Kemp 1996).

However, the overall developmental picture suggests that less mature musicians, say those in adolescence, emerge with distinct tendencies towards dependency. Besides reflecting a general educational trend identified by researchers such as Entwistle (1972), this may signify additional developmental trends important in musical performance. For example, this shift may be reflected by students who cease instrumental tuition because of a lack of intrinsic motivation or increasing discomfort with teachers' demands. We shall return to this notion a little later.

At this point we may wish to speculate whether certain implicit beliefs within music circles may also be reflected here as well as possibly causing drop-out. The view that pupils must initially learn the skills and knowledge of music in order to be fully initiated into the discipline before engaging in interpretative, imaginative, and creative activities might render the early stages of learning too uncomfortable for the more independent types.

One of McCrae and Costa's (1985) 'big five' factors, namely 'openness', relates to the independent, imaginative, creative, and curious type of person. It also appears to involve an analytical approach towards the perception of phenomena. At this point we may wish to speculate whether Witkin's theory of field dependence–independence operates within this 'space' as well. His theory of 'psychological differentiation' addresses individual differences of perception. The field-dependent person is dominated by the overall organization of a perceptual whole; field-independent types are more able to focus on specific parts of the field and able to do so more analytically. Cattell (1973) certainly maintained that field-independence was connected with his independence factor, capturing the perceptual style of the more autonomous. But Witkin's theory goes further than this by showing that field-independent types were more fully aware of their needs, feelings, and attributes as belonging to themselves, and that these things were separate from the surrounding environment. In line with the arguments above he also showed that the dimension was linked to maturity, the change occurring particularly at adolescence.

Several studies support the notion that mature musicians are indeed more field-independent. In their case this highlights a perceptual orientation which enables them to analyse, extract, and reorganize the elements of music. These features may well separate the trained musician from the more musically naïve. For example, Schmidt and Lewis (1987) cite research which claims that aural skills and sight-reading, musical creativity, and musical conservation tasks are all positively related to field-independence (King 1983; Matson 1978; Schmidt 1984; Schmidt and Sinor 1986). Furthermore, Ellis and McCoy (1990) found field-independent types were more able to identify musical forms. Similarly Ellis (1995) showed that they were more efficient in making judgements about musical textures.

The 'openness' factor of the 'big five' also appears to link with those aspects of creativity which were explored by the early investigators of creativity in the USA. Barron (1963), for example, whose pioneering work incorporated aspects of Asch's classic experiments with 'yielders' and 'non-yielders' in situations where group pressure to conform was applied, pursued the notions of tolerance of ambiguity and preference for complexity. Those who were able to resist group pressure were generally found to be the more creative types. Barron explained the difference between yielders and non-yielders in terms of the latter's capacity to deal with contradictory phenomena and cognitions. Witkin (1965) maintained that this very capacity to operate more comfortably with conflicting thoughts and feelings is a central characteristic of field-independent types.

MacKinnon's (1962) work with creative groups did much to establish the use of the Jungian personality inventory known as the Myers-Briggs Type Indicator (MBTI) in the USA. In recent years this test has become increasingly popular in the USA as well as in Britain, particularly in careers advice, and has been used with musicians in both countries. In the context of independence, what particularly emerged from MacKinnon's research was that creative people tended to be perceptive as opposed to judging types. Myers and McCaulley (1985) help explain the dimension in terms of the former being spontaneous and adaptable whereas the latter tend to be more decisive and organized. Musicians to not tend to emerge with any bias towards one preference, suggesting that as an occupational group they do not reveal particular creative tendencies. However, research with student composers shows that there is significant predominance of perceptive types, although this was less pronounced in professional composers (Kemp 1996).

The question which arises of course is the degree to which the education of musicians allows or encourages them to be free-thinking, autonomous, and flexible. As we have already observed, younger musicians appear to be characterized more by dependency, conformity, and control, and this may well be a reflection of their earlier tuition as instrumental performers. We shall certainly need to take a closer look at this issue later in the chapter when discussing styles of upbringing. Let it suffice to say here that, in terms of conforming and control, young musicians tend to display high levels of conscientiousness, indicating a drive to do one's best and revealing a persistence of effort often instilled by parents and teachers. It is interesting to observe how this pattern of discipline and sense of duty is replaced in mature performers by significant levels of expediency—described by Cattell as self-indulgence, slackness, and indolence. In terms of artistic types this factor may be better interpreted as an adherence to a personal code of conduct and standards and a tendency to reject social norms and those imposed by others.

SENSITIVITY

No discussion of musicians and the personal qualities which characterize them would be complete without mention of their sensitivity for, like Cattell's factor of self-sufficiency, it emerges as a stable trait in all groups of musicians regardless of age (Kemp 1996). Clearly, we need to be precise about a definition for musicians' sensitivity: Seashore referred to it in terms of sensory capacities, and whilst this aspect of perceptual skill is important—perception of pitch, dynamics, tempo and timbre—our study of the personality domain might be attempting to identify a less cognitive aspect of sensitivity. The Jungian Myers-Briggs Type Indicator may help us here since one of its bipolar dimensions dichotomizes 'sensing and intuition', suggesting that sensing relates to a conscious gathering of physical evidence by means of the senses. On the face of it one might be tempted to align this with sensitivity but for the fact that Cattell's definition stresses empathy, gentleness, imagination, and *intuition*—the kind of description assigned to the MBTI opposite pole of sensing, namely intuition. We might also see negative connections between sensitivity and Eysenck's psychoticism dimension.

Neither must we overlook the fact that Cattell's primary factor of sensitivity is embraced along with imagination as the two main components of his second-order factor of 'pathemia', unfortunately also referred to by some researchers as sensitivity. Pathemia has been described by Cattell as engaging in an indulgent life of feeling, proneness to day-dreaming, and emotional sensitivity, and certainly appears to characterize the musician, particularly composers. The contrasting pole of 'cortertia' as its label suggests, relates to a high level of cortical alertness in which feelings are kept well under control. It is important not to confuse the reader, but the MBTI dimensions of thinking versus feeling require mentioning at this point simply because research (Myers and McCaulley 1985) has shown that the feeling preference, as we might expect, overlaps with Cattell's sensitivity factor. This is interesting simply because it tends to reinforce Cattell's definition that pathemia represents an absence of logical thinking and organization, with the individual preferring to live more at the 'hypothalamic level'. Certainly, a high preponderance of musicians display significant levels on the MBTI feeling dimension, for example, 76 per cent of undergraduates and 84 per cent of professionals (Kemp 1996). If we combine the Jungian dimensions of intuition and feeling (as an approximation to Cattell's pathemia) we still find that a cluster of 48 per cent of undergraduate musicians and 63 per cent of professionals share these two characteristics. Furthermore, these percentages rise to 59 per cent and 74 per cent respectively in composers (Kemp 1996).

Jungian psychology suggests that these preferences not only identify people's strengths, they also assist in locating their 'inferior' characteristics. The underdeveloped aspects of intuitive–feeling types are sensing and thinking. Less developed sensing and thinking will often manifest themselves in a tendency to gloss over facts and details, and a preoccupation with broad experience of an impressionistic kind rather than the need to understand it by means of detailed analysis. What this suggests, together with Cattell's notion of pathemia, is that musicians are able to mobilize both upper and lower brain functions in developing a cognitive style which makes more extensive use of the subcortical areas of the brain. The point is well made by Gardner (1983) when he suggests that music

. . . can serve as a way of capturing feelings, knowledge about feelings, or knowledge about the forms of feelings, communicating them from the performer or the creator to the attentive listener. The neurology that permits or facilitates this association has by no means been worked out. Still, it is perhaps worth speculating that musical competence depends not upon cortical analytic mechanisms alone, but also upon those subcortical structures deemed central to feeling and motivation. (p. 124)

Certainly this corresponds with the earlier point that an important aspect of musical performance and response appears to be kinaesthetic, and that musical 'decision-making', particularly in the height of performance, may be less cerebral than is often supposed.

ANXIETY

Trait and state anxiety are not always easily separable either conceptually or in terms of measurement. Trait anxiety can be seen as a general predisposition to be anxious; state anxiety fluctuates according to the kinds of situation in which individuals find themselves. It is the former which is focused on here. For our purposes, Cattell's anxiety factor and Eysenck's neuroticism dimension will be viewed as being largely overlapping, although Cattell and Kline (1977) have maintained that neuroticism is an inappropriate term since it embraces a wider set of factors than those relating to anxiety. Nonetheless, they describe anxiety as being 'easily perturbed, worrying, emotional when frustrated, lax, uncontrolled, depressed, moody, hypochondriacal, shy, embittered, and of restricted interests' (pp. 121–2).

Amongst these kind of factors, adult musicians display particular tendencies towards the primary factors of emotional instability and ergic tension (a tendency to be tense and frustrated), as well as some evidence of suspiciousness, low self-sentiment, and apprehensiveness (Kemp 1996).

Wills and Cooper (1988) also identified high levels of neuroticism (as well as psychoticism) in popular musicians. Other research using an Eysenckian inventory showed that, amongst groups of other performing artists, musicians were particularly 'cynical, resigned, and world-weary' (Marchant-Haycox and Wilson 1992, p. 1065). Steptoe (1989) also tended to find a certain world-weariness in his study on stage fright and coping strategies in professional musicians, and he interpreted this as reflecting stressful aspects of their working lives.

The extensive body of research into anxiety in musicians, quite understandably, largely focuses on ways of dealing with the problem of performance anxiety behaviourally (see Chapter 12, this volume), and this emphasis on the debilitating aspects of anxiety frequently shifts our attention away from the small minority of researchers who have considered its facilitating effects. Clearly, however, the two are not distinct, and an inverted U-shaped relationship between anxiety and performance ability helps describe its performance-facilitating effects on one side and its debilitating aspects on the other. Cattell (1972) refers to the links between anxiety and motivation in that the former (presumably in its debilitating form) can be perceived as a degenerate form of motivation which cannot be mobilized for performance enhancement. If one takes this kind of view then, in education, it is a matter of finding the personal optimum point at which the change-over is likely to occur and identifying those environmental and technical aspects within the music and the performing context which 'tip the scales'.

Hamann and Sobaje (1983) showed that levels of anxiety in music students, and in this case, state anxiety, can actually facilitate performance; the quality of performances in high stress situations was superior to those in low stress conditions and yet were characterized by higher levels of state anxiety. However, this enhanced performance under the high stress condition was displayed most significantly by those students with the most musical experience; those with moderate or minimal experience displayed proportionately less enhancement. Later, Hamann (1985) managed to demonstrate the interrelationship between trait and state anxiety; those students with high trait anxiety experienced greater increases in state anxiety than those with lower trait anxiety. He also demonstrated the mediating effects of levels of task-mastery (technical proficiency in performance). Those students who experienced high trait anxiety and possessed high levels of task-mastery benefited more from high levels of state anxiety, than those who shared the same levels of trait anxiety but possessed low task-mastery levels. He concluded that high levels of performance skills in combination with high trait and state anxiety will lead to successful performances in stressful situations. Similarly, in his comprehensive review of the literature on performance anxiety, Lehrer (1987) concluded that frequent engagement in performance allowed anxiety to be best mobilized as a performance facilitator. On the other hand, any avoidance of performance in the form of extended periods of lay-off can incubate higher levels of debilitating anxiety.

What may eventually emerge from research of this kind is that the inverted U-relationship between anxiety and musical performance may not be uniform. For example, Gaudrey and Spielberger (1971) questioned the non-critical adoption of the Yerkes-Dodson Law suggesting that the interrelationship between anxiety and various forms of performance might be far more negative than positive. Unfortunately, space does not allow for a more detailed discussion of other aspects of anxiety. For example, Eysenck (1967) maintains that neuroticism and autonomic nervous system activation are linked in the form of an information processing loop. This was certainly a notion first developed by Freud (1964).

As we noted earlier, introverts will arrive at their optimum levels of arousal before extraverts in high stress situations because they have higher arousal rates. Thus two feedback loops, both involving levels of arousal, might well result in musicians who tend to be anxious introverts anyway, suffering over-arousal in stressful situations. Certainly, a fear of impending over-arousal might well result in anticipation of such events and has been referred to as 'catastrophizing'. Steptoe and Fidler (1987) found tendencies among amateur, student, and professional musicians to generate exaggerated fears of impending catastrophe which, in their view, was linked to state anxiety rather than neuroticism. This, however, is at odds with Gaudrey and Spielberger's (1971) view that people with high trait anxiety are more likely to perceive situations as threatening, generating levels of state anxiety and tendencies towards self-depreciation. Marchant-Haycox and Wilson (1992) similarly argued that emotional instability would predispose performing artists to symptoms of panic within situations apparently threatening. Powell and Enright (1990) referred to catastrophizing as a form of secondary anxiety—a tendency to 'worry about anxiety'. Such irrational thoughts are likely to increase physiological arousal and generate symptoms of sweating, nausea, increased heart rate, and shaking. These fears easily become maladaptive and, as Steptoe (1989) maintains, such off-task concerns which divert attention away from the performance will significantly increase the danger of committing errors.

GENDER ROLE STEREOTYPING

Research on the 'creative personality' dating from the 1950s and 60s suggested that creative types frequently display more characteristics of the opposite sex than is considered to be 'normal' amongst the general population (see, for example, Barron 1957; Hall and MacKinnon 1969; MacKinnon 1962). This phenomenon becomes even more pronounced when certain masculinity–femininity scales are adopted, of the kind incorporated into some of the earlier personality inventories. Later, Bem's (1974) theory of psychological androgyny challenged the bipolar nature of these scales and developed the notion that masculinity and femininity should be viewed as two separate dimensions. Her theory maintained that the two dimensions are quite independent—as well as being exclusively masculine or feminine, people could be strongly both, or, indeed, neither. This fourfold typology in which the third type was described as androgynous and the fourth, undifferentiated, appeared to generate the ideal vehicle with which to investigate creative types.

Certainly, personality research with musicians had earlier identified an interesting set of interactions on gender-related traits (Garder 1955; Martin 1976; Sample and Hotchkiss 1971). What was to emerge later was that the gender differences normally found in general populations were significantly eroded in groups of adult musicians, particularly in respect of those traits closely related to musicianship—aloofness, urgency, sensitivity, and self-sufficiency (Kemp 1982a). However, the same research which also involved a large group of musicians of secondary school age showed that the phenomenon did not occur until after the age of 15.

A few researchers have adopted the *Bem Sex Role Inventory* (BSRI; Bem 1974) to investigate the question further. For example, a study of conservatoire music students showed that, indeed, the women were identifiable as both feminine and masculine (i.e. androgynous); however, whilst the men emerged as more feminine they were identifiably lower in masculinity (Kemp 1985). Wubbenhorst's (1994) research with student teachers and performers also found most of them to be androgynous (48 and 38 per cent respectively). The remaining members of the two groups were more or less equally distributed amongst the other three BSRI types. This research, regardless of whether it adopted personality inventories or the BSRI, raises important issues. For example, it helps identify the kinds of demands that music makes upon the individual which can be interpreted as the temperamental requirements of musicianship. Csikszentmihalyi and Getzels (1973) maintained that these patterns of results 'can be explained in terms of task requirement . . . to use a full range of cognitive and emotional responses regardless of sex-linked, sociocultural expectations' (p. 102). This may well result in some musicians being perceived as sex-typed contrary to their own gender. Elsewhere (Kemp 1996) I have discussed several issues relating to these perceptions. For example, Ruch (1984) examined the underlying factor structure of the BSRI, and discovered that whereas the femininity scale comprised a loosely structured set of factors, those factors concerning masculinity were much more closely clustered. This, conceivably, suggests that in everyday existence women who do not display all the different manifestations of femininity may nevertheless still be typed as feminine. On the other hand, men may be required to adhere far more rigidly to their closely structured set of characteristics in order that their masculinity should not be questioned.

Although Bem (1981) has moved away somewhat from her original theory of androgyny, the central message of her theory still stands. In fact, in arguing that society should be more schematic in the way that children are socialized into developing their personal gender schemas, Bem has high-lighted important issues for those engaged in music education in schools. In current climates children who pursue music into and beyond adolescence may be in possession of the kind of personal autonomy which enables them to disregard sociocultural expectations as well as the necessary high motiva-tion towards music which allows them to continue regardless of the personal and social costs. Certainly, such notions may well account for the high drop-out rates from instrumental tuition, and clearly these drop-out rates might well help explain the change-over pattern in adolescence to which I have already referred.

As a final comment, it should perhaps be mentioned here that such manifestations of androgyny do not appear to be present in all groups of musicians. There is some evidence to suggest that music teachers are able to retain some of their gender-related traits, sometimes to the extent of re-ducing their levels on musicianship-related traits (Kemp 1982*b*). It is also interesting to speculate whether the playing of instruments perceived as being more 'macho' allows their male players to retain their masculinity. Some evidence in connection with brass and woodwind players suggests that this is in fact the case (Kemp 1985).

MUSIC PREFERENCES AND LISTENING STYLES

It goes without saying that our preferences for particular pieces of music and composers may well reflect deeper aspects of our individual differences, particularly in terms of our listening styles and perceptual processes. There is certainly a growing body of research into these questions, particularly in the form of work which attempts to develop deeper insights into the nature of musical preference by studying personality parameters.

Burt's (1939) early work considered whether Eysenck's fourfold typology (stable extravert, unstable extravert, stable introvert, and unstable introvert) might underlie people's preferences for both paintings and music. Stable extraverts, he maintained, should prefer classical or baroque music which was solid and predictable (e.g. Handel, Mussorgsky, and Brahms). Stable introverts also were attracted by classical and baroque styles whilst displaying a preference for intellectual and more cognitive music (e.g. Bach). On the other hand, unstable extraverts, in Burt's view, preferred romantic styles, vivid colours, strong contrasts, and the emotional and sensational content of the works of composers such as Wagner, Richard Strauss, Liszt, and Berlioz. Finally, unstable introverts, whilst being drawn to romantic styles, were attracted to impressionistic and mystical pieces which offer an escape from reality (e.g. Debussy or Delius).

Although Burt's early pioneering work is rarely cited, that of Payne (1967) has exerted a more lasting influence. Payne was particularly concerned with the notion that classical and romantic styles exemplify qualities quite irrespective of the musical styles of the eighteenth and nineteenth centuries. In her view the essential difference between these styles concerned form versus feeling. In classical styles form and structure, she maintained, are the primary instigators of expression; in romantic styles, form may well not be lacking but it will be a means to an end—to communicate subjective and emotional experience. The emotional content in classical music is more elusive, in romantic music the subject matter is concerned with mystery, abnormality, and conflict. Like Burt, Payne showed that neuroticism indeed operated as a powerful factor in people's preferences for these styles—neurotics tend to prefer romantic music. Similarly, Payne (1967) also speculated that music might be distinguishable as either extravert or introvert, and later, showed that introverts tended to prefer pieces that possess a formal structure whilst extraverts were attracted to music which reflected human and emotional concerns (Payne 1980).

Before leaving the issue of the music preferences of introverts and extraverts we need to return to the question of their different levels of reaction to arousal. Although this more physiological notion was not pursued by Burt and Payne it may be implicit in their findings. As we noted above extraverts prefer solid, weighty, vivid, vigorous, emotional, and sensational music, whereas that preferred by introverts might well be more intellectually restrained, mystical, deep, and introspective. Certainly, in respect of popular styles, Daoussis and McKelvie (1986) showed that extraverts demonstrated far stronger preferences for rock music than introverts, and that these differences were strongest in the case of hard rock.

Another promising area of investigation into aesthetic preferences and individual differences relates to work in listening strategies. Hargreaves and Colman (1981) showed that two general listening styles emerged in the listening strategies of adult education students—'objective–analytic' and 'affective'. These two styles appeared to differentiate between those listeners who adopt an objective view, focusing on technical aspects of the music, and those whose attitude was more 'affective', emotional, and generally more naïve. A third listening strategy, the 'associative', which had emerged in a pilot study involving children, interestingly, did not emerge. In some ways these findings accord with Hedden's (1973) earlier study which also found two distinct listening strategies amongst adults which he identified as cognitive and associative respectively.

Although these two investigations were carried out with music novices, the findings relate to Smith's (1987) work which attempted to identify fundamental differences between the listening strategies of music experts and untrained listeners. Smith claimed that the essential characteristic of experts' listening is that they enter into a form of partnership with the composer, 'going along' with his or her compositional processes—posing a problem, working at it, solving it, denying expectations, and finally, coming to a satisfactory conclusion. Smith maintained that this 'syntactic' form of listening employed by the expert could be contrasted with the 'non-syntactic' listening of the novice which emerged as more referential, emotional, or sensual. Smith's rather controversial view was that syntactic listening might well desensitize the ear by forcing the 'listener' into a predominantly non-acoustic world of musical syntax. On the other hand, the non-syntactic listener may well be able to perceive musical works more as entities. This relates well to Schmidt's (1985) speculation that field-dependent people's more global listening styles enable them to develop a greater sensitivity to the expressive aspects of music than the more analytic functioning of the field-independent types.

In fact, Witkin's theory may offer additional insights into our discussion about listening styles and preferences. Whilst clearly relating to the contrast between the field-independent individual's analytical approach to music and the field-dependent individual's holistic attitude, the theory might well help to explain individual differences in terms of a number of skills required of the trained and educated musician. For example, Ellis (1995) showed that field-independent students were superior at distinguishing between musical styles, and Ellis and McCoy (1990) cited research which suggested that the perception of thematic transformations and musical structures was more developed in field-independent students than others. As we noted earlier, aural skills, sight-reading, and certain aspects of musical creativity appear more developed in those identified as field-independent.

Finally, this section of the chapter should not close without a brief discussion about popular music preferences: brief, simply because the research to date is fairly sparse and fragmentary (see Zillmann and Gan, this volume). In their discussion concerning rock and punk music preferences Hansen and Hansen (1991) helpfully offer three contrasting theories; firstly, that people's preferences largely reflect their personalities—people gravitate towards particular styles according to their self-concepts and their perception of social reality; secondly, that listening to different types of music helps shape attitudes and personality—a social cognition theory; and thirdly, a combination of these—that the causal direction is two-way. Although not setting out to test these kinds of hypotheses, Rawlings *et al.* (1995) may have had them in mind when studying the links between levels of psychoticism and preferences for more aggressive styles of popular music. As we might expect, the more psychotic types—tough-minded individuals—were indeed attracted to hard rock, and in addition, were found to be more extraverted, impulsive, and venturesome. On the other hand, a preference for easy listening music was negatively associated with psychoticism. Furthermore, in a second study, Rawlings *et al.* showed that a tolerance for dissonance was also displayed by the psychotic types, particularly if they were also high on neuroticism.

Clearly, an inherent problem in pursuing punk and rock music preferences involves separating actual musical preferences from the social meanings that such music has for some types of young people. As Rawlings *et al.* point out, the social connotations linking music to aggressive, radical, and rule-breaking attitudes may well be quite independent of listeners' aesthetic and appreciative responses. This is consistent with Wheeler's (1985) finding that rock music preferences were not generally linked to appreciation of any other type of music. Furthermore, she indicated that such preferences were generally negatively linked to obedience, ambition, and intellectual pursuits. Hansen and Hansen (1991) also found a lack of interest in cognitive endeavour amongst heavy metal fans along with higher male hyper-sexuality, and machiavellianism, i.e. manipulative, cynical, or amoral forms of behaviour. In addition, they found that punk rock fans were more anti-authority and prone to crime than heavy metal fans, but less prone to drug involvement.

MUSICAL DEVELOPMENT, UPBRINGING, AND EDUCATIONAL ENVIRONMENT

A curious developmental pattern emerges from studies of musicians which have employed Cattell's inventories (Kemp 1995). In young musicians of secondary school age a clear pattern of 'good' upbringing is reflected: they appear to be the recipients of a type of nurturing that is encouraging and supportive, if not controlling—the kind of environment that is often viewed as being predominantly middle class. What is intriguing in this research is that after entry into music conservatoires these traits become reversed: the more talented students, either performers or composers, as well as profes-sionals, tend to lack conscientiousness, suffer from low self-sentiment, and are more dominant. There are a number of ways that these results may be interpreted which offer particular insights into the nurturing process required by young musicians. It may well be true that in the early stages of development the young musician is particularly dependent upon the kind of parental support and encouragement that instils good working habits and a conscientious attitude to practice. However, later on the achieving musician appears to be characterized by a set of traits which suggests a good deal of personal autonomy leading to the rejection of external forms of control. It may well be true that the lack of conscientiousness of the kind identified by Barron (1955) in various artistic types is interpretable as creative people needing to develop and impose their own internalized rule systems. Clearly this is a form of internal freedom and regulation which is implicit in creative thinking and production.

Again, it is unclear whether this developmental pattern is caused by a changing population—brought about by self- or externally-imposed selection processes, or whether it is a population that undergoes a gradual change from dependency on parents to a more autonomous attitude to personal destiny. Further research may disentangle this issue but in the meantime we might wish to speculate that there may be elements of both processes occurring simultaneously. Firstly, young children may be particularly dependent upon an encouraging environment but, at the same time, one in which the internal motivations of the individual are allowed to develop without too much parental interference. Davidson *et al.* (1996) have shown that the most successful young musicians certainly received parental encouragement over matters such as practice routines. However, research by Freeman (1991) suggests that such benefits might be fairly short term and that early promise is not always sustained, no matter how hard young musicians work. The research may well be indicating that the young musician requires a facilitating environment comprising sensitive tuition and encouragement but, at the same time, personal space, and freedom in which creativity and autonomy might blossom. Roe's (1967) view that too much loving and too little neglect does not produce a creative child may well have a semblance of truth in the case of the musician's upbringing.

CONCLUSION

It is hoped that this chapter might serve to demonstrate ways in which the more well-researched questions of music psychology might be further enlightened by the kinds of issues raised here. Research into the problematic area of human motivation, particularly related to artistic activity, remains in relative infancy, and may prove to be the missing piece of the jigsaw which will allow us to develop a clearer understanding of humanity's need and drive to participate in music and artistic pursuits generally. Cognitive psychology has made important in-roads into our understanding of the musician's conceptual and physical skills; what remains to be clarified is why the acquisition of these is so fundamentally important to particular groups of people. It may not be merely what these people can *do* that separates them from others, it may well prove to be the kinds of people that they *are*. Furthermore, it may well prove to be the latter that underlies the former and ensures ultimate success at whatever level. In the case of non-executant listeners it may be the latter that predisposes them to experience levels of pleasure and delight in music.

REFERENCES

Bachmann, M-L. (1991). *Dalcroze today: an education through and into music* (trans. D. Parlett). Clarendon, Oxford.

Barron, F. (1955). The disposition towards originality. *Journal of Abnormal and Social Psychology*, **51**, 478–85.

Barron, F. (1957). Originality in relation to personality and intellect. *Journal of Personality*, **25**, 730–42.

Barron, F. (1963). *Creativity and psychological health: origins of personal vitality and creative freedom*. Van Nostrand, Princeton, New Jersey.

Bem, S. L. (1974). The measurement of psychological androgyny. *Journal of Consulting and Clinical Psychology*, **42**, 155–62.

Bem, S. L. (1981). Gender schema theory: a cognitive account of sex typing. *Psychological Review*, **88**, 354–64.

Burt, C. (1939). The factorial analysis of emotional traits. *Character and Personality*, **7**, 238–54; 285–99.

Cattell, R. B. (1971). *Abilities: their structure, growth, and action*. Houghton Mifflin, Boston.

Cattell, R. B. (1972). The nature and genesis of mood states: a theoretical model with experimental measurements concerning anxiety, depression, arousal, and other mood states. In *Anxiety: current trends in theory and research*. Vol. 1 (ed. C.D. Spielberger), pp. 115–83. Academic, New York.

Cattell, R. B. (1973). *Personality and mood by questionnaire: a handbook of interpretive theory, psychometrics, and practical procedures*. Jossey-Bass, San Francisco.

Cattell, R. B. (1995). The fallacy of the five factors in the personality sphere. *The Psychologist*, **8**, 207–8.

Cattell, R. B. and Kline, P. (1977). *The scientific analysis of personality and motivation*. Academic, New York.

Costa, P. T., Jr and McCrae, R. R. (1992). *Revised NEO Personality Inventory (NEO-PI-R) and NEO Five-Factor Inventory (NEO-FFI) professional manual*. Psychological Assessment Resources, Odessa, Florida.

Csikszentmihalyi, M. and Getzels, J. W. (1973). The personality of young artists: an empirical and theoretical exploration. *British Journal of Psychology*, **64**, 91–104.

Daoussis, L. and McKelvie, S. J. (1986). Musical preferences and effects of music on a reading comprehension test for extraverts and introverts. *Perceptual and Motor Skills*, **62**, 283–9.

Davidson, J. W., Howe, M. J. A., Moore, D. G., and Sloboda, J. A. (1996). The role of family influences in the development of musical ability. *British Journal of Developmental Psychology*, **14**, 399–412.

Deary, I. J. and Matthews, G. (1993). Personality traits are alive and well. *The Psychologist*, **6**, 299–311.

Drevdahl, J. E. and Cattell, R. B. (1958). Personality and creativity in artists and writers. *Journal of Clinical Psychology*, **12**, 21–6.

Ellis, M. C. (1995). Field dependence–independence and texture discrimination in college non-music majors. *Psychology of Music*, **23**, 184–9.

Ellis, M. C. and McCoy, C. W. (1990). Field dependence/independence in college nonmusic majors and their ability to discern form in music. *Journal of Research in Music Education*, **38**, 302–10.

Entwistle, N. J. (1972). Personality and academic attainment. *British Journal of Educational Psychology*, **42**, 137–51.

Eysenck, H. J. (1967). *The biological basis of personality*. Thomas, Springfield, Illinois.

Eysenck, H. J. (1976). *The measurement of personality*. MTP, Lancaster.

Eysenck, H. J. (1992). Four ways five factors are *not* basic. *Personality and Individual Differences*, **13**, 667–73.

Freeman, J. (1991). *Gifted children growing up*. Cassell, London.

Freud, S. (1964). *New introductory lectures on psychoanalysis*, standard edition, Vol. XXII (trans. J. Strachey). Hogarth, London.

Garder, C. E. (1955). Characteristics of outstanding high school musicians. *Journal of Research in Music Education*, **3**, 11–20.

Gardner, H. (1983). *Frames of mind: the theory of multiple intelligences*. Basic Books, New York.

Gaudrey, E. and Spielberger, C. D. (1971). *Anxiety and educational achievement*. Wiley, Sydney.

Gordon, E. E. (1993). *Learning sequences in music: skill, content, and patterns*. G. I. A., Chicago, Illinois.

Hall, W. B. and MacKinnon, D. W. (1969). Personality inventory correlates of creativity among architects. *Journal of Applied Psychology*, **53**, 322–6.

Hamann, D. L. (1985). The other side of stage fright. *Music Educators' Journal*, **71** (8), 26–7.

Hamann, D. L. and Sobaje, M. (1983). Anxiety and the college musician: a study of performance conditions and subject variables. *Psychology of Music*, **11**, 37–50.

Hansen, C. H. and Hansen, R. D. (1991). Constructing personality and social reality through music: individual differences among fans of punk and heavy metal music. *Journal of Broadcasting and Electronic Media*, **35**, 335–50.

Hargreaves, D. J. and Colman, A. M. (1981). The dimensions of aesthetic reactions to music. *Psychology of Music*, **9** (1), 15–19.

Hedden, S. K. (1973). Listeners' responses to music in relation to autochthonous and experiential factors. *Journal of Research in Music Education*, **21**, 225–38.

Kemp, A. E. (1981b). The personality structure of the musician. I. Identifying a profile of traits for the performer. *Psychology of Music*, **9** (1), 3–14.

Kemp, A. E. (1981b). The personality structure of the musician. II. Identifying a profile of traits for the composer. *Psychology of Music*, **9** (2), 69–75.

Kemp, A. E. (1982a). The personality structure of the musician. III. The significance of sex differences. *Psychology of Music*, **10** (1), 48–58.

Kemp, A. E. (1982b). Personality traits of successful music teachers. *Psychology of Music* (Special Issue) Proceedings of the Ninth International Seminar on Research in Music Education, 72–5.

Kemp, A. E. (1985). Psychological androgyny in musicians. *Council for Research in Music Education Bulletin*, **85**, 102–8.

Kemp, A. E. (1995). Aspects of upbringing as revealed in the personalities of musicians. *Quarterly Journal of Music Teaching and Learning*, **5** (4), 34–41.

Kemp, A. E. (1996). *The musical temperament: the psychology and personality of musicians.* Oxford University Press, Oxford.

King, D. (1983). Field dependence/field independence and achievement in music reading. *Dissertation Abstracts International*, **43**, 2534A.

Lehrer, P. M. (1987). A review of the approaches to the management of tension and stage fright in musical performance. *Journal of Research in Music Education*, **35**, 143–52.

McCrae, R. R. and Costa, P. T., Jr (1985). Openness to experience. In *Perspectives in personality*, Vol. 1 (ed. R. Hogan and W. H. Jones), pp. 145–72. JAI, Greenwich, Connecticut.

McCrae, R. R. and Costa, P. T., Jr (1989). More reasons to adopt the five factor model. *American Psychologist*, **44**, 451–2.

MacKinnon, D. W. (1962). The nature and nurture of creative talent. *American Psychologist*, **17**, 484–95.

Marchant-Haycox, S. E. and Wilson, G. D. (1992). Personality and stress in performing artists. *Personality and Individual Differences*, **13**, 1061–8.

Martin, P. J. (1976). Appreciation of music in relation to personality factors. Unpublished PhD thesis, University of Glasgow.

Matson, D. L. (1978). Field dependence–independence in children and their response to musical tasks embodying Piaget's principle of conservation. *Dissertation Abstracts International*, **39**, 4798A.

Mischel, W. (1968). *Personality and assessment*. Wiley, New York.

Myers, I. B. and McCaulley, M. H. (1985). *Manual: a guide to the development and use of the Myers-Briggs Type Indicator* (2nd edn). Consulting Psychologists Press, Palo Alto, California.

Payne, E. (1967). Musical taste and personality. *British Journal of Psychology*, **58**, 133–8.

Payne, E. (1980). Towards an understanding of musical appreciation. *Psychology of Music*, **8** (2), 31–41.

Powell, T. J. and Enright, S. J. (1990). *Anxiety and stress management*. Routledge, London.

Rawlings, D., Hodge, M., Sherr, D., and Dempsey, A. (1995). Toughmindedness and preference for musical excerpts, categories and triads. *Psychology of Music*, **23**, 63–80.

Roe, A. (1967). Parent–child relations and creativity. Paper prepared for conference on child-rearing practices for developing creativity. Macalester College, MN, November 2–4.

Ruch, L. O. (1984). Dimensionality of the Bem sex role inventory: a multidimensional analysis. *Sex Roles*, **10**, 99–117.

Sample, D. and Hotchkiss, S. M. (1971). An investigation of relationships between personality characteristics and success in instrumental study. *Journal of Research in Music Education*, **19**, 307–13.

Schmidt, C. P. (1984). The relationships among aspects of cognitive style and language-bound optional perception to musicians' performance in selected aural discrimination tasks. *Journal of Research in Music Education*, **32**, 159–68.

Schmidt, C. P. (1985). Cognitive styles and musical behaviour. Unpublished paper presented at the Southeastern Music Education Symposium, Athens, Georgia, April 1985.

Schmidt, C. P. and Lewis, B. A. (1987). Field dependence/independence, movement-based instruction and fourth graders' achievement in selected musical tasks. *Psychology of Music*, **15**, 117–27.

Schmidt, C. P. and Sinor, J. (1986). An investigation of the relationships among music audiation, musical creativity, and cognitive style. *Journal of Research in Music Education*, **34**, 160–72.

Seashore, C. E. (1936). The psychology of music V: measurement of musical talent: the Eastern experiment. *Music Educators' Journal*, **23** (3), 24–5.

Smith, J. D. (1987). Conflicting aesthetic ideals in a musical culture. *Music Perception*, **4**, 373–92.

Stelmack, R. M. (1990). Biological bases of extraversion, psychophysical evidence. *Journal of Personality*, **58**, 293–311.

Stelmack, R. M. and Campbell, K. B. (1974). Extraversion and auditory sensitivity to high and low frequency. *Perceptual and Motor Skills*, **38**, 875–9.

Steptoe, A. (1989). Stress, coping and stage fright in professional musicians. *Psychology of Music*, **17**, 3–11.

Steptoe, A. and Fidler, H. (1987). Stage fright in orchestral musicians: a study of cognitive and behavioural strategies in performance anxiety. *British Journal of Psychology*, **78**, 241–9.

Storr, A. (1976). *The dynamics of creation*. Penguin, Harmondsworth.

Storr, A. (1989). *Solitude*. Fontana, London.

Weisen, A. (1965). Differential reinforcing effects of onset and offset of stimulation on the operant behaviour of normals, neurotics, and psychopaths. Unpublished doctoral dissertation, University of Florida.

Wheeler, B. L. (1985). Relationship of personal characteristics to mood and enjoyment after hearing live and recorded music and to musical taste. *Psychology of Music*, **13**, 81–92.

Wills, G. and Cooper, C. L. (1988). *Pressure sensitive: popular musicians under stress*. Sage, London.

Wilson, G. D. (1977). Introversion/extraversion. In *Personality variables in social behavior* (ed. T. Blass), pp. 179–218. Lawrence Erlbaum, Hillsdale, New Jersey.

Witkin, H. A. (1965). Psychological differentiation. *Journal of Abnormal Psychology*, **70**, 317–36.

Wubbenhorst, T. (1994). Personality characteristics of music educators and performers. *Psychology of Music*, **22**, 63–74.

3 | *Gender and music*

Susan A. O'Neill

INTRODUCTION

Historically in Western culture, men have dominated the music profession and occupied positions of power and privilege. Prior to the 1850s, the vast majority of orchestras refused to employ women. It was thought to be 'improper' for a woman to perform in public. Women were traditionally encouraged to play instruments such as the harp and keyboard which could be played as accompaniment to the voice and used to entertain family and friends in the home. They were discouraged from playing instruments such as the drums, woodwind, and brass, either because women were thought to be too weak (e.g. physical strength, lung capacity) or because it would 'spoil their appearance'. In 1904, an American conductor was quoted as saying, 'nature never intended the fair sex to become cornettists, trombonists, and players of wind instruments. In the first place, they are not strong enough to play them as well as men ... Another point against them is that women cannot play brass instruments and look pretty and why should they spoil their good looks?' (cited in Pugh 1991, p. 7).

In the past, women were not given the same opportunities as men for music education and training. Thus, few women were able to attain the high levels of performance achievement required for careers as professional musicians. Their lack of orchestral experience and education meant that women found it difficult to compose the large-scale, complex works that are associated with well known and respected male composers. The famous composer Sir Thomas Beecham was once quoted as saying 'there are no great women composers, never have been, and probably never will be' (cited in Pugh 1991, p. 33). Even if women did produce symphonies, concertos, and operas, they were rarely performed and received little publicity. Often the only way a woman could publish a composition was to do so under a man's name.

Today there are increasing numbers of women employed in professional orchestras and playing a much wider range of instruments (although they rarely equal the number of male musicians). The number of women composers is increasing and many have produced large-scale works which are considered to be equal to those by men (Pugh 1991). There are roughly twice as many girls learning to play instruments than boys (ABRSM 1994), and girls achieve a higher percentage of passes than boys in school music examinations (DES 1991). However, despite the increased opportunities and achievement of women in music, men continue to have more prominent roles in the music profession.

One explanation for this phenomenon stems from the growing body of research on *gender stereotypes* in music. Gender stereotypes refer to a range of physical, psychological, and social characteristics considered to be typical of males and females in a particular culture or social group. Gender stereotypes are pervasive in society and operate at many different levels (e.g. individual, interpersonal, society, cultural). However, as Unger and Crawford (1992) point out, in reality females and males share many traits, interests, behaviours, and even physical characteristics, and will often display characteristics or behaviour normally associated with the other sex. Thus, stereotyped beliefs may not accurately reflect the *actual* behaviour of males and females in the real world. For example, a boy may believe that the flute is an instrument 'just for girls', even though the majority of principal flute players in orchestras throughout the world are male.

All cultures differentiate the roles of females and males to some extent even though there is considerable variation both within and between different social groups (Maccoby 1988; Unger and Crawford 1992). The term *gender roles* is used to describe the behaviours that are considered appropriate for males and females in a particular culture. As children grow up they learn to accept and conform to their culture's stereotyped beliefs about the appropriate characteristics and behaviour for males and females. Gender roles are learned through exposure to males and females in the 'real world', in stories, and through the mass media. In music, both children and adults share culturally defined views. Gender stereotyped beliefs reinforce the idea that particular types of music, instruments, or occupations are 'masculine' or 'feminine', influencing gender differences in education, experience, opportunity, and even levels of aspiration. Each of these factors contribute to a complex, interrelated system which cannot be explained by a simple cause-and-effect relationship (Archer and Lloyd 1985; Unger and Crawford 1992).

This chapter explores several issues related to gender and music. I will begin by examining gender differences in musical aptitude and achievement, followed by boys' and girls' preferences for music and musical activities. I will then present a review of research on gender stereotyping of musical instruments and offer explanations for this phenomenon based on social and environmental factors which influence the preferences and behaviour of both sexes. Finally, I will take a broader approach to the topic and explore some of the ways in which gender role models may be used to help children overcome gender stereotyping in music.

Sex or gender?

Controversy and contradiction surround the use of the terms *sex* and *gender* in psychology. Some authors use the terms to differentiate between the biological and social aspects of the two sexes. The category of *sex* has been used to refer to biological distinctions (i.e. hormonal, anatomical, or chromosomal differences) between males and females, such as the criteria used to identify the sex of a newborn infant, whereas the category of *gender* has been used to infer the social traits and characteristics that are learned through socialization processes (Archer and Lloyd 1985; Unger 1979, 1992).

However, such a distinction between sex and gender is difficult to make in practice. Although biological differences contribute to gender differences they interact with the social environment and are mediated through our common sense beliefs about the behaviour we expect from males and females in our society and culture. Unravelling this complex interaction is no easy task. Maccoby (1988) cautions that research which attempts to examine the existence of sex differences in achievement should not assume at the outset the cause of any differences through choice of terminology. She proposed that the words sex and gender be used interchangeably, without any assumption that sex implies a biological cause or that gender results from socialization. This suggestion has subsequently been adopted by several authors such as Bem (1989), Archer (1992), Golombok and Fivush (1994), and will be used throughout this chapter.

Discussion of the use of the terms *sex* and *gender* in music research has received little attention. However an examination of the literature revealed a notable shift over the past two decades from studies which referred primarily to 'sex differences' and 'sex stereotyping' towards studies using 'gender differences' and 'gender stereotyping' respectively. Research carried out in the 1980s referred almost entirely to sex differences when discussing issues related to stereotyped associations of musical instruments or the roles of males and females in music. However, in the 1990s, most researchers either used the terms interchangeably or used the term gender exclusively. This change in terminology appears to reflect the growing concern among music educators over equal opportunities in boys' and girls' musical experiences and the increased recognition of the effects of social and environmental factors on the development of musical performance achievement.

GENDER DIFFERENCES IN MUSICAL APTITUDE
AND ACHIEVEMENT

Few researchers have *specifically* set out to investigate the question of whether there are gender differences (either biological or social) in musical aptitude or 'ability'. One reason for the lack of research in this area stems from the fact that there is no general agreement among researchers on what the precise definition of musical 'ability' should be (i.e. a general ability to perceive and understand musical structure or a number of distinct abilities which can be present or absent in varying degrees). Thus, any attempt to examine sex differences in musical aptitude or achievement is invariably based on weak theoretical and methodological ground. Additionally, few theoretical models of sex differences in performance achievement have been proposed as a basis for empirical investigation (Ussher 1992).

Nevertheless, a number of standardized tests have been designed by researchers who purport they are able to measure musical aptitude or 'ability' (e.g. Bentley 1966; Gordon 1979; Seashore 1919, 1960; Wing 1960). As a result, many schools use these tests to select those children who will be given the opportunity to engage in musical training and those children who will be denied the opportunity. Thus, a direct causal relationship is implied between musical aptitude and achievement. Given the fact that girls achieve a higher percentage of passes in school music examinations at all levels than boys (DES 1991), one might expect girls to score consistently higher on tests of musical aptitude. However, no reliable sex differences have been found in the musical aptitude of females and males based on tests of musical 'ability' or auditory perception (see review by Shuter-Dyson and Gabriel 1981). Where sex differences have been found, they have been explained in terms of the higher amount of musical training females had received compared to males (Gilbert 1942). Although sex differences have appeared on sub-tests of test batteries, the explanations that have been offered by researchers for these differences have been speculative and remain unsupported by empirical evidence (Shuter 1964; Shuter-Dyson 1979; Wing 1941).

Despite the lack of evidence for gender differences in musical aptitude, a gender reversal is apparent in the success and involvement of girls and boys, and men and women, in music. More girls than boys are involved in, and successful at, musical activities at school, whereas men dominate the music profession, achieving higher levels of success in their musical careers. Recent evidence suggests that musical achievement depends not only on the initial musical aptitude of the individual, but on a complex interaction involving cognitive, social, environmental, and motivational factors, and an individual's experience, education, aspirations, and attitudes towards music, and the process of musical training (e.g. Crowther and Durkin 1982; Howe *et al.* 1995; Manturzewska 1990; O'Neill and Sloboda, in press; Sloboda and Howe 1991; Sosniak 1985, 1990). Each of these factors distinguish males and females according to assumptions and expectations about masculinity and femininity in our culture. Thus, in order to understand gender differences in musical achievement, we must investigate gender stereotyping in girls' and boys' musical attitudes and behaviour.

GENDER DIFFERENCES IN MUSICAL PREFERENCES

There are striking gender differences in boys' and girls' preferences for music and musical activities. For example, Crowther and Durkin (1982) administered questionnaires to 12–18 year-olds that were designed to meas- ure their attitudes towards music. They found that although positive atti- tudes towards music increased with age for both sexes, girls reported more positive attitudes towards music than boys at all ages, with significant differences between the ratings of boys and girls in the lower age groups. Girls also rated listening to music more favourably than boys.

The researchers also administered a questionnaire designed to measure girls' and boys' participation in musical activities. Results indicated that girls reported themselves significantly more involved in singing in a choir and playing musical instruments than boys, and reported attending more concerts on average than boys. Girls also gave more favourable ratings for these activities than boys. With the exception of the highest age group, more girls than boys reported music to be an important school subject.

These findings were supported in a recent study by Eccles *et al.* (1993) who asked 865 children aged 7–10 to rate how much they valued mathematics, reading, sport, and music, and how good they thought they were in each domain. Their results showed gender-role stereotyped responses from both sexes. Boys reported more positive competence beliefs and values for sport than girls, whereas girls reported more positive competence beliefs and values for instrumental music than boys.

One explanation for these findings can be found in the results of studies investigating gender stereotyping of school subjects. For example, Colley *et al.* (1994) found that although 11–13 year-old females and males did not differ significantly in their rank-ordered preferences for music compared with eight other school subjects, higher rankings for music were associated with higher 'feminine' scores on the *Children's Sex Role Inventory* (Boldizar 1991). This finding suggests that music tends to be regarded by males and females as a 'feminine' subject and is therefore far more likely to attract, and be valued by, girls than boys.

However, evidence from recent research in the area of music information technology suggests that males' interest in music may be in the process of change (Comber *et al.* 1993). Researchers administered a survey to students aged 11–18 in order to obtain information on perceived competence with music technology and attitudes towards music technology. They found that males reported more positive attitudes towards, and confidence in using, music technology than girls. Comber and colleagues concluded that 'whilst boys seem to approach music technology with the self-assurance derived from many hours in front of a home computer, bolstered by a cultural stereotype (apparently accepted by many females) which says that technology is masculine, girls are more likely to express considerable anxiety and lack of confidence' (p. 129). Music information technology holds an attraction for boys which appears to be encouraging them to participate in music. Although many music educators welcome this development, the increase in male interest in this area may only serve to perpetuate the image of information technology as a masculine subject, thereby increasing the 'gender gap' in this area. As Comber and colleagues point out, further research is needed to identify the factors which contribute to inequalities in girls' and boys' involvement in a range of musical activities at school. In addition, more needs to be done by teachers in schools to devise teaching practices which address the problems that have been identified.

GENDER STEREOTYPING OF MUSICAL INSTRUMENTS

This section reviews the growing body of research on gender stereotyping of musical instruments. Although there is a great deal of overlap in the musical instrument preferences of males and females, research has demonstrated that gender stereotyped associations are influential in the preferences towards, and selection of, instruments by the two sexes. There is evidence to suggest that external or self-imposed restrictions are limiting the range of musical instruments available for boys and girls to select from, thereby also limiting their musical experience, participation in instrumental groups, and opportunities for careers in instrumental music.

'Masculine' and 'feminine' musical instruments

In a series of related studies, Abeles and Porter (1978) systematically examined the gender stereotyping of musical instruments. They asked undergraduate music and non-music students to determine the placement of eight instruments on a masculine–feminine continuum. Participants were presented with randomly ordered pairs of instruments and were asked to circle the instrument they considered to be the most 'masculine'. They found a perfect correlation of 1.00 for ranked gender ratings between the two groups. The most 'masculine' instruments were the drums, trombone, and trumpet; the most 'feminine' instruments were the flute, violin, and clarinet. The cello and saxophone were ranked in the middle. Other studies have reported similar findings. Griswold and Chroback (1981) found that undergraduate students at an American university, regardless of their sex, had gender stereotyped associations for certain instruments which were regarded as 'feminine' and 'masculine'. Crowther and Durkin (1982) also found sex differences in the instrumental choices of 12–18 year-old secondary pupils in England.

Do adults select gender 'appropriate' instruments for children to play?

Abeles and Porter (1978) also asked adults to select a musical instrument for their (hypothetical) daughter or son from a list of eight instruments as follows: cello, clarinet, drums, flute, saxophone, trombone, trumpet, and violin. They found a significant main effect for sex of child. Participants were more likely to choose a clarinet, flute, and violin for a daughter and drums, trombone, and trumpet for a son. There were no significant sex differences in the preferences shown for the cello and saxophone. In addition to demonstrating that particular instruments are associated with gender categories of 'masculine' and 'feminine', Abeles and Porter concluded that their results suggest but do not establish that parents may encourage their sons and daughters to select instruments based on gender stereotyped associations.

Their conclusions find support in past research involving gender stereotypes and parents' selection of toys. For example, Seavey *et al.* (1975) asked adults to interact and select a toy for a three-month-old infant dressed in a yellow jumpsuit. Half of the adults were told the infant was female and half were told the infant was male. Several toys were available for the adults to select from which included a masculine stereotyped toy (a small rubber football), a feminine stereotyped toy (a doll), and a neutral toy (a plastic ring). Perhaps not surprisingly, participants were more likely to select the doll for the infant labelled a girl. However, when the infant labelled was a boy, the adults were more likely to choose the gender neutral toy than either the football or the doll. In their review of gender labelling studies, Stern and Karraker (1989) found that on average adults were more likely to give dolls to infants labelled female, and masculine toys such as balls and tools to infants labelled male. However, when adults were asked to report their beliefs about the characteristics of either a boy or a girl infant, their descriptions did not vary significantly. Thus, the behaviour of adults does not necessarily correspond with their self-reported attitudes. As Golombok and Fivush (1994) point out, 'even if adults do not consciously believe they are making a distinction in the way they perceive a female versus a male infant, they nevertheless behave in very different ways depending on the given gender label . . . this is evidence of the pervasiveness of gender stereotypes' (p. 26). It is possible that a similar phenomenon exists among parents and teachers regarding musical instrument selection, although few studies have explored this issue.

Children's preferences for musical instruments: a function of gender?

Clearly, gender stereotyped associations of musical instruments are present in adults and adolescents. But do children hold similar gender stereotyped beliefs? Abeles and Porter (1978) showed girls and boys (aged 5–10) pictures and played tape recordings of eight musical instruments, asking them to indicate their preferences. The preference scores were then related to the scores of femininity/masculinity they obtained from adult participants in their first study. Results showed a significant age by sex interaction. The youngest children showed no difference in the extent to which girls and boys preferred instruments that were viewed by adults as feminine and masculine. However, the older children showed a gender divergence with the girls exhibiting a preference for feminine instruments and the boys exhibiting a preference for masculine instruments. The results also indicated that girls selected a wider variety of instruments along the masculine–feminine continuum, whereas boys' choices tended to be narrow and near the masculine end of the scale.

In a similar study, Delzell and Leppla (1992) showed children (aged 9–10) pictures of eight musical instruments and asked them to indicate the one they would prefer to learn to play. More girls than boys were found to prefer the flute, clarinet, and violin, and more boys than girls were found to prefer the drums, saxophone, and trombone. However, the majority of boys wanted to play either the drums or the saxophone, whereas the majority of girls showed a preference toward a wider selection of instruments.

In a recent study carried out by myself and Michael Boulton, we too found gender differences in the types of instruments boys and girls would be prepared to play (O'Neill and Boulton 1996). We examined the instrument preferences of 153 children aged 9–11 from the North West of England. The children were shown a pictorial array of six instruments (without performers) and were asked to name each of the instruments. The instruments included two 'feminine' instruments (flute and violin), two 'masculine' instruments (drums and trumpet), and two instruments that have featured much less in previous research in this area (piano and guitar). The children were then asked to rank order the instruments from the one they would most like to learn to play to the one they would least like to learn to play. Our findings indicated that girls showed a stronger preference for the flute, piano, and violin, whereas boys expressed a stronger preference for the drums, guitar, and trumpet.

In each of the above mentioned studies, researchers compared children's preferences for musical instruments with the way instruments are gender stereotyped by adults. Few studies have *directly* assessed children's own gender stereotyped associations of instruments. However, in the studies by Delzell and Leppla (1992) and O'Neill and Boulton (1966) this issue was investigated. Delzell and Leppla asked nine-year-old children to indicate which of 28 pairs of instruments they thought a girl would like to play (50 per cent of respondents), or a boy would like to play (50 per cent of respondents). The questions were randomly distributed to male and female participants. Their findings indicated that female participants were more accurate in predicting instruments boys would like to play, than male participants were at predicting instruments girls would like to play. The researchers attributed the girls' ability to predict boys' preferences to the fact that boys showed an interest in a limited number of instruments, whereas girls tended to show an interest in a greater variety of instruments, thus making it more difficult for boys to predict them.

Based on the findings from Delzell and Leppla, we asked the children in our study whether they thought any of the six musical instruments they were shown *should not be played* by girls, and separately, whether any of the instruments *should not be played* by boys (O'Neill and Boulton 1996). Our justification for asking the question in this form was that it enabled the children to select the instruments themselves and we wanted to ensure that the children had the opportunity to discount gender stereotyped associations if they believed that all the instruments were appropriate for members of each sex to play. Results indicated that boys and girls had similar ideas about which instruments should not be played by members of each sex. However, more boys than girls viewed the violin as 'inappropriate' for boys to play.

Why do children have gender stereotyped beliefs about musical instruments?

In order to answer this question and provide an explanation for our findings, we turned to the social psychological literature on gender role development. Research and theory suggests that one of the broad aspects of boys' gender role development is 'avoidance of femininity' (Archer 1984, 1992; David and Brannon 1976). This is thought to develop early in a boy's life, as early as the second year (O'Brien and Huston 1985), and extend into adulthood (Thompson and Pleck 1986). It manifests itself in avoidance of activities that are considered to be feminine. A similar phenomenon is thought to occur in girls, but at a later time in development. This has been called the 'gender intensification hypothesis' by Hill and Lynch (1982) who found evidence that at adolescence, but not before, achievement behaviour becomes more sex stereotyped and as such girls begin to disengage from activities that they view as masculine. Indeed, as Green (1993) found in an exploratory study of music, gender, and education, the opinions expressed by 78 music teachers working in secondary schools were that '*both* boys and girls tend to restrict themselves or find themselves restricted to certain musical activities and instruments for fear of intruding into the other sex's territory, where they might stand accused of a sort of musical transvestism' (original emphasis, p. 248).

One explanation for the restriction boys and girls face with regards to instrument selection is based on research into gender boundary violation

(Best 1983; Damon 1977; Sroufe *et al.* 1993; Thorne 1986; Thorne and Luria 1986). These studies have found that children, prior to adolescence, tend to respond in a negative manner towards peers who exhibit behaviour they consider inappropriate on the grounds of gender. For example, Sroufe *et al.* (1993) found that children who violated gender boundaries were less popular with their peers, and tended to be subjected to more hostile teasing, than those who adhered to gender boundaries. With regards to music, two recent studies lend some support to this idea. Howe and Sloboda (1992) interviewed 42 talented musicians aged 10–17 who were attending a specialist music school. Many of these young people (26 per cent) reported that they experienced some pronounced problems with their peer relationships prior to attending the specialist school. These problems included loss of popularity and increased bullying, often as a result of playing gender inappropriate instruments. These problems were so severe that some of the children even contemplated giving up. One male student reported, 'I remember on occasions thinking, I'd really like to stop the violin, because there was a lot of pressure in my old school to stop, because it wasn't a musical school, and they thought it was a bit iffy and strange' (p. 18). Many of the children who reported difficulties as a result of other children not valuing their accomplishments said they valued having the opportunity to be in an environment where they were with like-minded students.

Recently, we investigated the social outcomes children expect from their peers for playing particular instruments (O'Neill and Boulton 1995). Children were asked to rank order six instruments (piano, flute, guitar, trumpet, violin, drums) from the one they would most like to learn to play, to the one they would least like to learn to play. Then they were asked to think about their first choice instrument and state how they thought their classmates would react to each one of four hypothetical target children (a boy who played the participant's most, and separately, least favoured instrument, and a girl who played the participant's most, and separately, least favoured instrument). The children rated (a) how popular they thought the child would be, (b) how much they thought the child would be ignored by their classmates, and (c) how much they thought the child would be bullied or 'picked on' by their classmates. The order in which the children were asked to think about the four types of target child was randomized. We found that both female and male participants in our study thought that a child of the same sex as themselves would be liked less, and bullied more, by other children if they played an instrument that was viewed as 'gender inappropriate'. In other words, the boys who selected 'feminine' instruments as their least favourite, were more likely to expect negative outcomes from peers than the boys who selected masculine instruments. Girls were more likely to expect negative outcomes from peers if they had selected a 'masculine' instrument as their least favourite. These negative peer reactions are not trivial for children. Being subjected to bullying and being low in popularity are two of the most distressing, and potentially damaging, aspects of peer relationship problems that can occur during childhood (Boulton and Smith 1991, 1994; for review see Parker and Asher 1987). Thus, it would not be unreasonable to hypothesize that children would choose to behave in ways that minimize their risks for such negative reactions from peers. Given this recognition, it is surprising, as MacKenzie (1991) recently pointed out, that relatively little research has been carried out on the reasons why children decide to learn to play musical instruments or to avoid some or all of them altogether.

Are gender stereotyped preferences resistant to change?

Delzell and Leppla (1992) concluded from their research that although the gender associations of the instruments which lie on opposite ends of the masculine–feminine continuum (drums and flute) appeared to be salient in children's preferences, there appeared to be a lessening of gender association in the choices of instruments girls in particular would like to learn to play. This issue of change over time in girls' and boys' preferences for musical instruments was recently examined by Zervoudakes and Tanur (1994). They contacted 200 elementary schools, 200 high schools, and 200 colleges and universities across 50 states in the USA. The institutions were chosen at random and were asked to send programmes for band and orchestra performances from the 1960s, 70s, and 80s. From the 590 usable programmes that were returned, the researchers were able to glean information about who played in each institution's band/orchestra and what instruments they played. A major aim of their study was to investigate changes in the proportion of females who played 'feminine' and 'masculine' instruments across three time periods—1959–76, 1977–86, and 1987–90. The analysis showed an increase in the proportion of females playing both feminine and masculine instruments. However, at the high school and college levels, when the increased proportion of instrumentalists who were female was controlled by means of a partial correlation technique, the proportion of females playing feminine instruments increased over time, whereas the proportion of females playing masculine instruments either remained the same or decreased. Zervoudakes and Tanur suggested that 'the increasing participation of young women in high school and college bands seems to have served to perpetuate gender-based stereotypes of appropriate instruments' (p. 67).

The evidence pertaining to the elementary school level obtained by Zervoudakes and Tanur was much more encouraging in that it indicated that there was some limited increase over time in the proportion of girls playing masculine instruments, even when the overall increase in the number of females playing instruments was held constant. However, we should be cautious about accepting this latter result as being evidence that gender-based preferences for musical instruments are beginning to change. Zervoudakes and Tanur themselves concede that their data at the elementary school level were sparse and further research is needed before we can conclude with any confidence that girls are in fact playing a wider range of instruments than boys.

Overall, it appears as though little has changed with respect to gender stereotypes and music since research in this area began several decades ago. This is especially disappointing given that the efforts within schools to change children's views that participating in specific activities is either 'just for girls' or 'just for boys' have met with some success in other domains. For example, a recent study of children's views of gender stereotyping in sport found no consistent evidence that males and females believed that particular sports were appropriate for only one sex (Howat *et al.* 1995). Indeed, Archer and McDonald (1990) found that many 10–15 year-old girls reported that they participated in particular sports, such as soccer, that had previously been regarded as masculine. Researchers have also demonstrated that it is possible to change females' attitudes and behaviour towards the traditionally masculine subject of mathematics. By providing opportunities for girls to see and interact with female role models who work in mathematics/science related fields, and by teachers actively encouraging girls to become more involved in mathematics, some schools have been effective in persuading females towards higher levels of mathematical achievement (Licht and Dweck 1983; see also review by Fennema 1983). Although we should not conclude that gender stereotyping in fields such as sport and mathematics has been *eliminated*, research evidence suggests that the positive change which has taken place in these areas has not occurred with respect to music.

CROSSING THE GENDER DIVIDE IN MUSIC

Children's attitudes and behaviour towards music, musical activities, and instruments are influenced by their perceptions of gender differences in musical participation they observe in the adult world. Duveen and Lloyd (1986) argued that boys and girls construct a social understanding of gender differentiation from the social interactions they witness in everyday life. Despite the increasing number of women in music, there are far fewer female role models than male. For example, children are more likely to be exposed (primarily through the media) to male rock/pop musicians playing guitars and drums. Indeed, as Eccles *et al.* (1993) recently pointed out, '[instrumental music] is the only instance we know about in which the gender-role differentiated beliefs and self-perceptions in childhood are opposite to the gender differences in participation one observes in the adult world' (p. 845).

The fact that music is viewed by both boys and girls to be a 'feminine' subject means that only the most motivated boys are likely to become interested and involved in music at school. On the other hand, girls must balance their early musical interest and success with their perceptions of women in the 'real world' as inferior to men in the music profession (Green 1993).

Crowther and Durkin (1982) suggest that social and cultural norms and values perpetuate children's stereotyped beliefs about music at school. These beliefs may be reinforced by the stereotyped beliefs and behaviour of teachers, parents, and peers. According to Maccoby (1988), once a child understands gender categories, subsequent information may be integrated in terms of this influential classification and gender schemas (e.g. concepts such as masculine and feminine) are extremely resistant to change and disconfirmation. In a recent review of research on change in gender stereotypes in society, Golombok and Fivush (1994) concluded, 'it is apparent that gender stereotypes have remained relatively stable over the past 30–40 years. Although there have been many changes in the roles that females and males play in our society, beliefs about gender-related traits and characteristics have not undergone much change' (p. 36).

Although individuals' behaviour is usually consistent with their attitudes, subtle persuasion can alter attitudes and individuals tend to bias their recall of behaviour to correspond with their current attitudes (Ross *et al.* 1981, 1983). Thus, it would seem that schools, parents, and others in a position of influence need to do more to challenge children's gender stereotyped views of music and musical participation if boys and girls are to share positive attitudes towards music and have a wider choice of instruments to select from. Indeed, as Comber *et al.* (1993) recently pointed out, 'music education has the potential to play a major role in redressing the imbalance between the sexes' (p. 133). Despite this recognition, few studies have focused on changing children's stereotyped associations. However, there are two exceptions. Abeles and Porter (1978) found that it was possible to influence children's preferences for particular instruments by changing the mode of presentation. One group of children was presented with the sound and pictures of eight instruments using a widely adopted educational recording designed to introduce instruments to children. The second group of children (the control group) were played the same tune on all eight instruments and showed pictures of the instruments without players. The third group were presented with excerpts from another widely adopted educational recording and were shown pictures of instruments with female players holding 'feminine' instruments and male players holding 'masculine' instruments. The results indicated that although the mode of presentation did not influence the preferences of girls (who tended to select a wider range of instruments than the boys), a significantly higher proportion of boys selected fewer masculine instruments when they had been presented in an unbiased control group condition than in the other two conditions. Their findings indicate that both the type of music played, and the gender role models used, can lead to decreases in boys' preferences for masculine instruments.

A recent study by Bruce and Kemp (1993) found that it was possible to influence five to seven-year-old children's preferences for particular instruments by changing the sex-role model they saw playing particular instruments. For example, when children watched a concert in which the trombone player was female, over 20 per cent of the girls showed an interest in the trombone. However, in another concert at a different school, in which the trombone player was male, less than two per cent of the girls showed an interest in the trombone. A similar response was found in the boys' choice of flute. It would appear from their results that the identification of the same sex role models overcame the gender stereotyped associations of particular instruments. Future research should examine this possibility further if we are to overcome the self-imposed restrictions that apply to boys' and girls' preferences for learning to play particular musical instruments.

However, a word of caution may be necessary. According to Katz (1986), manipulations by adults to change boys' and girls' gender stereotyped beliefs appear to have little lasting impact on behaviour. There are two important reasons for this. First of all, short-term programmes are ineffective in changing the cultural context that maintains gender stereotyping. In music, this issue was recently highlighted by Green (1993) who concluded her paper on music, gender, and education by pointing out that 'to whatever extent teachers themselves provide opportunities and encouragement for girls and boys to cross sexual/musical boundaries, the complex process of labelling and self-fulfilment which circulates around this hidden agenda cannot be easily overcome; nor can the deeply-rooted sexual ideology which lies within this conundrum' (p. 250). The second issue involves the considerable pressure children experience from peers. It is necessary for girls and boys to be able to ignore the pressure exerted against them displaying gender inappropriate behaviour and crossing traditional gender boundaries. Both of these issues were raised by Unger and Crawford (1992) who stated that 'people in general are unaware of how the culture mandates sex-based dichotomies and punishes those who deviate' (p. 265). In order to overcome these problems it is necessary for children to have support from a variety of sources over a prolonged period of time. For example, Unger and Crawford found that high-achieving women tend to report having parental and social encouragement that enabled them to 'transcend gender typing'. Clearly, this is an area that could be explored further by researchers, and one which requires concerted effort on the part of parents, teachers, and those interested in helping children overcome gender differentiation in musical interests and participation.

REFERENCES

Abeles, H. F. and Porter, S. Y. (1978). The sex-stereotyping of musical instruments. *Journal of Research in Music Education*, **26**, 65–75.

Associated Board of the Royal Schools of Music (1994). *Making music: The Associated Board review of the teaching, learning, and playing of musical instruments in the United Kingdom*. ABRSM.

Archer, J. (1984). Gender roles as developmental pathways. *British Journal of Social Psychology*, **23**, 245–56.

Archer, J. (1992). Childhood gender roles: Social context and organization. In *Childhood social development: Contemporary perspectives* (ed. H. McGurk), pp. 31–61. Lawrence Erlbaum Associates, Hove.

Archer, J. and Lloyd, B. (1985). *Sex and gender*. Cambridge University Press, Cambridge.

Archer, J. and McDonald, M. (1990). Gender roles and sports in adolescent girls. *Leisure Studies*, **9**, 225–40.

Bem, S. L. (1989). Genital knowledge and gender constancy in preschool children. *Child Development*, **60**, 649–62.

Bentley, A. (1966). *Musical ability in children and its measurement*. Harrap, London.

Best, R. (1983). *We've all got scars: What boys and girls learn in elementary school*. Indiana University Press, Bloomington.

Boldizar, J. P. (1991). Assessing sex typing and androgyny in children: The Children's Sex Role Inventory. *Developmental Psychology*, **27**, 505–15.

Boulton, M. J. and Smith, P. K. (1991). Bullying and withdrawn children. In *Truants from life: Theory and therapy* (ed. V. Varma). David Fulton, London.

Boulton, M. J. and Smith, P. K. (1994). Bully/victim problems in middle-school children: stability, self-perceived confidence, peer perceptions, and peer acceptance. *British Journal of Developmental Psychology*, **12**, 315–29.

Bruce, R. and Kemp, A. (1993). Sex-stereotyping in children's preferences for musical instruments. *British Journal of Music Education*, **10**, 213–17.

Colley, A., Comber, C., and Hargreaves, D. J. (1994). Gender effects in school subject preferences: A research note. *Educational Studies*, **20**, 13–18.

Comber, C., Hargreaves, D. J., and Colley, A. (1993). Girls, boys, and technology in music education. *British Journal of Music Education*, **10**, 123–34.

Crowther, R. and Durkin, K. (1982). Sex- and age-related differences in the musical behaviour, interests, and attitudes towards music of 232 secondary school students. *Educational Studies*, **8**, 131–9.

Damon, W. (1977). *The social world of the child*. Jossey Bass, San Francisco.

David, D. S. and Brannon, R. (1976). The male sex role: our culture's blueprint for manhood, and what it's done for us lately. In *The forty-nine per cent majority: The male sex role* (ed. D. S. David and R. Brannon). Addison-Wesley, Reading, Mass.

Delzell, J. K. and Leppla, D. A. (1992). Gender association of musical instruments and preferences of fourth-grade students for selected instruments. *Journal of Research in Music Education*, **40**, 93–103.

Department of Education and Science (1991). *Music for ages 5 to 14: Proposals of the Secretary of State for Education and Science and Secretary of State for Wales*. HMSO.

Duveen, G. and Lloyd, B. (1986). The significance of social identities. *British Journal of Social Psychology*, **25**, 219–30.

Eccles, J., Wigfield, A., Harold, R. D., and Blumenfeld, P. (1993). Age and gender differences in children's self- and task perceptions during elementary school. *Child Development*, **64**, 830–47.

Fennema, E. (1983). Success in mathematics. In *Sex differentiation and schooling* (ed. M. Marland), pp. 163–80. Heinemann, London.

Gilbert, G. M. (1942). Sex differences in musical aptitude and training. *Journal of General Psychology*, **26**, 19–33.

Golombok, S. and Fivush, R. (1994). *Gender development*. Cambridge University Press, Cambridge.

Gordon, E. E. (1979). *Primary measures of music audiation: Test manual*. G. I. A., Chicago.

Green, L. (1993). Music, gender, and education: A report on some exploratory research. *British Journal of Music Education*, **10**, 219–53.

Griswold, P. A. and Chroback, D. A. (1981). Sex-role associations of music instruments and occupations by gender and major. *Journal of Research in Music Education*, **29**, 57–72.

Hill, J. P. and Lynch, M. E. (1982). The intensification of gender-related expectations during early adolescence. In *Girls at puberty: Biological and psychological perspectives* (ed. J. Brooks-Gunn and A. C. Petersen), pp. 201–29. Plenum, New York and London.

Howat, D., Fishwick, L., and Wolfson, S. (1995). Sex, sport and stereotypes: Children's attitudes towards the sexes in sport. Proceedings of the British Psychological Society London Conference, Vol. 3, p. 81.

Howe, M. J. A. and Sloboda, J. A. (1992). Problems experienced by talented young musicians as a result of the failure of other children to value musical accomplishments. *Gifted Education*, **8**, 16–18.

Howe, M. J. A., Davidson, J. W., Moore, D. G., and Sloboda, J. A. (1995). Are there early childhood signs of musical ability? *Psychology of Music*, **23**, 111–28.

Katz, P. A. (1986). Modification of children's gender stereotypical behaviour: General issues and research considerations. *Sex Roles*, **14**, 591–602.

Licht, B. G. and Dweck, C. S. (1983). Sex differences in achievement orientations: Consequences for academic choices and attainments. In *Sex differentiation and schooling* (ed. M. Marland), pp. 72–97. Heinemann, London.

Maccoby, E. E. (1988). Gender as a social category. *Development Psychology*, **24**, 755–65.

MacKenzie, C. G. (1991). Starting to learn to play a musical instrument: A study of boys' and girls' motivational criteria. *British Journal of Music Education*, **8**, 15–20.

Manturzewska, M. (1990). A biographical study of the life-span development of professional musicians. *Psychology of Music*, **18**, 112–39.

O'Brien, M. and Huston, A. C. (1985). Development of sex-typed play in toddlers. *Developmental Psychology*, **21**, 866–71.

O'Neill, S. A. and Boulton, M. J. (1995). Is there a gender bias towards musical instruments? *Music Journal*, **60**, 358–9.

O'Neill, S. A. and Boulton, M. J. (1996). Boys' and girls' preferences for musical instruments: A function of gender? *Psychology of Music*, **24**, 171–83.

O'Neill, S. A. and Sloboda, J. A. (in press). Effects of failure on children's ability to perform a musical test. *Psychology of Music*.

Parker, J. G. and Asher, S. R. (1987). Peer relations and later personal adjustment: are low-accepted children at risk? *Psychological Bulletin*, **102**, 357–89.

Pugh, A. (1991). *Women in music*. Cambridge University Press, Cambridge.

Ross, M., McFarland, C., Conway, M., and Zanna, M. P. (1983). Reciprocal relation between attitudes and behaviour recall: Committing people to newly formed attitudes. *Journal of Personality and Social Psychology*, **45**, 257–67.

Ross, M., McFarland, C., and Fletcher, G. J. O. (1981). The effect of attitudes on the recall of personal histories. *Journal of Personality and Social Psychology*, **10**, 627–34.

Seashore, C. E. (1919). *The psychology of musical talent*. Silver Burdett, New York.

Seashore, C. E., Lewis, D., and Saetveit, J. C. (1960). *Manual of instructions and interpretations for the Seashore Measures of Musical Talents* (2nd edn). The Psychological Corporation, New York.

Seavey, A. A., Katz, P. A., and Zalk, S. R. (1975). Baby X: The effect of gender labels on adult responses to infants. *Sex Roles*, **1**, 103–9.

Shuter, R. (1964). *An investigation of heredity and environmental factors in musical ability*. Unpublished Doctoral Dissertation, University of London.

Shuter-Dyson, R. (1979). Unisex or 'vive la difference'? Research on sex differences of relevance to musical abilities. *Bulletin of the Council for Research in Music Education*, **59**, 102–6.

Shuter-Dyson, R. and Gabriel, C. (1981). *The psychology of musical ability* (2nd edn). Methuen, London.

Sloboda, J. A. and Howe, M. J. A. (1991). Biographical precursors of musical excellence: An interview study. *Psychology of Music*, **19**, 3–21.

Sosniak, L. (1985). Learning to be a concert pianist. In *Developing talent in young people* (ed. B.S. Bloom), pp. 477–506. Ballatine, New York.

Sosniak, L. (1990). The tortoise, the hare, and the development of talent. In *Encouraging the development of exceptional skills and talents* (ed. M. J. A. Howe), pp. 149–64. British Psychological Society, Leicester.

Sroufe, L., Bennet, C., Englund, M., Urban, J., and Shulman, S. (1993). The significance of gender boundaries in preadolescence: Contemporary correlates and antecedents of boundary violation and maintenance. *Child Development*, **64**, 455–66.

Stern, M. and Karraker, K. H. (1989). Sex stereotyping of infants: A review of gender labelling studies. *Sex Roles*, **20**, 501–22.

Thompson, E. H., Jr. and Pleck, J. H. (1986). The structure of male role norms. *American Behavioral Scientist*, **29**, 531–43.

Thorne, B. (1986). Boys and girls together . . . But mostly apart: Gender arrangements in elementary schools. In *Relationships and development* (ed. W. W. Hartup and Z. Rubin). Lawrence Erlbaum Associates, Hillsdale, N.J.

Thorne, B. and Luria, Z. (1986). Sexuality and gender in children's daily worlds. *Social Problems*, **33**, 176–90.

Unger, R. (1979). *Female and male: Psychological perspectives*. Harper & Row, New York.

Unger, R. and Crawford, M. (1992). *Women and gender: A feminist psychology*. McGraw-Hill, New York.

Ussher, J. (1992). Sex differences in performance: Fact, fiction, or fantasy? In *Handbook of human performance*, Vol. 3 (ed. A. P. Smith and D. M. Jones), pp. 63–94. Academic Press, London.

Wing, H. D. (1941). A factorial study of musical tests. *British Journal of Psychology,* **31,** 341–55.

Wing, H. D. (1960). *Manual for standardised tests of musical intelligence.* NFER, Windsor.

Zervoudakes, J. and Tanur, J. (1994). Gender and musical instruments: Winds of change? *Journal of Research in Music Education,* **42,** 58–67.

PART II

Social groups and situations

4 | *Music and social influence*

W. Ray Crozier

The enjoyment of music is essentially a social experience. Music contributes to many of the ceremonies that mark the significant events in people's lives —weddings, funerals, bar-mitzvahs, parties, dances, church services, thanksgiving, and state ceremonies of commemoration, coronations, and political rallies, with their fanfares and anthems. Dancing provides a useful example of the reciprocal relationship where music influences, and is influenced by, social behaviour. Chandler (1993) offers insight into group processes in his account of English morris dancing, a form of folk dancing that can be traced back to the fifteenth century. Each side [team of dancers] comprised a number of specialist roles, and the performance required the contribution of all its members working together. At the same time, the repertory of any group was highly dependent on the skills and knowledge of tunes of its individual players, and it changed as the membership changed. Thus, the activity of the group reflected processes of conformity and innovation.

One important function that dances serve is to facilitate and regulate encounters between young men and women. For example, the country or 'barn' dance repertory consists of variations of arranged 'encounters' between partners. The rotation of partners that is integral to those dances means that a participant is not obliged to commit him or herself to the choice of one partner or to remain with a specific other person, but can meet briefly with a number of other people, smile, and make eye and physical contact with them. This arrangement helps to overcome the shyness and other difficulties that can be involved in initiating interaction with a member of the opposite sex. Furthermore, the process takes place in public, is structured, has clear codes of conduct, and can be overseen by parents or community leaders. A dance is a social activity of a particular kind, but it shares many of the properties of group processes that have been the focus of social psychological research. It is governed by the rules and norms that have evolved over time, and conformity to these rules is essential for the activity to continue. It is also a dynamic entity, whose members have different, possibly conflicting goals, and the dance must accommodate these if it is to be enjoyed by its participants and continue to serve a useful function. A social psychology of music needs to study the role that music plays in such group activities.

This role can be studied in two ways. One approach is to examine how responses to music are influenced by group processes. A second approach is to investigate how group processes are influenced by music and, more specifically, to consider what properties of music have what kinds of influence. In this chapter, we concentrate on social influence, as conformity and persuasion have long been regarded by social psychologists as fundamental to small group processes. We consider two further elements in social interaction processes, social identity and affect, that are involved in both social influence and musical experience. The chapter provides an analysis of selected significant research and evaluates explanations of the links between social influence and music.

SOCIAL INFLUENCE

The dominant theoretical framework for explaining conformity (see Levine and Russo 1987) has emphasized two kinds of dependence process: compliance and informational influence. Individuals depend on the group for social approval and acceptance, and they comply with the group because they anticipate being rewarded for doing so or punished for not doing so. In the second kind of process, individuals modify their position in the process of trying to understand the world by comparing their view of reality with that of the group. Compliance is more likely the greater the individual's dependence upon the group and the more public his or her response. Informational influence is greater when the situation is ambiguous and the individual is uncertain of his or her judgment.

Several studies have examined conformity in aesthetic judgments, including preferences for music. The typical study, as pioneered by Farnsworth and Beaumont (1929), takes an art object or a piece of music that can be described in different ways and assesses whether judgments about the object or music are influenced by 'prestige' manipulations of the descriptions. Research has examined prestige effects upon aesthetic judgments in different domains (see Crozier and Chapman 1981, for a review of these studies). We consider one study of music in some detail. Chapman and Williams (1976) selected those respondents to a survey who had expressed preference for 'progressive pop' music and antipathy towards 'serious' music and assigned them to one of three groups. In the 'high status' condition, participants were led to believe that a piece of music was an excerpt from work by a member of a progressive pop music group; in the 'low status' condition, the same piece was described as a piece of serious music, and in a control condition participants listened to the piece without description. There were significant differences between the three groups in their ratings of the same piece of music. Chapman and Williams attempted to test the hypothesis proposed by

Asch (1948) that changes in judgment brought about by prestige suggestions involve a cognitive re-organization of the material being judged, that is to say, the meaning of the music has changed. Students' ratings of the music on 12 rating scales were submitted to principal components analysis, and four components were interpreted as one evaluative factor and three descriptive factors—mood, activity, and conventionality. Prestige effects were found in four of the 12 scales, including scales on the descriptive factors. These differences in description were interpreted as showing that the music was perceived differently, rather than simply being liked more or less. Nevertheless, the evidence can only be regarded as tentative; only a minority of the scales are involved, and no analysis was carried out on factor scores.

A number of studies have investigated prestige effects. These have looked at the influence upon judgments of music (Rigg 1948), drama (Francès 1963), literary prose (Sherif 1935), and poetry (Michael *et al.* 1949; Das *et al.* 1955). Prestige is usually defined in terms of judgments made by experts. Exceptions are the study by Chapman and Williams (1976) which defined it in terms of reference group norms and a study of preferences for classical music by Rigg (1948) which was carried out during the Second World War; one group of subjects was informed that the piece was by Wagner and that he was Hitler's favourite composer, whereas the second group was simply told that the piece was by Beethoven. Although the studies do find statistically significant differences between prestige and control conditions, many questions remain about the generality of these findings. The experimental manipulations require that the stimuli are unfamiliar to subjects, that they show little variation in style, and that they are capable of sustaining alternative descriptions. All of these criteria mean that the stimuli lack any context for judgment. The labels attached to the stimuli may be the only cue that the subjects can use in making their responses. The research, too, is essentially empirical and is rarely, if ever, based on theoretical advances in understanding conformity and persuasion processes. Finally, there has been no systematic investigation of the phenomenon: the literature comprises a series of isolated experiments, and there have been no rigorous attempts to explore the robustness of effects or their limits. Despite these problems, there remains some evidence that stated musical preferences are subject to conformity effects.

Conformity was originally conceived in terms of the movement of the individual's responses in the direction of the majority view, producing greater consensus in the group. Moscovici (1980) provided evidence that the shift can also be in the opposite direction, with the majority moving towards a position advocated by a minority. Aebischer *et al.* (1983) compared the effects of majority and minority influence upon stated preferences for music. Participants were drawn from one type of French high school. Students indicated their preference for either hard rock or 'new wave' music and for either hard rock or 'contemporary' music, before learning of the results of an opinion survey. The majority preferred hard rock over both other forms. The experiment had two conditions, depending on what students were led to believe about the results of the survey. In the 'majority' condition they were informed that the survey showed that most students at their own type of school preferred new wave to hard rock. The hypothesis was that this information would change preferences in the direction of new wave. Those in the 'minority' condition were informed that most students in a different, lower status school preferred new wave to hard rock. Aebischer et al. argued that this other school would serve as a minority-influence outgroup, and their hypothesis was that the survey information would exert minority influence and would produce increased preference for new wave music. All participants made a second set of forced choice preferences between the different kinds of music, and analysis of the preference data found support for both majority and minority influence hypotheses. A second test was made of the indirect effect of influence upon preferences for contemporary music over hard rock. This would be an indirect effect in the sense that survey data had not mentioned contemporary music, but social influences changing preferences from hard rock towards new wave would necessarily also result in greater preference for contemporary music (because the assessments were forced-choice). Analysis showed that indirect effects were smaller than direct effects, nevertheless the influence of the minority upon preferences was significantly greater that that of the majority.

There have been few studies of social influence and musical preferences and the two studies we have examined in more detail seem to us to be among the best designed. They show that musical preferences are subject to social influence. In this respect, musical preferences are similar to attitude statements, other kinds of perceptual judgments, and aesthetic judgments of visual stimuli: Mugny et al. (1988) report a pattern of findings similar to Aebischer et al. when they investigated preferences for visual patterns varying in colour and complexity—when direct influence was assessed, the majority was more influential than the minority (particularly when the majority's alleged preferences ran counter to those endorsed by participants) whereas, for indirect influence, the reverse was found. Music seems to lend itself to this kind of research, in that the boundaries between different categories of contemporary music are permeable, and musical 'stimuli' lend themselves to plausible alternative descriptions, one of the main requirements of this research design. However, reviews of prestige effects more generally (Child 1972; Chapman and Williams 1976; Crozier and Chapman 1981) have concluded that these effects can be difficult to replicate. Clearly, further research is needed before we can identify the processes that underlie conformity effects upon judgments. We now consider the relevance of identity and self-presentation for explaining these effects.

Personal and social identity

The distinction between attitudes that are privately held and those that are publicly expressed is an important one for understanding social influence. It is often easier from the point of view of sustaining the group and one's position in it to remain silent, to 'pay lip service', or to appear neutral concerning a majority view counter to one's own position, and to reserve one's true position for another occasion. Similarly, although one's attitude might be changed by a persuasive minority argument, one might be reluctant to admit to this in the presence of the majority. Finnäs (1989) found differences between the music preferences that young people stated publicly and those that they privately endorsed, and these tendencies were larger among those whose preferences deviated most from the majority. He interpreted these trends in terms of subjects' self-confidence in their own beliefs, their beliefs about the preferences of the majority, and the social influence of the majority. Maass *et al.* (1987) have suggested that self-presentation motives can contribute to whether or not individuals admit to social influence.

Self-presentation motives have been extensively studied by researchers into social interaction processes. Much of this research has been influenced by Goffman's (1959) seminal analysis of the fundamental role of identity in social encounters. Issues of self and identity are complex and multi-faceted and have generated a large number of different theoretical terms. Despite the risk of reifying the self or divisions of it, drawing distinctions has heuristic value. A common distinction is between personal and social identity. Personal identity refers to an individual's unique qualities, values, and attributes, and reflects his or her personal history, whereas social identity refers to the social categories to which people belong, aspire to belong, or share important values with. The latter concept has received considerable attention from social psychologists, for example, Tajfel and Turner (1986) proposed that social identity is an important determinant of relationships within and between groups. When considering personal identity, some writers distinguish further between the private and the public self. The private self is the self that only you know, your own desires, aspirations, and beliefs about yourself, that you may or may not wish to communicate with others. The public self corresponds more closely to Goffman's conceptualization of identity and refers to the person you present to others, the enacted self, the you that others know. Any individual will aspire to be perceived in certain ways, to be popular, or thought physically attractive.

There is no direct evidence that issues of identity mediate between social influence and music, but there are many reasons why they might. The studies of social influence and music preference summarized above examined group processes only in a limited sense, as there was no face-to-face interaction, and responses could be made privately. Influence in these studies does not depend upon the pressure of an actual group, but is manipulated through reference to the preferences of other people or by attaching labels that imply that the music belongs to preferred categories. Prestige studies, more generally, manipulate the social status of the art object or music, by linking it with particular reference groups. Pieces are described as originating from a source that one identifies with, or feels that one ought to identify with, either because one aspires to be the sort of person who identifies with it or does not wish to be seen as the kind of person who does not.

Maass *et al.* (1987) have suggested that the potential loss of face before others is involved in whether someone admits to minority influence. More generally, the self-presentation perspective upon social interaction regards embarrassment as the consequence of a failure of one or more individuals to sustain their identity. Although there is no direct evidence, I would suggest that prestige effects may work, at least in part, through the fear of embarrassment. It would be embarrassing to admit that one was the kind of person who preferred a minor to a significant work or artist; if prestige was studied in a within-subjects design, my hunch would be that individuals would be embarrassed to have their change of judgment pointed out to them. Some indirect evidence comes from a study by Edelmann and Hampson (1979), where participants who were criticizing a painting became embarrassed when the interviewer suddenly announced that he was the artist. In his fictional account of a group of young men who work in a specialist record store, Hornby (1995) describes the embarrassment of one of his characters who inadvertently reveals his liking for a version of a record that the others regard as inferior; his preference is incompatible with a certain kind of identity and the implication is, of course, that preferences are not a matter of choice but are normative.

Support for this explanation of social influence can also be sought in the evidence that musical preferences have considerable implications for personal and social identity. Much of this evidence comes from studies of adolescents for whom issues of private and public self and social identifications are salient. Adolescence is also the period when the amount of time devoted to listening to music is at its peak (Larson *et al.* 1989; see also Chapter 9 of this volume). Larson (1995) argues that listening to music in adolescence, particularly solitary listening, plays an important part in attempts to explore and integrate a private self. Baumgartner (1992) found that people readily identified specific pieces of music with memories of significant events in their lives. Dittmar (1992, p. 89) has considered material possessions in terms of their capacity to symbolize the self. The notion of possession can be extended beyond ownership of music recordings to include musical taste—attitudes and preferences are, in an important sense, possessions (Abelson 1986) and the enacted self has to include, among its props, musical tastes that are appropriate to the self being presented.

Music relates to social identity, as Larson (1995, p. 548) suggests, 'music provides the security of identification with other like-minded peers. The teenager who deeply identifies with Guns-N-Roses gains the solidarity of being soul mates with millions of other youth. Identification with M. C. Hammer connects you to a different group of peers'. A number of studies have considered social identification with heavy metal, a form of rock music characterized by heavily amplified guitars and bass and by lyrics with an imagery of power, violence, and sexuality. Hansen and Hansen (1991) submitted judgments of the themes of heavy metal lyrics to factor analysis, producing a number of factors, identified as war and death, mental pain, drugs and suicide, 'bad sex' (prostitution, pornography, rape), the devil, and the occult. The social identity implications of heavy metal are also evident in the forms of clothing that are adopted by its supporters, and by the violent and 'bizarre' gestures and behaviour that are often exhibited at concerts. Singer *et al.* (1993) investigated relationships between self-reported rates of offending and the music preferences of a large, predominantly white, and affluent sample of American high school students. Students who expressed a preference for heavy metal reported significantly more offences than those who preferred other rock music styles. This relationship remained statistically significant when the influences of delinquent friends, amount of parental supervision, and school record were taken into account. Many other music styles that ultimately achieve mass popularity, such as jazz, rock 'n' roll, punk, and rap, also have their origins in the music preferences of minorities and are associated with challenging styles of dress, rebellious behaviour, and delinquency.

Musical preferences also reflect and promote gender identity. Larson (1995) found gender differences in adolescents' musical preferences and in their emotional responses to music. The music itself often addresses issues of gender identity. Middleton (1995) has provided a content analysis of the gender implications of the music and videotapes of the British group, the Eurythmics, in such terms. The songs and accompanying performance by Annie Lennox are interpreted as combining in an exploration of sex-stereotyped identities: 'The initial shocking androgynous persona . . . had Annie in a man's suit, with cropped hair, dyed orange; and several other looks played on the theme of appropriating male power . . . But increasingly, Annie also played ironically with traditional images of femininity (flouncy dresses, lace, soft-focus blond curls, etc.), and with markers of an equally stereotypic raunchy sexuality (black leather, low-cut bra, and so forth)' (pp. 476–7).

MUSIC, MOOD, AND SOCIAL INFLUENCE

Thus far, this chapter has considered whether musical preferences are subject to social influence. We now discuss whether music has a role in social influence processes, that is, we examine studies where music is treated as an independent variable. Here, research has been dominated by the related concepts of affect, arousal, emotion, and mood, and music is seen to contribute to social influence by virtue of its capacity to induce affect. There is little doubt that music has this capacity. This has long been the subject of much philosophical analysis (e.g. Langer 1976; Budd 1985) and there is psychological evidence that relates specific qualities of music to mood, including phrasing in singing (Sundberg 1982), melodic contour, and modality (Kastner and Crowder 1990; Gerardi and Gerken 1995). The relationship between music, mood, and social influence has also been a topic of research in advertising, marketing, and consumer behaviour (Bruner 1990). Finally, there has been considerable research into the role of affect in psychological processes, including 'attributional processing, decision-making, person impression formation, forming judgments about members of a group, and processing persuasive messages' (Hamilton *et al.* 1993, p. 41). The extent of this literature makes it impossible to provide an overview within the confines of a single chapter. Rather, we concentrate on three issues. First we consider briefly the qualities of music that have been shown to elicit affective responses. Second, we ask whether it is more useful to construe the effects of music in terms of arousal or in terms of different moods. Third, we consider how music-induced mood might have social influence. Here, we restrict our attention to research into individual responses. Many studies, especially in marketing and consumer research, have examined aggregate data, for example, measures of behaviour such as sales volume or the rate of customer flow through a department store. Aggregate data can be suggestive of the effects of mood, for example, Stack and Gundlach (1992) reported a significant correlation between the amount of air time devoted to country music on American radio and the suicide rate among the white (but not the black) urban population, a correlation that remained significant when they controlled statistically the effects of divorce rate, poverty, and availability of guns. However, in general, such data are not informative about the mechanisms mediating between music and social influence.

Affective responses to music

First, we briefly examine the kinds of moods that have been induced by music in the experimental literature. Much of this research has been in the field of marketing, as theme music in advertisements and background music in shopping centres have been regarded as having the potential to influence consumer behaviour. Bruner (1990) reviewed the literature on musical characteristics that induce mood. Some indication of the range of affective responses induced by music can be gleaned by a simple inspection and (admittedly subjective) grouping of the mood terms in the section of Bruner's paper summarizing empirical findings. There were 63 mentions of mood. The most common references (frequencies are in parentheses) were to: exhilarating/exciting/brilliant (13); tranquil/peaceful/serene (11); solemn/ serious/sacred/dignified (9); happy/joyful (9); sad/mournful (5). These terms also appear in the set of emotion rating scales used by Baumgartner (1992) in a study of the role of music in recalled personal experiences. Correlations between ratings were entered into multidimensional analysis, and a two-dimensional solution proved most interpretable. The two axes were labelled pleasure–displeasure (contrasting playful, cheerful, and joyous with tragic, mournful, and solemn) and degree of arousal (contrasting vigorous, triumphant, and [surprisingly] dignified with tranquil, sentimental, and soothing). These two axes seem to correspond closely to two of the three factors in Mehrabian and Russell's (1974) three-dimensional model of emotions: pleasure–displeasure, arousal–nonarousal, and dominance–submissiveness.

On the basis of a review of empirical studies, Bruner offered generalizations about the musical qualities that induce different moods. Excitement is produced by music in the major mode, that is fast, of medium pitch, uneven rhythm, dissonant harmony, and loud volume. Tranquillity is produced by music in the major mode, slow tempo, medium pitch, flowing rhythm, consonant harmony, and soft volume. Happiness is induced by the major mode, fast tempo, high pitch, flowing rhythm, consonant harmony, and medium volume. Serious music is in major mode, slow with low pitch, firm rhythm, consonant harmony, and medium volume. Sadness is produced by the minor mode, slow tempo, low pitch, firm rhythm, and dissonant harmony.

Arousal or mood?

Arousal is a central concept in many theories of affect. Research has utilized the concept to explain both musical preferences (see Chapter 5 of this volume) and social influence and group processes. Maass *et al.* (1987, pp. 68–9) offered an interpretation of findings from minority and majority influence studies in terms of arousal, specifically the tendency of high arousal which, they argued, was associated with pressures to conform to the group, to reduce attention to message cues. Arousal has also been combined with attribution processes to explain a range of social phenomena, for example, Patterson's (1976) account of interpersonal distance in social encounters—proximity increases arousal, but it is their interpretation of this that determines whether people maintain or change this distance: contrast your reaction to a stranger who sits beside you on a bus when other seats are vacant with your reaction when all other seats are occupied.

One of the attractions of explanations in terms of arousal is that it can be related to analyses of musical properties. In a series of experiments summarized by Konečni (1982), participants who were angered by being insulted by another person (actually a confederate of the researcher) subsequently preferred to listen to music of less complexity than participants who had not been insulted. Konečni interpreted anger as heightened arousal and musical complexity as a collative variable that is correlated with arousal: the insult raises the level of arousal and, because individuals prefer moderate levels of arousal, they try to attain their preferred level by choosing the less complex music. In an elaboration of the experimental design, participants had a subsequent opportunity to retaliate against the person who had insulted them by supposedly administering a mild electric shock. They listened to a piece of music while they were deciding whether or not to retaliate. The manipulated variables in the study were whether the participants had been insulted, or not, and the arousal level of the music, which itself varied along two dimensions, complexity and loudness. Angry participants who had been exposed to music that was both complex and loud punished the confederate more than did angered participants who heard music that was only complex or only loud, and more than those who had not been exposed to music at all. Affect induced by music has significant implications for social behaviour, in this case, aggression. Music did not, in itself, have a direct impact upon aggression, but amplified or moderated the, presumably strong, arousal produced by the insult.

Konečni's studies are among the most dramatic in the social psychology of music, but the basis of his explanation, that music is used to attain an optimal, moderate level of arousal, has been queried. There are situations where people seek out very high levels of arousal. Consider, for example, the multiple and cumulative sources of arousal at a contemporary club or 'rave': the noise and lighting; the close physical proximity, the sexual stimulation of proximity to the opposite sex, perfume, body odours, and flimsy dress; the possible influence of drugs and alcohol; the loudness, beat, and tempo of the music; feedback from one's own dancing movements and exertion. Reversal theory (e.g. Apter 1984) proposes that there is no universal tendency to prefer moderate levels of arousal, but that the preferred level depends on whether the individual is in telic, goal-directed, mode or in paratelic mode, where the activity itself rather than any goal is the focus of interest and is enjoyed for what it is. The telic mode is associated with arousal reduction and the paratelic mode with arousal-seeking. One possible interpretation of arousal reduction in Konečni's experiments is that anger has moved subjects from a paratelic mode into a telic mode as they attempt to solve the problem of dealing with their anger.

Galizio and Hendrick (1972) found that music influenced students' attitudes to messages about social issues such as pollution, poverty, and the abolition of boxing. The message was communicated to different groups either through song accompanied by guitar, unaccompanied singing, or a dramatic spoken presentation. There was more movement of attitudes when the sung message was accompanied by guitar compared with the unaccompanied musical version (although there was no statistical difference between the sung and spoken messages). The researchers interpreted these findings in terms of an arousal model of persuasion. However, ratings of the messages on mood scales showed differences not only on scales apparently related to arousal but also on scales referring to loving, warm, serious, sad, and contented that have been shown by other studies to load on dimensions other than arousal.

Other approaches have examined the influence of affect upon social behaviour in terms of specific moods or emotions without relying upon a general concept of arousal. A variety of experimental paradigms have used music to induce different moods, to study their effects upon anxiety (Smith and Morris 1977), persuasion (Schwarz *et al.* 1991), consumer behaviour (Bruner 1990), memory (Blaney 1986), and person perception (Hansen 1989). As far as this research is concerned, music is but one tool in the researcher's repertory for inducing affect. One of the advantages of emphasizing different moods is that it reflects findings that factors in addition to arousal can be elicited by music. Furthermore, there is evidence that 'positive' and 'negative' moods have different implications for information processing. These differences have often been interpreted in terms of a distinction between deliberate, analytical processing of information, on the one hand, and more heuristic, less analytical processing on the other. Thus, Petty and Cacioppo (1986) have distinguished between a direct route to persuasion where the contents of a message are closely analysed and the arguments are evaluated in the light of the recipient's own knowledge and beliefs, and a peripheral route where the message is not analysed and the recipient is influenced by other factors such as the source of the message. Hamilton *et al.* (1993) argue that evidence shows that positive moods tend to elicit more heuristic processing whereas negative moods induce more deliberate analytical processing.

These approaches suggest that properties of music can contribute in various ways to social influence. Unfortunately, there has been little attempt to manipulate music in a systematic way, nor have there been attempts to look at the interaction between music and different properties of persuasive messages. Schwarz *et al.* (1991) have proposed that tests of the hypothesis that music affects direct processing require experimental designs where the effectiveness of the direct route can be assessed, for example, by varying the number and strength of arguments. However, studies that have specifically examined the persuasive effects of music have either failed to manipulate the strength of different messages (Galizio and Hendrick 1972) or have focused upon a single, simple message (Gorn 1982). It has been argued that music encourages peripheral processing, particularly in the interpretation of studies of purchasing behaviour (Bruner 1990), but this conclusion is premature in the absence of more systematic research.

Attention, conditioning, and priming

Given that music can induce various moods, how might these have social influence? One means is by influencing attentional processes. Milliman (1982) found that the tempo of background music influenced customers' behaviour: they walked more slowly through the store and made, on average, more purchases when the music was slower rather than faster. Stratton and Zalanowski (1984) suggested that slow music gives rise to closer attention to a task. Chebat et al. (1993) studied relationships among musical tempo, visual cues, attentional processes, and time perception. Music did not have direct effects upon judgments of mood or measures of attention or time perception, but it did act as a moderating variable. In the absence of music, elevated levels of mood—pleasure, arousal, and submissiveness—were associated with less attention, and less attention was associated with longer time estimates. Visual stimulation was positively correlated with both attention and time estimation. All these relationships were modified by musical tempo. When music was slow, estimates of time were longer when visual stimulation was high than when stimulation was low; in the fast music condition, visual stimulation had no effect upon time estimation. Musical tempo also interacted with visual stimulation to influence attentional processes. When music was slow, mood was positively related to time estimation; when music was fast, there was no significant association. Music clearly can have complex relationships with mood and attention.

A further means of influence is through conditioning, where a previously neutral stimulus, e.g. a commercial product, is repeatedly paired with an (unconditioned) stimulus that already elicits a positive affective response, and through a process of conditioning itself elicits this response. For example, Gorn (1982) influenced the frequency of choosing pens by pairing the pens with music that had been either rated as liked or disliked. This process might explain the effectiveness of music in advertising, for example of the use of the largo from Dvořák's *Symphony No. 9* in a television advertisement for bread. However, there are many limitations on classical conditioning as an explanation of social influence. Conditioning can be difficult to establish; for example, Gorn's results have not always been replicated (Bruner 1990, p. 99). Furthermore, the pairing of stimuli in persuasion campaigns is often non-arbitrary. In the bread advertisement, an attempt is made to make the advertisement as a whole convey an impression of a sentimental, English rural past, and the music, voice, props, and setting all combine to create this impression. This suggests a process like *priming*, where a network of associations that are linked by shared mood connections is activated by music.

Hansen (1989; Hansen and Hansen 1991) argued that material that is not analysed in depth might nevertheless be analysed schematically, where cues in the material activate existing schemas which influence subsequent processing by priming relevant categories of information. She has tested this model in several studies of heavy metal lyrics and videos. Music videos that contained sex-stereotyped themes primed perceptions of subsequent video-taped social encounters, influencing recall of schema-relevant material and also ratings of the likeability and trait characteristics of characters in the tapes (Hansen 1989). Calfin *et al.* (1993) found that participants expressed different attitudes to sexual activities depending on whether they had viewed an erotic video of music by Madonna, a romantic video with Amy Grant, or neither video. Hansen and Krygowski (1994) showed that the effects of priming were magnified when participants' physiological arousal levels were raised through exercise.

Mood might interact with the extent of processing. Specifically, music that induces a positive mood might lead to more simplified, heuristic processing. This might be more likely when differences between decision alternatives are small, when the individual is not clear about his or her preferences, or there is so much information available that the costs of detailed processing are high. In these circumstances, music might have a significant impact upon decision-making. Decision-making may also involve self-perception processes, where the person imagines him or herself in the post-decision situation in order to estimate how happy they would feel about the decision alternatives. Music-induced mood might mean that this imaging is more likely to access positive associations. Schwarz *et al.* (1991) have proposed a number of such mechanisms relating mood to persuasion, but there has been no research that has examined these where different moods have been induced by music. The literature largely comprises investigations of consumer behaviour, and the moods induced in these studies are not representative of the range of moods that can be induced by music; in particular, 'negative' moods, such as anger, anxiety, or sadness, are under-represented. The relationship between mood and information processing can be understood either in terms of cognitive capacity or motivation. Music-induced happiness might lead to heuristic strategies or to adopting a less stringent criterion for reaching a decision either because the mood disrupts processes or makes less working memory capacity available for them, or because there is little motivation to invest effort in any detailed processing of information. Again, there is little evidence. Chebat *et al.* (1993) suggest that musical tempo interacts with mood to affect information processing, rather than there being a direct link between music and processing. Whether these effects are simple or complex requires further investigation. We need to consider too whether it is tempo that is the significant factor, given the emotional richness of the excerpts from Mozart's *Symphony No. 41* that served as experimental stimuli.

Relationships between affect, cognition, and social processes have been extensively studied in recent years and many models are potentially available to account for links between properties of music and social influence. There have been, as yet, few empirical studies that make use of music's capacity to induce a range of moods or that examine social influence in interpersonal settings rather than in preferences for consumer products.

CONCLUSIONS

We have reviewed evidence that musical preferences are subject to majority and minority influence. These studies manipulate social influence by providing information about the preferences of groups with whom participants identify, and this led us to consider the role of identity processes in conformity and social influence. Studies that have looked at the effects of music on social influence have concentrated on the capacity of music to elevate arousal or to induce mood. There has been considerable theoretical development in this area, but research has yet to take full advantage of the capacity of music to induce a range of moods. The phenomena we have considered have traditionally been viewed as fundamental to small group processes, and the emphasis in explanation has been upon the *interindividual* and the *situational* levels (see Chapter 1 of this volume). However, research into social influence and music has seldom looked in any detail at social interaction processes and, as we have seen, there has been a tendency for experiments to test the effects of information that is presented to subjects for their private judgments. Perhaps in consequence, there seems to be a shift in explanations towards the *intraindividual* level, and research into social influence in general, and the role of affect in particular has adopted a more cognitive approach.

We believe that the relationship between music and social influence is a complex topic that requires different levels of explanations. The need to consider conformity and minority influence effects, identity processes and affect as jointly affecting social behaviour can be illustrated by recent studies of heavy metal. The music, lyrics, performance, videos, and appearance of performers and fans combine to present a particular identity that appeals to some, but not all young people. Those who express a preference for heavy metal are more likely than their peers to show other psychological characteristics, for example, antisocial behaviour (Singer *et al.* 1993). We would predict that representation of a piece of music as heavy metal could serve as a stimulus in studies of majority and minority influence processes. Yet it is surely no accident that the properties of heavy metal music are associated with a particular identity. They are integral to the attraction of this identity and their capacity to induce affect contributes to the associated behaviour. Suggestive evidence comes from a study of behaviour in a mental health hospital which reported that there was a significantly higher frequency of aggressive and difficult behaviour when 'hard rock' and 'rap' background music was played than when 'easy listening' and 'country' music was played (Harris *et al.* 1992). Psychologists have yet to provide explanations for the relationships between the affective and the identity implications of music and behaviour. Musically and culturally, there is some distance between the morris and barn dances of this chapter's first examples and the heavy metal and hard rock of the final examples. However, we have shown that both examples draw attention to aspects of small group processes to which music makes an important contribution.

REFERENCES

Abelson, R. P. (1986). Beliefs are like possessions. *Journal for the Theory of Social Behaviour*, **16**, 223–50.

Aebischer, V., Hewstone, M., and Henderson, M. (1983). Minority influence and musical preference: innovation by conversion not coercion. *European Journal of Social Psychology*, **14**, 23–33.

Apter, M. J. (1984). Reversal theory, cognitive synergy, and the arts. In *Cognitive processes in the perception of art* (ed. W. R. Crozier and A. J. Chapman). North-Holland, Amsterdam.

Asch, S. E. (1948). The doctrine of suggestion, prestige, and imitation in social psychology. *Psychological Review*, **55**, 250–76.

Baumgartner, H. (1992). Remembrance of things past: music, autobiographical memory, and emotion. *Advances in Consumer Research*, **19**, 613–20.

Blaney, P. H. (1986). Affect and memory: a review. *Psychological Bulletin*, **99**, 229–46.

Bruner, G. C. (1990). Music, mood, and marketing. *Journal of Marketing*, **54** (4), 94–104.

Budd, M. (1985). *Music and the emotions*. Routledge and Kegan Paul, London.

Calfin, M. S., Carroll, J. L., and Shmidt, J. (1993). Viewing music videotapes before taking a test of premarital sexual attitudes. *Psychological Reports*, **72**, 475–81.

Chandler, K. (1993). *Ribbons, bells, and squeaking fiddles: The social history of morris dancing in the English South Midlands, 1660–1900*. Hisarlik Press, London.

Chapman, A. J. and Williams, A. R. (1976). Prestige effects and aesthetic experiences: adolescents' reactions to music. *British Journal of Social and Clinical Psychology*, **15**, 61–72.

Chebat, J-C., Gelinas-Chebat, C., and Filiatrault, P. (1993). Interactive effects of musical and visual cues on time perception: an application to waiting lines in banks. *Perceptual and Motor Skills*, **77**, 995–1020.

Child, I. L. (1972). Esthetics. In *Annual review of psychology* (ed. P. H. Mussen and M. R. Rosenzweig). Annual Reviews Inc., Palo Alto.

Crozier, W. R. and Chapman, A. J. (1981). Aesthetic preference: prestige and social class. In *Psychology and the arts* (ed. D. O'Hare). Harvester Press, Brighton, Sussex.

Das, J. P., Rath, R., and Das. R. S. (1955). Understanding versus suggestion in the judgment of literary passages. *Journal of Abnormal and Social Psychology*, **51**, 624–8.

Dittmar, H. (1992). *The social psychology of material possessions.* Harvester Wheatsheaf, Hemel Hempstead.

Edelmann, R. J. and Hampson, S. E. (1979). Changes in non-verbal behaviour during embarrassment. *British Journal of Social and Clinical Psychology*, **18**, 385–90.

Farnsworth, P. R. and Beaumont, H. (1929). Suggestion in pictures. *Journal of General Psychology*, **2**, 362–6.

Finnäs, L. (1989). A comparison between young people's privately and publicly expressed musical preferences. *Psychology of Music*, **17**, 132–45.

Francès, R. (1963). Limites et nature des effets de prestige-II. Notoriété de l'auteur et jugement de l'oeuvre. *Journal de Psychologie*, **4**, 437–56.

Galizio, M. and Hendrick, C. (1972). Effect of musical accompaniment on attitude: the guitar as a prop for persuasion. *Journal of Applied Social Psychology*, **2**, 350–9.

Gerardi, G. M. and Gerkin, L. (1995). The development of affective responses to modality and melodic contour. *Music Perception*, **12**, 279–90.

Goffman, E. (1959). *The presentation of self in everyday life.* Doubleday, New York.

Gorn, G. C. (1982). The effects of music in advertising on choice behavior: a classical conditioning approach. *Journal of Marketing*, **46**, 94–101.

Hamilton, D. L., Stroessner, S. J., and Mackie, D. M. (1993). The influence of affect on stereotyping: the case of illusory correlations. In *Affect, cognition, and stereotyping: interactive processes in group perception* (ed. D. M. Mackie and D. L. Hamilton). Academic Press, New York.

Hansen, C. H. (1989). Priming sex-role stereotypic event schemas with rock music videos: effects on impression favorability, trait inferences, and recall of a subsequent male–female interaction. *Basic and Applied Social Psychology*, **10**, 371–91.

Hansen, C. H. and Hansen, R. D. (1991). Schematic information processing of heavy metal lyrics. *Communication Research*, **18**, 373–411.

Hansen, C. H. and Krygowski, W. (1994) Arousal-augmented priming effects. *Communication Research*, **21**, 24–47.

Harris, C. S., Bradley, R. J., and Titus, S. K. (1992). A comparison of the effects of hard rock and easy listening on the frequency of observed inappropriate behaviors: control of environmental antecedents in a large public area. *Journal of Music Therapy*, **29**, 6–17.

Hornby, N. (1995). *High fidelity.* Victor Gollancz, London.

Kastner, M. P. and Crowder, R. G. (1990). Perception of the major/minor distinction: IV. Emotional connotations in young children. *Music Perception*, **8**, 189–202.

Konečni, V. J. (1982). Social interaction and musical preferences. In *The Psychology of Music* (ed. D. Deutsch). Academic Press, New York.

Langer, S. K. (1976). *Philosophy in a new key.* Harvard University Press, Cambridge, MA.

Larson, R. W. (1995). Secrets in the bedroom: adolescents' private use of media. *Journal of Youth and Adolescence*, **24**, 535–50.

Larson, R. W., Kubey, R., and Colletti, J. (1989). Changing channels: early adolescent media choices and shifting investments in family and friends. *Journal of Youth and Adolescence*, **18**, 583–600.

Levine, J. M. and Russo, E. M. (1987). Majority and minority influence. In *Review of personality and social psychology*, Vol. 8 (ed. C. Hendrick), pp. 13–54. Sage, Newbury Park, CA.

Maass, A., West, S. G., and Cialdini, R. B. (1987). Minority influence and conversion. In *Review of personality and social psychology*, Vol. 8 (ed. C. Hendrick), pp. 55–79. Sage, Newbury Park, CA.

Mehrabian, A. and Russell, J. A. (1974). *An approach to environmental psychology*. MIT Press, Cambridge, MA.

Michael, W. B., Rosenthal, B. G., and DeCamp, M. A. (1949). An experimental investigation of prestige-suggestion for two types of literary material. *Journal of Psychology*, **28**, 303–23.

Middleton, R. (1995). Authorship, gender, and the construction of meaning in the Eurythmics' hit recordings. *Cultural Studies*, **9**, 465–85.

Milliman, R. E. (1982). Using background music to affect the behavior of supermarket shoppers. *Journal of Marketing*, **46**, 85–91.

Moscovici, S. (1980). Toward a theory of conversion behavior. *Advances in Experimental Social Psychology*, **13**, 209–39.

Mugny, G., Gachoud, J-P., Doms, M., and Perez, J. A. (1988). Influences majoritaire et minoritaire directe et indirecte dans un paradigme de choix ésthetiques. *Schweizerische Zeitschrift für Psychologie/Revue Suisse de Psychologie*, **47**, 13–23.

Patterson, M. L. (1976). An arousal model of interpersonal intimacy. *Psychological Review*, **83**, 235–45.

Petty, R. E. and Cacioppo, J. T. (1986). The elaboration likelihood model of persuasion. *Advances in Experimental Social Psychology*, **19**, 123–205.

Rigg, M. G. (1948). Favorable versus unfavorable propaganda in the enjoyment of music. *Journal of Experimental Psychology*, **38**, 78–81.

Schwarz, N., Bless, H., and Bohner, G. (1991). Mood and persuasion: affective states influence the processing of persuasive communications. *Advances in Experimental Social Psychology*, **24**, 161–99.

Sherif, M. (1935). An experimental study of stereotypes. *Journal of Abnormal and Social Psychology*, **29**, 371–5.

Singer, S. I., Levine, M., and Jou, S. (1993). Heavy metal music preference, delinquent friends, social control, and delinquency. *Journal of Research in Crime and Delinquency*, **30**, 317–29.

Smith, C. A. and Morris, L. W. (1977). Differential effects of stimulative and sedative music on anxiety, concentration, and performance. *Psychological Reports*, **41**, 1047–53.

Stack, S. and Gundlach, J. (1992). The effect of country music on suicide. *Social Forces*, **71**, 211–18.

Stratton, V. and Zalanowski, A. (1984). The effect of background music on verbal interaction. *Journal of Music Therapy*, **21**, 16–26.

Sundberg, J. (1982). Perception of singing. In *The psychology of music* (ed. D. Deutsch). Academic Press, New York.

Tajfel, H. and Turner, J. C. (1986). The social identity theory of intergroup behavior. In *Psychology of inter-group relations* (ed. S. Worchel and W. G. Austin). Nelson-Hall, Chicago.

5 | Experimental aesthetics and everyday music listening

Adrian C. North and David J. Hargreaves

The occasional experiment in the psychology of music is even today being carried on under conditions so artificial that the findings bear little relation to the affairs of real life. (P. R. Farnsworth 1948)

We suggested in Chapter 1 that one important feature of the social psychology of music should be the reciprocity of the individual and the social world. The present chapter addresses this reciprocity directly by describing a small but growing number of studies which concern how theories of musical preference might be applied to and be mediated by the everyday environments in which people usually listen to music. Whilst the majority of research on the music–situation relationship has concerned various aspects of consumer behaviour (see Chapter 14), several studies conducted mainly by Vladimir Konečni in California and ourselves and colleagues in Leicester have approached the issue from the perspective of traditional laboratory research on experimental aesthetics. This chapter reviews these studies.

Although used frequently, the very definition of the term 'experimental aesthetics' raises important issues. First, what do we mean by the word 'experimental'? This certainly implies many of the qualities that a behavioural science ought to satisfy, such as control of extraneous variables in the laboratory. However, some have argued that this approach may be of only limited use (see, for example, Konečni 1982; Persson and Robson 1995). If a theory is to explain behaviour in its entirety then it goes without saying that research based solely in a laboratory cannot be adequate. At some point, research must be carried out under real world conditions, and focus on the mundane, everyday circumstances of music listening: a comprehensive theory of musical preference should tell us, for example, why a piece makes drivers tap their fingers on the car steering wheel as well as why a first-year undergraduate in a psychology laboratory likes a certain computer-generated tone sequence.

Second, what exactly do we mean by an 'aesthetic' response to music? When music critics and musicologists discuss the term, they often seem to be considering a form of peak experience involving a profound affective response to a great or famous piece. However, mundane 'tapping-on-the-wheel' responses to music are almost certainly more common than such peak musical experiences: if they were not then scrapyards would be full of the vehicles wrecked by drivers who have been intoxicated by the music on their in-car stereos! In short, if experimental aesthetics is to achieve its full potential of explaining music listening behaviour then it must at some point begin to explain our responses to music as it is experienced in the real world. This chapter begins with a brief review of the new experimental aesthetics that has dominated research on musical preference over the past 30 years, before discussing some of the studies that have attempted to take these theories out of the laboratory.

THE NEW EXPERIMENTAL AESTHETICS

With its publication in 1876, Gustav Fechner's *Vorschule der Äesthetik* established experimental aesthetics as the second oldest topic in experimental psychology. Fechner's approach emphasized the basic building blocks of aesthetic preferences such as responses to simple shapes and geometrical forms, and with this he tested the notion of the 'aesthetic mean', namely the idea that beauty is associated with the absence of extremes. This idea can be traced back to the writings of Plato, who wrote in the *Statesman* that the arts are 'on the watch against excess and deficit . . . [in that] the excellence and beauty of every work of art is due to this observance and . . . a standard removed from the extremes'. Similarly, Aristotle wrote in the *Nichomachean ethics* that 'A master of any art avoids excess and deficit but seeks the intermediate and chooses this'. These ideas perhaps came to maturity in the work of Daniel Berlyne who adopted a psychobiological approach in founding 'the new experimental aesthetics' (e.g. Berlyne 1971, 1972, 1974). He characterized research within this approach as possessing one or more of the following features:

'1. It concentrates on collative properties of stimulus patterns. Collative properties (of which more will be said later) are "structural" or "formal" properties, such as variations along familiar–novel, simple–complex, expected–surprising, ambiguous–clear, and stable–variable dimensions.
2. It concentrates on motivational questions (see Berlyne 1960, 1970, 1971).
3. It studies nonverbal behavior as well as verbally expressed judgements.
4. It strives to establish links between aesthetic phenomena and other psychological phenomena. This means that it aims not only to throw light on aesthetic phenomena but, through the elucidation of aesthetic problems, to throw light on human psychology in general.' (Berlyne 1974, p. 5).

Berlyne (1971) proposed a theory based on this approach which has dominated research efforts up to the present day. The theory states that preference for

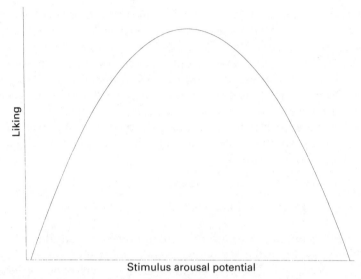

Fig 5.1 The relationship between liking for music and its arousal potential.

stimuli is related to their 'arousal potential', which is the amount of activity they produce in areas of the brain such as the reticular activating system. Stimuli with an intermediate degree of arousal potential are liked most, and this degree of liking gradually decreases towards the extremes of arousal potential. This means that there is what might be called an inverted-U relationship between preference and stimulus arousal potential (see Fig. 5. 1), and this relates to the well-known Wundt curve (Wundt 1874) as well as to the arguments of Fechner, Plato, and Aristotle.

Stimuli of moderate arousal potential are liked most because, on their way to the higher brain, the fibres of the reticular system pass through both pleasure and displeasure centres. The former has a lower threshold level and a lower asymptotic level than the latter. With low degrees of arousal only the pleasure centre is activated so that liking increases with arousal. At slightly higher degrees of arousal the displeasure centre also becomes activated, so that the relationship between arousal and liking begins to level off. At high degrees of arousal, the pleasure centre has already reached its asymptotic degree of activation whilst activation in the displeasure centre continues to increase, and this causes liking to decrease.

Berlyne stated that the stimulus variables which mediate arousal fall into three categories: 'psychophysical' variables, which are the intrinsic physical properties of the stimulus such as musical tempo; 'ecological' variables, which are the learned associations between the stimulus and other events or activities of biological importance; and 'collative' variables, which are the informational properties of the stimulus such as its degree of novelty/familiarity or complexity. Berlyne (1971) proposed that the collative variables are the 'most significant of all for aesthetics' (p. 69), and they have dominated research with several studies supporting the proposed inverted-U relationships between liking and laboratory manipulations of both novelty/familiarity and complexity (see reviews Finnäs 1989; Hargreaves 1986).

However, research on Berlyne's theory has been criticized on two grounds, and these form the basis for the remainder of this chapter. The first criticism relates to Berlyne's (1974) claim that the new experimental aesthetics 'strives to establish links between aesthetic phenomena and other psychological phenomena' (p. 5). Konečni (1982) argues very persuasively that 'the vast majority of research studies . . . have treated aesthetic preference and choice as if they, and the process of appreciation itself, normally occur in a social, emotional, and cognitive vacuum, as if they were independent of the contexts in which people enjoy aesthetic stimuli in daily life' (p. 498). Konečni points out that music is something enjoyed 'in the stream of daily life' (p. 500), for example in shops, restaurants, whilst doing housework, and so on. We clearly need to establish whether Berlyne's theory can be used to explain musical preferences in everyday listening situations. This issue has been investigated either directly or indirectly in four areas: the 'plugging' of songs on the radio; the preference-feedback hypothesis; acculturation and familiarity; and complexity and tempo.

MUSICAL PREFERENCE IN EVERYDAY LIFE

Radio plugging

The majority of music radio stations base their programming on the 'playlist'. This is a list of records that the stations intend to broadcast frequently, and can be crucial to the chances of a record reaching the top 40 (see Denisoff 1975; Hirsch 1969; Rothenbuhler 1985). One obvious implication of the playlist is that certain records will presumably become more familiar to listeners than others, and this can be related to Berlyne's assertion that there should be an inverted-U relationship between liking and familiarity. The effects of radio plugging on liking for music have been investigated in four studies.

Wiebe (1940) investigated 24 songs just prior to their release to the broadcasting networks, and divided the songs into 'better liked' and 'less liked' groups on the basis of subjects' initial liking ratings. He found that subjects' liking for 'better liked' songs decreased over time whether or not they had been plugged. However, plugging did increase liking for 'less liked' songs, whereas the absence of plugging was associated with liking for these songs decreasing. Erdelyi (1940) investigated the relationship between the frequency with which 20 songs were played on the radio and sales of their sheet music. Both measures were consistent with an inverted-U function, showing a clear gradual increase and subsequent decrease over time. More importantly, the results for 18 of the 20 songs indicated that 'plugging systematically *precedes* sales' (p. 699, our emphasis) by approximately 13 days, and this supports Berlyne's prediction that variations in familiarity should *cause* rather than follow variations in liking.

Jakobovits (1966) approached radio plugging from the perspective of what he termed 'stimulus satiation'. He claimed that plugging should cause increased liking at first because exposure leads to people learning more about the stimulus ('semantic generation'). However, after a given point, further exposure no longer provides new information about the stimulus ('semantic satiation'), and Jakobovits claimed that this should lead to decreased liking. His analyses of two separate sets of songs yielded near-identical results. The sales of songs rose and fell as plugging increased, and more importantly, the more frequently that songs were plugged, so the quicker that their popularity increased and decreased. This again suggests that increasing familiarity influences liking.

Although these three studies were not explicitly set in Berlyne's theoretical framework, their results nevertheless correspond closely with the predictions of an arousal-based theory: the degree and frequency of naturalistic exposure to real songs brought about by radio plugging is related directly to their popularity, whether this is measured by subjects' liking ratings or by sales charts. A more recent study of radio plugging by Russell (1987) explicitly supported Berlyne's theory. In a first experiment, he showed that the higher the chart position a recording reached and the longer it spent in the charts, so the more familiar it was to subjects (see also Russell 1986). In a second experiment he obtained some (albeit weak) evidence that subjects' liking for the songs over the period of their chart run could be described as an inverted-U curve. This seems to support Berlyne's theory in that naturalistic exposure to music leads directly to increasing familiarity, and this in turn leads to a waxing and waning in liking. Russell also argues that one possible reason for subjects' liking ratings following only a weak inverted-U pattern is the existence of 'a self-regulating mechanism which decreases exposure once likeability begins to decline' (p. 187). This mechanism is a central feature of the preference-feedback hypothesis.

The preference-feedback hypothesis

The studies of radio plugging described above hint at the potential ability of Berlyne's theory to explain variations in liking for music to which people have been exposed naturalistically, and the preference-feedback hypothesis (see Sluckin *et al.* 1983) attempts to formalize this approach. The hypothesis separates stimuli into two classes. Class B stimuli, whose degree of familiarity is *not* under voluntary control, should produce an inverted-U relationship between liking and familiarity as a result of Berlyne's arousal-based process. Surnames might be an example of such stimuli whose cultural prevalence is near impossible to control (Colman *et al.* 1981*a*). National anthems or the theme tunes of favourite television programmes might be corresponding musical examples.

According to the preference-feedback hypothesis, there should be a different relationship between liking and familiarity with Class A stimuli. The familiarity of such stimuli *is* under voluntary control, and *at any given moment in time*, Class A stimuli should give rise to a positive relationship between liking and familiarity: the most liked Class A stimulus is the most familiar. This is because when familiarity with Class A stimuli is about to become super-optimal (i.e. and about to be disliked) we deliberately avoid further exposure to them, and only recommence this when familiarity has subsided. Christian names are an example of such stimuli whose cultural prevalence can be controlled (Colman *et al.* 1981*b*) since we are obviously free to decide what we call our children. This means that *over time* our familiarity with a Class A stimulus should not show a single inverted-U peak, but should rather wax and wane in cycles as we continually halt and recommence exposure to it. There are several musical examples of this, such as the continued revivals in the popularity of works, composers, and even musical styles both in culture as a whole and individuals' own private listening choices (see Chapters 1 and 6). However, as yet there is only limited and equivocal formal evidence concerning applications of the preference-feedback hypothesis to music (North and Hargreaves 1996*a*; North and Hargreaves, in press, *a*; but see also Colman *et al.* 1986).

Acculturation and familiarity

Two other studies have taken a developmental approach to musical familiarity by operationalizing it in terms of age and acculturation. Increased familiarity with a musical culture (i.e. acculturation) is presumably related to age, since people are exposed to more stimuli as they get older. Hargreaves and Castell (1986) found that liking for obscure folk songs peaked at a later age than did liking for more familiar nursery rhymes: through acculturation, older people had been overexposed to the nursery rhymes, but had had sufficient cultural exposure to develop liking for the less prevalent, obscure songs. Colman *et al.* (1975) found similar developmental effects on preferences for common and uncommon words.

We investigated this issue (North and Hargreaves 1995*a*) by suggesting that the effects of familiarity/acculturation should interact with the complexity of the music in question. As people become more familiar with a stimulus, it should become more predictable and therefore less subjectively complex and arousing to them: in other words, the more familiar people are with something so the better they know it. This means that complex, highly arousing stimuli should become quite familiar before they evoke moderate levels of arousal: simple, relatively unarousing stimuli will evoke moderate levels of arousal at much lower levels of familiarity (see Heyduk 1975). We asked subjects from five age groups across the life span to name and also rate their liking for as many styles of jazz, classical, and rock and pop music as they could (e.g. be-bop, chamber music, and heavy metal respectively). Figures 5.2(a) and (b) show that both of these measures peaked at an earlier age and degree of acculturation for comparatively simple styles (in this case rock and pop) than they did for other more complicated styles (e.g. jazz and classical). Complex music was able to sustain a greater degree of naturalistic exposure than simple music before tolerance began to tail off, and this corresponds with Berlyne's theory. (See also LeBlanc (1991) and LeBlanc *et al.* (1993) for a different theoretical approach.)

Complexity and tempo

In another study (North and Hargreaves 1996*b*) we looked specifically at the effects of complexity on preferences for the music played in a Student Union cafeteria. The results were consistent with Berlyne's theory in that moderate complexity music was preferred by diners. Furthermore, diners were invited to state which aspects of the cafeteria they would like to change (e.g. the decor), and they were less likely to mention the music as one of these when moderately complex pieces were playing. However, musical style mediated these effects since moderately complex organ music was liked less than new age music of the same complexity level: real-life music varies in several ways (such as its style), and it may be important to accept that these complicate the relationships revealed in laboratory studies.

Kellaris (1992) also investigated Berlyne's theory in a naturalistic music listening situation. He measured the tempo of the music played by the same band at various American-Greek social events, and looked at the relationship between this psychophysical variable and the duration of the subsequent applause. His findings supported Berlyne in that pieces of moderate tempo were applauded the longest. This unobtrusive measure of musical preference could well be employed in a variety of future studies.

In conjunction, these studies of musical preference in everyday life do seem to support Berlyne's theory: naturalistic exposure to real music is associated with liking for it in a way that is consistent with preference for moderately-arousing stimuli. The effects of familiarity on preference seem to occur whether caused explicitly through deliberate repeated presentations of

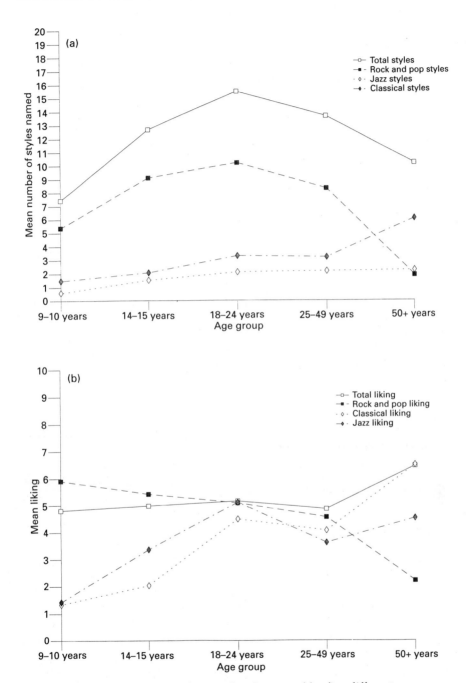

Fig 5.2 (a) The mean number of musical styles named by five different age groups. (b) The mean liking for musical styles named by five different age groups.

particular songs, or more implicitly through gradual acculturation to musical styles: they also occur whether preference is measured by verbal ratings, by the ability to name musical styles, or by the sales figures of songs. There is also evidence that familiarity actually *causes* liking, and that we need to consider the degree to which exposure is voluntary. Everyday musical preferences seem to be further mediated by complexity, tempo, and style. It should be made clear that, given their nature, the studies described above were obviously unable to provide direct evidence on the specifically arousal-based processes that supposedly underlay the effects demonstrated. Nevertheless, the sheer consistency of findings that have resulted from such methodological diversity seems persuasive in its own right. It is also interesting to note the extent to which these findings correspond with recent studies of broader cultural influences on music (see Chapter 6; Martindale 1990).

Other everyday factors

Although the focus of this chapter is on theories within experimental aesthetics, we should also mention a small number of other studies carried out by Konečni which take an experimental approach to other aspects of the everyday realities of music listening. Breckler, Allen, and Konečni (1985) investigated the manner in which subjects organized their exposure to different types of music (e.g. square waves, baroque, 'soft rock 'n' roll') which varied in terms of how pleasing they were. Subjects were told that they must listen to all the different types of music, although the ordering of this was up to them. 'Subjects chose the aversive ones early in the session and reserved the most pleasing ones for the end. Runs of aversive stimuli were interspersed with exposure to moderately pleasing ones . . . [and] the most pleasing type [of stimulus] was chosen in the longest runs' (Breckler *et al.* 1985, p. 459). Similar results were found when male subjects were exposed to photographs of, for example, assault victims, furniture, and nude females.

In an earlier short series of studies, Konečni (1984; Karno and Konečni 1992) demonstrated that the messages which artists attempt to communicate through their work are rarely recognized by the perceiver (see also North and Hargreaves, in press, *b*). For example, subjects were unable to identify correctly the intended subject of pop music lyrics (even when the performers' identities were revealed). Also, re-ordering of the movements from Beethoven's quartets and sonatas had little effect on subjects' enjoyment of them. Artists' explicit and implicit messages are usually missed by their audience. More studies of such everyday realities in music listening are needed badly. For example, large sums of money are spent on pop music videos, but does performer attractiveness/image influence preference or record sales (see North and Hargreaves, in press, *c*)? We do not always listen to music when we have the opportunity, so what are the circumstances that cause us to want to listen in the first place?

ENVIRONMENTAL EFFECTS ON MUSICAL PREFERENCE

Arousal-based factors

We mentioned earlier that Konečni (1982) had criticized research on Berlyne's theory for ignoring the social, emotional, and cognitive circumstances of music listening behaviour. In a series of complex and carefully controlled studies in the late 1970s, Konečni addressed this issue himself by investigating the effects of the immediate listening situation *on* musical preference. In reviewing these studies, Konečni (1982) emphasized that 'People listen to music while working, talking, eating, engaging in sexual intercourse ... What music does to people at different times, why they choose to listen to it so much, why they choose a particular type of music while engaged in a particular activity—all of these are important and unanswered questions' (p. 500).

Konečni characterized the music listener as a mood and emotion-optimizing organism, and specifically investigated interactions between the arousal evoked by an experimental situation and that evoked by (usually the complexity and/or volume of) music. He proposed that these sources of arousal were linked by a feedback loop such that listeners will expose themselves to music that will moderate their level of arousal. Konečni then drew on Berlyne's theory by arguing that, within this loop, situationally- and musically-evoked arousal are summed by the listener so that musical selections should indicate an attempt to moderate and optimize arousal evoked by the listening situation: furthermore, subsequent responses to the listening situation should indicate an attempt to moderate and optimize arousal evoked by music. For example, listeners in a highly arousing situation should choose to listen to simple, low complexity music that should reduce their level of arousal to a moderate level. This in turn should reduce the probability of listeners exhibiting behaviour that is associated with highly aroused states (e.g. aggressive acts). This is because we are 'engaged in a constant exchange with the social and non-social environment, of which the acoustic stimuli are a part' (Konečni 1982, p. 501).

A good example of this approach comes from Konečni *et al.* (1976). In the first part of the study, an experimental group of subjects was insulted repeatedly by a confederate of the experimenters who posed as a subject: pilot work had already established that this would bring about a high degree of arousal in subjects. In the next part of the study, subjects chose to listen to short melodies of either high or low complexity. Pilot studies had established that, under normal conditions, subjects forced to choose between the two types of music would listen to each on an equal number of occasions: control subjects in the main study followed this pattern. However, subjects who had been insulted (and were therefore highly aroused) chose to listen to the simple, relatively unarousing melodies for about 70% of the time. This indicates that they used their musical selections as a means of reducing arousal brought about by the listening situation to a moderate, comfortable level: aspects of the listening situation interacted with musical preference in line with the view of individuals as mood- and emotion-optimizers. 'The findings . . . show that a socially induced change in a listener's emotional state may strongly affect that person's aesthetic choice' (Konečni 1982, p. 503).

Konečni and his colleagues pursued several lines of further enquiry, of which we will mention just two here. Konečni (1979) described how the probability of aggressive behaviour could be reduced significantly if its musical consequences were positive (i.e. arousal-optimizing music) rather than negative (i.e. music that would further polarize subjects' arousal). Similarly, we often listen to music in the course of *another activity*, and Konečni and Sargent-Pollock (1976) found that subjects' musical preferences were mediated by the concurrent tasks they were given. Carrying out a complex task and listening to complex melodies should both involve processing a large amount of information, and should therefore place strain on the people's limited processing resources. Konečni and Sargent-Pollock showed that asking subjects to carry out complex tasks caused them to choose to listen to simple rather than complex melodies. It seems that subjects were deliberately selecting simple, undemanding music so as to compensate for the demands of the task. In summary, Konečni's work shows that musical preference is determined by an interaction between the music and the listening situation. The chosen music reflects an attempt to bring about an optimal, moderate level of arousal, and to compensate for any excessive demands of the listening situation.

Arousal and appropriateness

Clearly, arousal is only one factor amongst many which surround the everyday realities of musical preference. Konečni (1982) notes that 'I am not denying the importance of other factors that may affect aesthetic choice, including . . . the appropriateness of listening to a particular piece of music in a given situation' (p. 501). As we noted earlier, there have been two major criticisms of research on Berlyne's theory. The first, dealt with in the previous sections, is that the music listening *situation* has been neglected. Our own research in Leicester has attempted to address this first criticism whilst also considering a second, namely that the *prototypicality* or *appropriateness* of music for a listening situation may be as important in explaining musical preference as the variables considered by Berlyne.

Authors including Martindale (e.g. Martindale and Moore 1988, 1989; Martindale *et al.* 1990; Martindale *et al.* 1988; Moore and Martindale 1983) and Whitfield (e.g. Whitfield 1983; Whitfield and Slatter 1979) have investigated the importance of stimulus *prototypicality*, which may be defined as the degree to which a given stimulus is typical of its class. For example, sandy brown dogs with four legs are more typical of the category 'dog' than are albino dogs with three legs. The preference for prototypes model proposed by these authors states that preference increases (or may at times be in a U-shaped relationship) with prototypicality. Typical instances of a category should be preferred because they give rise to a stronger activation of the relevant cognitive representations.

This strength of activation occurs because the representations of typical stimuli are activated more frequently (see, for example, Martindale and Moore 1988). For example, we are more frequently exposed to sandy brown dogs with four legs than to albino dogs with three legs: the former should give rise to stronger activation of the category 'dog', and should therefore be preferred. Perhaps the most important aspect of these studies on preference for prototypes is their demonstration that the prototypicality of real-life artistic stimuli may be a stronger determinant of preference than are their arousal-evoking qualities: this contrasts with Berlyne's (1971) claim that the collative variables (e.g. complexity, familiarity, etc.) are the 'most significant of all for aesthetics' (p. 69).

This is useful in the context of the present chapter because the concept of prototypicality provides a framework for investigating the appropriateness of music for a listening situation. Konečni's research suggests that appropriate music may be that which brings about a moderate level of arousal (e.g. simple music when we are angry). However, we can also characterize appropriateness in a different way by defining it in terms of the extent to which a given piece is *typical* of the music usually played in the situation in question (e.g. organ music in a church). In short, the prototypicality model predicts that typical/appropriate music should be preferred because it leads to stronger category activation.

North and Hargreaves (in press, *d*) investigated the musical preferences of participants in local yoga and aerobics classes. There was an inverted-U relationship in both classes between ratings of liking and complexity assigned to the music played, and this is consistent with Berlyne's theory. However, members of both classes also produced positive relationships between liking and appropriateness which was defined as the extent to which the music was *typical* of that usually played in the classes: this is consistent with the preference for prototypes model. Also, these latter relationships explained as much of the variance in subjects' preferences as did the inverted-U relationships with complexity. These findings suggest that arousal might be only one of a number of factors in determining responses to music in everyday situations, and that appropriateness/prototypicality might also be important.

Two further studies investigated the relative importance of arousal and typicality in shaping musical preference in real-world situations. North and Hargreaves (1996c) asked independent groups of subjects either to exercise or relax, and gave them the option of listening to arousing or unarousing music. Perhaps unsurprisingly, subjects preferred to listen to arousing music whilst exercising and relatively unarousing music whilst relaxing. They also judged their musical selections as being typical of the music usually experienced in their given listening situations. That is, typicality outweighed arousal-moderation in determining musical preferences in these situations: if subjects had instead followed the latter strategy they would have chosen, for example, arousing music whilst relaxing. The results of this experiment were supported by a questionnaire study in which subjects responded to verbal descriptions of 17 situations (North and Hargreaves 1995b), and reported preferring, for example, quiet, relaxing music before going to bed.

Rather than moderating their level of arousal, subjects in these studies were selecting typical/appropriate music for the situation in question. This parallels the laboratory research described above in suggesting that category activation may be more important than arousal-moderating processes in determining preference. Rather than suggesting that moderate levels of arousal are always preferred, it might be more accurate to say that people prefer typical musically-evoked levels of arousal which help them to achieve a particular situational goal, be this low, moderate, or high arousal. (See also Apter (1984) on how cognitive factors mediate preferred arousal levels). There are times (e.g. when exercising) when we want to be highly aroused, and we can use arousing music to help achieve this. Similarly, there are times when we want to moderate an unpleasantly high level of arousal (e.g. in Konečni's studies), and we can use relatively unarousing music to help achieve this. The arousal-based goal of a situation is critical. Perhaps music becomes typical and appropriate for a situation because it helps listeners to achieve arousal-based goals.

It might at first sight seem rather obvious to say that liking for music is influenced by its appropriateness for the listening situation. However, the very obviousness of the idea strengthens the case for the kind of experimental aesthetics we have advocated throughout this chapter. If such mundane, social psychological influences are so prevalent that they seem obvious, they must presumably be a major factor in determining preference: it therefore makes sense to attempt to incorporate them into existing aesthetic theories if those theories are to explain adequately music listening behaviour.

Four further points should be made here. First, it seems likely that musical appropriateness should cause liking rather than vice versa: if liking caused music to be perceived as appropriate then an upbeat song such as 'She Loves

You' by The Beatles might be considered appropriate for even a morose situation such as a funeral! Second, it is possible that other cognitive factors may mediate any underlying effects of arousal-based goals on musical appropriateness (see also Behne 1996): parties and making love might both induce similarly high levels of arousal, but would be accompanied by quite different choices of music. Third, the listener's more general preferences should mediate appropriateness effects: fans of heavy rock would not necessarily enjoy or want to listen to choral music just because they were at a meeting of a choral society. Musical appropriateness is likely only to *increase* the probability of a positive aesthetic response, or *increase* the likelihood of our deciding to expose ourselves to appropriate music.

Finally, the extent of appropriateness effects on actual listening selections will obviously depend on the availability of music that fits the situation: it is impossible to listen to the optimal music for a given situation if you do not first have access to it. However, in the modern world, our access to appropriate music is increasing rapidly. There is a growing number of radio stations that play only certain specific types of music (so-called 'narrow-casting'); pre-recorded music is becoming affordable to ever larger sections of the population; radio sets, tape recorders, and compact disc players are becoming increasingly portable; and the technology even exists for a system in which any piece of music may be downloaded at will from the internet onto portable laptop computers on a 'pay-per-play' basis. In short, it is becoming increasingly easier for all people to listen to the music they want to, when they want to, wherever they want to: technological advances mean that this trend is likely to continue.

EFFECTS OF MUSIC ON RESPONSES TO THE ENVIRONMENT

A further small group of studies has investigated the opposite relationship to that discussed above: does music affect responses to the situation in which it is heard? Research on this issue has investigated whether the arousal-evoking qualities of music can be used to explain responses to other stimuli in the environment. The general conclusion is that they can, and these make an interesting adjunct to the studies reviewed in Chapter 14 on the effect of music on consumers' responses to commercial environments.

Indeed, two investigations have attempted to link explicitly these commercially-oriented studies with experimental aesthetics. North, Hargreaves, and Binns' (1995) study of television advertisements found that moderate rather than high complexity music led to the highest ratings of liking for the advertisement; liking for the visual component of the advertisement; and estimated probability of buying the advertised chocolate bar (see also Marshall and Cohen (1988); and Chapter 14). Second, North and Hargreaves' study in a university cafeteria (which was described earlier) also investigated a range of responses to the dining area itself (see North and Hargreaves 1996*d*). These responses were derived from Mehrabian and Russell's (1974) model of environmental psychology. This states that responses to an environment may be classified as approach and avoidance behaviours, which are the extent to which we desire to physically stay, explore, communicate with others, and be satisfied with tasks performed in a given environment.

To test whether these responses could be mediated by background music we set up an advice stall in the cafeteria offering leaflets on student welfare issues, and investigated the effects of different levels of musical complexity (i.e. low, moderate, and high) on responses to the stall itself and the cafeteria in general. The results were consistent with Berlyne's theory: moderate complexity music led generally to most people visiting the stall; diners requiring the least amount of coercion by the experimenters to persuade them to complete a questionnaire about the cafeteria; and the most positive ratings on this questionnaire of liking for the cafeteria, and willingness to return to it. Furthermore, only moderate complexity music led to responses that were more positive than those obtained in a silent, no music condition. Responses to the music seemed to become associated with responses to the listening environment: the strength of antipathy toward the environment when low and high complexity music was played is perhaps best demonstrated by one diner who threatened to punch one of us unless he agreed to 'turn that ******* music off'!

Perhaps the best known demonstration of the link between music and situational behaviour is provided by Konečni *et al.*'s (1976) study which we described earlier. In a third part of the experiment, insulted subjects were able to retaliate against the person who had insulted them *before* they chose between listening to the simple and complex melodies. Previous studies had already shown that such retaliation would have the effect of reducing subjects' level of arousal. When subjects retaliated then they were less likely to select simple melodies than were subjects who did not 'let off steam'. In other words, subjects who did not retaliate were still highly aroused and continued to select arousal-reducing music, whereas subjects who did retaliate returned to a more moderate level of arousal that was reflected in their musical preference. This suggests that 'the execution of actions directed at social targets effects the actor's emotional state, which, in turn, regulates subsequent behaviour' (Konečni 1982, p. 503). It seems as though our responses to the listening situation *interact* with our musical selections.

We investigated this interaction between responses to the music and responses to the situation in a study of task performance (North and Hargreaves 1996*e*). Konečni and Sargent-Pollock's (1976) study (described earlier) showed that the demands of music and a concurrent task competed for cognitive space in determining preference. Subjects doing complex tasks compensated for this by listening to simple rather than complex music, and

Konečni (1982) suggests that this might explain why a driver turns down the car radio in heavy traffic. Loud (i.e. arousing) music should place greater processing demands on drivers, and so by turning down the radio, they release processing capacity that can then be devoted to driving. We tested a variation of this basic idea: if arousing music takes up cognitive space, performance on a driving task should be worse when it is carried out in the presence of arousing (cognitively-demanding) than of relatively unarousing (undemanding) music. We asked subjects to play a motor racing computer game in the presence of these two types of music, and found that arousing music did indeed lead to slower lap times (i.e. worse performance). This effect also interacted with the difficulty of the task so that performance was worst when subjects had a difficult task/arousing music combination, and best when subjects had a simple task/unarousing music combination. These findings suggest that musically-evoked arousal can indeed interact with responses to the listening situation.

CONCLUSION

In summary, this chapter has described how theories of musical preference operate in everyday contexts. Moreover, these everyday listening contexts can influence responses to music, and music can influence responses to everyday listening contexts. These studies have some interesting implications for several aspects of our everyday musical preferences. For example, the notion of arousal state goals might explain why we might turn down the radio when driving in busy traffic (i.e. we moderate unpleasantly high arousal), but play loud music at lively parties (i.e. we maintain pleasantly high arousal). Similarly, the importance of typicality/appropriateness can explain why the wedding march might move us to tears of happiness in a church, but tears of boredom elsewhere. The interaction between music and the listening situation on task performance also has implications for many of the everyday activities that we carry out to a musical accompaniment. For example, it might explain how the quality of students' essays might be influenced by the music they listen to as they work and the difficulty of the essay itself. There may be times when the music we want to listen to will actually worsen our performance. Similarly, Konečni's results also indicate how musically-evoked arousal reduction might be able to reduce aggression in characteristically violent settings. Indeed, the framework set out by Konečni suggests a relationship between music and any other variable that may influence arousal (e.g. temperature, crowding, time of day, anxiety, etc.): the wider practical applications/implications of this relationship may reveal several more specific environmental factors which mediate the role of music in everyday life.

Also, if music can affect responses to the environment, this should be of interest to those who use music to influence consumer behaviour in commercial settings (see Chapter 14). In particular, two of the studies described above show that the 'wrong' types of music attract listeners' attention (North and Hargreaves 1996b) and can be less effective than silence (North and Hargreaves 1996d), whereas the 'right' types of music can lead to people visiting its source, and being more open to persuasion (North and Hargreaves 1996d). Moreover, complexity, style, and typicality/appropriateness are important defining features of the 'right' kinds of music.

The relationship between music and the listening situation also has important theoretical consequences. The studies described in this chapter illustrate the potential of theories of experimental aesthetics to account for responses to real music experienced under naturalistic circumstances. Also, if the situation interacts with our responses to music, then it is only possible to arrive at a comprehensive explanation of musical behaviour by carrying out investigations in the context of the everyday environments and activities in which we are conventionally exposed to music: the 'social vacuum' that typifies most laboratory research may indeed be an inadequate means of investigating musical preference. To paraphrase the quotation from Farnsworth (1948) with which we began this chapter, experiments in the psychology of musical preference should be carried out under conditions which relate to the affairs of real life. In conclusion, we hope that arguments such as these have demonstrated our belief that the social psychology of music needs experimental aesthetics as much as experimental aesthetics needs the social psychology of music.

REFERENCES

Apter, M. J. (1984). Reversal theory, cognitive synergy, and the arts. In *Cognitive processes in the perception of art* (ed. W. R. Crozier and A. J. Chapman). North-Holland, Amsterdam.

Behne, K. E. (1996). The development of 'Musikerleben' in adolescence. In *Perception and cognition of music* (ed. I. Deliège and J. Sloboda). Lawrence Erlbaum, London.

Berlyne, D. E. (1960). *Conflict, arousal, and curiosity*. McGraw-Hill, New York.

Berlyne, D. E. (1970). Motivational problems. In *Proceedings of the International Conference on Psychology of Human Learning*, Vol. 1 (ed. J. Lindhart). Institute of Psychology, Czechoslovak Academy of Sciences, Prague.

Berlyne, D. E. (1971). *Aesthetics and psychobiology*. Appleton-Century-Crofts, New York.

Berlyne, D. E. (1972). Experimental aesthetics. In *New Horizons in Psychology 2* (ed. P. C. Dodwell). Penguin, Harmondsworth.

Berlyne, D. E. (1974). The new experimental aesthetics. In *Studies in the new experimental aesthetics: steps towards an objective psychology of aesthetic appreciation* (ed. D. E. Berlyne). Halsted Press, New York.

Breckler, S. J., Allen, R. B., and Konečni, V. J. (1985). Mood-optimizing strategies in aesthetic-choice behaviour. *Music Perception*, **2**, 459–70.

Colman, A. M., Walley, M. R., and Sluckin, W. (1975). Preferences for common words, uncommon words, and non-words by children and young adults. *British Journal of Psychology*, **66**, 481–6.

Colman, A. M., Sluckin, W., and Hargreaves, D. J. (1981a). The effect of familiarity on preference for surnames. *British Journal of Psychology*, **72**, 363–9.

Colman, A. M., Hargreaves, D. J., and Sluckin, W. (1981b). Preference for Christian names as a function of their experienced familiarity. *British Journal of Social Psychology*, **20**, 3–5.

Colman, A. M., Best, W. M., and Austen, A. J. (1986). Familiarity and liking: direct tests of the preference-feedback hypothesis. *Psychological Reports*, **58**, 931–8.

Denisoff, R. S. (1975). *Solid gold: the popular record industry*. Transaction Books, New Brunswick, NJ.

Erdelyi, M. (1940). The relation between 'radio plugs' and sheet sales of popular music. *Journal of Applied Psychology*, **24**, 696–702.

Farnsworth, P. R. (1948). Sacred cows in the psychology of music. *Journal of Aesthetics*, **7**, 48–51.

Fechner, G. T. (1987). *Vorschule der Äesthetik*. Breitkopf and Hartel, Leipzig.

Finnäs, L. (1989). How can musical preferences be modified? A research review. *Bulletin of the Council for Research in Music Education*, **102**, 1–58.

Hargreaves, D. J. (1986). *The developmental psychology of music*. Cambridge University Press, Cambridge.

Hargreaves, D. J. and Castell, K. C. (1986). Development of liking for familiar and unfamiliar melodies. *Paper presented at the Eleventh International Seminar of the International Society for Music Education, Frankfurt, Germany.*

Heyduk, R. G. (1975). Rated preference for musical composition as it relates to complexity and exposure frequency. *Perception and Psychophysics*, **17**, 84–91.

Hirsch, P. (1969). *The structure of the popular music industry*. Survey Research Center, University of Michigan, Ann Arbor.

Jakobovits, L. A. (1966). Studies of fads: 1. The 'hit parade'. *Psychological Reports*, **18**, 443–50.

Karno, M. and Konečni, V. J. (1992). The effects of structural interventions in the first movement of Mozart's symphony in G Minor K.550 on aesthetic preference. *Music Perception*, **10**, 63–72.

Kellaris, J. J. (1992). Consumer esthetics outside the lab: preliminary report on a musicial field study. *Advances in Consumer Research*, **19**, 730–4.

Konečni, V. J. (1979). Determinants of aesthetic preference and effects of exposure to aesthetic stimuli: social, emotional, and cognitive factors. In *Progress in experimental personality research (Volume 9)* (ed. B. A. Maher). Academic Press, New York.

Konečni, V. J. (1982). Social interaction and musical preference. In *The psychology of music* (ed. D. Deutsch). Academic Press, New York.

Konečni, V. J. (1984). Elusive effects of artists' 'messages'. In *Cognitive processes in the perception of art* (ed. W. R. Crozier and A. J. Chapman). Elsevier Science Publishers, Amsterdam.

Konečni, V. J. and Sargent-Pollock, D. (1976). Choice between melodies differing in complexity under divided-attention conditions. *Journal of Experimental Psychology: Human Perception and Performance*, **2**, 347–56.

Konečni, V. J., Crozier, J. B., and Doob, A. N. (1976). Anger and expression of aggression: effects on aesthetic preference. *Scientific Aesthetics/Sciences de l'Art*, **1**, 47–55.

LeBlanc, A. (1991). Effect of maturation/aging on music listening preference: a review of the literature. *Paper presented at the Ninth National Symposium on Research in Music Behaviour, Canon Beach, Oregon, U.S.A.*

LeBlanc, A., Sims, W. L., Siivola, C., and Obert, M. (1993). Music style preferences of different-age listeners. *Paper presented at the Tenth National Symposium on Research in Music Behaviour, University of Alabama, Tuscaloosa, Alabama, U.S.A.*

Marshall, S. K. and Cohen, A. J. (1988). Effect of musical soundtracks on attitudes toward animated geometric figures. *Music Perception*, **6**, 95–112.

Martindale, C. (1990). *The clockwork muse: the predictability of artistic change*. Basic Books, New York.

Martindale, C. and Moore, K. (1988). Priming, prototypicality, and preference. *Journal of Experimental Psychology: Human Perception and Performance*, **14**, 661–70.

Martindale, C. and Moore, K. (1989). Relationship of musical preference to collative, ecological, and psychophysical variables. *Music Perception*, **6**, 431–55.

Martindale, C., Moore, K., and West, A. (1988). Relationship of preference judgements to typicality, novelty, and mere exposure. *Empirical Studies of the Arts*, **6**, 79–96.

Martindale, C., Moore, K., and Borkum, J. (1990). Aesthetic preference: anomalous findings for Berlyne's psychobiological theory. *American Journal of Psychology*, **103**, 53–80.

Mehrabian, A. and Russell, J. A. (1974). *An approach to environmental psychology*. MIT Press, Cambridge, Mass.

Moore, K. and Martindale, C. (1983). Preference for shapes varying in color, color typicality, size, and complexity. *Paper presented at the International Conference on Psychology and the Arts, Cardiff*.

North, A. C. and Hargreaves, D. J. (1995*a*). Lifespan influences on tolerance for musical styles. *Submitted for publication*.

North, A. C. and Hargreaves, D. J. (1995*b*). Situational influences on reported musical preference. *Submitted for publication*.

North, A. C. and Hargreaves D. J. (1996*a*). Liking for musical styles. *Submitted for publication*.

North, A. C. and Hargreaves, D. J. (1996*b*). Responses to music in a dining area. *Journal of Applied Social Psychology*, **26**, 491–501.

North, A. C. and Hargreaves, D. J. (1996*c*). Musical preference when relaxing and exercising. *Submitted for publication*.

North, A. C. and Hargreaves, D. J. (1996*d*). The effects of music on responses to a dining area. *Journal of Environmental Psychology*, **16**, 55–64.

North, A. C. and Hargreaves, D. J. (1996*e*). Music and driving game performance. *Submitted for publication*.

North, A. C. and Hargreaves, D. J. (in press, *a*). Subjective complexity, familiarity, and liking for popular music. *Psychomusicology*.

North, A. C. and Hargreaves, D. J. (in press, *b*). Affective and evaluative responses to pop music. *Current Psychology.*

North, A. C. and Hargreaves, D. J. (in press, *c*). The effect of physical attractiveness on responses to pop music performers and their music. *Empirical Studies of the Arts.*

North, A. C. and Hargreaves, D. J. (in press, *d*). Responses to music in aerobic exercise and yogic relaxation classes. *British Journal of Psychology.*

North, A. C., Hargreaves, D. J., and Binns, A. S. (1995). The effects of musical complexity and style on responses to television advertisements. *Submitted for publication.*

Persson, R. S. and Robson, C. (1995). The limits of experimentation: on researching music and musical settings. *Psychology of Music*, **23**, 39–47.

Rothenbuhler, E. W. (1985). Programming decision-making in popular music radio. *Communication Research*, **12**, 209–32.

Russell, P. A. (1986). Experimental aesthetics and popular music recordings: pleasingness, familiarity, and chart performance. *Psychology of Music*, **14**, 33–43.

Russell, P. A. (1987). Effects of repetition on the familiarity and likeability of popular music recordings. *Psychology of Music*, **15**, 187–97.

Sluckin, W., Hargreaves, D. J., and Colman, A. M. (1983). Novelty and human aesthetic preferences. In *Exploration in animals and humans* (ed. J. Archer and L. Birke). Van Nostrand Reinhold, London.

Whitfield, T. W. A. (1983). Predicting preference for familiar, everyday objects: an experimental confrontation between two theories of aesthetic behaviour. *Journal of Environmental Psychology*, **3**, 221–37.

Whitfield, T. W. A. and Slatter, P. E. (1979). The effects of categorization and prototypicality on aesthetic choice in a furniture selection task. *British Journal of Psychology*, **70**, 65–75.

Wiebe, G. (1940). The effect of radio plugging on students' opinions of popular songs. *Journal of Applied Psychology*, **24**, 721–7

Wundt, W. M. (1874). *Grundzuge der Physiologischen Psychologie.* Engelmann, Leipzig.

PART III

Social and cultural influences

6 | Products, persons, and periods: historiometric analyses of compositional creativity

Dean Keith Simonton

Anyone well versed in the European music tradition must have some acquaintance with such compositions as the *Missa Papae Marcelli*, the *Brandenburg Concerti, Eine kleine Nachtmusik, Tristan und Isolde, La Mer, Das Lied von der Erde,* and *Le Sacre du Printemps*. Such persons would also show some familiarity with the composers responsible for these masterpieces: Palestrina, Bach, Mozart, Wagner, Mahler, Debussy, and Stravinsky. And, finally, these well-educated individuals will have some awareness of the musical periods in which these composers conceived their works, whether the Renaissance, Baroque, Classical, Romantic, Post-Romantic, Impressionist, or Modern eras. Moreover, musicologists devote considerable amount of time to discussing these and other products, persons, and periods in order to discern the nature of composition, the basis for a composer's achievements, or the changes in musical style. Yet these three entities are not merely of interest to musicologists. Psychologists, too, can learn a great deal about musical creativity by a careful examination of the compositions, the composers, and the compositional eras that define the European music tradition.

Of course, there are multiple ways psychologists might go about extracting good behavioural science from the available material. One option is to conduct laboratory experiments, such as is done in experimental aesthetics. For example, experimenters might make modifications in a piece of classical music in order to determine whether these changes influence aesthetic preference (e.g. Karno and Konečni 1992). Although this approach has many attractive features, in this chapter I would like to discuss an alternative line of attack that is much less common. This method is called *historiometry*, 'a scientific discipline in which nomothetic hypotheses about human behaviour are tested by applying quantitative analyses to data concerning historical individuals' (Simonton 1990, p. 3). The utility of this approach should become quite evident as we review some of the major historiometric findings concerning the product, person, and period aspects of compositional creativity.

PRODUCTS

'By their fruits ye shall know them' says St. Matthew. This surely holds for the works of the great classical composers, and in two distinct senses. First, by listening to the compositions of a Beethoven or Tchaikovsky or Schoenberg, we come to recognize their manner of conceiving and organizing musical ideas. Aficionados of classical music can often identify the composer of a piece after only a few bars even if they have never heard the work before, so long as the composer is well known to them. Second, and more dramatically, composers would not even be known to us at all if they composed absolutely nothing that would inspire anyone to listen to their work. In fact, there are thousands of composers who failed to produce a single piece of fruit that is still consumed in the concert hall, opera stage, or recording studio. These are the unknowns of the repertoire. Fortunately, historiometric research has shed light on both of these aspects of the compositional product.

Compositional style

Content analysis is a technique for assessing the attributes of personal documents, artifacts, and creative products. An impressive variety of content analytical methods have been devised for studying music compositions (e.g. Brook 1969; Cerulo 1989; Lomax 1968). Rather than review all of these schemes, I focus here on the subset that (a) deal specifically with the compositions that make up the classical repertoire and (b) are objective enough to take the form of computer programs.

Identifying composers

Paisley (1964) was interested in whether a computer could identify the distinctive style of major classical composers. He started with a thematic dictionary that presented the principal melodies of the classical repertoire. This dictionary included an index presenting just the pitches of the themes translated into a C tonic key (i.e. either C major or C minor). Taking just the first four notes of the themes composed by a group of eminent composers, Paisley had the computer calculate the two-note transition frequencies for the three transitions connecting these four notes. Having set aside a test batch of themes by the same composers that was not used to estimate the transition frequencies, Paisley then checked to see if the mystery composers could be correctly identified. The test was affirmative. Each composer had a characteristic way of putting melodies together that could be detected right from the beginning of each theme. Moreover, when there was any ambiguity, the ambiguities made perfect sense. For example, it should not surprise us that the early melodies of Beethoven could often pass for melodies by Haydn. Beethoven greatly admired the older master and went specifically to Vienna in order to study under him!

Paisley's surprising results have been replicated by applying the same general approach to the first six notes (or the first five two-note transitions) of 15 618 themes by 477 classical composers (Simonton 1980*b*; see also Simonton 1980*a*, 1989*b*). This same basic method has also been used to gauge an extremely important facet of musical style—the predictability of its thematic content.

Melodic originality

Simonton (1980*b*, 1984) took Paisley (1964) a step further. First, he began with a much larger sample, namely 15 618 themes by 477 classical composers spanning from the Renaissance to the 20th century. These products and the persons who created them more or less represent almost 100 per cent of the classical repertoire performed and recorded by the middle of this century (cf. Moles 1958/1968). Then, rather than taking the first four notes, Simonton took the first six notes, yielding five two-note transitions between the consecutive pitches that open each theme. Next, a computer tabulated the frequencies of the various two-note transitions across all the themes, for which the probability of each transition could be easily calculated. These two-note transition probabilities were then used to measure the improbability of each of the 15 618 themes. An improbable theme is one that contains two-note transitions that are extremely rare, whereas a probable theme is one containing transitions that are extremely common. From this calculation it was easy to define a variable called *repertoire melodic originality*, which measures how rare a theme is with respect to the rest of the classical repertoire.

A series of investigations have demonstrated the utility and validity of the computer's calculations (Simonton 1993*b*, 1994*a*). In the first place, after listening to violin performances of melodies, naïve subjects tend to rate themes scoring objectively higher in melodic originality as subjectively higher on 'arousal potential' (Martindale and Uemura 1983). In addition, melodic originality calculated according to two-note transition probabilities correlates very highly with scores estimated from three-note transition probabilities (Simonton 1984).

More importantly, computer generated estimates of melodic originality correlate in a predictable manner with other attributes of a musical composition (Simonton 1993*b*, 1994*a*). Thus, themes composed in a minor key score higher in originality than those in a major key (Simonton 1987), and themes taken from vocal music score lower on originality than themes taken from instrumental music (Simonton 1980*b*). Furthermore, independent of the distinction between major and minor keys and between instrumental and vocal works, chamber music (sonatas, quartets, etc.) features melodies with more originality than concert music (symphonies, tone poems, etc.), while the latter class of compositions contain more originality than works written for the theatre (opera, ballet, etc.) (Simonton 1980*b*, 1986*a*). Melodic originality also varies according to the formal structure of the piece (Simonton 1987). For instance, minuet and scherzo movements generally contain themes of lower originality than those found in sonata-allegro movements. The computer-calculated gauge of originality even correlates with the tempo and rhythm of a composition (Simonton 1987). For example, faster tempi are associated with themes having lower originality, and themes with relatively common time signatures (e.g. 4/4 or 3/4) tend to feature less originality than themes with relatively rare time signatures (e.g. 5/4).

Because compositions on large forms are almost invariably constructed from multiple themes, we can use the melodic originality of each theme to generate a second content analytical measure, namely originality variation (Simonton 1986*a*, 1987). This basically assesses the degree of variability in originality as a composition unfolds. Originality variation is associated with other compositional characteristics in a manner that further validates the computerized measure. Hence, variation in originality is greater in multiple-movement works than in single-movement works (Simonton 1987) and with works with long performing times (Simonton 1989*b*), suggesting that the composer uses such variation as a device to maintain attention for longer, more complex works. Interestingly, the same pattern holds for variation in metric originality, or the use of diverse and often unusual time signatures, an attribute that correlates positively with melodic originality variation (Simonton 1987). As further support for the notion that melodic originality is varied as vehicles to grab an audience's attention, we can cite one final empirical result: the very first symphony a composer offers the world tends to score much higher on melodic originality variation (Simonton 1995). The neophyte composer is evidently trying to pull out all the stops!

As intriguing as these diverse findings may be, the chief utility of the above computerized measure of melodic structure concerns not style but rather substance, namely the actual aesthetic impact of a musical composition.

Aesthetic success

Music is often referred to as the 'universal language'. It is a form of communication that can transcend national boundaries and historical periods. Yet as any communication, a musical composition may be more or less successful. In classical music, certainly, some works have become universally admired and appreciated, becoming the 'warhorses' of the repertoire. Other works, even pieces by the very same composers, are much less successful, either because they communicate their message so ineffectively or because they lack a message worth communicating. In any case, we can take a work's aesthetic success as a gauge of how well a composition is bridging the hiatus between the composer and his or her audience. Below we look at two different ways of assessing aesthetic success, one objective and the other subjective.

Objective indicators

The most direct historiometric approach to the assessment of aesthetic success is simply to count how often different compositions appear in catalogues of recorded performances, music appreciation textbooks, student scores, concert and record-buying guides, thematic dictionaries, anthologies of great music, and music histories, dictionaries, and encyclopaedias (Simonton 1980*a,b*). Because these counts correlate very highly with how often a work is performed in classical repertoire (Simonton 1983), they can be used as measures of popularity in the repertoire.

There are several interesting predictors of this archival index of repertoire popularity. First, vocal works tend to be less popular than instrumental works, on the average (Simonton 1980*a,b*, 1986*a*). This difference may reflect the fact that a vocal composition is often encumbered by the text which restricts the accessibility of the piece even when written in one of the world's most widely distributed languages. Second, concert music tends to be the most popular, chamber music the least, with church and theatre compositions falling somewhere between (Simonton 1980*b*, 1986*a*). Third, compositions in the larger forms, such as symphonies, ballets, and operas, tend to be more popular than compositions in the smaller forms, such as overtures, bagatelles, and art songs (Simonton 1980*a,b*, 1986*a*).

But this is not all: the computer-generated scores on melodic originality also predict repertoire popularity! In particular, the popularity of a composition is an inverted backwards-J function of originality, as shown in Fig. 6.1 (Simonton 1980*b*, 1987). That is, the most successful works fall in the middle range, whereas those compositions whose themes are either very low in melodic originality or very high will be less popular, on the average. However, if the choice is between low and high originality, the former will more likely receive the accolades. Furthermore, this is not the only melodic attribute that exhibits this relationship. Similar inverted-U functions hold for melodic originality variation and for metric originality (Simonton 1987). What makes these results especially interesting is that similar inverted-U functions have often been noted in experimental aesthetics as well. Berlyne (1971) has styled this functional relation the 'Wundt curve', linking it with his optimal-arousal theory of aesthetic appreciation.

The implications of these findings are provocative: the comparative popularity of the compositions that make up the classical repertoire is not

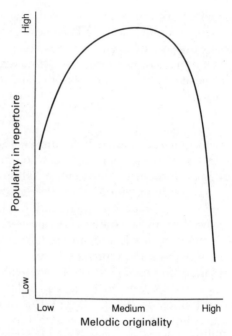

Fig 6.1 The curvilinear relationship between repertoire popularity and melodic originality for 15 618 themes in classical music (Simonton 1983).

arbitrary. The more frequently performed pieces are objectively different from the esoterica of the repertoire. Indeed, the discriminating characteristics can be discerned by a mere computer, just as a mere computer could be programmed to recognize composers' styles. Needless to say, the data do not show that differential popularity is solely a consequence of melodic structure. On the contrary, many other factors are involved as well, such as form, medium, and content. In fact, studies show that the larger the musical composition, the less influence the melodies have by themselves (Simonton 1980*b*). Even so, the conclusion remains that, as Haydn once put it, 'melody is the main thing'.

Subjective indicators

Admittedly, the foregoing results presume that repertoire popularity is a worthy criterion of aesthetic success. Not everyone might agree. Perhaps something more is needed than simply to count the citations received in various archival sources. Maybe what we require is a human being to provide subjective evaluations. For example, one musicologist has rated thousands of compositions on the criteria of aesthetic significance and listener accessibility (Halsey 1976). Are these human judgements also predictable? The answer is affirmative. Let us begin by noting that repertoire popularity, aesthetic significance, and listener accessibility are all positively correlated with each other (Simonton 1986a, 1989b). In other words, for the most part, the most well-known works in the classical repertoire are deemed both artistically important and reasonably intelligible. As a consequence, sometimes factors that influence one criterion of aesthetic success will influence another criterion in much the same way. For instance, 'fifth' symphonies, when compared to symphonies with different ordinal positions, tend to be rated higher in *both* aesthetic significance and listener accessibility, a trend well exemplified by several 'fifths' between Beethoven and Shostakovitch (Simonton 1995). In contrast, whereas vocal music tends to score higher in aesthetic significance than does instrumental music, it also tends to score lower in listener accessibility, just as we saw earlier for repertoire popularity (Simonton 1986a).

In addition, compositional attributes like melodic originality do not display the same functional relationship with these subjective assessments of aesthetic success. On the one hand, aesthetic significance tends to be a positive function of both melodic originality and originality variation (Simonton 1986a). On the other hand, listener accessibility tends to be a negative function of these same two content analytical variables (Simonton 1986a). Both of these tendencies differ from the curvilinear function found for repertoire popularity. Still, this departure actually leads us to a provocative explanation for that very curvilinear relationship. Popular works must be both significant and accessible, and yet significant compositions score high in melodic originality and originality variation while accessible compositions score low on these same thematic attributes. The peak of the curve then represents the compromise between these two contradictory tendencies. Compositions with a moderate amount of melodic originality and originality variation will be aesthetically significant without being too inaccessible.

PERSONS

When historiometricians study eminent personalities, famous classical composers are often included in the sample. For instance, Cox (1926) conducted an interesting study of 301 geniuses of Western civilization, which included several composers, such as Palestrina, Bach, Handel, Haydn, Mozart, Beethoven, Rossini, Mendelssohn, and Wagner. Besides estimating IQ scores for these individuals, she also assessed them on 67 character traits. Cox showed that the great classical composers were very similar to other eminent personalities, except that they were above average on the desire to excel, persistence in the face of obstacles, quiet determination, originality of ideas, degree of aesthetic feeling, but below average in intellectual and physical activities. Cox's study has been followed up by many other historiometric researchers. White (1931), for example, showed how famous composers tend to be somewhat less versatile than most luminaries. That is, they tend to concentrate on writing music to the exclusion of making achievements in other areas in the arts and sciences. There are no Goethes or Leonardo da Vincis among the great composers.

However, the bulk of the historiometric research on the person aspect of compositional creativity has focused on how composers achieve distinction. Closely associated with this question is the issue of whether it is even meaningful to claim that some composers have attained more eminence than others have.

Stability of eminence

It was Paul Farnsworth (1969), in his classic *Social psychology of music*, who first systematically examined the matter of whether 'taste was lawful'. By combining surveys of musicologists and performers with historiometric assessments of eminence using encyclopaedias and histories, he was able to prove that the differential distinction of the classical repertoire is highly consistent and stable. This is a fact that is often overlooked by enthusiasts who want to debate whether Bach or Beethoven or Mozart is *the* greatest composer. What these controversies ignore is that none has entered the debate with the serious suggestion that it is Gebel or Türk or Lickl who actually deserve this distinction. In fact, Simonton (1991*b*) has reanalysed the eminence measures collected by Farnsworth (1969) along with other measures compiled more recently (e.g. Simonton 1977*b*, 1991*a*) in order to demonstrate that these assessments have the same psychometric properties as the best instruments in psychology. Despite the intrusion of some measurement errors, the differential renown of classical composers is explained by a single, underlying factor that is extremely stable over time and that accounts for an impressive percentage of the total variance.

This empirical fact raises the next issue: what is the basis for this single latent factor behind all eminence indicators? The answer is creative productivity (Simonton 1977*b*, 1991*a*). The greatest composers tend to start making contributions to the repertoire at a young age, produce at exceptional output rates, and continue to produce to the very end of their lives. Not only is lifetime output the single best predictor of a composer's eminence, it is also a good predictor of the aesthetic success of individual works. The most productive composers generate the compositions that score highest on both aesthetic significance and repertoire popularity (Simonton 1980*b*, 1986*a*).

One especially remarkable finding about this productivity is that only a small proportion of the composers account for the bulk of the repertoire (Dennis 1955; Moles 1958/1968; Simonton 1987). In fact, only a little over a dozen creators account for about half of all music heard in the concert and recital halls, opera and ballet theatres, and recording studios. This elitist distribution of output is characteristic of outstanding achievers in other domains as well (Simonton 1993*a*).

Antecedents of eminence

If individual differences in productivity are so central to the achievement of distinction, what underlies this variation in output? A respectable number of historiometricians have tried to address this question either directly or indirectly. The first such investigation was that conducted by Galton (1869), who devoted a whole chapter to classical composers. In line with his eugenic views, Galton showed that composers tended to form family pedigrees, the most famous of which is the prolific Bach family. However, as elsewhere in psychology, the nature–nurture enigma makes interpretation of these results difficult. Lineages like these may just as well reflect environmental influences, such as the availability of role models (Simonton 1977*b*, 1988) and the early onset of specialized music training (Simonton 1986*b*, 1991*a*). To offer a specific example, the earlier composers begin music lessons, the earlier they begin composition, the sooner they have their first successful product, and the greater their total lifetime output as well as their average annual output rate (Simonton 1991*a*).

Furthermore, other variables affect the attainment of distinction that are clearly not genetic in nature. For example, ordinal position in the family seems to be a factor, the great classical composers having a high likelihood of being the first born (Schubert *et al.* 1977), a developmental influence that sets them apart from luminaries in other artistic endeavours. At a less personal level we can cite the impact of geographical marginality, that is, when a composer is born and raised far from the centres of musical activity for a particular historical period. Such provincials tend to be less prolific than their more cosmopolitan contemporaries (Simonton 1977*b*), and even are prone to write compositions that score lower in both repertoire popularity and aesthetic significance (Simonton 1986*a*). The only saving grace here is that those born at the musical periphery create works that score lower on melodic originality variation and thus score higher on listener accessibility (Simonton 1986*a*).

One last antecedent of compositional eminence must be mentioned: the exceptional precocity of the great classical composers (Simonton 1977*b*, 1991*a*). Not only do the more famous composers differ from the less famous composers on this variable, but in addition great composers tend to be more precocious than eminent personalities in other domains of achievement (Ludwig 1995; Simonton 1986b). Those composers who most dominate the classical repertoire show musical talent early, start formal lessons at a young age, and begin composing when still very young. At this point it is difficult to determine how much of this precocity is due to inherited musical ability and how much is the result of role models and other social influences.

PERIODS

We now turn to the last of three perspectives that have been the subject of historiometric research on compositional creativity—consecutive intervals across historical time. Actually, we should speak of two distinct types of periods, those within the careers of individual composers and those within the course of the history of the musical tradition.

Composers' careers

As noted earlier, notable composers tend to have long careers (Simonton 1977b, 1991a). They begin composition early and end it late. Besides the tremendous output that results, a long productive life often means that the greatest contributors will go through more than one compositional phase. These phases may be stylistic, such as the three distinct periods in Beethoven's output, or they may concern genre, such as seen in Schumann's progression from smaller to larger forms. Whatever the specifics, the career cannot always be considered a homogeneous entity, but rather it may consist of 'mini-careers' in sequence. The progression of the career from one phase to another may have multiple determinants. Some of these determinants may be endogenous in nature, whereas other determinants may be exogenous.

Endogenous factors

Any creative career will exhibit an intrinsic transformation that is not dictated by external circumstances. Most obviously, there is abundant evidence that the output of compositions tends to vary with age (Dennis 1966; Lehman 1953; Simonton 1989a,b). The output rate first increases until it attains a peak somewhere in the thirties or forties, and then gradually declines thereafter. This longitudinal trend has two curious aspects, however. First, the placement of the peak varies according to the type of composition. Creativity in smaller forms, such as art songs and piano pieces, tends to maximize earlier in the career, while creativity in the larger forms, such as symphony and opera, will maximize when they composer is more mature (Lehman 1953). Second, there exists a strong relationship between quantity and quality of compositional output. Those periods in which a composer generates the most total works tend to be the same periods in which they generate their best work, whether gauged by repertoire popularity, aesthetic significance, or listener accessibility (Simonton 1977a, 1980b, 1986a, 1991a). This means that the ratio of hits to total attempts tends to stay relatively constant across the career (Simonton 1977a).

Compositional creativity also exhibits some significant stylistic changes over the years as well. To begin with, the melodic originality of the thematic material tends to increase with age, although a decline will often set in after around age 56 (Simonton 1980a,b, 1987). Furthermore, those periods in which a composer is the most prolific are likely to be those in which the average level of melodic originality declines (Simonton 1986a, 1987). Hence, productivity can bear an inverse relationship to originality. Finally, Martindale (1990) has shown how the amount of 'primordial' thought (or 'primary process') tends to decline during periods of major stylistic changes. In fact, Beethoven's three main stylistic periods are clearly demarcated by Martindale's content analytical measure.

Exogenous factors

Naturally, the endogenous unfolding of compositional creativity is vulnerable to all kinds of intrusive events and circumstances that impinge on the creator's daily life. Certainly the amount of creative output may be deflected upward or downward by various conditions. For instance, the output of compositions tends to decline during those periods in which the composer suffers from serious physical illness (Simonton 1977a). On the other hand, it could be that certain transient mental states can increase the level of creative output. At least, Weisberg (1994) showed that Robert Schumann became far more productive during his manic periods.

Still more intriguing are the ways that a composer's style may be responsive to outside influences. For example, although physical illness causes a decline in output, it spurs an increase in melodic originality (Simonton 1980a, 1987). Originality also increases when the composer is experiencing considerable stress due to various life changes, such as marriage, parenthood, deaths in the family, job changes, legal problems, and so forth (Simonton 1980a, 1987). Perhaps the most fascinating of these stylistic shifts is the 'swansong phenomenon' (Simonton 1989b). The works appearing shortly before a composer's death tend to exhibit a cluster of characteristics that set these late works apart from the pieces appearing earlier in the career. In particular, these swansongs are more likely to be relatively short and to contain themes that score lower in melodic originality, and yet which enjoy higher repertoire popularity and aesthetic significance. It is as if composers are trying to get out one final masterpiece that can serve as a capstone to their creative careers.

Musical traditions

The periods that define the changes in music traditions, like those that define a composer's career, are subject to both exogenous and endogenous factors.

Exogenous influences

Let us begin at the grandest level possible by observing that there are periods in history that are rich in great composers and there are periods that show a near or complete absence of compositional activity. These generational fluctuations occur both for a civilization as a whole, and for individual nations within that civilization (Kroeber 1944; Simonton 1988). These ups and downs in compositional activity tend to correspond to movements in other creative domains, such as literature, philosophy, and science (Simonton 1975, 1976). Curiously, it is not just the quantity of creative output that may roughly correspond in several creative endeavours, but certain stylistic movements may be approximately synchronized as well. The genuine existence of these cross-media artistic styles has been empirically demonstrated for music, architecture, painting, and poetry (Hasenfus *et al.* 1983). Hence, we may meaningfully refer to Baroque, Neoclassical, or Romantic styles that permeate all the artistic products in a given era.

Some of this cross-media stylistic correspondence may ensue from influences linking the various artistic activities. Yet, this synchrony may also reflect some underlying sociocultural forces (Simonton 1994*b*). Appreciable evidence exists, for instance, that the occurrence of warfare exerts a profound effect on compositional creativity. In the first place, works composed under wartime conditions tend to score higher in repertoire popularity and yet lower in listener accessibility (Simonton 1986*a*). In addition, the thematic material produced under these adverse circumstances tends to feature more variation in melodic and metric originality (Simonton 1986*a*, 1987), and the melodies themselves tend to be more jagged in shape, with more chromatic transitions (Cerulo 1984). We observed earlier that stresses in the composer's personal life can leave traces in his or her compositions. A parallel repercussion holds for stresses that take place on a more global scale. If comparable influences operate on other forms of artistic expression, some degree of coherence would emerge in the stylistic changes.

Endogenous influences

Even so, we must also recognize that many of the trends that characterize music history may ensue from the inner workings of the music tradition itself, independent of any external influences. To begin with, there is reason to believe that some of the ups and downs in the appearance of major composers across time are a result of role-modelling effects (Kroeber 1944; Simonton 1975, 1988). The outcome are autoregressive time series in which musical activity tends to cluster into specific 'golden ages'. During these periods a large number of compositions are produced, both in quantity and in quality (Simonton 1980b). Moreover, stylistic changes can often be driven by an internal impetus. In Martindale's (1990) evolutionary theory, primordial content in musical compositions should oscillate in a manner that corresponds to influential stylistic movements, and there is evidence showing that this is indeed the case (Martindale and Uemura 1983). Furthermore, both melodic originality and originality variation display systematic trends over time that seem to indicate that compositional style is governed by some factors endogenous to the musical tradition (Simonton 1980a,b, 1986a). In particular, because the composers of each generation are compelled to exhibit more originality than those of the preceding generation, the complexity and richness of the compositions will constantly increase over time.

I would like to close by mentioning a fascinating finding that connects the periods of the composer's career with the periods of the historical tradition (Simonton 1980b). Young composers produce works that conform closely with the prevailing stylistic fashions of their day. But as they mature, their compositions become ever more distinctive and independent of that tradition.

PROSPECTS

Historiometry has tremendous potential as a broad technique for developing a psychology of compositional creativity. Because the method permits the incorporation of biographical information about composers' lives and careers, historiometric studies can examine musical creativity as it actually occurs within creative persons. Moreover, this approach allows the investigator to examine the impact of the sociocultural context, and thereby study the periods of musical creativity. In addition, because music is the most mathematical of all forms of artistic expression, its products are quite amenable to computerized content analyses. This potential has already been illustrated in some of the studies reviewed here, but the methods have ample room for future development. Perhaps a day will come when a computer can directly access all the digital information on a compact disk, and then convert it directly to useful measures of various aesthetic parameters, such as melodic, rhythmic, harmonic, instrumental, and structural originality or style. Furthermore, we have not even touched upon the application of historiometric techniques to other musical traditions, such as jazz, rock, or pop (see, for example, Jackson and Padgett 1982; Peterson and Berger 1975). In truth, historiometry can be applied to any form of music that has a history that narrates the coming and going of products, persons, and periods.

REFERENCES

Berlyne, D. E. (1971). *Aesthetics and psychobiology*. Appleton-Century-Crofts, New York.

Brook, B. S. (1969). Style and content analysis in music: The simplified 'Plaine and Easie Code'. In *The analysis of communication content* (ed. G. Gerbner, O. R. Holsti, K. Krippendorff, W. J. Paisley, and P. J. Stone), pp. 287–96. Wiley, New York.

Cerulo, K. A. (1984). Social distuption and its effects on music: An empirical analysis. *Social Forces*, **62**, 885–904.

Cerulo, K. A. (1989). Variations in musical syntax: Patterns of measurement. *Communication Research*, **16**, 204–35.

Cox, C. (1926). *The early mental traits of three hundred geniuses*. Stanford University Press, Stanford, California.

Dennis, W. (1955). Variations in productivity among creative workers. *Scientific Monthly*, **80**, 277–8.

Dennis, W. (1966). Creative productivity between the ages of 20 and 80 years. *Journal of Gerontology*, **21**, 1–8.

Farnsworth, P. R. (1969). *The social psychology of music* (2nd edn). Iowa State University Press, Ames, Iowa.

Galton, F. (1869). *Hereditary genius: An inquiry into its laws and consequences*. Macmillan, London.

Halsey, R. S. (1976). *Classical music recordings for home and library*. American Library Association, Chicago.

Hasenfus, N., Martindale, C., and Birnbaum D. (1983). Psychological reality of cross-media artistic styles. *Journal of Experimental Psychology: Human Perception and Performance*, **9**, 841–63.

Jackson, J. M. and Padgett, V. R. (1982). With a little help from my friend: Social loafing and the Lennon–McCartney songs. *Personality and Social Psychology Bulletin*, **8**, 672–7.

Karno, M. and Konečni, V. J. (1992). The effects of structural interventions in the first movement of Mozart's Symphony in G Minor K. 550 on aesthetic preference. *Music Perception*, **10**, 63–72.

Kroeber, A. L. (1944). *Configurations of culture growth*. University of California Press, Berkeley, California.

Lehman, H. C. (1953). *Age and achievement*. Princeton University Press, Princeton, New Jersey.

Lomax, A. (ed.). (1968). *Folk song style and culture*. American Association for the Advancement of Science, Washington DC.

Ludwig, A. M. (1995). *The price of greatness: Resolving the creativity and madness controversy*. Guilford Press, New York.

Martindale, C. (1990). *The clockwork muse: The predictability of artistic styles*. Basic Books, New York.

Martindale, C. and Uemura, A. (1983). Stylistic evolution in European music. *Leonardo*, **16**, 225–8.

Moles, A. (1968). *Information theory and esthetic perception* (trans. J. E. Cohen). University of Illinois Press, Urbana, Illinois. (Original work published 1958.)

Paisley, W. J. (1964). Identifying the unknown communicator in painting, literature and music: The significance of minor encoding habits. *Journal of Communication*, **14**, 219–37.

Peterson, R. A. and Berger, D. G. (1975). Cycles in symbol production: The case of popular music. *American Sociological Review*, **40**, 158–73.

Schubert, D. S. P., Wagner, M. E., and Schubert, H. J. P. (1977). Family constellation and creativity: Firstborn predominance among classical music composers. *Journal of Psychology*, **95**, 147–9.

Simonton, D. K. (1975). Interdisciplinary creativity over historical time: A correlation analysis of generational fluctuations. *Social Behaviour and Personality*, **3**, 181–8.

Simonton, D. K. (1976). Do Sorokin's data support his theory?: A study of generational fluctuations in philosophical beliefs. *Journal for the Scientific Study of Religion*, **15**, 187–98.

Simonton, D. K. (1977a). Creative productivity, age, and stress: A biographical time-series analysis of 10 classical composers. *Journal of Personality and Social Psychology*, **35**, 791–804.

Simonton, D. K. (1977b). Eminence, creativity, and geographic marginality: A recursive structural equation model. *Journal of Personality and Social Psychology*, **35**, 805–16.

Simonton, D. K. (1980a). Thematic fame and melodic originality in classical music: A multivariate computer-content analysis. *Journal of Personality*, **48**, 206–19.

Simonton, D. K. (1980b). Thematic fame, melodic originality, and musical zeitgeist: A biographical and transhistorical content analysis. *Journal of Personality and Social Psychology*, **38**, 972–83.

Simonton, D. K. (1983). Esthetics, biography, and history in musical creativity. In *Documentary report of the Ann Arbor Symposium*, Session 3, pp. 41–8. Music Educators National Conference, Reston, Virginia.

Simonton, D. K. (1984). Melodic structure and note transition probabilities: A content analysis of 15 618 classical themes. *Psychology of Music*, **12**, 3–16.

Simonton, D. K. (1986a). Aesthetic success in classical music: A computer analysis of 1935 compositions. *Empirical Studies of the Arts*, **4**, 1–17.

Simonton, D. K. (1986b). Biographical typicality, eminence, and achievement style. *Journal of Creative Behavior*, **20**, 14–22.

Simonton, D. K. (1987). Musical aesthetics and creativity in Beethoven: A computer analysis of 105 compositions. *Empirical Studies of the Arts*, **5**, 87–104.

Simonton, D. K. (1988). Galtonian genius, Kroeberian configurations, and emulation: A generational time-series analysis of Chinese civilization. *Journal of Personality and Social Psychology*, **55**, 230–8.

Simonton, D. K. (1989a). Age and creative productivity: Nonlinear estimation of an information-processing model. *International Journal of Aging and Human Development*, **29**, 23–37.

Simonton, D. K. (1989b). The swan-song phenomenon: Last-works effects for 172 classical composers. *Psychology and Aging*, **4**, 42–7.

Simonton, D. K. (1990). *Psychology, science, and history: An introduction to historiometry.* Yale University Press, New Haven, Connecticut.

Simonton, D. K. (1991a). Emergence and realization of genius: The lives and works of 120 classical composers. *Journal of Personality and Social Psychology*, **61**, 829–40.

Simonton, D. K. (1991*b*). Latent-variable models of posthumous reputation: A quest for Galton's G. *Journal of Personality and Social Psychology*, **60**, 607–19.

Simonton, D. K. (1993*a*). Creative genius in music: Mozart and other composers. In *The pleasures and perils of genius: Mostly Mozart* (ed. P. F. Ostwald and L. S. Zegans), pp. 1–28. International Universities Press, New York.

Simonton, D. K. (1993*b*). Esthétique et créativité en musique classique: Ce que les ordinateurs peuvent décrypter à partir des six premières notes. *Bulletin de Psychologie*, **46**, 476–83.

Simonton, D. K. (1994*a*). Computer content analysis of melodic structure: Classical composers and their compositions. *Psychology of Music*, **22**, 31–43.

Simonton, D. K. (1994*b*). *Greatness: Who makes history and why*. Guilford Press, New York.

Simonton, D. K. (1995). Drawing inferences from symphonic programs: Musical attributes versus listener attributions. *Music Perception*, **12**, 307–22.

Weisberg, R. W. (1994). Genius and madness? A quasi-experimental test of the hypothesis that manic-depression increases creativity. *Psychological Science*, **5**, 361–7.

White, R. K. (1931). The versatility of genius. *Journal of Social Psychology*, **2**, 460–89.

7 | *The roles of music in society: the ethnomusicological perspective*

Andrew H. Gregory

Most studies on the psychology of music are set within the context of Western musical and cultural traditions. However, in many other cultures both the style of the music and its role in society are quite different. This area of study is particularly interesting both for its own sake and because it allows conclusions from studies on the psychology of Western music to be looked at from a different perspective.

The study of music in different societies is known as ethnomusicology. This is a hybrid discipline; at one extreme musicologists whose interests lie in the structure of the music and the instruments, and at the other extreme anthropologists whose primary concern is culture and the roles played by music within it. It is this latter approach to ethnomusicology which is most relevant to the social psychology of music. Merriam (1964), in his book on the anthropology of music, gives his definition of ethnomusicology as the study of music in culture. Nettl (1980), in a general overview of the subject, similarly suggests 'the study of music *in* and *as* culture; the study of how people use, perform, compose, and think about music; and of their general attitudes toward it'. Merriam stresses that ethnomusicology is an approach to all types of music, not just to non-Western music. He also makes a distinction between the uses and the functions of music. The uses comprise the ways in which music is employed in a society, but the music may or may not have a deeper function such as emotional expression, aesthetic enjoyment, or entertainment.

To read about these topics without being able to listen to the actual music gives a very incomplete picture. Two books which both contain musical examples on records or compact discs are a series of introductory essays on the music of many cultures edited by May (1980), and a review of the traditional music of indigenous people by Blumenfeld (1993). In general, references have been given to these or other books in preference to more specialized journal articles.

TRADITIONAL ROLES OF MUSIC

In many societies music is not an independent art form to be enjoyed for its own sake, but is an integral part of the culture. Music may accompany every human activity from the cradle to the grave, including lullabies, games, dancing, work, healing, battle, rites and ceremonies, including weddings and funerals. The style of this music is frequently very different from that of Western music. Bebey (1975) describes the traditional music of black Africa: 'African musicians do not seek to combine sounds in a manner pleasing to the ear. Their aim is simply to express life in all its aspects through the medium of sound'. He also stresses that to understand African music it must be studied within the context of traditional African life.

Africa has hundreds of different societies, each with their own traditions and with different roles for music, but in the majority of them music forms an integral part of all activities. In other cultures elsewhere in the world, music may also be integrated into many human activities or restricted to only a limited number. Similarly, all members of a society may take part in musical activities or there may be a small number of skilled musicians. The main traditional uses of music will now be discussed, some of which are common to nearly all societies, but others are almost unique.

Lullabies

Lullabies are one of the most universal forms of music, and found in all cultures, obviously reflecting the universal need to calm infants in every society. There have been few cross-cultural comparisons of lullabies, but in general they tend to have smooth descending contours, slow tempo, relatively simple structure, and repetition. Unyk *et al.* (1992) found that lullabies from several different cultures were judged as simpler in form than other songs from the same cultures, and were more likely to be judged as lullabies if they contained a higher proportion of descending intervals. This parallels the observation that soothing infant-directed speech also tends to show smooth descending contours (Papoušek and Papoušek, 1981).

Games

Children's games are another universal activity where music and song are found. The songs are often related to dancing, skipping, or other rhythmic activities following from the rules of the games. Children's games may be quite different from any adult activities, or may be a mirror of, or a preparation for, adult life. Bebey (1975) describes the musical games played by children in some African societies as a form of musical training which prepares them to participate in all areas of adult activity, and their games may copy both the activity and the associated music. In Europe, children's games on the whole seem to form a different world, which may well reflect the fact that children tend to be brought up separated from the adult world.

Whenever populations have moved, the music of children's games has usually been incorporated into the new culture. Bilby (1985) describes Caribbean children's game songs which derive from both European and African roots. Many of the songs have a call-and-response form, and include memory games, ring games, and stone-passing games. Some, such as the well-known song 'Brown Girl in the Ring' seem to be derived from British melodies, but others, such as 'Manuel Road' (Emmanuel Road), where the children pass stones in rhythm as they sing, show clear signs of the much stronger African rhythms (Fig. 7.1).

Work music

In Europe, the use of music and song to accompany work has all but died out, although sea shanties are probably the most recent surviving form, and provide an excellent example of the use of music to help in the strict rhythmic coordination necessary in sailing. Hugill (1961) gives a good review of British sea shanties. They were always associated with work, and there was a superstitious taboo against singing them ashore. The songs developed over the time of the great sailing shops from rhythmic shouts through chants to tuneful songs. The form of the songs closely matched the task. One form comprising alternating solo and chorus lines, as in 'Blow the Man Down', was used for intermittent tasks like hauling sails (Fig. 7.2). The other form usually had longer verses and chorus, as in 'A-rovin' and 'Shenandoah', and was used for continuous operations such as the capstan or windlass.

In most traditional African societies, music accompanies the rhythm of work in the fields, and also indoor activities such as grinding and pounding. Nkeita (1988) describes teams of men from the Frafra people of Ghana who cut grass accompanied by musicians. They swing their cutlasses to the rhythm of the music, with a remarkable effect on the speed of the grass cutting. In Jamaica, work songs were a traditional part of the musical heritage of the country, with group songs for digging, timber sawing and rice beating. These sings usually have a call-and-response structure, with a leader singing solo lines answered by a chorus, and they probably derive from both African and European traditions. Work songs are most common for group working, but are also sung by individuals, either to help keep a rhythm or to relieve the monotony.

Dancing

Dancing to music is found in a wide variety of forms in all cultures, either as an integral part of ceremonies, or for its own enjoyment. It is often difficult to know which is the primary activity, music or dance. Is the music just

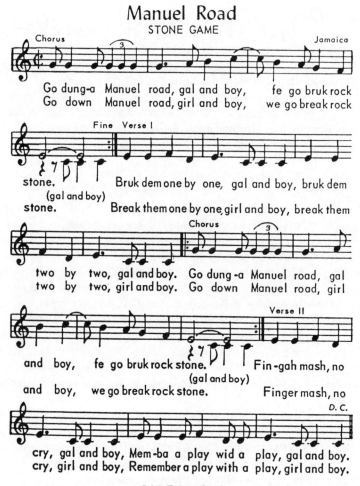

Manuel Road
STONE GAME

Jamaica

Go dung-a Manuel road, gal and boy,   fe go bruk rock
Go down Manuel road, girl and boy,   we go break rock

stone.   Bruk dem one by one, gal and boy, bruk dem
(gal and boy)
stone.   Break them one by one, girl and boy, break them

two by two, gal and boy. Go dung-a Manuel road, gal
two by two, girl and boy. Go down Manuel road, girl

and boy, fe go bruk rock stone.   Fin-gah mash, no
(gal and boy)
and boy, we go break rock stone.   Finger mash, no

cry, gal and boy, Mem-ba a play wid a play, gal and boy.
cry, girl and boy, Remember a play with a play, girl and boy.

DIRECTIONS:

Players are seated on the ground in a close circle. Each player has one stone in front of him. On
the first beat, or "Go", he picks up his stone and
on the third beat, or "Manuel", places it in front of
the player to his right. Continue passing the stones
around the circle from one to the other, always pick-
ing them up on the first beat and putting them down
on the third.

The song continues to be sung as many times as
desired, only faster each time. New verses may be
improvised. Players who fumble or make mistakes
must leave the circle.

Description by Marion Roberts. © 1959 C.R.S.

Fig 7.1 Stone game 'Manuel Road' from Jamaica (Cooperative Recreation Service).

BLOW THE MAN DOWN

Fig 7.2 'Blow the Man Down'. A Halyard Shanty, coordinating hauling on a rope (Hugill 1961).

an accompaniment to the dance, or is the dance a movement to the music? Certainly in many societies music and dance are intricately interlinked. Arom (1991) describes music in sub-Saharan Africa as being a motor activity, almost inseparable from dance, and comments that hearing music will often immediately give rise to a movement of the body. Most Central African vernacular languages have no words for pure music, nor for the concepts of melody or rhythm. Melody is only thought of as representing the words it conveys, and then becomes song. Rhythm is thought of as the stimulus for the bodily movement to which it gives rise, and is given the name of the dance. Chernoff (1979) points out that the dance gives the implied beat, which is not always physically present, in African and Afro-American music, and that one is incomplete without the other. Waterman (1952) also emphasizes the importance of the subjective beat in African music, which is not always actually played. He stresses that to appreciate African music it is necessary to develop a 'metronome sense'. European music emphasizes the main beats, the upbeat and the downbeat. African musicians assume that their audience is mentally supplying these fundamental beats, and will elaborate their rhythms around this mental beat, often using polyrhythms, the interplay of two or more simple meters, and offbeat melodic accents. An example of polyrhythm from Ewe drumming in Ghana is given by Chernoff (1979) and illustrated in Fig. 7.3. A bell and two drums, the high-pitched Kagan and the larger, lower-pitched Kidi, each play simple repetitive rhythms in the introductory section of a dance called Adzogbo. However, the relationship of the rhythms is complex. The bell's pattern is played three times while the Kidi's pattern is played four times. The main beat is not stressed musically, but exists in the dance and in the minds of the musicians and listeners. Thus African music needs to be danced to, physically or mentally, in order to appreciate it fully.

Fig 7.3 Example of African polyrhythm, showing the beats of a bell and two drums, and the position of the main beat, marked X (Chernoff 1979).

Storytelling

The telling of stories, with song or recitation to music, has a long historical tradition in many cultures. The medieval wandering minstrel is a typical example. This tradition is still strong over a wide area of south-west Asia, such as Afghanistan, Azerbaijan, and Turkey. The travelling bard, the *ashiq*, sings epic stories and tales, keeping an age-old oral tradition, often accompanying himself on the *saz*, a long-necked lute (Blumenfeld 1993).

In West Africa the *griots* are professional musicians who play a vital role in traditional African life. Bebey (1975) gives an excellent description of their activities. Some are attached to the houses of noblemen, while others are independent and wander from village to village. They sing stories from the past, providing a living archive of their societies' traditions, and also stories of the present. They know everything that is going on, and their songs spread gossip and slander. Those who belong to the household of a nobleman will sing his praises and recite his genealogy, but independent *griots* will sing the praises of anyone who will pay them, and slander anyone who refuses. The *griot* is both despised and feared, perhaps the cultural equivalent of a tabloid newspaper.

In equatorial Africa the equivalent of the *griot* is the player of the *mvet* or harp–zither. He combines the function of musician, dancer, storyteller, and keeper of the oral traditions of the society. However, he does not usually improvise songs to praise the rich, as the *griot* does, and so is held in higher esteem.

Ceremonies and festivals

Religious and state or local ceremonies are one of the most widespread occasions for music throughout the world, ranging from church bells to ceremonial fanfares on trumpets to greet a new ruler. Nkeita (1988) describes the use of music in ceremony in Africa, and points out that music may either set the mood for the actions or provide an outlet for the feelings they generate. Drumbeats may create a mood of mourning for the death of a chief or a sense of pageant for the installation of a new ruler. The formal part of any ceremony is often followed by music and dancing which allows an emotional expression of feelings.

Ceremonies for individual members of society are also important, and music is an essential element of every marriage, initiation ritual, and funeral in most cultures. Several African societies have special music for the birth of twins, which is considered a very special occasion.

Battle

Music has frequently been used both before battle to inspire the armies, and on the battlefield to intimidate the enemy and also to give signals to troops. The history of military music is reviewed by Farmer (1912, 1950), and also in Hart's (1990) survey of the drum. Trumpets were widely used in ancient Egypt, Greece, and Rome, and in ancient India the kettledrum was combined with trumpet and conch shells. During the Crusades the Saracens rode into battle playing trumpets, drums, cymbals, and pipes. The Christians adopted the Saracen kettledrum, and over the next few centuries the barrel drum, side-drum, and bass drum were added. In the middle of the eighteenth century the Turkish army of the Ottoman empire marched to the sounds of shawm, fife, kettledrum, tenor drum, bass drum, cymbals, and triangle. This brilliant percussion sound was soon adopted by European armies, and also by European composers wishing to write 'Turkish' music.

By the time of the Renaissance the armies of Europe had worked out musical languages to communicate information in battle. The cavalry used the trumpet to issue commands, while the drums gave commands to the infantry. Changes in the drum rhythm signalled march, alarm, approach, assault, battle, retreat, or skirmish. It was considered dishonourable to wound a drummer, although the capture of the enemy's drums was symbolically very important.

Communication

Many languages in the world are tonal, where the pitch of a vowel is linguistically important. However some languages, such as the Bantu group,

Fig 7.4 Musical intonation of two Bantu words (Bebey 1975).

and many central African languages, have a much more subtle stress and intonation pattern. Both the pitch of a level tone and a glide that is rising or falling may be linguistically significant, and each syllable has its own pitch, intensity, and duration. Bebey (1975) states that in Bantu these may be so precise that each word can be written on a musical stave (Fig. 7.4). It must however be stressed that it is the pitch of a given syllable relative to that of neighbouring syllables that is linguistically significant. Thus different speakers will not necessarily use the same absolute pitch levels. In these languages music cannot be dissociated from speech, and to play music is to speak. The music in many ceremonies and dances is thus speaking directly to the participants. Bebey (1975) describes how, during the initiation ceremony into manhood of the Adiukuru people of the Ivory Coast, the tom-toms assume the role of humans and speak to the young men, who answer them back.

This ability to represent language musically is the basis of the talking drum found in some African societies. This is a small, two-headed, hour-glass shaped drum, with cords fastened to the membrane. The drum is held under the armpit, so pressure on the arm can vary the tension of the skins, and thus the pitch of the drum. This instrument is particularly found in West Africa, and can accurately convey the intonation changes of spoken language. Another way of talking with drums is to use two drums of different pitches, as the Ashanti do, or to vary the pitch of a single drum by striking it in different ways (Chernoff 1979).

The other form of talking drum in Africa is a large slit drum, usually made from a length of hollow tree-trunk, leaving a cylinder with one or two longitudinal slits, differing in size. There is no membrane, but striking the drum near one or other of the slits produces one of two possible tones, which can be heard over a great distance. Bebey (1975) describes these drums in detail, and the form of the messages, which are usually coded following the rhythm of the language, using just a few simple phrases. These are the bases of the stories of the bush telegraph given by early European travellers in Africa, by which messages could travel rapidly over a long distance.

Personal symbol

The Saami people (Lapps) have a unique musical tradition where each individual person has their own special song or *joik*. This becomes a personal acoustic symbol, and is often sung when herding reindeer. Parents can give a *joik* to their child, or lovers can give a *joik* to each other as a gift (Blumenfeld 1993).

Although the Saami *joik* is a unique tradition, Herzog (1938) describes a custom of the American Indians of the central prairies, where each person at one time in his life was expected to have a vision. Children were sent out to stay by themselves without food or sleep until a vision appeared, usually an animal which would give the child certain powers, a name, and often one or more personal songs. However these songs were usually kept secret by the individual until near the time of death.

Ethnic or group identity

Music is a powerful means of creating a sense of belonging, either to a particular ethnic group or to a place. Stokes (1994) states 'Music is socially meaningful . . . largely because it provides means by which people recognize identities and places, and the boundaries which separate them'. Stokes describes the boundary between 'Irish' and 'British' identities in Northern Ireland as being patrolled and enforced by musicians. The parades by Protestant Orangemen with fife and drum bands define the central city space in Belfast as the domain of Ulster Protestants and of British rule. On the other hand 'Irish traditional' music, which is often considered to be 'Catholic' music, is widely played in bars and clubs, and defines the Catholic areas of the city.

The Aboriginal people of the Northern Territory of Australia also have a strong relationship between musical performance, social identity, and rights to geographical area. Magowan (1994) describes how their ancestral law relates individuals and clans to spirit ancestors, by rights to land through mythological links. These rights are asserted in paintings, songs, and dances, all of which associate people with places. Songs belong to particular clans, and may only be sung by someone belonging to that clan or related clans. The meaning of the song texts are analogues connecting people with places.

In British popular music Cohen (1994) has shown how discourses, both oral and in the musical press, have created a distinctive 'Liverpool sound' as opposed to both a 'Manchester sound' and a 'London sound'.

The political use of music is a strongly related topic. Rhodes (1962) describes an example from Ghana. After the Ashanti people submitted to British rule in 1900, whenever the Governor appeared for a *durbar* he was greeted ceremonially with drum music. The Ashanti used talking drums which translated the text of an old war song 'Slowly but surely we shall kill . . .', whose meaning was clear to everyone except the British.

Salesmanship

At markets all over the world, song and music are used to attract the attention of passers-by in the hope of selling wares. The old London street cries are a well-known example of this custom, where each seller had a distinctive cry so that matches, lavender, and all kinds of food could be recognized by sound in a crowded market. An excellent review of street music is given by Scholes (1938), and Bridge (1921) describes many of the old London street cries, two of which are shown in Fig. 7.5. African markets still keep this tradition, where sellers of all manner of goods will sing their praises in song (Bebey 1975).

Healing

In many traditional societies music serves a healing function. The harp–lute players of West Africa are often associated with healing, and the players act as healers or soothsayers. In traditional Mali society music has a sacred healing role both for the individual and for society. Music is believed to facilitate communication with the ancestors, the spirits, and the Creator, and to harmonize the forces of the visible and the invisible world. Yaya Diallo, who was brought up in the traditions of Mali, describes the use of music, particularly drum rhythms, for healing (Diallo and Hall 1989). He describes the technique of the musician in trying to find a musical rhythm that has a calming and stabilizing effect on the patient, and then continuing it for several hours, helping to restore the disturbed individual to inner balance. He emphasizes the use of musical monotony, and points out that it is similar to other practices such as autosuggestion, affirmations, and mantra recitation, which are only effective through prolonged repetition.

Native Americans believe that music has a magical power for curing people, but can only be used by ceremonial practitioners who have had years of learning. They also believe that too much use of this power will weaken it. Herzog (1938) describes a Navaho belief that a man should not sing a curing song more than three times a year, or he will be stricken by the disease he is trying to cure. Giving songs away is also held to divide and thus weaken the power (clearly a useful explanation if the cure does not work).

Will you buy my dish of Eels?

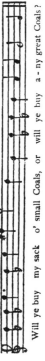

Will ye buy my sack o' small Coals, or will ye buy a - ny great Coals?

Fig 7.5 London street cries (Bridge 1921).

Trance

Trance is a special state of consciousness which usually occurs in a religious context. It may feature a convulsive state, accompanied by cries, trembling, loss of consciousness, and falling. In many different traditional cultures music is used to induce trance states in individuals during special ceremonies. Diallo and Hall (1989) describe trance occurring during the dances of members of secret societies in Mali. Kartomi (1980) describes several art forms in Bali that are associated with trance. In the *Calonarang* drama some performers enter into trance and perform a dagger stabbing dance with no apparent injury, while the *kecak* is a trance choir dance performed to appease the gods. In Sumatra the *dabus* ceremony comprises men singing Arabic songs to the accompaniment of the *rabana*, a form of tambourine. This produces a trance-like state of extreme religious concentration, when they are able to perform feats such as tolerating extreme heat.

Rouget (1985) gives a detailed review of the relations between music and trance. He rejects the simple view that music directly causes trance states, pointing out that the forms of the relations between music and trance are quite different in different cultures. Rouget describes the role of music as 'socializing' the trance, where the precise relation between music and trance will depend upon the conventions of each particular society. Music may trigger a trance state or calm it, and in different cultures trance may be induced by loud or quiet music, the human voice, drums, or other instruments. Rouget concludes that music is one component of the factors causing trance states, usually an essential one, but that many other cultural factors are important.

Rouget (1985) analyses trance as being associated with two different aspects of religion, shamanism and possession. The word 'shaman' originally comes from the Tungus people of Siberia, but is now used for similar religious practices in south-east Asia and all the Americas. In all these cultures the shaman's trance is conceived of as a journey to the 'upper' or 'lower' worlds, undertaken in the company of the spirit he embodies. It is a voluntary trance, where the shaman gains control over the spirit. In possession it is not the person who visits the spirits in their world, but the spirits who visit him or her. It is essentially an involuntary trance where the spirit gains control over the person. These two forms of trance are associated with quite different uses of music.

Possession is associated everywhere with music and dance, and these both play their part in inducing trance. Often music and dance may act together to produce the emotional state favourable to trance. All kinds of music may produce possession trance, although there are some frequently recurring characteristics such as breaks or abrupt changes in rhythm, or a simultaneous accelerando and crescendo. Within a culture trance music may be characterized by a particular scale or mode, such as the Phrygian mode in ancient Greece, which was associated with the cult of Dionysus, but the scale is a cultural signal and does not have intrinsic emotional properties. It should be noted that it is the dancers, who are members of the cult, who go into trance, not the musicians playing who are external to the cult.

Blacking (1973) describes the possession dance of the Venda people of the Northern Transvaal, and shows the importance of both the music and the social environment. The rhythms of the possession dance do not send every Venda into a trance, but only those who are members of a cult, and then only when they are dancing in their own homes. The effectiveness of the music thus depends very much on the context, but ultimately it depends upon the music.

The shaman, in contrast, is in every case the musical performer for his own entry into trance. Other musicians are present to assist and to take over when he goes into trance, and to help bring him out safely. The Siberian or Eskimo shaman traditionally uses the drum to induce trance. This has led some authors to speculate about the power inherent in the physical sound of the drum but, as with possession music, other instruments are used in different cultures. In general it is the cultural significance of the music rather than its intrinsic properties which are important for inducing trance.

Personal enjoyment

In many societies people enjoy music, singing, and dancing independently of any celebration and festival. In many African villages people will congregate in the evenings in an open place and spontaneous music-making and dancing will occur. Some of the music may be specifically for entertainment, while other music may be that normally reserved for other occasions. Different groups of musicians may take turns, and this is particularly the time when children participate in the musical life of the community.

Many instrumentalists play for personal enjoyment when they are alone. Nkeita (1988) mentions how in East Africa the sight of a lonely wayfarer playing the hand-piano is quite common, and that children looking after flocks may be given or make flutes or pipes and will play them for their own enjoyment.

COURT AND RELIGIOUS MUSIC

Societies which have developed separated social classes tend to have different styles of music for each group. A ruling class would develop its own court music, and religious groups their own forms of music. The common people, whilst being aware of this music at secular or religious ceremonies, would have quite different styles of music for singing, dancing, working, and other activities. Folk music can be defined in these forms of society as the traditional popular music of the common people.

Court music

The cultures of the Far East in particular have developed this pattern of socially differentiated musical styles. Japan had ancient court music for rituals and dancing, while the common people were entertained by bards and storytellers singing with musical accompaniment, and by drama and theatre. These included the traditional *noh* drama with singing and an instrumental ensemble, and later the *Kabuki* theatre and the *bunraku* puppet theatre, in both of which music is an essential part of the performance (Malm 1980).

In ancient China, local traditions of folk songs, minstrel music, and narrative song developed alongside court music. Confucius himself commented on the rise of secular music and lamented the decline of ritual and ceremonial music. The Ch'ing dynasty (seventeenth to nineteenth century AD) was energetic in the promotion of traditional Chinese arts. Regional theatre was introduced to the court and led to the flowering of the Peking opera, which became popular throughout China (Han and Mark 1980).

In India, music was traditionally considered to be of divine origin, and the temples were cultural centres, training dancers, musicians, and singers. The courts and homes also encouraged the performing arts, and many rulers and often their wives were proficient musicians. Historically there was a close relationship between the court and the people, all of whom showed a respect for tradition. The two great Indian epics, the *Mahabharata* and the *Ramayana* were constantly retold in forms of drama, dance, and song, and had great popularity throughout India. During the Mughal empire the Muslim rulers followed the tradition of supporting the performing arts in their courts, but regarded it as secular entertainment in contrast to the Hindu reverence for music. The extensive court patronage of music meant that musicians were playing for a highly knowledgeable audience, and Indian classical music flourished in court circles (Wade 1979).

The Islamic empire developed rapidly following the founding of Islam, and at first music was not approved of and classified as one of the 'forbidden pleasures', along with wine and women. In fact the Qur'an does not contain any statement against music, and Mohammed was only opposed to the licentiousness associated with the three. However, the original legal schools of Islam justified their negative attitude on the basis of 'tradition'. During the first dynasty music did begin to flourish, and the court in Damascus became a cultural centre, where traditional Arabic and Persian music were both popular. During the following dynasty Arabic music flourished, and this period is considered the Golden Age of Islamic culture. The Arabic style was complimented by a new 'romantic' Persian style in Baghdad, and in Cordoba a distinctive Andalusian style began to develop. After the destruction of Baghdad by the Mongols, the cultural centres moved to Persia and central Asia, and the Christian reconquest of Spain led to the expulsion of the Moors and their music to North Africa. Traditional Arabic music is still performed in Egypt, Lebanon, Syria, and Iraq, but is strictly elitist, having been developed in the courts (Pacholczyk 1980).

Religious music

In some societies religion has been the main force behind the development of music, while other religions use no music and may even disapprove of music, as with orthodox Islam. Religious music may be public music with which most of the members of the society are involved, or music performed by religious communities for their own spiritual devotions. Some isolated religious communities have maintained the same musical style for several hundred years, and have preserved some very old musical traditions. One example is the ancient chanting style of Tibetan monks from Gyütö Tantric college, which is still maintained, although the college was closed during the Chinese invasion and is re-established in India. The vocal quality of the chanting sounds quite unusual, as the singers produce low bass notes with unusually rich overtones (Blumenfeld 1993).

Musical drama often developed from religious plays. In Java, where most plays and music have a religious basis, traditional stories are enacted by the *Wayang Kulit,* a puppet play with two-dimensional puppets accompanied by a small *gamelan,* a bronze percussion ensemble, and also by the *Wayang orang,* a human theatre with a larger double *gamelan* ensemble.

DEVELOPMENTS

The emergence of a cultured class in many societies led to the development of 'art music', which is listened to for personal enjoyment. This often developed from court or religious music. In some regions it has remained very close to its original source, as with classical Arabic music in the Middle East. In Europe however, Western classical music has evolved and incorporated music from many sources, including folk music and military music.

Some of the most striking developments in music have arisen from the mass population movements of the last few centuries, where musical traditions have travelled with the people, and different traditional musics have combined together to create new music. The European immigrants to America took their folk music with them, and many European folk melodies can be traced in the folk songs of the USA. Where groups of immigrants remained together there was a flourishing of folk song which created a sense of identity for each ethnic community. Also, singers and instrumentalists from different areas of each country were brought together and there was a great cross-fertilization of musical ideas. African music travelled to the Americas with the slave trade, and relatively unchanged African music and song can clearly be heard in some parts of the Caribbean and South America. Elsewhere, however, many new forms of music developed, with the inter-mixing of African and European music, such as Caribbean dance music, soul, and jazz. This field has been reviewed by many authors, particularly Waterman (1952), and illustrates how changes in society can often lead to consequent developments in music.

In conclusion it is clear that the very wide range of variation in the role of music and musicians within different societies shows the cultural determination of many aspects of the psychology of music. For example, those societies such as the pygmies where all members engage in a very skilled level of musical activity, illustrate the potential for musicianship in every-one. On the other hand nearly all societies contain individuals who are exceptionally skilled musicians, expressing their skills in a form determined by the particular culture. Cross-cultural studies show that listeners in general have difficulty in perceiving the emotions expressed by unfamiliar music from another culture (Gregory and Varney 1996; Morey 1940). Emotional expression in music thus seems to be culturally determined rather than being an inherent property of the music.

It is evident that one can only begin to understand the music of another culture if one understands the culture. The strongest example of this is traditional African music which only makes sense if one knows the rhythm of the dance which it accompanies, but the principle applies to all forms of music. True understanding of the music would only come from complete immersion in the culture, but a knowledge of the historical and cultural significance of any music is important for its appreciation.

I am grateful to John Baily for valuable comments on a draft of this chapter.

REFERENCES

Arom, S. (1991). *African polyphony and polyrhythm.* Cambridge University Press, Cambridge.

Bebey, F. (1975). *African music: a people's art.* Lawrence Hill, Westport, CT.

Bilby, K. (1985). Caribbean crucible. In *Repercussions: a celebration of African-American music* (ed. G. Haydon and D. Marks). Century, London.

Blacking, J. (1973). *How musical is man?* University of Washington Press, Seattle.

Blumenfeld, L. (1993). *Voices of forgotten worlds. Traditional music of indigenous people.* Ellipsis Arts, Roslyn, N.Y.

Bridge, F. (1921). *The old cryes of London.* Novello, London.

Chernoff, J. M. (1979). *African rhythm and African sensibility.* University of Chicago Press, Chicago.

Cohen, S. (1994). Identity, place and the 'Liverpool sound'. In *Ethnicity, identity and music: the musical construction of place* (ed. M. Stokes). Berg, Oxford.

Cooperative Recreation Service. *Caribbean folk songs and games.* Cooperative Recreation Service Inc., Delaware, Ohio.

Diallo, Y. and Hall, M. (1989). *The healing drum: African wisdom techniques.* Destiny, Rochester, VT.

Farmer, H. G. (1912). *The rise and development of military music.* Reeves, London.

Farmer, H. G. (1950). *Military music.* Parrish, London.

Gregory, A. H. and Varney, N. (1996). Cross-cultural comparisons in the affective response to music. *Psychology of Music,* **24**, 47–52.

Han, K-h. and Mark, L. L. (1980). Evolution and revolution in Chinese music. In *Musics of many cultures* (ed. E. May). University of California Press, Berkeley.

Hart, M. (1990). *Drumming at the edge of magic: a journey into the spirit of percussion.* Harper SanFrancisco, San Francisco.

Herzog, G. (1938). Music in the thinking of the American Indian. *Peabody Bulletin,* May 1938, 8–12. [Reprinted in Shelemay (1990)]

Hugill, S. (1961). *Shanties from the seven seas.* Routledge and Kegan Paul, London.

Kartomi, M. J. (1980). Musical strata in Sumatra, Java, and Bali. In *Musics of many cultures* (ed. E. May). University of California Press, Berkeley.

Magowan, F. (1994). 'The land is our märr (essence), it stays forever': The *yothuyindi* relationship in Australian Aboriginal traditional and popular musics. In *Ethnicity, identity, and music: the musical construction of place* (ed. M. Stokes). Berg, Oxford.

Malm, W P. (1980). Some of Japan's musics and musical principles. In *Musics of many cultures* (ed. E. May). University of California Press, Berkeley.

May, E. (ed.) (1980). *Musics of many cultures.* University of California Press, Berkeley.

Merriam, A. P. (1964). *The anthropology of music.* Northwestern University Press, Evanston, Illinois.

Morey, R. (1940). Upset in emotions. *Journal of Social Psychology,* **12**, 333–56.

Nettl, B. (1980). Ethnomusicology: definitions, directions, and problems. In *Musics of many cultures* (ed. E. May). University of California Press, Berkeley.

Nkeita, J. H. K. (1988). *The music of Africa.* Gollancz, London.

Pacholczyk, J. M. (1980). Secular classical music in the Arabic Near East. In *Musics of many cultures* (ed. E. May). University of California Press, Berkeley.

Papoušek, M. and Papoušek, H. (1981). Musical elements in the infant's vocalization: their significance for communication, cognition, and creativity. In *Advances in infancy research,* Vol. 1 (ed. L. P. Lipsett), pp. 163–224. Ablex, Norwood, N.J.

Rhodes, W. (1962). Music as an agent of political change. *African Studies Bulletin,* **5**, 14–22. [Reprinted in Shelemay (1990)]

Rouget, G. (1985). *Music and trance: a theory of the relations between music and possession.* University of Chicago Press, Chicago.

Scholes, P. A. (1938). Street music. *The Oxford companion to music.* Oxford University Press, Oxford.

Shelemay, K. K. (ed.) (1990). *The Garland library of readings in ethnomusicology. Vol. 3. Music as culture.* Garland, New York.

Stokes, M. (ed.) (1994). *Ethnicity, identity, and music: the musical construction of place.* Berg, Oxford.

Unyk, A. M., Trehub, S. E., Trainor, L. J., and Sellenberg, E. G. (1992). Lullabies and simplicity: a cross-cultural perspective. *Psychology of Music,* **20**, 15–28.

Wade, B. C. (1979). *Music in India: the classical traditions.* Prentice-Hall, Englewood Cliffs.

Waterman, R. A. (1952). African influence on the music of the Americas. In *Acculturation in the Americas* (ed. S. Tax). University of Chicago Press, Chicago. [Reprinted in Shelemay (1990)]

8 | Musical tastes and society

Philip A. Russell

Links between musical tastes and society manifest themselves in various ways and at various levels, particularly those levels described as *social-positional* and *ideological* (see Chapter 1). For example, different types of music tend to appeal to different social groups—the audience at a heavy metal concert will probably have little in common, in terms of age, social class, and lifestyle, with the audience at an opera house. One major section of the present chapter reviews empirical data on these sorts of associations between musical tastes and sociodemographic variables. A second major section is devoted to an analysis of social influences on musical tastes. People's musical tastes do not develop in isolation—they are subject to a variety of social influences, including those stemming from family, peers, education, and the media. These two sections are prefaced by a brief consideration of the problems of measuring musical tastes and by an outline of the concepts of taste cultures and taste publics.

MEASURING MUSICAL TASTES

Musical tastes are most usefully defined as *stable, long-term preferences* for particular types of music, composers, or performers (Abeles 1980; Price 1986). Thus, a person can have a taste for country music or jazz or for the music of Mozart or the Grateful Dead. This chapter follows the consensus of the literature in using the terms taste and preference interchangeably (although see LeBlanc 1982).

In everyday life, people's musical tastes are identifiable by the music they choose to listen to, the recordings they buy, and the live music performances they attend. More formally, tastes may be measured by means of such devices as musical preference ratings and laboratory measures of listening time (Abeles 1980; Wapnick 1976).

The variety of measures of musical taste, the fact that most empirical studies use only a single measure of taste, and the fact that different studies tend to use different measures, combine to raise questions about the validity and the equivalence of the various measures and about the comparability of studies. For example, do verbally expressed preferences always correspond with actual listening or with recording buying? These issues have not been examined systematically, although there are suggestions that the correspondence between different taste measures can vary from good to poor (Fink *et al.* 1985; Geringer 1982).

Further problems attach to attempts to categorize music types. Investigations of musical tastes usually involve the specification of a number of types of music. The number of types may be as few as two, as in some early studies which simply distinguished between popular and classical music. More often, there are a handful of categories, such as blues, country, folk, jazz, opera, rock, and soul. No study, however, can hope to include all possible categories, partly because the number of categories is huge and partly because the definitions, boundaries, and appropriateness of categories are debatable. Most major categories can be subdivided into many subcategories (for example, there are many distinct styles of jazz—Gridley 1985). The problem of music categorization has increased in recent years, with the proliferation of music types and hybrids, and the breakdown of boundaries between traditional categories (Dallin 1977; Gridley 1983). Further discussion of the problem of categorization can be found in Zillmann and Gan (Chapter 9, this volume).

An additional consideration is that studies of musical tastes are invariably conducted 'in the abstract', without specifying *contexts* for the music. Yet, in everyday life, music has a multiplicity of functions for listeners (Rosing 1984) and people listen to it in a variety of contexts—when dancing, working, relaxing, driving, and so on. Although this suggests that musical tastes are likely to vary contextually, this aspect has received little study (although see Chapter 10, this volume).

TASTE PUBLICS AND TASTE CULTURES

In the age of mass communication, people have access to an enormous diversity of music. The listening potential offered by live music is greatly expanded by recorded and broadcast music, giving a choice of music spanning national, cultural, social, and historical divides. Individuals only have time to listen to a fraction of this music, and the choices they make define their personal tastes. People sharing a taste for a particular type of music can be described as members of a *taste public* who subscribe to a *taste culture*. In coining these terms, Gans (1974) intended them to have social class implications (see below), but they have also come to be used in a more general way. A music taste public is a social group comprising devotees of a particular type of music or performer (for example, opera buffs or Elvis fans) and a music taste culture is the set of aesthetic values they share (for example, 'Elvis Is King').

THE SOCIAL STRUCTURE OF MUSIC TASTE PUBLICS

In theory, it is possible to imagine a comprehensive taxonomy of taste cultures and publics, with each taste culture defined in terms of musical values and choices, and its taste public described in terms of such sociodemographic variables as sex, age, social class, and ethnic group. This taxonomy would comprise a huge number of partially overlapping taste cultures and publics, the nature and composition of which would change over time as music and society change. In practice, the difficulties involved in categorizing music types and in specifying social groups make such a taxonomy unachievable. It is possible, however, to identify some associations between tastes and social variables. As well as basic social demographic variables, these associations involve subcultures and lifestyles.

Social class

Relationships between musical tastes and social class, usually defined in terms of socio-economic status and occupational category, have been reported in a number of studies. Some of these studies have been based directly on Gans' (1974) theories linking taste cultures with social class. Gans identified five general taste cultures in the United States, referred to as 'high culture', 'upper-middle culture', 'lower-middle culture', 'low culture', and 'quasi-folk low culture'. These cultures are assumed to be ranged along a socio-economic, social class continuum. For example, upper-middle culture is held to be the culture of 'the vast majority of America's upper–middle class, the professionals, executives and managers' (Gans 1974, p. 81), and quasi-folk low culture that of 'many poor people, who work in unskilled blue collar and service jobs' (Gans, p. 93). Gans recognized, however, that the relationships between cultural tastes and social class are merely probabilistic, and also that the classification of tastes into a small number of discrete taste cultures, and their associated publics, is simply a convenient analytic device for dealing with a much more complex reality in which the boundaries and definitions of tastes are considerably blurred. Moreover, within each class level, there exist more discrete and homogeneous taste publics, differentiated by such factors as age, ethnic group, and home region.

Although Gans provided impressionistic descriptions of the various taste cultures in terms of such factors as their preferred art and literature and their responses to mass media, these descriptions included few musical examples, so there is little on which to base specific predictions about relationships between social class and *musical* taste cultures. One obvious prediction, however, concerns classical music, which, as a putative element of 'high culture', should be preferred more by higher socio-economic status groups. This prediction is consistent with some empirical findings. Hargreaves (1986, Chapter 7) reviewed four representative studies, three of which reported that a positive attitude to classical music was more likely to be found among higher status groups (although, overall, popular music was preferred to classical music and this may be true even for higher status groups).

Further evidence of an association between a taste for classical music and membership of higher socio-economic status groups comes from concert attendance data. In an American national, cross-sectional, social survey cited by DiMaggio and Useem (1978), where the measure was concert attendance during the previous 12 months, only four per cent of blue collar workers were consumers of symphonic music, compared to 14 per cent of managerial workers and 18 per cent of professionals. Similar differences were evident for opera and ballet. Differences in the consumption of popular music (folk, jazz, rock), however, were less marked, with 20 per cent of blue collar workers, 26 per cent of managers, and 33 per cent of professionals having attended popular music concerts. Income and education were also related to classical music consumption, with people earning over $15 000 a year, or having had a college education, being much more likely to have attended classical music concerts than those earning less than $5000, or having had less than a high school education. DiMaggio and Useem also presented other data showing that education was a better predictor of the consumption of symphonic music, opera, and ballet (and of high culture generally) than was income.

Comparable British data were reported by Pegg (1984): surveys of the audience at live music events revealed that classical music concerts had a preponderance of people from the upper-middle and middle classes, while folk concerts had a majority from the middle and working classes. This study also found evidence of class effects in the self-reported preferences of schoolboys. Public schoolboys, who came predominantly from upper-middle and middle class homes, were more likely to give classical music as their favourite music than were state schoolboys, from mainly working class homes.

The data on the association between a taste for classical music and social class, then, seem best summarized as showing that although classical music tends to be a minority taste among all social classes, it is *less* of a minority taste among people from higher socio-economic groups. The other side of this associative coin is that a taste for popular music is somewhat more common among the lower socio-economic groups.

Given that popular music is an extremely heterogeneous category (Christenson and Peterson 1988), we might also anticipate class differences in tastes for various popular music subcategories. Findings in this area are rather difficult to summarize, however, partly because of the categorization problem, and partly because of the rapidly changing popularity of popular music styles and performers. Although several studies have presented evidence that social class membership is not randomly distributed across various popular music subcategory taste cultures, these studies permit few easy generalizations about the precise relationships between social class and these taste cultures (Denisoff and Levine 1972; Dixon 1982; Fox and Wince 1975).

One generalization for which there is some empirical support, however, is that among teenagers and young adults, middle class tastes tend to be rather more 'progressive' and less 'mainstream' than working class tastes. This tendency may be manifest in various ways. Robinson and Hirsch (1972) found that late-1960s, middle class American teenagers were less likely to cite Top 40 hits as favourites and more likely to favour social protest songs, compared to working class teenagers. Murdock and McCron (1973) found that middle class pupils at an English comprehensive school in the 1970s were more likely to be fans of 'progressive' rock groups (for example, Genesis, Yes, Pink Floyd) than were working class pupils, who were correspondingly more likely to prefer mainstream Top 20, American soul, and West Indian reggae artists. Tanner (1981), in a study of Canadian school pupils, also found a tendency for middle class senior high school pupils to be less likely to favour Top 40 music than their working class classmates, although this class difference was not evident among junior high school pupils.

These studies suggest that allegiance to different types of popular and rock music tends to differentiate, to some extent, along class lines. Given that the studies were carried out some years ago, however, it is unclear how, or indeed whether, this tendency manifests itself in contemporary popular music.

Further associations between musical tastes and social class were evident in Peterson and DiMaggio's (1975) analysis of the country music taste public in the United States, which used data from audience surveys of country music radio stations, concert attendance, record buying, and questionnaires. Although Peterson and DiMaggio concluded that a taste for country music could not be equated with a distinct social class, it is clear from their data that, among the country music taste public, the working class and lower-middle class sectors were over-represented, and the upper-middle class sector was under-represented.

Age

Although the empirical literature on musical tastes contains numerous references to age effects, these effects have not been studied very systematically and it is difficult to discern more than a few general trends. One is a tendency for popular music, in its various forms, to appeal more to younger people. The existence of a distinctive youth, 'teenage' culture, centring on popular music, has long been recognized, and the commercially-slanted popular music of the best-seller charts has traditionally been aimed at this taste public (Coleman 1961; Frith 1983; Zillmann and Gan, Chapter 9, this volume). Relevant data are sparser than might be expected, but do tend to confirm expectations. Not only is the taste for popular music in general stronger, and tastes for other music types (especially classical) weaker, among teenagers than among older age groups (Denisoff and Levine 1972), but the teenage group shows a stronger preference for *current* popular hits (Fox and Wince 1975).

Age effects relating to other aspects of musical tastes are also scattered through the literature. For example, Peterson and DiMaggio (1975) reported that country music fans were concentrated in the 25–49 age range, with few teenagers and over-50s. Tolhurst *et al.* (1984) found that people in the age range 20–30 preferred soft rock and country music over light classical and classical music, while this preference was reversed among the over-40s.

The general fact that the preferences of young and older people tend to be different is amenable to various explanations. The most obvious explanation is that people's tastes change as they grow older. There is, however, little evidence to support this explanation. Indeed, the evidence is that, on the contrary, musical tastes formed in youth tend to persist into and across the adult years, especially in the case of popular music. Holbrook and Schindler (1989) found evidence of the persistence of musical tastes in tests of preference for popular music hit songs, using a sample of people aged 16–86 years. People's most preferred songs from among those presented were those which had been hits when the respondents were in their late adolescence or early adulthood (maximum preference was for hits from the period when the respondents were about 23 years old). This persistence of tastes, coupled with the changes which take place over time in the popularity of musical styles and artists among the young, results in each generation having its own defining music and performers. Stipp (1990) argues that the connection between age and popular music tastes is so strong that a person's age can be reliably predicted from a knowledge of his or her favourite 'golden oldies'. For example, fans of Elvis Presley, who was at the peak of his popularity in the late 1950s and early 1960s, are likely to be currently in their 50s, while devotees of Bob Dylan, whose popularity heyday was slightly later, tend to be a few years younger.

It is unclear, however, whether age differences in musical tastes are explainable wholly in terms of taste persistence effects, or whether a degree of age-related taste change is also involved. For example, the fact that classical music tastes are more common among older age groups may reflect more people from these age groups having acquired a taste for this genre in their youth. Alternatively, a taste for classical music may be something which tends to develop at later ages, or with more prolonged exposure to this kind of music. Clarification of this issue may require longitudinal, as opposed to the existing cross-sectional, studies of the relationships between age and musical tastes.

Gender

Gender is rarely a primary variable in studies of music preferences but is commonly included as an incidental one. Reviews of some of the literature on gender effects, most of which relates to the music preferences of school-children or college students, are provided by Abeles (1980), Christenson and Peterson (1988), and Finnäs (1989). These reviewers all come to the con-clusion that males are more likely than females to prefer music described as 'hard' or 'tough', while females are more likely to prefer music which is 'softer' and more romantic. Music which tends to appeal more to males includes hard rock, progressive rock, heavy rock, rock 'n' roll, heavy metal, and, sometimes, jazz. Females are more likely to have stronger preferences for mainstream pop, pop hits, folk, classical, and for dance-oriented music such as disco.

The correspondence between these gender differences in music tastes and conventional general gender stereotypes is obvious. Frith (1983) related the existence of gender differences in the music preferences of British working class teenagers to differences in male and female cultures, lifestyle expecta-tions, and general gender roles. Among this particular social group, the career opportunities for girls were more limited, so that their aspirations tended to focus more on finding a husband and establishing a home, hence their greater orientation to softer and more romantic 'love song' music, and to dance music, which provided a social context for meeting potential marriage partners. This apparent link between gender role and musical tastes prompts the speculation that, in social groups where differences in the gender roles of men and women are less distinct, sex differences in musical tastes will also be less marked, although relevant data are lacking.

Ethnic and cultural factors

The existence of distinctive national, cultural, and ethnic group musics suggests that musical tastes tend to segregate along national, cultural, and ethnic lines. One aspect of this segregation is that within multi-ethnic and multicultural societies, such as exist in the United States and Britain, differ-ent ethnic and cultural groups have different musical tastes. Such differences have not been studied very systematically, but the literature provides some examples, including marked differences in the preferences of American blacks and whites. For example, Denisoff and Levine (1972) found that, among the college population, the most preferred music of blacks was soul

(Motown) and jazz, while for whites it was folk and rock. Dixon (1982), working with 16 music genres, also found that the most popular music of blacks was soul, whereas this was only the twelfth most popular genre among whites. The most popular music of whites, soft folk/country rock, was only the ninth most popular with blacks. In Dixon's study, these ethnic differences were evident even after the partialling out of any effects of age, education, and musical involvement. Further evidence of a strong link between musical tastes and ethnic factors is Peterson and DiMaggio's (1975) finding that the American taste public for country music was overwhelmingly white.

Subcultures, lifestyles, and values

The associations between taste cultures and sociodemographic variables documented in the preceding sections are often only weakly probabilistic. For example, although people with a taste for country music *tend* to be middle-aged, lower-middle, or working class, and white, not only does this taste public contain people from other demographic groups, but there are many people who belong to this particular demographic group who do not subscribe to the country music taste culture. The existence of relatively weak correlations between musical tastes and social demography means that demographic variables can only be crude predictors of tastes. A more complete understanding of taste publics has to embrace additional factors, including those which can be summarized as relating to subcultures, lifestyles, and values (Lewis 1992).

Some music taste cultures are associated with more or less distinct subcultures within society (Lull 1992). A subculture is essentially a particular way of life which stands apart, in various ways, from mainstream culture, and which is characterized by particular patterns of behaviour and values. In some subcultures, musical tastes are central to the values of the subculture, as in the case of punk and heavy metal subcultures. In other subcultures, particular musical tastes are evident but less definitive: for example, gay and lesbian subcultures. Lull also distinguishes between 'aesthetic' and 'oppositional' musical subcultures. An aesthetic musical subculture is one centring on a particular minority interest music, such as jazz, classical, or ethnic music. Minority musics receive only limited media coverage and exist on the fringes of mainstream culture. Lewis (1992) points out that, in such taste cultures, the music often contains elements which are part of a wider iconography. An example is heavy metal subculture, where the key aesthetic elements include Satanic images, visual excesses in performance, and distinctive clothing and hair styles. Oppositional music subcultures are associated with loosely organized resistance to conventional social institutions and values, and have ideological and political components: the Jamaican subculture centring on reggae music is one example. Music subcultures can, however, also be supportive of the power structure of the society in which they exist (for example, country music in the USA) or alternative and coexisting (for example, New Age music).

It is evident, then, that in subscribing to a music taste culture, people are often associating with a particular lifestyle and a wider set of values. This linkage of music taste cultures with wider aspects of lifestyle is further exemplified by the reported associations between tastes for certain kinds of popular music and adolescent behavioural problems. Teenagers with preferences for heavy metal, hard rock, and rap music are reportedly more likely to display such traits as low school achievement, delinquent and antisocial behaviour, drug-taking, recklessness, and suicidal tendencies, relative to peers with other preferences (Arnett 1992; Martin *et al.* 1993; Singer *et al.* 1993; Took and Weiss 1994). The problems of interpreting such associations, however, become evident when it is remembered that both musical tastes and behavioural problems may be correlated with a variety of other factors, including personality, social class, and education.

GENERAL THEORIES OF THE RELATIONSHIP BETWEEN SOCIAL STRUCTURAL AND MUSICAL TASTES

Given that there are links between social structure and musical tastes, how are these associations to be explained? This question has parallels in the wider context of theories of the relationships between social structure and: (a) culture in general, discussed by various theorists (Peterson 1976; Rosengren 1981); and (b) music types (Adorno 1941; Shepherd 1977). Links between social structure and musical tastes are open to two distinct broad interpretations, reflecting different notions about the direction of causality. One interpretation is that musical taste differences are the products of social stratification; that is, social structure influences music tastes. The other is that musical tastes are one of the many factors which determine social stratification; that is, music tastes influence social structure. Both interpretations probably have some validity, because it is likely that social structure and musical tastes constitute sets of *mutual influences*. For example, the differentiation of music into different types, which forms the basis for the existence of different taste cultures, is probably, at least in part, a response to the differing needs of different social groups. But, at the same time, the differences in musical tastes between these social groups almost certainly serve (along with many other factors) to amplify and reinforce the distinctions between the groups, and so represent one of the ways in which groups 'construct' themselves, a point which is developed below in the section on group identification.

SOCIAL INFLUENCES ON MUSICAL TASTES

Social influences on musical tastes take many forms and operate at various levels. For descriptive convenience, these influences can be classified as stemming from various specific sources, such as socialization, education, peers, and the media. In reality, the influences are unlikely to be truly discrete, but rather comprise a complex, interacting system.

Socialization and education

The socialization of individuals involves a host of influences, stemming from parents, other family, peers, and society generally, and serving to perpetuate systems of behaviour, beliefs, attitudes, and values. There is reason to suppose that this intergenerational reproduction of culture will extend to the aesthetic domain, including musical tastes. Some of the associations between musical tastes and social demography, noted in preceding sections, may reflect this process. For example, the tendency for a taste for classical music to be more common among the upper-middle class could reflect the fact that children growing up in upper-middle class homes are more likely to encounter classical music and to experience positive values associated with it. Furthermore, to the extent that there are class differences in education, home influences might be reinforced by influences from school and other educational sectors (DiMaggio and Useem 1978), including possible differences in formal musical training (Crozier and Chapman 1981).

If this analysis is correct, a family belonging to a particular taste public is likely to provide a set of influences which increase the likelihood of its children becoming members of that taste public. There are, however, several problems with this argument. One is the difficulty of empirically disentangling the various influences, particularly as they may also intersect with differences in personality and intelligence (Crozier and Chapman 1981). This may be why pertinent empirical data are hard to come by. Even more problematically, the data which do exist suggest that family and educational influences are likely to be quite weak (Thompson 1993). The role of music in reinforcing the 'generation gap' between young people and people of their parents' generation (see the section below on peer influences) suggests possible limitations on the influences of family and school on the musical tastes of children. Consistent with family factors having a minimal influence, when young people listen to music, they tend to be alone or with peers, not with their family (Christenson and DeBenedittis 1986; Larson and Kubey 1983). That school influences are also likely to be minimal, is suggested by the generally scant success of formal educational attempts to shift adolescent tastes towards classical and away from popular music, by exposure and instruction (studies reviewed by Finnas 1989), and by the distinction drawn by pupils between the 'serious' music of school and the 'popular' music with which they more naturally align (Vulliamy 1978).

One area in which socialization effects might be expected is that of gender differences in musical tastes, noted above. These taste differences may be linked with the differing ways in which boys and girls are socialized, and so with the differing gender roles of men and women and with broader social and cultural patterns (Christenson and Peterson 1988). This suggestion is consistent with the previously-noted link between gender taste differences and gender role differences, but detailed confirmatory evidence is lacking.

A further consideration with regard to socialization in general, is that music taste cultures may themselves form part of the socialization environment and so play a role in shaping social attitudes and behaviour (Hansen and Hansen 1991). A possible example is the influence of gender 'messages' in the lyrics of popular music on gender role socialization. These messages tend to reflect conventional gender role values, so the fact that pre-teenage children 'eavesdrop' on them means that the messages may contribute to the maintenance of restrictive gender role socialization (Christenson *et al.* 1985; Christenson and DeBenedittis 1986).

Group identification and cohesion

People's musical tastes may reflect a tendency to listen to, and to enjoy, the same music as is listened to by other people they like, or with whom they seek to identify (Lewis 1992). Such identification may be especially evident in the musical tastes of young people (see the following section), but it also occurs in other contexts, including that of social class (DiMaggio and Useem 1978). Although socialization and education may account, at least in part, for intergenerational social class continuities in musical tastes, these factors do not in themselves explain why different social groups have different musical tastes. Why, for example, is the upper-middle class more likely to have a taste for classical music? One relevant consideration here is that subscribing to a particular musical taste culture may be one way in which people seek to identify with a specific social class. The different musical tastes of different classes are part of a much broader panoply of class difference norms relating to tastes, interests, values, attitudes, and behaviour. These norms serve simultaneously to reinforce between-class differences and to promote within-class solidarity. Musical tastes, then, along with such factors as style of dress, manner of speech, and political affiliation, help establish an individual's membership of a particular class and promote class cohesion.

This argument can be extended to cover identification with ethnic and other social groups, and with subcultures. Links between musical tastes and subcultures have already been discussed. Someone with a taste for heavy metal music, for example, is likely to be identifying with a range of extra-musical lifestyle factors and values and with other people who also sub-scribe to these factors and values.

Peer influences

Perhaps the most remarked example of the role of music in group identi-fication and cohesion concerns young people. The distinctive musical tastes of the young serve to separate them from their parents and older people generally (the 'generation gap') and also act as a framework for a set of socially shared meanings and common states of awareness through which individuals identify with others in their peer group (Coleman 1961; Frith 1983; Riesman 1950; Zillmann and Gan, Chapter 9, this volume). Within this general context of youth culture, musical taste differences also serve to align young people with various, more specific teenage and adolescent groups and subcultures, such as the British Teddy Boy of the 1950s, whose lifestyle centred on rock 'n' roll music; hippies; punks; new romantics; and many more (Savage 1988). Beyond these broad generalizations, data which would permit statements about the specific roles of peers in shaping one another's tastes, and the about the particular mechanisms involved, seem lacking. For example, it is unclear how much the shared tastes of young people stem from direct peer contact, rather than from the indirectly shared experience resulting from media targeting of youth taste cultures (see the following section). Also, what aspects of peer contact are likely to be important? For example, how much are the emerging tastes of young people influenced by slightly older youth role models, or by popular or dominant 'taste leaders' within the peer group?

Media influences

The music media include recorded music, music radio, music television, music video, and the music press (newspapers, magazines, and books). These com-prise a complex set of factors which intersect with one another, with the per-formance and promotion of live music, and with musical tastes. More broadly, the music media are part of what has long been recognized, particularly in the case of popular music, as a music industry (MacDougald 1941). Other aspects of this industry include musicians, composers, producers, promoters, policy-makers, programmers, presenters, disc jockeys, and the consumers of the music, who include record buyers, radio listeners, and concert goers.

An important aspect of the relationships between the media and musical tastes is the fact that there are different media sectors catering for different taste publics. This is clearly exemplified by commercial music radio in the United States, where a large number of radio stations, many of them specializing in a particular type of music, such as country, 'golden oldies', or album-oriented rock, cater for a listening audience which is fragmented into many different taste publics (Barnes 1988). Although precise data are not available, it is highly probable that there is good correspondence between the size of the audience for a particular type of music and the number of stations broadcasting that type of music. For example, minority tastes, such as classical and jazz, have relatively few outputs. This correspondence can be seen as one example of a general correlation, probably existing throughout the music industry, between the media resources devoted to a music type and the size of the audience for it. This correlation tends to be reflected in such factors as the number of professional musicians performing, concerts promoted, and recordings made.

This correspondence between media provision and tastes is consistent with the media *reflecting* the needs and demands of taste publics—the bigger the demand for a particular type of music, the more media resources allocated to it. There are, however, grounds for believing that, as well as reflecting tastes, the music media also, to some extent, *create and shape* tastes (Frith 1983; Rothenbuhler and McCourt 1992). Perhaps the most commented-upon aspect of the shaping effect of the media is that of airplay exposure upon the popularity, and so the sales, of popular music recordings. At its most extreme, this takes the form of 'hyping' or 'plugging', as exemplified in 'payola'—payments to radio station employees to promote particular recordings (Denisoff 1975). This practice is based on the assumption that the likeability of recordings is enhanced by repetition (see Chapter 5, this volume) and by endorsement by an 'authority' or 'role model' figure, normally the disc jockey (see Chapter 4, this volume). Hyping and plugging usually centre on individual recordings or artists, but these processes, operating over time and over a number of cases, have the potential for wider effects in relation to the shaping of tastes for music types.

Moreover, hyping and plugging are merely particularly conspicuous aspects of a wider set of selection processes operating at various levels within the music industry (Hirsch 1969, 1972). For example, whether a composer's work is actually performed and recorded depends upon its selection by performers and producers. Whether a recording is actually made depends upon its acceptability to recording executives in charge of the purse-strings. Before a recording reaches the public, it will have to go through a further series of selection processes to do with release, promotion, inclusion on radio station playlists, and so on. In effect, the music industry thus operates a variety of 'filters' which can either block or facilitate the exposure of musical styles to audiences (Lopes 1992; Rothenbuhler and McCourt 1992), and which can, therefore, shape musical tastes.

Although it seems likely, then, that the media both reflect and shape musical tastes, the relative importance of these two sets of processes is hard to evaluate. In the final analysis, perhaps they are virtually inextricable. Their relative importance may also vary in different contexts and with the particular music concerned.

The potential of the music media for shaping tastes has led some commentators to express concern that media effects can lead to an undesirable *massification* of musical tastes. As it applies to culture in general, the massification hypothesis rests on the assumption that the rise of effective mass communications has produced mass media and a consequent tendency toward mass culture (MacDonald 1964; McQuail 1994). Mass culture comprises a set of cultural products manufactured specifically for the mass market. It is seen as replacing the diversity of earlier culture, marked by regional, ethnic, occupational, and class differences, with a standardized and homogenized culture which is everywhere the same. With regard to music, the dissemination of popular music, especially through recordings and radio, has indeed, on the face of it, led to a degree of massification of musical tastes within cultures. This is reflected, for example, in the publication of *national* charts of best-selling recordings, and in the fact that different radio stations (both national and local) which focus on current recordings tend to have highly similar playlists (Rothenbuhler and McCourt 1992). As Peterson and DiMaggio (1975) have argued, however, the notion of a largely homogenized popular music culture is a gross oversimplification. While there are signs that the emergence of the mass music media has been accompanied by a break-up of the older patterns of diversity in musical tastes, which had been differentiated along regional, ethnic, and other lines, there is little evidence of homogenization. Indeed, the data reviewed in some of the preceding sections of the present chapter present a picture which is essentially that of a large number of relatively specialized musical taste cultures, both within popular music and across music generally. This picture is consistent with the more general observation that contemporary, 'post-industrial' society is characterized by a variety of specialized media catering for the needs of a large number of specific taste cultures, and that the mass media have declined in size and importance (Maisel 1973).

CONCLUSIONS

The evidence of the foregoing sections leaves little doubt about the existence of integral links between musical tastes and society. Beyond this broad conclusion, however, the nature of these links is surprisingly difficult to specify precisely. There are several reasons for this. One is that the links appear to be complex and multifarious, and so are difficult to pin down empirically. This is true, for example, of the relationships between musical tastes and socialization and education, and of the interaction of musical tastes and the media. In such cases, there are a large number of potentially interlinked factors, the individual effects of which are extremely difficult to isolate. Moreover, most of the available data are, inevitably, purely correlational, making it difficult to be sure of the direction of causality. A final complication is that, because both music and society exist in a state of sometimes rapidly-changing flux, data, and the theories linked to them, may quickly become outdated.

All of the areas reviewed would benefit from the collection of more, and better, empirical data: some specific suggestions identified in the course of this chapter include the need for:

(1) more up-to-date information on the relationships between tastes and sociodemographic variables such as social class and subculture, and including longitudinal studies of age-related taste differences;
(2) more detailed studies of the influences of family, education, and peers on the development of musical tastes;
(3) similarly more detailed studies of the roles of the media as reflectors *versus* shapers of musical tastes.

That said, the complex and intractable nature of the processes involved makes the collection of such data a challenging task.

REFERENCES

Abeles, H. F. (1980). Responses to music. In *Handbook of music psychology* (ed. D. A. Hodges). National Association for Music Therapy, Lawrence, KS.

Adorno, T. W. (1941). On popular music. *Zeitschrift für Sozialforschung*, **9**, 17–49.

Arnett, J. (1992). The soundtrack of recklessness: musical preference, and reckless behaviour among adolescents. *Journal of Adolescent Research*, **7**, 313–31.

Barnes, K. (1988). Top 40 radio: a fragment of the imagination. In *Facing the music: a Pantheon guide to popular culture* (ed. S. Frith). Pantheon, New York.

Christenson, P. G. and DeBenedittis, P. (1986). Evesdropping on the FM band: children's use of radio. *Journal of Communication*, **36**, 27–38.

Christenson, P. G. and Peterson, J. B. (1988). Genre and gender in the structure of music preferences. *Communication Research*, **15**, 282–301.

Christenson, P. G., Debenedittis, P., and Lindlof, T. (1985). Children's use of audio media. *Communication Research*, **13**, 327–44.

Coleman, J. (1961). *The adolescent society*. Free Press, New York.

Crozier, W. R. and Chapman, A. (1981). Aesthetic preferences: prestige and social class. In *Psychology and the arts* (ed. D. O'Hare). Harvester, Brighton.

Dallin, L. (1977). *Listeners' guide to musical understanding*. William C. Brown, Dubuque, IA.

Denisoff, R. S. (1975). *Solid gold: the popular record industry*. Transaction Books, New Brunswick, New Jersey.

Denisoff, R. S. and Levine, M. H. (1972). Youth and popular music. A test of the taste culture hypothesis. *Youth and Society*, **4**, 237–55.

DiMaggio, P. and Useem, M. (1978). Social class and arts consumption: the origins and consequences of class differences in exposure to the arts in America. *Theory and Society*, **5**, 141–61.

Dixon, R. D. (1982). Musical taste cultures and taste publics revisited: a research note of new evidence. *Popular Music and Society*, **8**, 2–9.

Fink, E. L., Robinson, J. P., and Dowden, S. (1985). The structure of music preference and attendance. *Communication Research*, **12**, 301–18.

Finnas, L. (1989). How can musical preferences be modified? A research review. *Bulletin of the Council for Research in Music Education*, **102**, 1–58.

Fox, W. S. and Wince, M. H. (1975). Musical taste cultures and taste publics. *Youth and Society*, **7**, 198–224.

Frith, S. (1983). *Sound effects: youth, leisure, and the politics of rock*. Constable, London.

Gans, H. J. (1974). *Popular culture and high culture: an analysis and evaluation of taste*. Basic Books, New York.

Geringer, J. M. (1982). Verbal and operant music listening preferences in relationship to age and musical training. *Psychology of Music*, Special Issue, 47–50.

Gridley, M. C. (1983). Clarifying labels: jazz, rock, funk, and jazz-rock. *Popular Music and Society*, **9**, 27–34.

Gridley, M. C. (1985). *Jazz styles: history and analysis*. Prentice-Hall, Englewood Cliffs, N.J.

Hansen, C. H. and Hansen, R. D. (1991). Construction personality and social reality through music: individual differences among fans of punk and heavy metal music. *Journal of Broadcasting and Electronic Media*, **35**, 335–50.

Hargreaves, D. J. (1986). *The developmental psychology of music*. Cambridge University Press, Cambridge.

Hirsch, P. (1969). *The structure of the popular music industry*. Institute for Social Research, Ann Arbor, MI.

Hirsch, P. (1972). Processing fads and fashions: an organization-set analysis of cultural industry systems. *American Journal of Sociology*, **77**, 639–59.

Holbrook, M. B. and Schindler, R. M. (1989). Some exploratory findings on the development of musical tastes. *Journal of Consumer Research*, **16**, 119–24.

Larson, R. and Kubey, R. (1983). Television and music: contrasting media in adolescent life. *Youth and Society*, **15**, 13–31.

LeBlanc, A. (1982). An interactive theory of music preference. *Journal of Music Therapy*, **19**, 28–45.

Lewis, G. (1992). Who do you love? The dimensions of musical taste. In *Popular music and communication* (ed. J. Lull). Sage, London.

Lopes, P. D. (1992). Innovation and diversity in the popular music industry, 1969 to 1990. *American Sociological Review*, **57**, 56–71.

Lull, J. (1992). Popular music and communication: an introduction. In *Popular music and communication* (ed. J. Lull). Sage, London.

MacDonald, D. (1941). The popular music industry. In *Radio research 1941* (ed. P. F. Lazarsfeld and F. N. Stanton). Duell, Sloan, and Pearce, New York.

MacDonald, D. A. (1964). A theory of mass culture. In *Mass culture* (ed. B. Rosenberg and D. M. White). Free Press, London.

McQuail, D. (1994). *Mass communication theory*. Sage, London.

Maisel, R. (1973). The decline of mass media. *Public Opinion Quarterly*, **37**, 159–70.

Martin, G., Clarke, M., and Pearce, C. (1993). Adolescent suicide: music preference as an indicator of vulnerability. *Journal of the American Academy of Child and Adolescent Psychiatry*, **32**, 530–5.

Murdock, G. and McCron, R. (1973). Scoobies, skins, and contemporary pop. *New Society*, **29**, 690–2.

Pegg, C. (1984). Factors affecting the musical choices of audiences in East Suffolk, England. In *Popular music 4: performers and audiences* (ed. R. Middleton and D. Horn). Cambridge University Press, Cambridge.

Peterson, R. A. (1976). The production of culture. *American Behavioral Scientist*, **19**, 669–84.

Peterson, R. A. and DiMaggio, P. (1975). From region to class, the changing locus of country music: a test of the massification hypothesis. *Social Forces*, **53**, 495–506.

Price, H. E. (1986). A proposed glossary for use in affective response literature in music. *Journal of Research in Music Education*, **34**, 151–9.

Riesman, D. (1950). Listening to popular music. *American Quarterly*, **1**, 359–71.

Robinson, J. P. and Hirsch, P. M. (1972). Teenage response to rock and roll protest songs. In *The sounds of social change* (ed. R. S. Denisoff and R. A. Peterson). Rand McNally, Chicago.

Rosengren, K. E. (1981). Mass media and social change: some current approaches. In *Mass media and social change* (ed. E. Katz and T. Szecsko). Sage, London.

Rosing, H. (1984). Listening behaviour and musical preference in the age of 'transmitted music'. In *Popular music 4: performers and audiences* (ed. R. Middleton and D. Horn). Cambridge University Press, Cambridge.

Rothenbuhler, E. W. and McCourt, T. (1992). Commercial radio and popular music: processes of selection and factors of influence. In *Popular music and communication* (ed. J. Lull). Sage, London.

Savage, J. (1988). The enemy within: sex, rock, and identity. In *Facing the music: a Pantheon guide to popular culture* (ed. S. Frith). Pantheon, New York.

Shepherd, J. (1977). The musical coding of ideologies. In *Whose music? A sociology of musical languages* (ed. J. Shepherd, P. Virden, G. Vulliamy, and T. Wishart). Latimer, London.

Singer, S. I., Levine, M., and Jou, S. (1993). Heavy metal music preference, delinquent friends, social control, and delinquency. *Journal of Research in Crime and Delinquency*, **30**, 317–29.

Stipp, H. (1990). Musical demographics. The strong impact of age on music preferences affects all kinds of businesses. *American Demographics*, August, 48–9.

Tanner, J. (1981). Pop music and peer groups: a study of Canadian high school students' responses to pop music. *Canadian Review of Sociology and Anthropology*, **18**, 1–13.

Thompson, K. P. (1993). Media, music, and adolescents. In *Early adolescence: perspectives on research, policy, and intervention* (ed. R. M. Lerner). Lawrence Erlbaum, Hillsdale, New Jersey.

Tolhurst, G. C., Hollien, H., and Leeper, L. (1984). Listening preferences for music as a function of age. *Folia Phoniatricia*, **36**, 93–100.

Took, K. J. and Weiss, D. S. (1994). The relationship between heavy metal and rap music and adolescent turmoil: real or abstract? *Adolescence*, **29**, 613–23.

Vulliamy, G. (1978). Culture clash and school music: a sociological analysis. In *Sociological interpretations of schooling and classrooms: a re-appraisal* (ed. L. Barton and R. Meighan). Nafferton, Driffield.

Wapnick, J. (1976). A review of research on attitude and preference. *Bulletin of the Council for Research in Music Education*, **48**, 1–20.

PART IV

Developmental issues

9 | Musical taste in adolescence

Dolf Zillmann and Su-lin Gan

In this chapter, we first sketch the enormity of adolescents' consumption of, and apparent fascination with, various forms of music. After a brief excursion into the massification versus diversity controversy over popular music, we present and critically analyse efforts at explaining the enjoyment of music by adolescents on the basis of their own introspective assessments and rationalizations. We then turn to the mostly experimental social–psychological exploration of music appreciation, and we ascertain the influence of social, individual, and situational factors in light of the available research evidence. Much attention is given to the great appeal of music expressing defiance of authority and of music celebrating love found or bemoaning love lost. The chapter concludes with an abridged review of social–psychological research that addresses the question of whether or not the massive consumption of particular forms of popular music, especially music of the rebellious variety, can foster and strengthen socially and societally relevant beliefs and dispositions of adolescents.

MUSIC CONSUMPTION BY ADOLESCENTS

The magnitude of adolescent involvement with music is perhaps best indicated by the staggering sales figures of the recording industry. Frith (1987), in tracing the development of this industry, reported that, regarding mainstream rock 'n' roll music alone, annual sales exceeded $1 billion as early as 1967. In 1973, annual sales had reached $2 billion; and in 1978, the $4 billion mark was surpassed, and sales may have been as high as $7 billion. This explosion in the rock 'n' roll market, at least in part due to the increasing purchase power of youths (Eliot 1989), contrasted sharply with a decline in the sales of classical music. Such sales, which had a market share of 25 per cent in the 1950s, dwindled to a mere 5 per cent in comparison. Estimates of more recent years put the popular music market at $10 billion for 1993 and at over $12 billion for 1994 (Geter and Streisand 1995). These economic figures translate to staggering music-consumption times. It has been estimated that from seventh to 12th grade, American teens average 10 500 hours of elected exposure to popular music (Davis 1985). Such times approximate those spent in the classroom from kindergarten through high school.

Prior to the advent of music television, according to estimates provided by Lyle and Hoffman (1972), about a quarter of American 10 year-olds listened to music for at least four hours daily; another third listened for up to three hours daily. The listening times increased substantially for teens, especially for female teens. A quarter of male teens listened to music for at least four hours daily; half listened for up to three hours. Female teens topped these figures, with almost half of them listening for at least four hours, and with the other half listening for up to three hours daily.

A representative survey of 12–14 year-olds by Brown *et al.* (1986) yielded similar figures for the consumption of music television. Exposure by white Americans approached four hours, and that by African Americans exceeded four and a half hours daily. Additional music consumption amounted to more than three daily hours, with the consumption by males below, and that by females above, the average. This group of adolescents, then, appears to consume music for most of their wake time outside of school—more than seven hours a day, according to these estimates.

Sun and Lull (1986) reported more moderate, yet nonetheless surprisingly high consumption times, for a sample of California high-school students. On average, the students watched two hours of music television daily. Again, the females outdid the males, reaching an average of two and a half hours on weekends.

The extraordinary appeal of music to adolescents is also evident from a recent Irish leisure survey conducted by Fitzgerald *et al.* (1995). Both male and female teens around 16 years of age placed their interest in music above all else. Abrams (1959) had much earlier reported similar findings for British youth. Music consumption, then, may be considered the primary leisure objective of adolescents—at least in industrialized societies that afford adolescents sufficient leisure time as well as the privilege and the means to choose freely from among entertaining alternatives.

Larson and Kubey (1983) explored the social circumstances of such pre-occupation with music in a survey with Midwestern high-school students and observed that listening occurred primarily in privacy (69 per cent of all incidents), mostly in the solitude of the teens' own personal rooms. Only in a minority of cases was music consumed in the company of friends (23 per cent), and it was rarely consumed with family members (eight per cent). These investigators also discovered that adolescents' music consumption is tied to their homes (82 per cent). Consumption in public places is the exception (18 per cent).

These observations accord well with techno-economical analyses (Andreasen 1994), suggesting that most American adolescents now enjoy the luxury of their own private room outfitted with a colour television set, a video recorder, and tape and disk audio equipment. Other industrial societies are not far behind. For instance, Frith (1987) reported that as early as 1984 in Britain almost all adolescents (97 per cent) owned audio recorders that allowed music consumption in privacy.

The fact that adolescents consume their music mostly alone in a private situation has not received much attention. Sociological analyses have concentrated on the public manifestations of music consumption (e.g. Clark 1974; Frith 1981; Henry 1989; Kotarba and Wells 1987; Savary 1967; Shepherd 1991; Weinstein 1991) and, although most insightful in terms of their focus, have treated private consumption as secondary, if not as irrelevant. As we shall see later, the psychological analysis of this neglected phenomenon complements the sociological explorations by elucidating the motives for the private and essentially non-social consumption of music.

MASSIFICATION, MUSICAL GENRES, AND DIVERSITY

Adolescent music is created, for the most part, by adolescents. However, the production and distribution of the resulting musical recordings—the essential trade item of the music business—are controlled by an industry that answers the dictate of profit maximization. On grounds of the apparent commercialization of music, and based on the erroneous notion that profits necessarily grow with the massiveness of industrial production, various cultural analysts (Adorno 1962; MacDonald 1957; Rosenberg 1957) projected a massification of taste. Adorno (1950) was most explicit in condemning music as a commodity; and because of what he deemed to be an exploitative industry involvement, he lumped together all popular musical genres as inferior forms. He berated 'that whole sphere of music whose lifeblood is standardization: popular music, jazz, be it hot, sweet, or hybrid' (p. 312). Musical standardization, he insisted, gives the music consumer no choice. 'Products are forced upon him' (p. 314). Adorno, then, distinguished only two genres: serious music for a musically educated elite, and pop for the masses.

Adorno's conception differs sharply from that offered by Shils (1961), who recognized that profits from industrial production do not linearly increase with the number of identical items produced, and who projected an ever increasing diversity of cultural products as a result of industrial capabilities. The process that fosters the expected diversity in musical products, even guarantees it, has been detailed by Epstein (1994) and termed *saturation marketing*. Briefly, it is the market success of groups with a particular sound that leads other groups to endless imitations that saturate the market; this saturation then gives the commercial advantage to groups that come up with a novel, engaging sound. Imitations again saturate the market, more new sounds have to be created, and so on without end. The profit motive thus does not get in the way of diversity. It ensures creativity. It instigates innovation. And to the extent that adolescents show an interest in diverse offerings, it actually enhances the diversity of adolescent music.

In this connection, Gans (1966) proposed that the consumption of cultural products is not undifferentiated but socially stratified. He conceived specific *taste cultures* as aggregates of persons who are similarly predisposed to consume items of similar content. Regarding the consumption of adolescent music, the existence of such cultures or subcultures has been established for some time (e.g. Denisoff and Levine 1972; Frith 1978; Hebdige 1979; Lewis 1972). We shall later discuss the social side of these taste cultures, also called taste publics, but now concentrate on what content similarity might mean in the realm of adolescent music.

In terms of stimulus properties, adolescent music is probably more varied than alternative forms. Its rhythms range from slow and gentle to rapid and forceful, and the associated melodic structures vary from sensitive and tender to disorganized and wild. The instrumentation may be simplistic or complex, starting with the drum-and-guitar essentials and advancing to sophisticated orchestration. Vocalization is particularly diverse, ranging from melodic singing to emotional moaning and groaning and seemingly uncontrolled screaming. Lyrics, the linguistic accompaniment of this music, analogously cover the spectrum of themes from requited and unrequited love to discontent with life at large and defiance of authority in particular. Moreover, conventional instrumentation and vocalization are often complemented, even overpowered, with forceful sounds generated by electronic means.

Structuring such diversity is no easy matter, and generally accepted clusters of adolescent music have never been constructed on the basis of all facets of the existing stimulus variation. Instead, numerous classifications have been employed, often with implied rather than explicated criteria for class formation. The results are vaguely specified genres, often involving extramusical criteria (such as mannerism and style of clothing of music performers or consumers).

In some of the earlier investigations of musical preferences (Fox and Wince 1975; Skipper 1973), a mere five genres were distinguished: pop and rock, hard rock/rhythm 'n' blues, jazz, folk, and classical. Chapman and Williams (1976), working with British youths, discerned 10 genres: classical, folk, reggae, jazz, rock, soul, progressive, ballads, Motown, and the Osmonds. The music of the Osmonds might, of course, be more appropriately considered a musical style than a genre proper. In efforts at being exhaustive, Christenson and Peterson (1988) saw fit to work with 26 music classes, only 22 of which they considered true genres. Blues, heavy metal, disco, funk, punk, and gospel entered their scheme. Yet finer distinctions concerned, for instance, art rock, southern rock, Christian rock, and psychedelic rock, as well as older new wave and post-new wave new music. Deihl *et al.* (1985) elected to reduce this list to 10 classes, but arrived at genres that differed markedly from those employed earlier. They drew on classical, country and western, jazz, rock, punk, soul, and folk music, but added opera, beautiful music, and big band. Working with Swedish adolescents, Roe (1985) found another set of 10 genres workable: classical, folk, country, mainstream pop, rock, punk, reggae, new wave, 60s protest songs, and jazz. Finally, in dealing with music television, Tapper *et al.* (1994) distinguished between seven adolescent genres only: rap, soul, country, heavy metal, pop, classic rock, and alternative rock.

As can be seen, the classification of music consumed by adolescents shows considerable variance and discrepancies. Some of the variance undoubtedly derives from musical innovation, with newly created genres, such as rap, superseding dated ones, such as the style of the Osmonds. Another portion is the likely result of the often careless adoption of genre labels suggested by music critics and conveniently supplied by the music industry. For the most part, however, the difficulty in deciding on genres is simply due to the complexity and multidimensionality of the musical products to be classified. As long as different investigators continue to focus on different dimensions and use different sets of criteria for their classifications, genre discrepancies are unavoidable, and generalizations about genre-to-subculture linkages are necessarily tenuous. Lewis (1987) characterized this imperfect linkage as 'ragged and incomplete' (p. 210).

In light of the indicated imprecision in the delineation of musical genres, as well as in recognition of the thematic variation within declared genres, psychological analyses have often ignored genre distinctions and created their own pertinent classifications. For instance, an interest in particular consequences of the musical and lyrical expression of defiance of authority led to the classification of popular music by the degree of manifest defiance, irrespective of specific genre considerations (Bleich *et al.* 1991). Similarly, themes such as the celebration of found love versus the lamentation of lost love have been employed to study preferences within related genres (Gibson *et al.* 1995). Nonetheless, to the extent that adolescents have been shown to recognize and distinguish genres with sufficient reliability, the conventional genre differentiations of popular music are most useful in exploring music-dependent behaviours (Roe 1985; Zillmann and Bhatia 1989). At times, it also proved useful to cross-vary obtrusive genres with dimensions of focal interest, creating subdivisions such as violent and non-violent rap (Johnson *et al.* 1995) or politically radical versus non-political rap (Zillmann *et al.* 1995).

MUSIC ENJOYMENT AND ITS RATIONALIZATION

The enjoyment of music by adolescents has been assessed in ratings to determine genre differences, as well as apparent preferences by age, gender, ethnicity, and social class of consumers. Skipper (1973), for instance, observed that American undergraduates enjoyed popular music and rock more than classical music; hard rock and rhythm 'n' blues along with folk music appreciably less; and jazz the least. Such genre assessments are bound to vary over time (Deihl *et al.* 1985) and may be of historical interest, but they provide little insight into motives for, and benefits from, music consumption. Comparisons across social groupings are more stable and potentially revealing. In these terms, Skipper observed that classical music held more appeal for females than for males, more for whites than for African Americans; and perhaps more importantly, that its appeal correlated with social-class standing, diminishing sharply for groups of inferior rank. The appeal of folk music, although altogether somewhat lower than that of classical music, followed the same pattern. In contrast, the appeal of popular music and rock, except for lesser appeal to African Americans, was uniform across gender and social standing. Again in contrast, the appeal of hard rock and rhythm 'n' blues and of jazz was exactly opposite to that of classical and folk, favouring males over females, African Americans over whites, and lower over higher social standing. Dizon (1981) examined ethnicity-defined preferences with a set of 17 genres and obtained similar differentiations. African Americans were partial to rhythm 'n' blues, jazz, soul, and spirituals, but deemed folk and bluegrass music unattractive.

The indicated gender differences were also observed in British 14–15 year-olds (Chapman and Williams 1976). Classical music was more highly rated by females than males; and rock, the genre receiving the highest scores overall, was more highly rated by males than females. Educational ambition, used as a secondary variable, proved to be of no appreciable consequence for music enjoyment by genre. If anything, classical music held particularly low appeal for the more ambitious youngsters. This is in stark contrast to observations on slightly older pupils. Working with 14–18 year-old British youths, Frith (1981) noted individualized tastes for folk and classical music in top-stream pupils, whereas the educationally less ambitious and musically less discriminating ones were drawn to mainstream pop. This pop group derogated all alternative genres.

Factor-analytical explorations with Swedish adolescents by Roe (1983, 1985) further substantiated the indicated relationships between discriminating and peer-dependent music preferences. Roe determined that, in terms of enjoyment, rock clusters with punk and new wave music, and classical music clusters with jazz and folk music. The two clusters were negatively correlated, and strongly so. Youths drawn to rock and its kin, then, showed little interest in classical music and related genres, and youths attracted to classical music deemed rock relatively unattractive.

The assessment of ratings of enjoyment is often associated with efforts at learning about adolescents' motives for their music consumption. The methodology employed in such querying is known as the uses-and-gratifications approach (Rosengren *et al.* 1985). Characteristically, respondents indicate to which degree they think their music consumption and enjoyment derives from a set of motives that is provided as an item list. On occasion, respondents are asked to articulate their perceptions, which are then categorized by the investigators. Uses-and-gratification probes are also directed at circumstances under which music is consumed, such as social situations and prevalent moods. Respondents might also be queried about their perceptions regarding the social and societal influence of music consumption.

Gantz *et al.* (1978), for instance, queried American college undergraduates and found that they believed to consume the music of their choice mostly because it relieves tension, distracts from bothers, helps pass time, and relieves boredom. Lesser reasons given were that listening to popular music helps set a wanted mood, fills silence, and makes one feel less alone. Roe (1985) used an extended list of motives, but also included music's presumed capacity to relax, set the right mood, help pass time, diminish feelings of loneliness, fill noxious silence, and make time seem to go faster. He added perceptions such as that music is good to dance to, is compatible with one's lifestyle, and offers lyrics that express one's feelings. Ratings of music's capability to set desired moods, to inspire dancing, and to fit one's lifestyle formed a primary factor. This capacity was considered most important. Further factors were formed by the ratings concerning seemingly faster passage of time, on the one hand, and an interest in lyrics along with their ability to express the listener's feelings, on the other. The subjective acceleration of time passage was deemed moderately important, and that of feeling understood, oddly, least important.

Focusing on the enjoyment of music videos, Sun and Lull (1986) reduced a list of 18 items to four factors: information/social learning, passing time, escape/mood, and social interaction. The ratings averaged within factors indicated that college students considered the need to lighten the burden of passing time (MTV watching passes time when I am bored, nothing better to do) their most important motive. The ratings of escape/mood (e.g. relieves tension, gets/keeps me in a mood, makes me feel less alone) and social interaction (be/do with friends, conversation topic) indicated utter indifference (i.e. both means fell within one-tenth of the scale midpoint between agreement/disagreement). In contrast, the students showed disagreement with the items of the information/social learning factor, essentially denying to be motivated by a desire to learn about self/others, the future and how to do things, or by a need for factual information, to understand the world, to be shown how to act, and to have one's own ideas supported. Working with 12–14 year-olds, Brown *et al.* (1986) created similar structures on intuitive grounds and observed a diversion component to receive the highest ratings. As reasons for watching music videos, the youngsters indicated the video's capacity to excite, to help them fight loneliness, to create a good mood, to relax, to get away from worries. Wanting to learn to dance and to see the latest fashion, as well as being with friends, also emerged as important motives. On the other hand, few of the interviewees thought that they cared to watch because they would learn things about themselves, gain a better understanding of their personal problems, or feel sexy.

Berry (1990) explored the fascination with rap of African American teens aged 13–18. She noted that rap was by far the best-liked genre of her sample of teens (47 per cent). Slow love songs (18 per cent) and soul and rhythm 'n' blues (16 per cent) followed, with the appeal of other genres falling off sharply. More importantly, Berry did not provide a motive list for ratings, but let the teens articulate their own perception of reasons for their prefer-ence for rap. The large majority of answers implicated rap's beat with its attraction (e.g. the beat is live, kickin'). Rapping along was another per-ceived motive. Other teens merely restated the fact that rap holds appeal (e.g. I just love it), and few (7 per cent) claimed that they are drawn to rap because it tells what's going on.

The media-preference research of Lyle and Hoffman (1972) illustrates the technique of asking situation-specific questions. Essentially, it posits an ex-periential state and calls for an indication of likely choices in this state (e.g. when you just want to relax/be entertained, when someone has hurt your feelings/made you angry, or when you feel lonely). Listening to one's pre-ferred music was the dominant media choice in all these situations. How-ever, in states of hurt and anger, both 12 and 16 year-olds indicated going off by themselves as a similarly likely alternative. The younger pupils, especially the girls, additionally thought that, when lonely, they might want to talk to somebody. An emerging maturation difference, also observed by Larson *et al.* (1989), further indicates that, with increasing age, teens tend to embrace music more strongly—at the expense of television as an initially preferred medium.

Finally, investigators have employed survey methodology to ascertain adolescents' perception of the effects of consuming popular music. Gantz *et al.* (1978), for instance, reported that college undergraduates expressed relatively strong agreement with statements like music exposure stimulates sexual activity or helps persons deal with their own problems. In contrast, the students recorded little agreement with assertions such as that music exposure would make persons more rebellious toward authority or lead to a breakdown of morals. Leming (1987) probed the influence issue in a more roundabout manner, asking 'Has a song ever influenced the way you think about an important topic?' At age 13, 23 per cent of his teens thought to have been influenced. By age 16, 70 per cent thought to have succumbed to influence at one point or another.

The analysis of the exploration of the influence of adolescent music on adolescents' beliefs and dispositions, by openly asking adolescents about the possibility of such influence, reveals the limitations of this procedure.

Clearly, what adolescents can report are their perceptions or opinions. These opinions are based on presumption rather than careful observation of causal connections between exposure to music and resultant behaviours. They are, additionally, subject to self-serving distortion. Moreover, the potential influence of familiarity with prevalent, mostly media-disseminated views about the issues cannot be ignored. All this is to say that adolescents' perception may be insightful on occasion, but cannot possibly be accepted as evidence of actual influences. The study of adolescents' opinions concerning the effects of music consumption certainly has merit in its own right and may be highly informative and useful. Care must be taken, however, that information about opinions is not misconstrued as evidence of the object of the opinions. Irrespective of whether or not popular music enhances libido, for instance, it may be of interest to know that college students believe their music to have such an effect. Similarly, surveying adolescents' opinions concerning the appeal of the music of their choice—why they like it and what it does for them—constitutes potentially valuable opinion research.

Nonetheless, the collecting of opinions obviously does not help establish that particular elements of music, no matter how firmly adolescents and others believe them to be responsible for the appeal of the music or its immediate effects on moods and dispositions, actually mediate the appeal or effects in question. It should be recognized that adolescents, when queried about causes of appeal and effects, are likely to provide explanations that have been provided either by their peers, their parents, or the media. In this connection, Berry's (1990) analysis is suggestive. When her teens, in contrast to procedures typically employed in uses-and-gratifications research, were not given a prepared list of reasons for the liking of rap, they mostly restated the fact that they liked the music (I like to rap. I like it. I love it. I just love it. etc.). The teens' responses exemplify a fundamental aesthetic privilege: persons are entitled to like and enjoy aesthetic stimulation without having to justify their behaviour to others or to themselves. As a matter of course, they are not compelled to analyse and scrutinize their preferences and to know exactly why they like what. On the other hand, as enthusiasts rather than as scientists, music consumers have developed a discourse that allows them to convey their beliefs about the causes and effects of music enjoyment, and the use of such discourse is evident in adolescent groups already (Frith 1981). As far as motives for music consumption and preferences are concerned, there is reason to believe that many adolescents think to know them, on occasion with great subjective certainty. This circumstance appears to legitimize enquiries into believed motives and consequences. Still, as indicated earlier, it would seem likely that the information attainable reflects more what adolescents have been told by sources such as MTV or pop-music magazines (Clarke 1983) than original inferences they made on their own.

Be this as it may, efforts at integrating the available survey findings are frustrating and yield little consistency. Whereas the indicated gender and ethnic music preferences hold up, responses to the basic question 'Why do you like your music?' are exceedingly varied and show little consistency across surveys. For instance, Roe (1985) found the perceived capacity for mood enhancement to be a primary attractant. Findings reported by Brown *et al.* (1986) are consistent with this assessment, but findings reported by Gantz *et al.* (1978) accord mood enhancement little significance, and Sun and Lull's (1986) respondents were totally ambivalent about the mood issue. Similarly, music's perceived ability to make one feel less alone is an important attractant according to the findings of Brown *et al.*, but a rather unimportant one according to those of Gantz *et al.* If there is some consistency, it concerns music as a time passer. The investigations by Gantz *et al.*, Roe, Sun and Lull, and Brown *et al.* agree in ascribing primary importance to music's diversionary capacity. According to these observations, then, the appeal of music for adolescents is viewed as being determined primarily by a need for diversion and secondarily by a host of enumerated needs whose magnitude has not been agreed upon.

The frequent use of the uses-and-gratifications approach in studying the appeal of adolescent music contrasts sharply with the exceedingly scarce use of experimental research in this domain. Experimentation into the basic aesthetics of the music of adolescence is virtually non-existent. What does exist are eclectic studies that explore the effects of mostly extramusical components and conditions on the enjoyment of music.

The fact that pre-adolescents are already partial to fast-tempo, highly rhythmic music has been established by an investigation of Wakshlag *et al.* (1982). Six and seven year-olds were provided with musical selections differing in tempo and rhythm and allowed to choose among them. The methodology of selective-exposure research (Zillmann and Bryant 1985) was employed. That is, the children's actual choices were unobtrusively recorded, and distortions that accrue to the creation of awareness of being observed, as well as of having to rate the music, were avoided. Irrespective of gender, the children strongly favoured fast-tempo, highly rhythmic, and seemingly arousing over slower-tempo, less rhythmic, and seemingly non-arousing music.

Cantor and Zillmann (1973) thought physiological excitation to be an essential aspect of adolescents' enjoyment of music and tested this expectation with college students who were or were not aroused by non-musical means prior to exposure to rock music. Music appreciation, assessed in ratings, proved to be more intense after pre-arousal than in the absence of pre-arousal. Residual excitation from prior stimulation, when not recognized as such, thus was shown to be capable of enhancing at least the enjoyment of adolescent music that is supposed to be exciting. Excitement that apparently derives from exposure to music, then, may be considered a salient component of adolescents' enjoyment of music.

Zillmann and Mundorf (1987) further explored the consequences of music-associated excitement for appreciation. Specifically, they manipulated rock-music videos by interspersing sexual or violent images in themes pertaining to sex and violence in order to create additional excitement from the involvement of these extramusical stimuli. The students' greater excitedness from the inclusion of sexual images greatly enhanced their enjoyment of the music as such. It also enhanced specific appreciation effects, such as considering the music more creative and ecstatic, and rating the quality of vocalization and the band's performance as superior. Except for ratings of creativeness, the effects of involving images of violence were similar, but comparatively weak. Hansen and Hansen (1990a) also probed the implications of the involvement of arousing sexual images for the enjoyment of rock music. Creating the variation in imagery by selection rather than manipulation, they observed the same facilitation of global music appreciation as well as aspects of musical performance and lyrical quality.

The findings are consistent with predictions from excitation-transfer theory (Zillmann 1983, 1996). Essentially, the observations accord with the proposal that adolescents, as a rule, do not consider their reaction to music a composite of various identifiable contributions made by specific stimuli within, or external to, the music. Rather, they form an overall impression of their aesthetic reaction to the musical presentation. They cannot, or they simply do not, isolate exactly what it was that excited them. They attribute, *de facto* and without elaboration, their reaction *in toto* to the complex stimulus situation to which they have been exposed. To the extent, then, that excitation instigated by images intensifies the affective reaction to the focal stimulus, namely enjoyable adolescent music, the music and all its facets are more intensely enjoyed.

In a series of imaginative studies, Konečni (1982) addressed some basic issues of music aesthetics. However, since his explorations concern the experiential context in which music is consumed more than music enjoyment *per se*, we shall review this research in connection with situational music preferences.

SOCIAL FACTORS IN MUSIC PREFERENCE

The analysis of adolescent groups that form around particular musical genres or subgenres (e.g. Brake 1985; Frith 1981; Hebdige 1979; Henry 1989; Savary 1967) must be considered to have spawned some of the most intriguing conceptions concerning adolescent's fascination with the music of their choice. The fact that a cultural product, music, can serve as the defining, central condition in the formation and organization of interactive groups has led to the idea of competing culture classes (Peterson and DiMaggio 1975), taste cultures (Gans 1966), or youth cultures (Epstein 1994) that are rather independent of social-class standing. Musical preferences, then, seemed to bring adolescents together, often despite pronounced differences in social-class standing (Denisoff and Levine 1972; Peterson and DiMaggio 1975).

Conceptually, the impetus for seeking and joining a taste culture is usually linked to adolescent maturation; specifically, to the transition from parental protection and guidance to self-determination and independence. The family is abandoned, to a degree, in favour of peer affiliation. The shift into a new social aggregate does not occur in random fashion, however, but is presumed to be controlled by numerous factors. Peers who, for whatever sound or trivial reason, are admired at this time define social attractants, and their preferred music is likely to become the affiliating party's choice (Johnstone and Katz 1957). Once a group that focuses on a particular musical genre is formed in this fashion, its members benefit in at least two ways. First, they have defined themselves as members of a cultural elite (in their own perception) and attain the emotional gratifications of belonging. Second, they have defined themselves as distinct and different from other peer groups and attain the gratifications of being somehow superior (in their own perception). Grossberg (1990) illustrates this dual process with rock fans: 'Rock 'n' roll fans enact an elitism in their relation to music . . . Rock 'n' roll does not belong to everyone . . . The boundary is always drawn' (p. 115). Inclusion in this elite implies exclusivity. And as Frith (1981) observed, the stronger the involvement with a particular music genre, the more likely the disparagement of competing ones. For extremely engaged youngsters, he stated, the 'standard mode of criticism of other tastes was abuse' (p. 206). Such abuse serves, of course, a self-distinguishing function.

It should be noted that, as soon as one goes beyond the small, readily observable, intact group, taste cultures are poorly defined. They are, for the most part, hypothetical constructs. Or, as Grossberg (1990) put it, they are cultures in name only (i.e. they are nominal groups). Surely, nobody is able to stake out the actual taste publics of heavy metal, reggae, or folk music. These publics, as they lack empirical grounding (Epstein 1994), are illusory (Brake 1985) or imagined cultures (Zillmann and Bhatia 1989). In psychological terms, however, they are real in that presumptions about their existence, their size, and their specific social manifestations, erroneous as they may be on occasion or as a rule, exert considerable influence on the presumers' actual behaviour. In fact, it is the imagined taste culture that, as a true mass-culture phenomenon, necessitates the expression of group membership to the rest of the world. In small, interactive groups, members know each other's preference. Additionally, this preference could be directly

conveyed to rival groups for the purpose of distancing. Members of imagined groups, in contrast, have to project their belonging to a mass audience
composed of individuals of whom they have scant or no personal knowledge, this audience involving members of the same imagined taste culture
as well as members of opposing imagined taste cultures. An apparent need
for expressing affiliation and belonging, on the one hand, and indifference or
defiance, on the other, characterizes, of course, adolescent behaviour in connection with their musical preferences. Members of a particular imagined
musical-taste culture not only blare their preferred sounds from radios and
recorders in cars and homes to an undifferentiated public, but also exhibit
themselves with membership-defining attire, hair style, and mannerisms.
The indicated need to express oneself by close adherence to unique styles is
thought to typify adolescence. The use of obtrusive styles is thought to
secure 'attachment to . . . a . . . mythical elite' (Brake 1985, p. 12) and at the
same time demarcate from the mainstream and other class ascriptions.

The logic here is essentially that of conspicuous consumption (Veblen
1899). The exhibition of one's musical taste is used to distinguish oneself. Or
as Frith (1981) so succinctly put it: 'All adolescents use music as a badge'
(p. 217), apparently as a badge of distinction. For instance, adolescents
in foreign countries that embrace Western culture can easily distinguish
themselves by exhibiting a strong interest in popular Western music, which
is exactly what the better educated students tend to do (e.g. Cuthbert 1985;
Rauth 1982; Reddi 1985). But the paradigm also applies to adults who, by
flashing their musical sophistication, make themselves members of an
imagined elite. In this regard, Adorno's (1962) deification of the classics,
along with his denunciation of popular music, oddly parallels the reverse
proclamations of rock fans. His taste exhibition certainly makes him a
member of an elitist taste culture. However, the paradigm is broader yet. It
applies to extramusical phenomena as well. It applies, for instance, to
imagined sportsfan cultures (Zillmann and Paulus 1993) and to fashion at
large (Simmel 1904).

The wealth of proposals concerning the social influence of musical
preference and its expression stands in contrast to a scarcity of pertinent
empirical investigations. The badge function of preference has, nonetheless,
been directly addressed in two investigations.

Disguised as a study on video dating, Zillmann and Bhatia (1989) exposed
students of the opposite gender to tapes that showed male or female models
who introduced themselves and then, among other things, confessed to love
either classical, country, soft rock, or heavy metal music. In a control condition, no mention was made of a musical preference. Preference confession
was found to exert considerable influence on the perception of the models.
In the eyes of men, women who confessed to love classical music became
more sophisticated, those who confessed to love heavy metal less so. In the

eyes of women, men confessing to love classical music or heavy metal neither gained nor lost sophistication. They became less sophisticated, however, when confessing to love country music. Romantic attraction to the models was also influenced by the exhibition of musical taste. Allegiance with country music proved detrimental to the appeal of both men and women. In line with the perception of sophistication, women's appeal gained from the confession of love for classical music, but decreased from a confession of love for heavy metal. Somewhat unexpectedly, men's appeal increased markedly with the declaration of fascination with heavy metal, presumably because they were perceived to be especially exciting, beautiful, sexy, and fun at parties.

The question of whether the sharing of musical taste, essentially of sharing membership in the same taste culture, influences perceptions and attraction was also addressed. Men proved to be more strongly attracted to women within their own taste culture than to women outside of it. For women, in contrast, taste-culture membership was of little moment. They were greatly attracted to the exciting men wearing the heavy metal badge, irrespective of their own musical preference.

Sargent and Weaver (1996) used a simplified procedure in exploring music's badge function further. These investigators included the hard rock genre and observed, among other things, that students affiliating with hard rock or heavy metal lose sophistication while gaining rebelliousness. Together with the observations reported by Zillmann and Bhatia (1989), the findings also suggest that soft rock, as a mainstream preference, has little impact on perception. To wear the mainstream music badge, then, is useful for adolescents who want to be like most others and get lost in the crowd. Some desire to defy majority interest and practice appears to be necessary for adolescents to want to carry the banner of unique, distinct, and potentially defiant musical groups. But in sum, the findings confirm that the declaration of allegiance to a musical culture, in whatever form, amounts to a most meaningful statement about the declarer. Among adolescents, these statements seem especially important in choosing friends and rejecting others. They are by no means socially inconsequential.

Zillmann *et al.* (1995) also examined the implications of membership in an imagined musical taste culture for group cohesion and personal self-esteem. Specifically, these investigators used self-categorization (Turner 1985) and social identity theory (Hogg and Abrams 1990; Tajfel 1982) to predict that fascination with rap, an almost pure African American musical art form, might give African American adolescents feelings of belonging and thus enhance their self-esteem. Especially the politically radical variety of rap that, with its assault on white supremacy, highlights a common and presumably unifying cause, was expected to affect group cohesion and self-esteem. However, no such consequences of involvement with rap of any kind could be observed in African American high-school students. The often asserted and occasionally theory-based cognitive and affective benefits of attachment to musical taste groups, then, remain to be demonstrated.

INDIVIDUAL FACTORS IN MUSIC PREFERENCE

The search for social causes of adolescent involvement with music has, no doubt, provided valuable insight into their musical preferences. However, the discussion of social causes has been dominant to a point where altern-ative causes have been neglected. The focus on small interactive groups has been so strong that the lone music consumer has been forgotten—despite the fact that adolescents consume most of their music in solitude. This is not to say that social influences have been overrated. It is to say that alternative influences exist and are deserving of attention. In all probability, the various influences intertwine, and their respective contributions to the formation of musical preference will have to be ascertained eventually. For now, we shall turn to factors that reside in the individual (rather than the group) and try to discern their influence on adolescents' musical preference.

The expression of defiance of authority is, no doubt, the most obtrusive feature of some forms of adolescent music. Hard rock, especially the heavy metal genre, but also much of rap, musically and lyrically indulge in rebellion. The social conventions of the older generations are assaulted, and defiance of freedom-restricting authority by parents, the educational system, and society at large is openly celebrated. Whatever those who are perceived to control the lives of adolescents cherish and hold dear is torn down in the lyrics, and whatever is perceived as being dreaded and abhorred by them finds a way into the music. The result is music with pounding rhythm, squealing instrumentation, and screamed vocalization. The lyrics essentially demand that adolescents be left alone (e.g. 'Papa Don't Preach' by Madonna, 'Another Brick in the Wall', which proclaims 'We don't need no education' by Pink Floyd, or 'Fuck tha Police' by Niggaz With Attitude), or they simply report the liberties taken despite supervisory impositions (e.g. 'Living in Sin' by Bon Jovi). The performers' attire and make-up tend to challenge stand-ards of hygiene; and their mannerisms, such as crotch-grabbing and pelvic thrusting, give further support to a juvenile manifesto proclaiming that 'we do what we want!'.

Heavy metal, which serves the defiance agenda most directly, in fact defines an intriguing extreme of music in that its intrinsic stimulus prop-erties seem devoid of aesthetic quality. As the music is designed to offend the aesthetic sensitivities of those thought to curtail vital adolescent free-doms (the motto being, the more they hate it, the better it makes us, the adolescents, feel), it can only have a modest amount of *absolute musical meaning* (Hargreaves 1986; Meyer 1956). Its initially entirely *referential musical meaning* seems to attain and then hold great appeal, however, to sizable subsections of the adolescent population.

Defiance is also served, however, by social gatherings and movements that centre around music without lyrics lamenting established control. For instance, European adolescents are recently drawn to dance music in which vocalization is secondary and synthetic musical elements are dominant. This fast-paced, hectic music is often associated with organized defiance against prevailing authority in favouring such matters as the decriminalization of drugs or the criminalization or offences against the environment.

It has been proposed that the celebrant musical expression of defiance of established social conventions and its enforcers does not hold uniform appeal to all adolescents, but that the enjoyment of such expression presupposes defiant dispositions. More specifically, Bleich *et al.* (1991) suggested that only adolescents who had difficulties with their parents, in school, or with societal institutions in general, and who developed resentment against these agencies, would be attracted to the exhibition of defiance in rock and rap. Adolescents who had harmonious relations with the indicated agencies would lack the experiential basis for the enjoyment of defiance, and musically-expressed defiance simply could not provide needed support and thus resonate pleasantly.

Bleich *et al.* put this individual-difference concept to the test by determining adolescents' rebelliousness on the basis of their problems with authority. Working with high-school students in a rural area, these investigators then ascertained the students' enjoyment of videos of defiant and non-defiant popular music, as well as the students' ownership of recordings of defiant and non-defiant music. The findings concerning both music enjoyment and ownership of recordings showed the expected pattern of rebellious youths, as compared to non-rebellious youths, enjoying defiant music more and non-defiant music less. Rebellious adolescents, then, were partial to music consistent with their disposition. Rebellious youths are apparently pre-disposed to enjoy defiant music. It would seem likely that, at least in rural areas similar to those in which this study was conducted, they often enjoy their music in solitude. The affective benefits of a match between disposition and musical expression do not depend on the presence of others. The presence of disposition-sharing others is likely to enhance the indicated benefits, however.

A recent investigation by Robinson *et al.* (1996) replicated and extended the findings of Bleich *et al.* (1991). Rebellious college students proved to be partial to defiant hard rock. Their non-rebellious counterparts, in contrast, sided with soft non-rebellious rock. Additionally, psychoticism (Eysenck and Eysenck 1976) was found to be redundant with rebelliousness. Both rebelliousness and psychoticism entail egocentricity, callousness, and a pro-pensity for aggressive behaviour, and both appear to predispose adolescents to enjoy musical defiance. Extraversion and neuroticism, however, proved to be unrelated to the enjoyment of defiant rock.

In related research by Hansen and Hansen (1991), punk rock fans emerged as those least accepting of authority and, hence, as most appreciative of the defiance obtrusive in punk. Male heavy metal fans were found to be high in machismo and machiavellianism (i.e. they tended to be hypersexual, disrespectful, amoral, manipulative, and cynical). Arnett (1991) added a wide range of reckless behaviours, including drug use and dangerous driving. Female heavy metal fans were found to be similarly reckless, with irresponsible drug use and sexual behaviour often extending to shoplifting and vandalism. Sensation-seeking (Zuckerman 1979) was found to be high in both male and female heavy metal followers.

Irrespective of these rather unflattering specifications of the personality of punk and heavy metal zealots, hard rock has been linked to the trait of sensation-seeking (Dollinger 1993), which further expresses itself in a broad, many genres encompassing interest in music. The latter was also observed in an investigation by Litle and Zuckerman (1986). Moreover, sensation-seeking has been found to be negatively related to the appeal of bland, soundtrack-type music. The trait of conservatism (Glasgow *et al.* 1985), on the other hand, has been linked to a preference for bland and simplistic music.

Gender might also be treated as an individual-difference variable. Frith (1981), for instance, saw fit to generalize that female adolescents, compared to male adolescents, are more strongly drawn to soft, danceable music and pay more attention to lyrics, especially those pertaining to romance.

Romance, or sex in updated language, constitutes the second large domain of adolescent music themes. Whether expressing the active search for a partner, the happy stage of being satisfied with one, the breaking up of a relationship, or the experience of isolation and deprivation, love songs have always been in the fore of popular music (Carey 1969). The focus on romance obviously does not prevent that love songs differ markedly in hedonic valence. Songs of unrequited love, of lost love, and of heartless abandonment are clearly on the negative side. In stark contrast, the glorification and exuberance about love found and happiness is obviously positive. Seeking exposure to such joyous themes is in line with hedonic considerations and predictions from mood-management theory (Zillmann 1988*a,b*); seeking exposure to saddening lament is not, at least not directly so. Mood-management theory essentially posits that persons, in arranging their stimulus environment, make choices that help diminish bad moods, that convert bad to good moods, and that sustain and enhance good moods. It is puzzling, then, why adolescents, on occasion at least, are drawn to music of distinctly negative hedonic valence. It may be argued, however, that persons who acutely suffer from romantic disappointments might find solace in the expression of similar disappointment by others. Perhaps it is a desire to feel understood in one's suffering—suffering that is highly personal and private and that cannot be readily shared with friends—that can best be satisfied by love-lamenting songs by co-suffering others whose music can be consumed in the protection of solitude.

In their pioneering study of adolescents' musical taste, Johnstone and Katz (1957) sought to clarify the situation by linking dating frequency to the consumption of happy-in-love versus frustrated-in-love songs. They worked with female high-school students who were organized in social clubs, separated frequent from infrequent daters, and ascertained the teens' preference for happy or blue music. In a first study, infrequent daters indicated a clear preference for happy music. Frequent daters, in contrast, showed a preference for blue music. Unfortunately, exactly the opposite preference was obtained in a second study conducted in a different club. The inconsistent findings were attributed to differences in the social dynamics of the clubs. The preference issue, however, was left unresolved.

Gibson *et al.* (1995) explored the appeal of love-lamenting, love-celebrating, and love-unrelated popular music for both female and male white and African American high-school students who experienced loneliness to different degrees. The teens indicated their enjoyment of music videos with white or African American male and female performers. Prior to participation in the music study, the teens' subjective experience of loneliness had been ascertained (Russell *et al.* 1980). On the basis of their scores, teens were classified as lonely or not lonely. The enjoyment of love-lamenting music (e.g. 'How Could You Leave Me All Alone?' by Shanice) proved to be unaffected by loneliness. Music unrelated to love was equally unaffected. The enjoyment of love-celebrating music (e.g. 'Good For Me' by Amy Grant), in contrast, was strongly influenced by loneliness, but differently so for the genders. Consistent with expectations from mood-management theory, lonely females enjoyed love-celebrating popular music more than did their less lonely counterparts. Counter to such expectations, however, lonely males found love-celebrating music rather unenjoyable—certainly less enjoyable than did their less lonely counterparts. In agreement with observations reported by Frith (1981), the female teens enjoyed all forms of love music much more than did the male teens. And possibly because of the tradition of sad musical themes in the blues, African Americans enjoyed the love-lamenting music more than did whites. The absence of an effect of loneliness on the enjoyment of love-lamenting music, however, still leaves unclear why sad love themes hold appeal and to whom they do. It also remains to be explained why lonely male teens, relatively speaking, fail to enjoy and potentially shun the musical celebration of love.

Consistent with the finding that lonely female teens enjoy music capable of making them feel better, whereas lonely male teens tend to behave counterproductively, Wells and Hakanen (1991) observed that female high-school students were more emotionally responsive to popular music at large than were male students, and that these female students used music more directly for the purpose of mood enhancement. These investigators also attempted to discern taste cultures on the basis of emotional benefits sought in music consumption. According to their findings, teens' favourite music is to radiate excitement, happiness, love, confidence, and hope. It is to ignore and minimize grief, fear, anger, and sadness.

Wells and Hakanen also related emotional benefits from music consumption to genres and observed four preference clusters: mainstream consumers who committed themselves to the most popular genres, pop, rock, and new wave; indifferent consumers who showed minimal variance in relatively low ratings of all genres considered; music lovers who showed minimal variance in relatively high ratings of all genres considered; and heavy rockers who committed themselves to rock and heavy metal and downgraded everything else. Interestingly, these clusters derived from music usage did cut across social class and ethnicity. Only gender could not be ignored in the construction of such taste cultures. This gender complication, along with the findings concerning music lovers and indifferents who fail to commit to a singular genre or even a small number of genres, again points to the problems in constructing taste cultures in which a fascination and preoccupation with particular genres is matched up with particular socio-economic classes.

SITUATIONAL FACTORS IN MUSIC PREFERENCE

The taste culture concept is further complicated by situationally defined differences in music preference. Such differences are at times imposed by customs and traditions. For instance, at a formal dinner with friends, a rock enthusiast might serve up classical music. But more importantly, the appetite for music, when satisfied by free choice, varies considerably across experiential states and emotions. The same person, when acutely depressed, is likely to exercise a different musical choice than when elated and in a celebrant mood. Mood-management theory (Zillmann 1988*a,b*) addresses the utility of these choices and predicts them on the basis of prevailing mood states.

Konečni (1979, 1982) initiated the study of situation-specific influences on music preference and its affective consequences. He demonstrated, for instance, that angry persons, presumably because they do not want to be distracted from preparing retaliatory actions, prefer simple melodies over complex ones. When relaxed, these persons show the opposite preference. Moreover, he showed that persons, when combating a noxious stimulus environment, tend to choose non-arousing and soothing music, such as selections from Bach, Haydn, and Vivaldi. Under different emotional circumstances they may favour wild and uncontrolled music, such as hard rock.

North and Hargreaves (1996) extended this research by demonstrating that the appeal of musical features clusters differently in different consumption situations. Specifically, British college students were instructed to imagine themselves in situations such as being at an end-of-term party with friends, at a nightclub, jogging with their Walkman on, washing-up, ironing clothes, being in the countryside, in a French restaurant, at a posh cocktail reception, making love, and being in church. They then indicated the characteristics of the music they would like to hear in this situation. Some of these characteristics were properties of the music (e.g. sensual, exotic, loud), others were experiential or response properties (e.g. familiar, nostalgic, invigorating). Broad genres were included as well (jazz, pop, classical). Factor analysis of these characteristics showed pop positively linked to excitement and homeliness. It proved antithetical to melancholy. Classical music and jazz were positively linked to sophistication, and classical music proved antithetical to excitement. More important here, pop was considered desirable in situations like being at a nightclub, while jogging, when doing the dishes, and when ironing (ratings above six on a 0–10 scale). It was deemed inappropriate for situations like dining in a classy restaurant, at bedtime, while making love, when wooing someone for a dinner for two at home, and in church (ratings below four). Classical music, in contrast, was sought out for French dining and was deemed undesirable for parties with friends, in nightclubs, while jogging, and when doing the dishes. Jazz turned out to be the music of cocktail parties. It was rejected for parties with friends, jogging, work around the house, family gatherings, Sunday mornings, at bedtime, and in church.

The investigations by Konečni and by North and Hargreaves charted the scope of situational determination of musical choices, and along with it they established the multiple genre appreciation by many music consumers that such determination implies. Unfortunately, these investigations are not specific to adolescents' musical tastes. They did not involve the genres and subgenres that are popular with youth and hence leave unclear the choices that adolescents would make in specific situations. One study exists (Gibson *et al.* 1995), however, that very clearly demonstrates the situational determination of adolescents' choices of adolescent music, and it does so under conditions of totally restricted choice of music. Teens were asked to imagine themselves having just learned that their love for a person is reciprocated or that their romantic steady has abandoned them in favour of another partner. They were asked which of their recordings they were likely to listen to when getting home to the privacy of their personal room. Their choices were coded for love-celebrating and love-lamenting content, as well as for content unrelated to love. The findings suggest a tacit understanding of mood management.

Teens imagining to be love-happy preferred love-celebrating music more than fourfold over alternative music. Teens imagining to be love-sick, in contrast, preferred love-lamenting music more than threefold over the alternatives. The latter preference indicates that for love-distraught persons it may be distressing to see others happy-in-love, whereas it may be soothing to feel understood by similarly suffering performers—illusory as this presumed empathy must be. The indicated preferences were found regardless of the teens' classification as lonely or not, suggesting that these preferences are situationally determined and potentially short-lived rather than a part of personality. It should be added, however, that the reported affect-specific musical preferences were far stronger in female than in male teens. They also tended to be more pronounced in African Americans than in whites.

The fact that only one study dealing with mood-specific musical choices by adolescents could be found points to a neglect of situational factors, relative to social and individual factors. In view of the importance of adolescents' moods and moodiness, states they seek to influence and alter by exposure to music, the need for clarifying research is apparent.

SOCIETAL CONSEQUENCES OF ADOLESCENT MUSIC

This chapter addressed social, individual, and situational factors that influence the formation of musical tastes in adolescence. Except for music's immediate impact on hedonic states and moods, it bypassed extramusical consequences for adolescents, especially long-term effects on dispositions and behaviours unrelated to music proper. Assertions of such effects abound, of course. Presumably as a result of the obtrusive defiance of parental control and associated societal precepts, many parents, educators, and clergy consider the juveniles' consumption of music causally implicated with the development of violent inclinations and irresponsible sexual dispositions (Gladstone 1984; Moore *et al.* 1979). Personal observation and the habitual misinterpretation of correlational research findings seem to lend support to these contentions. For instance, growing nihilism has been projected on the basis of the sheer frequency of references to death in rock music (Plopper and Ness 1993) or images of death in music television (Davis 1984). Moreover, fascination with heavy metal, found to be associated with drug abuse, has been held accountable for such abuse (King 1988), although this musical preference may be a rather unimportant and incidental aspect of the expression of rebellion and sensation-seeking. Even after relatively careful analysis of the research literature it tends to be concluded that rock and related music exert a negative influence on adolescent development, and recommendations of how best to counteract this influence are being made (Brown and Hendee 1989).

It should at least be indicated here that the social–psychological investigation of the presumed consequences of adolescents' consumption of the music of their choice has begun and started to replace apprehension-based effect speculations with clarifying effect demonstrations. For instance, exemplary research by Roe (1983, 1987) has generated considerable support for the proposal that pupils' academic success or failure shapes their musical taste, this shaping being rather independent of social-class considerations. Successful pupils develop an interest in non-controversial mainstream musical forms, including classical music. Failing pupils, 'move instead toward socially disapproved and oppositional music and at the same time orient themselves more fully to school peer groups' (1987, p. 227). The indicated causal chain reverses that of the frequent argument that assigns responsibility for the development of scholastic disinterest and defiant attitudes to involvement with adolescent music. However, once defiance is embraced, prolonged preoccupation with music such as heavy metal appears to further the experience of alienation and rejection. Davis and Kraus (1989) observed that extreme consumption of this music tends to be associated with strong feelings of loneliness, if not abandonment.

Also, politically salient contentions such as that ethnically confrontational rap (i.e. rap in which rebellious African American men articulate their contempt for white supremacy) would alienate whites and possibly further solidarity in African American youths, thereby promoting rather than defusing social friction, could not be supported. According to research by Zillmann *et al.* (1995), consumption of radical rap neither alienated whites nor fostered solidarity in African Americans. In fact, radical rap was observed to promote ethnic tolerance, making white youths more supportive of non-radical African American youths and less supportive of radical white youths.

On the other hand, research into short-term exposure effects shows socially undesirable effects with considerably consistency. Hansen and Hansen (1990*b*), for instance, observed greater acceptance of deviant behaviours in college students after exposure to defiance-laden, rock-music videos. Johnson *et al.* (1995) similarly demonstrated that exposure to violent rap, compared to exposure to non-violent rap, made African American youngsters of an inner-city boys club (11–16 year-olds) more accepting of violence and less willing to put efforts into scholastic advancement. Greater acceptance of violence was also observed in female adolescents (Johnson *et al.* 1995). Hansen (1995) competently reviewed this literature and elaborated the cognitive mechanisms that mediate the perceptual and judgmental effects under consideration.

Notwithstanding these beginnings, in view of the enormity of music's role in adolescent development it must be said that, on the whole, social psychology has paid little attention to this obtrusive and apparently highly significant aspect of socialization. It can only be hoped that this neglect will be duly appreciated and eventually inspire much needed research into the developmental consequences of adolescents' involvement with their music, especially with the ever more explicitly defiant varieties of music.

REFERENCES

Abrams, M. (1959). *Introduction to the sociology of music*. Seabury, New York.

Adorno, T. (1950). A social critique of radio music. In *Reader in public opinion and communication* (ed. B. Berelson and M. Jarowitz), pp. 309–316. Free Press, Glencoe, IL.

Adorno, T. (1962). *Einleitung in die Musiksoziologie* [Introduction to the sociology of music]. Suhrkamp Verlag, Frankfurt-am-Main.

Andreasen, M. S. (1994). Patterns of family life and television consumption from 1945 to the 1990s. In *Media, children, and the family: Social scientific, psychodynamic, and clinical perspectives* (ed. D. Zillmann, J. Bryant, and A. C. Huston), pp. 19–36. Erlbaum, Hillsdale, NJ.

Arnett, J. (1991). Heavy metal music and reckless behavior among adolescents. *Journal of Youth and Adolescence*, **20**(6), 573–92.

Berry, V. T. (1990). Rap music, self-concept and low income black adolescents. *Popular Music and Society*, **14**(3), 89–107.

Bleich, S., Zillman, D., and Weaver, J. (1991). Enjoyment and consumption of defiant rock music as a function of adolescent rebelliousness. *Journal of Broadcasting and Electronic Media*, **35**(3), 351–66.

Brake, M. (1985). *Comparative youth culture: The sociology of youth cultures and youth subcultures in America, Britain, and Canada*. Routledge and Kegan Paul, London.

Brown, E. F. and Hendee, W. R. (1989). Adolescents and their music: Insights into the health of adolescents. *Journal of the American Medical Association*, **262**(12), 1659–67.

Brown, J. D., Campbell, K., and Fischer, L. (1986). American adolescents and music videos: Why do they watch? *Gazette*, **37**, 19–32.

Cantor, J. R. and Zillmann, D. (1973). The effect of affective state and emotional arousal on music appreciation. *Journal of General Psychology*, **89**, 97–108.

Carey, J. T. (1969). Changing courtship patterns in the popular song. *American Journal of Sociology*, **74**, 720–31.

Chapman, A. J. and Williams, A. R. (1976). Prestige effects and aesthetic experiences: Adolescents' reactions to music. *British Journal of Social and Clinical Psychology*, **15**, 61–72.

Christenson, P. G. and Peterson, J. B. (1988). Genre and gender in the structure of music preferences. *Communication Research*, **15**(3), 282–301.

Clark, R. M. (1974). The dance party as a socialization mechanism for black urban pre-adolescents and adolescents. *Sociological and Social Research*, **58**(2), 145–54.

Clarke, P. (1983). Teenagers' coorientation and information seeking about pop music. *American Behavioral Scientist*, **16**(4), 551–65.

Cuthbert, M. (1985). Cultural autonomy and popular music: A survey of Jamaican youth. *Communications Research*, **12**(3), 381–93.

Davis, D. M. (1984, November). *Nihilism in music television.* Paper presented to the Mass Communication Division of the Speech Communication Association annual convention, Chicago, IL.

Davis, S. (1985, Summer). Pop lyrics: A mirror and molder of society. *Et cetera,* pp. 167–9.

Davis, M. H. and Kraus, L. A. (1989). Social contact, loneliness, and mass media use: A test of two hypotheses. *Journal of Applied Social Psychology,* **19**(13), 1100–24.

Deihl, E. R., Schneider, M. J., and Petress, K. C. (1985). Dimensions of music preference: Factor analytic study. *Communications,* **11**(3), 51–9.

Denisoff, R. S. and Levine, M. (1972). Youth and popular music: A test of the taste culture hypothesis. *Youth and Society,* **4**, 237–55.

Dixon, R. D. (1981). Musical taste cultures and taste publics revisited: A research note of new evidence. *Popular Music and Society,* **8**(1), 2–9.

Dollinger, S. J. (1993). Personality and music preference: Extraversion and excitement seeking or openness to experience? *Psychology of Music,* **21**, 73–7.

Eliot, M. (1989). *Rockonomics: The money behind the music.* Franklin Watts, New York.

Epstein, J. S. (1994). Misplaced childhood: An introduction to the sociology of youth and their music. In *Adolescents and their music: If its too loud, you're too old* (ed. J. S. Epstein), pp. xiii–xxxiv. Garland, New York.

Eysenck, H. J. and Eysenck, S. B. G. (1976). *Psychoticism as a dimension of personality.* University of London Press, London.

Fitzgerald, M., Joseph, A. P., Hayes, M., and O'Regan, M. (1995). Leisure activities of adolescent children. *Journal of Adolescence,* **18**, 349–58.

Fox, W. S. and Wince, M. H. (1975). Musical taste cultures and taste publics. *Youth and Society,* **7**(2), 198–224.

Frith, S. (1978). *The sociology of rock.* Constable, London.

Frith, S. (1981). *Sound effects: Youth, leisure, and the politics of rock 'n' roll.* Pantheon, New York.

Frith, S. (1987). The industrialization of popular music. In *Popular music and communication* (ed. J. Lull), pp. 53–77. Sage Publications, Newbury Park, CA.

Gans, H. J. (1966). Popular culture in America: Social problem in a mass society or asset in a pluralistic society. In *Social problems: A modern approach* (ed. H. S. Becker), pp. 549–620. Wiley, New York.

Gantz, W., Gartenberg, H. M., Pearson, M. L., and Shiller, S. O. (1978). Gratifications and expectations associated with pop music among adolescents. *Popular Music and Society,* **6**, 81–9.

Geter, T. and Streisand, B. (1995, September 25). Recording sound sales: The music industry rocks and rolls to the newest financial rhythms. *U.S. News and World Report,* 67–8, 70, 72.

Gibson, R., Aust, C. F., Hoffman, K., and Zillmann, D. (1995). *Implications of adolescent loneliness for the enjoyment of love-lamenting and love-celebrating popular music.* Paper presented at the annual convention of the Speech Communication Association, San Antonio, TX, November 1995.

Gladstone, B. (1984, April 30). MTV sparks sex, violence concern. *Cablevision.*

Glasgow, M. R., Cartier, A. M., and Wilson, G. D. (1985). Conservatism, sensation-seeking and music preferences. *Personality and Individual Differences,* **6**(3), 395–6.

Grossberg, L. (1990). Is there rock after punk? In *On record* (ed. S. Frith and A. Goodwin), pp. 111–23. Pantheon, New York.

Hansen, C. H. (1995). Predicting cognitive and behavioral effects of gangsta rap. *Basic and Applied Social Psychology*, **16**(1–2), 43–52.

Hansen, C. H. and Hansen, R. D. (1990a). The influence of sex and violence on the appeal of rock music videos. *Communication Research*, **17**, 212–34.

Hansen, C. H. and Hansen, R. D. (1990b). Rock music videos and antisocial behavior. *Basic and Applied Social Psychology*, **11**(4), 357–69.

Hansen, C. H. and Hansen, R. D. (1991). Constructing personality and social reality through music: Individual differences among fans of punk and heavy metal music. *Journal of Broadcasting and Electronic Media*, **35**(3), 335–50.

Hargreaves, D. J. (1986). *The developmental psychology of music*. Cambridge University Press, Cambridge.

Hebdige, D. (1979). *Subculture: the meaning of style*. Methuen, London.

Henry, T. (1989). *Break all rules!: Punk rock and the making of a style*. UMI Research Press, Ann Arbor, MI.

Hogg, M. A. and Abrams, D. (1990). Social motivation, self-esteem and social identity. In *Social identity theory: Constructive and critical advances* (ed. D. Abrams and M. A. Hogg), pp. 28–47. Springer-Verlag, New York.

Johnson, J. D., Adams, M. S., Ashburn, L., and Reed, W. (1995). Differential gender effects of exposure to rap music on African American adolescents' acceptance of teen dating violence. *Sex Roles*, **33**(7/8), 597–605.

Johnson, J. D., Jackson, L. A., and Gatto, L. (1995). Violent attitudes and deferred academic aspirations: Deleterious effects of exposure to rap music. *Basic and Applied Social Psychology*, **16**(1–2), 27–41.

Johnstone, J. and Katz, E. (1957). Youth and popular music: A study in the sociology of taste. *American Journal of Sociology*, **62**(6), 563–8.

King, P. (1988). Heavy metal music and drug abuse in adolescents. *Postgraduate Medicine*, **83**(5), 295–301, 304.

Konečni, V. J. (1979). Determinants of aesthetic preference and effects of exposure to aesthetic stimuli: Social, emotional and cognitive factors. In *Progress in experimental personality research* (ed. B. A. Maher) Vol. 9, pp. 149–97. Academic Press, New York.

Konečni, V. J. (1982). Social interaction and musical preference. In *The psychology of music* (ed. D. Deutsch) pp. 497–516. Academic Press, Orlando, FL.

Kotarba, J. A. and Wells, L. (1987). Styles of adolescent participation in an all-ages, rock 'n' roll nightclub: An ethnographic analysis. *Youth and Society*, **18**(4), 398–417.

Larson, R. and Kubey, R. (1983). Television and music: Contrasting media in adolescent life. *Youth and Society*, **15**, 13–31.

Larson, R., Kubey, R., and Colletti, J. (1989). Changing channels: Early adolescent media choices and shifting investments in family and friends. *Journal of Youth and Adolescents*, **18**(6), 583–600.

Leming, J. S. (1987). Rock music and the socialization of moral values in early adolescence. *Youth and Society*, **18**(4), 363–83.

Lewis, G. H. (1972). *Side-saddle on the golden calf: Social structure and popular culture in America*. Goodyear, Pacific Palisades, CA.

Lewis, G. H. (1987). Patterns of meaning and choice: Taste cultures in popular music. In *Popular music and communication* (ed. J. Lull), pp. 198–211. Sage, Newbury Park, CA.

Litle, P. and Zuckerman, M. (1986). Sensation seeking and musical preferences. *Personality and Individual Differences*, **7**(4), 575–7.

Lyle, J. and Hoffman, H. R. (1972). Children's use of television and other media. In U. S. National Institute of Mental Health *Television and social behavior. Reports and papers: Vol. IV. Television in day-to-day life: Patterns of use* (ed. E. A. Rubinstein, G. A. Comstock, and J. P. Murray), pp. 129–256. U.S. Government Printing Office, Washington, DC.

MacDonald, D. (1957). A theory of mass culture. In *Mass culture: The popular arts in America* (ed. B. Rosenberg and D. M. White), pp. 59–73. Free Press, Glencoe, IL.

Meyer, L. B. (1956). *Emotion and meaning in music*. University of Chicago Press, Chicago.

Moore, M. C., Skipper, J. K., and Willis, C. L. (1979). Rock and roll: Arousal music or a reflection of changing sexual more? In *Love and attraction: An international conference* (ed. M. Cook and G. Wilson), pp. 481–6. Pergamon Press, Oxford.

North, A. C. and Hargreaves, D. J. *Situational influences on reported musical preference*. Manuscript submitted for publication.

Peterson, R. A. and DiMaggio, P. (1975). From region to class: The changing focus of country music. *Social Forces*, **53**, 497–506.

Plopper, B. L. and Ness, M. E. (1993). Death as portrayed to adolescents through top 40 rock and roll music. *Adolescence*, **28**(112), 793–807.

Rauth, R. (1982). Back in the USSR: Rock and roll in the Soviet Union. *Popular Music and Society*, **8**(4), 3–11.

Reddi, U. (1985). An Indian perspective on youth culture. *Communication Research*, **12**(3), 373–80.

Robinson, T. O., Weaver, J. B., and Zillmann, D. (1996). Exploring the relation between personality and the appreciation of rock music. *Psychological Reports*, **78**, 259–69.

Roe, K. (1983). *Mass media and adolescent schooling: Conflict or co-existence?* Almqvist and Wiksell International, Stockholm.

Roe, K. (1985). Swedish youth and music: Listening patterns and motivations. *Communication Research*, **12**(3), 353–62.

Roe, K. (1987). The school and music in adolescent socialization. In *Popular music and communication* (ed. J. Lull), pp. 212–30. Sage Publications, Newbury Park, CA.

Rosenberg, B. (1957). Mass culture in America. In *Mass culture: The popular arts in America* (ed. B. Rosenberg and D. M. White), pp. 3–12. Free Press, Glencoe, IL.

Rosengren, K. E., Wenner, L. A., and Palmgreen, P. (1985). *Media gratifications research*. Sage, Beverley Hills.

Russell, D., Peplau. L. A., and Cutrona, C. E. (1980). The revised UCLA loneliness scale: Concurrent and discriminant validity evidence. *Journal of Personality and Social Psychology*, **39**, 472–80.

Sargent, S. L. and Weaver, J. B. (1996). *Exploring the impact of expressed media preferences on perceptions of opposite gender peers*. Paper presented at the annual conference of the International Communication Association, Chicago, May 1996.

Savary, L. M. (1967). *The kingdom of downtown: Finding teenagers in their music*. Paulist Press, New York.

Shepherd, J. (1991). *Music as social text*. Polity Press, Cambridge, MA.

Shils, E. (1961). Mass society and its culture. In *Culture for the millions?: Mass media in modern society* (ed. N. Jacobs), pp. 1–27. Van Nostrand, Princeton, NJ.

Simmel, G. (1904). Fashion. *International Quarterly*, **10**, 130–55.

Skipper, J. K., Jr. (1973). How popular is popular music?: Youth and diversification of musical preferences. *Popular Music and Society*, **2**(2), 145–54.

Sun, S-W. and Lull, J. (1986). The adolescent audience for music videos and why they watch. *Journal of Communication*, **36**(1), 115–25.

Tajfel, H. (ed.). (1982). *Social identity and intergroup relations*. Cambridge University Press, Cambridge.

Tapper, J., Thorson, E., and Black, D. (1994). Variations in music videos as a function of their musical genre. *Journal of Broadcasting and Electronic Media*, **38**(1), 103–13.

Turner, J. C. (1985). Social categorization and the self-concept: A social-cognitive theory of group behavior. In *Advances in group processes: A research annual* (ed. E. J. Lawler), Vol. 2, pp. 77–121. JAI Press, Greenwich, CT.

Veblen, T. (1899). *Theory of the leisure class*. Macmillan, New York.

Wakshlag, J. J., Reitz, R. J., and Zillmann, D. (1982). Selective exposure to and acquisition of information from educational television programs as a function of appeal and tempo of background music. *Journal of Educational Psychology*, **74**, 666–77.

Weinstein, D. (1991). *Heavy metal: A cultural sociology*. Lexington, New York.

Wells, A. and Hakanen, E. A. (1991). The emotional use of popular music by adolescents. *Journalism Quarterly*, **68**(3), 445–54.

Zillmann, D. (1983). Transfer of excitation in emotional behavior. In *Social psychophysiology: A sourcebook* (ed. J. T. Cacioppo and R. E. Petty), pp. 215–40. Guilford Press, New York.

Zillmann, D. (1988a). Mood Management: Using entertainment to full advantage. In *Communication, social cognition, and affect* (ed. L. Donohew, H. E. Sypher, and E. T. Higgens), pp. 147–71. Erlbaum, Hillsdale, NJ.

Zillmann, D. (1988b). Mood management through communication choices. *American Behavioral Scientist*, **31**(3), 327–40.

Zillmann, D. (1996). Sequential dependencies in emotional experience and behavior. In *Emotion: Interdisciplinary perspectives* (ed. R. D. Kavanaugh, B. Zimmerberg, and S. Fein), pp. 243–72. Erlbaum, Mahwah, NJ.

Zillmann, D. and Bhatia, A. (1989). Effects of associating with musical genres on heterosexual attraction. *Communication Research*, **16**(2), 263–88.

Zillmann, D. and Bryant, J. (ed.). (1985). *Selective exposure to communication*. Erlbaum, Hillsdale, NJ.

Zillmann, D. and Mundorf, N. (1987). Image effects in the appreciation of video rock. *Communication Research*, **14**(3), 316–34.

Zillmann, D. and Paulus, P. B. (1993). Spectators: Reactions to sports events and effects on athletic performance. In *Handbook on research in sport psychology* (ed. R. N. Singer, M. Murphey, and L. K. Tennant), pp. 234–69. Macmillan, New York.

Zillmann, D., Aust, C. F., Hoffman, K. D., Love, C. C., Ordman, V. L., Pope, J. T. *et al.* (1995). Radical rap: Does it further ethnic division? *Basic and Applied Social Psychology*, **16**(1 and 2), 1–25.

Zuckerman, M. (1979). *Sensation seeking: Beyond the optimal level of arousal*. Erlbaum, Hillsdale, NJ.

10 | Environmental factors in the development of musical performance skill over the life span

Jane W. Davidson, Michael J. A. Howe, and John A. Sloboda

INTRODUCTION

The ethnomusicologist, J. Messenger, who was studying the Anang Ibibo Tribe in Nigeria in 1958, gave the following account of their musical activities:

We were constantly amazed at the musical abilities displayed by these people, especially by the children who, before the age of five, can sing hundreds of songs, both individually and in choral groups, and, in addition, are able to play several percussion instruments and have learned dozens of intricate dance movements, calling for incredible muscular control. We searched in vain for the 'non-musical' person, finding it difficult to make enquiries about tone-deafness and its assumed effects because the Anang language possesses no comparable concept . . . They will not admit, as we tried so hard to get them to, that there are those that lack the requisite abilities. This same attitude applies to the other aesthetic areas. Some dancers, singers, and weavers are considered more skilled than most, but everyone can dance and sing well (Messenger 1958, pp. 20–2).

Evidently, among the Anang Ibibo it is believed that everyone is capable of very high levels of musical expertise. That view is not widely shared in the West, but there is some evidence that, appearances notwithstanding, most people do have some musical skills. Musical response research undertaken in western Europe (e.g. Lecanuet 1996; Papoušek 1996; Zenatti 1976) has demonstrated that even before birth, responses to music occur. As the child matures, there is some kind of 'musical learning' process in which the grammatical rules of the musical language of the particular culture are unconsciously synthesized. For example, by the age of 10, most children are capable of discriminating between musical sequences which fit the rules of their specific musical language from those that do not (Sloboda 1985), and most are able to make appropriate judgements of the emotional character of musical pieces (Gardner 1973). By adulthood, provided that tasks do not re-quire specialized musical vocabulary, notation, or long-term memory train-ing skills, even people who have not been given specific training in music can make judgements based on musical structure that are often very similar to those of the musically-trained (e.g. Bigand 1990; Deliège and El Ahmahdi 1990). Thus, there is evidence that some sort of developmental process occurs, with learning about music and its structures taking place 'naturally' in all individuals as a result of exposure to the musical products of the culture.

In the Anang culture, it is apparent that these musical response skills are built upon by engagement in musical performance. Indeed, theirs is a cul-ture in which everyone participates in performance, enjoying the social engagement, manual, and expressive skills which music brings to their everyday lives. In western Europe, such regular involvement in musical per-formance is rare nowadays, yet it is known that in eighteenth-century Venice, certain orphanages (notably La Pietà where Vivaldi taught) estab-lished a cultural ambience in which musical expertise was valued and encouraged, and where all the children acquired performance skills to a high standard (Howe 1990; Kunkel 1985). Generally speaking, however, engaging in musical performance is a minority interest and activity, and because the experience of being a performer is unfamiliar, most people are unaware of how performance skills are developed. The tendency has been to label these achievements as being the consequence of special 'gifts' or 'talents' that are believed to involve some form of special biological endowment, possessed by only a minority of people.

The 'gifts' and 'talents' explanation of musical achievement is consistent with the determinist belief that abilities are largely hereditary. In reality, whilst it is true that individual biological differences play a significant role in human development (see Chapter 2), explaining musical achievement only or mainly in terms of 'gifts' and 'talents' denies the many varied and poten-tially vital environmental influences which affect development (Hargreaves 1994; Radford 1994). Indeed, one of the most commonly cited kinds of evidence for the importance of a gift or talent in music is so-called 'perfect pitch'. Yet, empirical studies of the past 30 years suggest that a particularly systematic exposure to musical stimuli in early childhood is required for 'perfect pitch' to emerge (Sergeant 1969). There is also evidence to suggest that with a sufficiently persistent approach, excellent pitch discrimination can be learned by any determined person (Cuddy 1968; Brady 1970). Levitin (1994) has argued that most measures of perfect pitch in fact draw on two independent abilities, pitch memory and pitch labelling (the ability to name a remembered pitch). When Levitin measured pitch memory in a task in which pitch labelling was not required (singing well-known popular songs from memory), over two-thirds of an unselected sample of college students demonstrated some evidence of a good pitch memory.

Researching the life span

Most of the existing research has relied on retrospective methods, drawing on biographical information about highly successful adult musicians. One such study by Manturzewska (1990), recruiting established adult professional musicians, used both structured and semi-structured interviews and questionnaires to ask an array of retrospective questions, ranging from ancestry to extrinsic and intrinsic motivations and obstacles to career advancement at different stages of life. A major problem with such methods is the unreliability of memory over the life span when information has been held in memory for a long time, since it is often difficult to discover the point at which it was learned. For, example, we may understand the concept of blue as a colour, yet few if any of us can remember when we learned the characteristics that comprise blue. In other words, there is a semantic memory, but no episode connected to the meaning. Even in terms of episodes, features are often merged or forgotten even when the episodes are key life events like getting married, or graduating from university (Rubin 1986). Therefore, it is highly likely that in activities like music practice which occur on a daily basis, the specific details such as increases in the quantity of time spent practising, or even feelings towards individual teachers, may become hazy over time. As a result, it can be difficult to disentangle, retrospectively, the various influences.

How, then, can the environmental influences on the development of musical performance skills be observed accurately? It would be desirable to observe directly the circumstances surrounding the emergence of musical skill, tracing young people from birth until the time at which musical competence has been achieved. In practice, however, doing that would be extremely difficult. Very large samples would need to be observed since only a minority of children actually begin learning musical instruments at all, and only a minute proportion of these learners persist to become skilled musicians. A more realistic approach is to interview young people at various stages of learning: from those who learned for less than a year, through to some who have been studying for 15 years. With this approach, the learners' actual engagement in their own musical development can be examined. Since many such interviewees would be very close in time to the events they were asked to recall, it would also be possible to use a structured interview technique, the young person and the parent or guardian being interviewed independently, so that corroborative evidence for responses could be sought.

The social and educational value of exploring the emergence of such specialist skills is obvious. As part of this process, it is essential to explore a variety of music learning experiences, and not only those of the most successful individuals. Therefore, at one extreme it would seem important to study individuals on a learning trajectory similar to virtuoso professional adult performers such as Tamsin Little and Yo Yo Ma, but at the other extreme it would be essential to examine young people who have given up all formal and leisure involvement in music. In our recent research, we studied the range of learners by examining the experiences of five different groups of young people who were all matched for socio-economic status, sex, age, and musical instrument studied. The first group attended a specialist music school ('specialists'), the second group comprised of children who had failed to gain a place at this school ('rejected specialists'), the third group included children whose parents had only inquired about attending the school ('passive interest specialists'), the fourth group were all learners of musical instruments, but music was only one of many other hobbies ('non-specialist instrumentalists'). The fifth group had all studied for at least six months, but all had given up at least a year prior to the interviews ('given-up instrumentalists'). Objective differences in musical competence between the five groups were confirmed by examining their achievements in Associated Board and Guildhall School of Music grades. Here it was discovered that the 'specialists' had achieved the highest grade levels, 'given-up instrumentalists' the lowest, and the other groups, intermediate levels.

Thus, we believe that our research provides data which can usually inform about the environmental circumstances in which musical skills do and do not emerge. In the sections which follow, we examine the findings of our own research project alongside the existing research literature to elaborate the picture of how musical performance skills emerge over the life span.

EARLY CHILDHOOD SIGNS OF MUSICAL ABILITY

Anecdotes referring to early signs of musical abilities are commonly cited in the biographies of virtuoso musicians. These stories include a special attraction to musical sounds, spontaneous early singing and imitation of tunes, and playing correctly tunes on a keyboard or wind instrument. For instance, it is said that Stravinsky amazed his parents as a two-year-old by imitating the performances of local peasant singers (Gardner 1984). Scheinfeld (1956) claimed that the majority of virtuoso instrumentalists have shown some special ability before the age of five, supporting the idea that some special signs are present prior to instruction on an instrument. However, whilst this evidence is consistent with the suggestion that there exist special indicators of inherent high ability, it is equally possible that the children concerned may simply have had more exposure to music in their everyday environments than other children, and as a consequence of familiarity display more musical signs.

The few empirical studies which look at accomplished professional musicians and which rely on data obtained from reliable sources (Manturzewska

1990; Sloboda and Howe 1991; Sosniak 1985, 1990) provide little support for the idea of early musical signs. Our recent study (full details can be found in Howe *et al.* 1995) confirmed this as the ages at which musical behaviours first occurred in the five different study groups did not vary greatly, with the mean ages of these activities starting being:

(1) 1.40 years for the infant moving to music;
(2) 1.94 years for the child showing a liking for musical sounds;
(3) 2.31 years for being attentive to music;
(4) 4.43 years for requests to become involved in musical activities.

Only in early singing was there a significant difference between the groups, with the specialist children singing on average six months earlier than all the other children at the mean age of 1.70 years. The reason why singing occurred earlier in the specialist group may be that these children's parents engaged in more musical activities with their children than the other parents.

THE ACQUISITION OF MUSICAL SKILLS

Research on the acquisition of various kinds of expertise shows that of a number of factors, the most directly effective activity for skill acquisition is deliberate practice. For example, Chase and Ericsson (1981) document the process of memory skill acquisition. At the start of their study a learner, SF, had the normal memory span of seven plus or minus two for the immediate recall of numerical items (Miller 1956). However, SF's memory span increased dramatically over 200 hours of systemic practice of the task. However, at the end of this period, memory span for other materials, such as recall of randomly sequenced letters of the alphabet, remained essentially unchanged. The effect of practising was specific to the items practised, numbers.

Music practice

Ericsson, Krampe, and Tesch-Romer (1993) obtained specific information about amounts of 'formal practice' (scales, pieces, and technical exercises) undertaken by student violinists. They discovered a clear relationship between proficiency and accumulated practice. The best students in the performance class of the conservatory had accumulated around 10 000 hours of practice by the age of 21, whereas the less accomplished students in the pedagogy department had accumulated only half that amount, on average.

With this finding in mind, we anticipated that our young instrumentalists would differ significantly in the amounts of formal practice they had undertaken (details in Sloboda *et al.* 1996). As expected, there were indeed large differences in the quantities of formal practice being done across the different groups of children in our study. These differences in quantities of practice between groups were enormous, with the specialists doing more than four times the practice of the non-specialist instrumentalists. The differences were apparent extremely early in the learning process, within the first two years of taking up a musical instrument, and were present in children from as young as six years of age. The specialist practice figures were similar to those reported by Ericsson *et al.* (1993).

As stated earlier, we discovered objective differences between the groups by collecting data about the children's examination achievements in musical grades. Indeed, we noted that the specialist group progressed through the grade examinations much quicker than the others. However, when we examined the relationship between grade level and accumulated practice directly, by computing the mean numbers of hours of practice amassed between grades, we found that there were in fact no group differences. In other words, it took the same number of hours of practice to achieve a given grade level, regardless of which group participants belonged to. We conclude from these data that the earlier achievements of the specialists are a direct result of having accumulated the required hours of practice at a faster rate than the other groups.

So, deliberate practice has significant effects on learning. Krampe and Ericsson (1995) have demonstrated in a study of adult pianists that deliberate practice needs to be maintained throughout adulthood if skill development is to occur as the years pass. Indeed, they discovered that deliberate and effortful practice was a critical factor in the advancement and continuance of the career in old age.

The central importance of practice in the development of musical expertise has been challenged in anecdotes about individuals who appear to perform to incredibly high standards without having had formal experiences to learn. However, examining the biographies of some of these 'exceptional' individuals, we believe that the practice model does indeed fit their stories. Two very different individuals help us to explore these issues: the autistic mono-savant, NP, who was studied by Sloboda *et al.* (1985) and Louis Armstrong, the New Orleans jazz trumpeter, studied by Collier (1983).

NP was an individual with very low mental accomplishments in all areas of his life but musical performance. In his early twenties, after one listening, he could perform an entire movement of a Grieg piano sonata. Exploring his biography, Sloboda *et al.* (1985) discovered that NP had spent almost all of his early life listening obsessively to Western tonal music on the radio. Indeed, his attention was entirely directed towards music, his mental activities being largely constrained to assimilating and retaining the musical structural information. A series of tape recordings made between the ages of five and eight demonstrated that NP's performing skills emerged through trial and error.

Having spent many hours at the keyboard, by adulthood NP's repro-
ductions of tonal pieces were staggering feats of memory, but they were not
always note-perfect. The inaccuracies revealed a profound knowledge of
Western tonality as they always fitted a possible structural solution to a
harmonic sequence that had been established. NP's abilities were completely
restricted to tonal music, for when Sloboda *et al.* asked him to play a piece
by Bartok which drew on an unfamiliar whole tone scale, he floundered
completely. Thus, his musical knowledge was profound, but highly circumscribed, related entirely to the musical material to which he had been
exposed over his life.

The second individual, Louis Armstrong, did not receive a formal musical
education, but had frequent exposure to musical stimuli from a very early
age. In New Orleans, the streets were filled with tonk bands. Indeed, in early
childhood, Louis Armstrong sang in street corner choirs, where there were
ample opportunities for freely exploring music over an extended time
period. He used to sit and watch jazz performances, and through trial and
error and interactions with older, more experienced players he had many
opportunities to discuss, play, and so develop his own ideas.

The fact that NP and Louis Armstrong never engaged in practice activities
that were set and coached by a specific teacher did not mean that they had
not undertaken thousands of hours of practice. We have data to confirm this
view, with our high achieving young instrumentalists carrying out many
more hours of informal, entirely self-motivated practice than the low
achievers. Since, overall, our high achievers always did less informal than
formal practice (practice set by teachers), perhaps the combination of informal with formal practice helped to sustain the individuals through the
learning process. It is important to emphasize that the children who eventually gave up playing did not engage in any informal practice activities. It
seems likely, therefore, that a free exploration of music is important for skill
acquisition. Whether practice is a combination of formal and informal tasks,
or informal tasks alone, high quantities of time are required engaging in
these activities for skills to develop.

Of course, specifying practice as informal and formal still leaves much
unsaid. Efficacy of practice will depend on more than the sheer amount of it.
For instance, Gruson (1988) and Miklaszewski (1989) discovered that the
structure of the practice was important. In Miklaszewski's study of a single
pianist, he discovered that fragments of the piece were often worked on for
extended periods of time, and that as the practice progressed the length of
the sections the pianists chose to work on tended to increase. Within this
sectioning strategy, the most frequently observed behaviour was playing a
section in an alternately fast or slow tempo. Gruson (1988) concluded from
her observations of young learners that practising actually represents a
sequence of transitions from controlled to automatic processing of the

musical materials which are built up from smaller to larger units. Hallam (1995), in a study examining 22 professional musicians, showed that the practice strategies themselves are highly individualized and that there is no simple correspondence between a particular practice strategy and success as a performer. The successful professional musicians employed a very wide variety of practice strategies ranging from holistic approaches to a piece to serial strategies similar to those employed by Miklaszewski's pianist. With little previous research, the area still needs a lot of work in order to be fully understood.

The technical and expressive aspects of musical performance

Practice itself is an activity in which both technical and expressive features are explored and learned. These skills are distinguishable constituents of musical expertise, but, expertise in music is regarded as the synthesis of these elements; without one, the performer is regarded as lacking in a significant aspect of his or her artistry (Coker 1972). In the West, technical, mechanistic aspects of performance have been regarded as learnable skills; but the expressive aspects have been considered as being more instinctive or natural. On reflection, this view seems illogical since recent research has established quite firmly that, although any one expert's use of expression may differ from any other's (Sloboda 1985), thus allowing for artistic originality or idiosyncrasy, expressive performance is nonetheless rational, or rule-governed.

There are five characteristics which attest to the rationality of expressive performance. First, it is *systematic*: that is to say, there is a clear relationship between the use of particular expressive devices (e.g. slowing, accenting, etc.) and particular structural features of the music, such as metrical or phrase boundaries (Todd 1985). Secondly, expressive performance displays *communicability*, in that listeners are better able to infer structural features of the music when expression is present than when it is absent. Thirdly, it shows *stability*: a given expert can very closely reproduce the same expressive performance on occasions which might be separated by some months (e.g. Shaffer 1984). Fourthly, expressive performance displays *flexibility*: an expert performer can attenuate, exaggerate, or change the expressive contour to highlight different aspects of the music (e.g. Davidson 1993; Palmer 1989). Fifth and finally, it shows *automaticity*: an experienced performer is not always aware of the details of how an expressive intention is translated into action (e.g. Gabrielsson 1988). This comes about through over-learning of consistent intention-performance mappings, which could not be established unless they were systematic and rule-governed. If expression is rule-governed why then is it described as the product of instinct?

Performance expression

Like many performance skills, the details of musical expression are often not available to the performer him or herself, and certainly not in a form that can be easily verbalized. Additionally, expressive performance is controlled, at least in part, by gestures which pre-exist in other non-musical domains of human activity (such as motion, vocalizations of emotion). Their application to music performance may come about by a process of analogical learning, where the shape of the whole gesture is transferred from the non-musical domain to a musical structure in a single act of recognition, rather than an analytic note-by-note construction, or a process of cumulative learning. The verification of the appropriateness of the transfer may be made through the monitoring of the emotional effect on the performer 'as listener', rather than at an analytic level. There are a whole range of plausible reasons why some performers may be able to access these gestural analogies more easily than others, and the detailed exploration of these reasons constitutes a possible 'deconstruction' of the notion of musical 'talent'.

Sloboda (1991) has shown that musical passages that elicit strong emotional responses from trained and untrained listeners tend to share certain structural features, thus suggesting a structure–emotion link. Most of these features concern creation and resolution of tensions and expectancies of various sorts. For instance, enharmonic changes, and other similar violations of expectancy seem to be associated with the emotions related to 'shivers down the spine' or 'goose bumps'. Expressive devices which intensify or exaggerate the tension or expectation-provoking characteristics of these structures are likely to enhance their emotional effect. Thus, it seems that musicians who have had many strong emotional reactions to music may be better equipped to mobilize knowledge of the emotional consequences of expression in their performance.

Research on emotional reactions to music (Pinchot *et al.* 1990; Gabrielsson and Lindström 1993) suggest that there are a number of childhood circumstances which determine the extent to which musical experiences will elicit strong emotional reactions of an appropriate kind. It is possible to distinguish broadly between emotional responses to music which are determined by its content (of the type described above) and those which are determined by its context. Contextual responses may be both positive (as when the music is associated with some pleasant event, such as a party) or negative (as when the music is taking place is a situation of anxiety, threat, or humiliation).

Sloboda (1990) studied autobiographical memories of emotional responses to music in childhood and showed that individuals with a lifelong commitment to music were much more likely to report strong emotions to musical content than those individuals who were not involved with music, or who considered themselves unmusical. Besides the structures of the music itself, Sloboda (1990) discovered that the timbre of the instrument also had a strong impact on some individuals' emotional associations and responses to music. For example, one young woman reminisced:

I was seven years-old, and sitting in the morning assembly ... The music was a clarinet duet, classical, probably by Mozart. I was astounded at the beauty of the sound. It was liquid, resonant, vibrant. It seemed to send tingles through me. I felt as if it was a significant moment. Listening to this music led to me learning to play first the recorder and then to achieve my ambition of playing the clarinet (Sloboda 1990, p. 37).

People who did not have a commitment to music were more likely to report negative, contextually-based emotions. Nearly all such negative emotions were generated in learning situations in which some attempt to perform or respond to the music was criticized by teachers. In contrast, the individuals reporting content-based responses to music were most likely to have experienced the music in situations of low external threat (such as the home, the concert hall, alone or with friends, and without performance expectation). It seems as though some of the contextual experiences in the 'non-musicians' were strong enough to lead to disengagement from music, and caused experiences of anxiety to be triggered whenever later attempts to attend to musical content were made.

These data suggest how it might come about that individuals begin to differ in their emotional responsivity to music from an early age, and indeed, hint at some of the intrinsic motivators which may stimulate children to practise at music. Here, we would cite the anecdotal examples of our successful young interviewees whose engagement in their informal music-making activities included generally 'having fun' on their instruments.

As the examination of the early signs of musical ability showed, and as the emotional response data hint, the role of other people is vital in the music learning process.

KEY 'OTHERS' IN THE LEARNING OF MUSICAL SKILLS

Parents

Parents may have a major influence upon the nature and form of a child's accomplishments (Baumrind 1989; Csikszentmihalyi *et al.* 1993). Although a stable family environment may not always be necessary in order to reach a high level of achievement, as the cases of both NP and Louis Armstrong attest, a stable and structured family life when it exists can contribute towards sustaining and motivating learning activities.

Some evidence suggests that musically outstanding individuals tend to have parents who attend lessons and support practice (Howe and Sloboda 1991a,b; Manturzewska 1986; Sloboda and Howe 1991; Sosniak 1985, 1990). But, it seems that the support needs to be of a particular kind. For example, there exists considerable evidence that one of the most crucial ways to aid intellectual growth is through the interactions that take place between parent and child, so long as the interactions are non-threatening to the child's sense of self-esteem (e.g. Bruner 1973).

A particularly interesting bibliographic analysis has been carried out by Lehmann (in press). By cross-referencing a pool of names of piano prodigies given in three different sources, a sample of 14 individuals was extracted about whom substantial biographical evidence is available (including Handel, Bach, Mozart, Beethoven, Mendelssohn, Chopin, Liszt, and Debussy). Thirteen of the 14 received regular supervision of practice from a family member (usually a parent), and 12 had periods of life when they lived in the same house as their teacher (whether parent or not), suggesting a quasi-parental role for the teacher.

In our own study (Davidson *et al.* 1996), we pursued the role of parents through asking questions about parental involvement in their children's lessons and practice and their personal involvement in music over the learning period of the child. The results showed that the most successful children had parents who were most involved in their lessons. These parents typically received regular feedback from teachers in the form of speaking to the teacher at the end of the lesson; or were present in the lessons, often taking notes. This level of involvement was sustained for up to 12 years. In contrast, the parents of children who were least successful were the least involved in their children's lessons in the early years of playing an instrument.

All parents (mothers and fathers equally) were uniformly and moderately involved in initiating the child's practice. This was typically in the form of giving them some verbal reminder to go and practise. In the actual practice session, parents from all groups tended to ask questions or offer advice about practice, rather than have no involvement or directly supervise the practice, but proportionally more parents from the specialist groups were involved with the child's practice than parents in the other groups.

In terms of the parents' own involvement in music making and listening, we discovered that although the parents of the specialist learners were most involved in music they were not performing musicians; typically, they did no more than listen to music at home. Once the children began learning an instrument, these parents increased their own involvement in music, whereas very little change occurred for the parents of the children who eventually ceased playing.

In summary, it appears that parents do have a crucial influence on their child's progress in musical skill acquisition.

Siblings

Musical investigations in general have paid little attention to the role siblings may have in the child's musical development. The general developmental literature reveals that siblings can have key influences over one another. For instance, older siblings generally display more teacher behaviour towards their younger siblings (Berndt and Bulleit 1985); and younger siblings, as young as 12 months-old, are found to imitate their older siblings (Abramovitch *et al.* 1979), often treating the older siblings as teachers (Dunn and Kendrick 1982). In addition, there appears to be a gender difference in the influence of older siblings, with older sisters being perceived as more effective instructors than older brothers (Cicirelli 1976).

We examined sibling influence by asking respondents to assess the influence of each sibling. Where there was a positive or negative influence, respondents were also asked to specify further the type of influence (e.g. inspired by the sibling). It turned out that the vast majority of individuals rated their eldest sibling as having a neutral or positive influence. Positive reports of siblings were most common in the specialist and rejected specialist groups.

Concerning the form of influence exerted by siblings, the majority of our respondents indicated that they were either inspired by the sibling musically, or had imitated the sibling. Interestingly, ten respondents indicated that their siblings had bullied them in some way, but six of these individuals reported that this had a positive, rather than a negative, influence, and were in the specialist group.

The sibling data were also examined to ascertain whether positive or negative influences predominated when the sibling's gender, age, or instrument played were taken into account. However, analyses revealed that there were no significant effects of any of these potentially influencing factors.

One way to account for the differing influence of siblings across the five groups might be in terms of the family dynamics and how the music learner's own motivations have been developed. We know, for example, that the participants in the specialist and rejected specialist groups were given the most support by their parents in their musical activities before and during formal instruction. Therefore, the siblings may be mirroring the parental pattern of support by either listening to, or participating in, lessons and practice of the young music learner. Thus, the sibling seems also to contribute towards providing external motivation.

For the groups with less parental involvement, it is less likely that siblings will be perceived to have a positive influence on the young music learner. Thus, even though a child in the given-up instrumentalist group may have imitated their sibling by starting lessons, this activity would not have been followed up by high levels of parental support, and therefore, a positive influence of the sibling might not be obtained.

Peers

Musical tastes and attitudes seem to be particularly constitutive of social roles in the school years (particularly in the 11–16 age range). There is considerable evidence that children hide their real musical interests in order to appear to conform to group norms (e.g. Finnäs 1987). Because high levels of classical musical accomplishment are unusual in most school contexts, musical children can receive considerable negative feedback from their peers, who consider musical activity to be 'weird' or 'sissy'. Howe and Sloboda (1992) reported a number of instances where able young musicians found peer attitudes to their music to be disabling to the extent that they even considered giving up playing. Many children found it crucial to be in an environment (such as a specialist music school) where other children shared their values. Some of the effects of peer response seem gender-specific, and there is evidence that children expect negative reactions from peers for playing musical instruments that are generally favoured by members of the opposite sex (O'Neill and Boulton 1996). Since some classical instruments (such as the flute) are generally seen as 'girls'' instruments, there is some suggestion that boys may experience higher levels of peer discouragement than girls.

Professional performers

There has been little systematic study of the influence of professionals on young learners. However, a current investigation exploring aspiring teenage musicians' attitudes on music and its role in their lives, by Jane Davidson and Jonathan Smith (personal communication), suggests that highly skilled professionals who are either known to young learners personally, or who have been heard and seen via radio, recording, or video can act as highly positive motivators to a child's desire to learn a musical instrument. In their sample of 28 student musicians aged 14–20 years, virtually all mentioned 'being inspired' by professionals. Here are two particularly interesting and contrasting examples:

Sixteen year-old female violinist:

I had already started violin lessons, and I suppose it was going OK. You know, I liked the instrument, and my Dad used to help me with the practice, but then I saw Nigel Kennedy on the TV, and I thought: 'Wow, he's great!' I suppose it's a bit like being a fan or something. He's great because he plays so fantastically, and he's a really cool person. He's not at all stuck up, like lots of classical musicians. I want to be like him: mellow and technically brilliant. He's my idol!

Fourteen year-old male oboist:

My dad is a professional accompanist, and he performs with this really good oboist. When I was really little they were at my house practising, and the oboist asked if I was going to be a musician. I said that I was going to be an oboist. I suppose I just said that because the man was there.

It was really, really hard when I started because I couldn't get a squeak out of the reed, but I used to listen to them rehearse and I suppose I wanted to be like that oboist. Then this absolutely amazing thing happened when, through the family, I got Leon Goossens' oboe. Can you believe it—Leon Goossens' old oboe! He had been such a fantastic player. I've got all his old records and his old oboe!

Although it is impossible to identify the relative contribution to musical success these professional players might have had on the child's development, the two examples above demonstrate how a positive expansion of the child's vision of what musical performance can be was made. Csikszentmihalyi *et al.* (1993) suggest that professionals give children identity models about which they construct and develop their concept of 'self'.

Teachers

The role of teachers in the development of skills has been studied widely. Emphasis has been placed on the effect of teachers' expectations on learner achievement, with low achievement and low teacher expectation being found to be highly correlated (Rosenthal and Jacobson 1968; Blatchford *et al.* 1989). However, much of this research has focused on classroom contexts, in which the teacher works alone with large groups of children (i.e. 25–35 children at a time). In music instrument learning, particularly in Britain, the teaching context is usually very different, with the teacher most often working in one-to-one or small group settings (typically six children or less).

The scant literature on music tuition has focused on the role of the initial teacher. Some reports (for instance, Howe and Sloboda 1991*b*; Sosniak 1985) suggested that the first teachers were regarded by the young music learners as significant influences on their musical skill acquisition, with many young musicians attributing their increasing interest in a particular instrument to having established a good personal relationship with the teacher.

In our studies (Davidson *et al.*, in press) we examined four specific areas related to the initial and last or current teacher on the main instrument (i.e. the instrument that individuals considered to be their best instrument, and the one on which they concentrated their attentions): the child's perceived characteristics of the teachers; the role of gender in the perception of teacher characteristics; the frequency of and reasons for changes of teacher; the proportions of lessons taught in group or one-to-one settings. We discovered that there were significant differences between our groups of learners in the ways in which they attributed characteristics to their teachers.

The children who successfully acquired musical skills were more likely than the less successful children to have regarded their initial teacher as a friendly, chatty, relaxed, and encouraging person. In addition, successful learners were more likely to perceive their current teachers as more friendly, chatty, and relaxed than their first teachers. Indeed, in analysis of the adjectives children used to describe their teachers, it was apparent that first teachers of the musically successful children were rated as having better 'personal quality' factors than the children who ceased music tuition; that is, they demonstrated such characteristics as friendliness and chattiness. In comparison, the current or most recent teachers of the most successful music learners had many 'professional qualities' attributed to them: for instance, being a good teacher and player. Those children who had given up lessons did not differentiate in any way between the notion of 'personal' and 'professional' teacher characteristics. Whilst it is impossible to know whether the teachers were truly different in their characteristics (since there was no objective measure, only the subjective student reports), the differences in characteristics *perceived* by the children in our study suggest that, in the early stages of learning, personal characteristics of teachers are important to promote musical development. At later stages, it is more important that teachers should be perceived to have good performance and professional skills.

Examination of the data for gender differences revealed that 'pushiness' was the only characteristic differentiated between boy and girls, with boys perceiving both first and last teachers as being more pushy. Since Rutter (1987) argues that boys are generally trained more for high achievement, this result might support the idea that teachers may demand more and therefore be more pushy in their treatment of males than females. This finding is particularly interesting when it is noted that the specialist group was the only group to have revealed sex differences for pushiness, suggesting that high achieving boys are pushed more than high achieving girls.

We also discovered that all but the group who ceased playing studied with more teachers on average than the other groups on their main instruments (2.5 teachers on the main instrument). One possible reading of these results is that more frequent changes of teachers may assist the child's musical development. Indeed, next to the practical external reason of moving house, these three groups attributed the search for a better teacher as the most frequent reason for changing teachers.

Another teacher characteristic which clearly differentiates between the groups was whether the instruction was individual or in small groups. The three most successful groups generally received individual instruction, whereas the other children mainly received group tuition. This final result has quite far-reaching implications. It suggests that if a child wishes to achieve high levels of expertise, he or she is likely to benefit from the attention of a teacher on a one-to-one basis.

In summary, it appears that a number of individuals contribute significantly to the child's desire to learn, often providing an external source of motivation for wanting to, and then actually engaging in, instrumental learning and performance.

CONCLUSION

Overall, the empirical results discussed in this chapter have demonstrated that musical performance skills do not just happen, but instead develop in fairly predictable ways out of specific environmental circumstances. It has been demonstrated that there are a number of common features in the backgrounds of those who successfully acquired musical skills: a supportive parent, a friendly teacher, ample opportunities to practise coupled with high levels of investment in formal practice, and informal musical engagement.

In sum, our chapter has outlined a number of rather unsurprising key influences on the development of musical skill which one would have thought would be easy to implement in most educational situations. Yet, why do young people in modern Western society not achieve the universally high levels of musical competence attributed to members of non-Western societies such as the Anang Ibibo? We believe that in our society, counter to the simple and effective environmental influences, runs the whole current of the 'art' culture, which promotes the notion that most people are incapable of high achievement, and, through the increasing professionalization and specialization of musical activity, makes access to appropriate training more and more difficult. We are not sanguine that any society such as ours which commodifies and sells music and musical expertise will ever be able to deliver musical skill to the majority of its population.

REFERENCES

Abramovitch, R., Corter, C., and Lando, B. (1979). Sibling interaction in the home. *Child Development*, **50**, 997–1003.

Baumrind, D. (1989). Rearing competent children. In *Child development today and tomorrow* (ed. W. Damon). Jossey Bass, San Francisco.

Berndt, T. J. and Bulleit, T. N. (1985). Effects of sibling relationships on pre-schoolers' behaviour at home and at school. *Development Psychology*, **21**, 761–7.

Bigand, E. (1990). Abstraction of two forms of underlying structure in a tonal melody. *Psychology of Music*, **19**, 45–59.

Blatchford, P., Burke, J., Farquhar, C., Plewis, I., and Tizard, B. (1989). Teacher expectations in infant school: associations with attainment and progress, curriculum coverage and classroom interaction. *British Journal of Educational Psychology*, **59**, 19–30.

Brady, P. T. (1970). Fixed-scale mechanism of absolute pitch. *Journal of the Acoustical Society of America*, **48**, 883–7.

Bruner, J. (1973). *Beyond the information given: studies in the psychology of knowing.* Norton, New York.

Chase, W. G. and Ericsson, K. A. (1981). Skilled memory. In *Cognitive skills and their acquisition* (ed. J. R. Anderson), pp. 141–89. Erlbaum, Hillsdale, NJ.

Cicirelli, V. G. (1976). Siblings helping siblings. In *Children as tutors* (ed. V. L. Allen). Academic, New York.

Collier, J. L. (1983). *Louis Armstrong: an American genius.* Oxford University Press, New York.

Coker, W. (1972). *Music and meaning: a theoretical introduction to musical aesthetics.* Free Press, New York.

Cuddy, L. L. (1986). Practice effects in the absolute judgement of pitch. *Journal of the Acoustical Society*, **43**, 1069-76.

Csikszentmihayli, M., Rathunde, K. and Whalen, S. (1993). *Talented teenagers: the roots of success and failure.* Cambridge University Press, Cambridge.

Davidson, J. W. (1993) Visual perception of performance manner in the movements of solo musicians. *Psychology of Music*, **21**, 103–13.

Davidson, J. W., Howe, M. J. A., Moore, D. G., and Sloboda, J. A. (1996). The role of parental influences in the development of musical ability. *British Journal of Developmental Psychology*, **14**, 399–412.

Davidson, J. W., Howe, M. J. A., Moore, D. G., and Sloboda, J. A. (in press). The role of teachers in the development of musical ability. *Journal of Research in Music Education.*

Deliège, I. and El Ahmahdi, A. (1990). Mechanisms of cue extraction in musical groupings: a study of perception on Sequenza VI for viola solo by Luciana Berio. *Psychology of Music*, **19**, 18–44.

Dunn, J. and Kendrick, C. (1982). *Siblings: love, envy, and understanding.* Harvard University Press, Cambridge, MA.

Ericsson, K. A., Krampe, R. T. and Tesch-Romer, C. (1993). The role of deliberate practice in the acquisition of expert performance. *Psychological Review*, **100**, 363–406.

Finnäs, L. (1987). Do young people misjudge each other's musical tastes? *Psychology of Music*, **15**, 152–66.

Gabrielsson, A. (1988). Timing in music performance and its relation to music experience. In *Generative processes in music: the psychology of performance, improvisation, and composition* (ed. J. A. Sloboda). Oxford University Press, Oxford.

Gabrielsson, A. and Lindström, S. (1993). On strong experiences of music. *Jahrbuch der Deutschen Gesellschaft für Musikpsychologie*, **10**, 114–25.

Gardner, H. (1973). Children's sensitivity to musical styles. *Merrill-Palmer Quarterly*, **19**, 67–72.

Gardner, H. (1984). *Frames of mind.* Heinemann, London.

Gruson, L. (1988). Rehearsal skill and musical competence: Does practice make perfect? In *Generative processes in music: the psychology of performance, improvisation, and composition* (ed. J. A. Sloboda). Oxford University Press, Oxford.

Hallam, S. (1995). Professional musicians' approaches to the learning and inter-pretation of music. *Psychology of Music*, **23**, 111–29.

Hargreaves, D. J. (1994). Musical education for all. *The Psychologist*, **7**, 357–8.

Howe, M. J. A. (1990). *The origins of exceptional ability*. Blackwell, Oxford.

Howe, M. J. A. and Sloboda, J. A. (1991a). Young musicians' accounts of significant influences in their early lives: 1. The family and the musical background. *British Journal of Music Education*, **8**, 39–52.

Howe, M. J. A. and Sloboda, J. A. (1991b). Young musicians' accounts of significant influences in their early lives: 2. Teachers, practising, and performing. *British Journal of Music Education*, **8**, 53–63.

Howe, M. J. A. and Sloboda, J. A. (1992). Problems experienced by talented young musicians as a result of the failure of other children to value musical accom-plishments. *Gifted Education*, **8.1**, 16–18.

Howe, M. J. A., Davidson, J. W., Moore, D. M., and Sloboda, J. A. (1995). Are there early childhood signs of musical ability? *Psychology of Music*, **23**, 162–76.

Krampe, R. and Ericsson, K. A. (1995). Acquisition and maintenance of high-level skill in violinists and pianists: the role of deliberate practice. Paper presented at VIIth European Conference on Developmental Psychology, Krakow, 1995.

Kunkel, J. H. (1985). Vivaldi in Venice: an historical test of psychological propositions. *Psychological Record*, **35**, 445–57.

Lecanuet, J-P. (1996). The foetal stage. In *Musical beginnings: origins and development of musical competence* (ed. I. Deliège and J. A. Sloboda). Oxford University Press, Oxford.

Lehmann, A. C. (in press). The acquisition of expertise in music: efficiency of deliberate practice as a moderating variable in accounting for sub-expert per-formance. In *Perception and cognition of music* (ed. I. Deliège and J. A. Sloboda). Lawrence Erlbaum, Hillsdale, NJ.

Levitin, D. J. (1994). Absolute memory for musical pitch: evidence from the production of learned melodies. *Perception and Psychophysics*, **56**, 414–23.

Manturzewska, M. (1986). Musical talent in the light of biographical research. In *Musikalishe Begabung funden und forden* (ed. S. Bosse). Verl, Munchen.

Manturzewska, M. (1990). A biographical study of the life-span development of professional musicians. *Psychology of Music*, **18**, 112–39.

Messenger J. (1958). Esthetic talent. *Basic College Quarterly*, **4**, 20–4.

Miklaszewski, K. (1989). A case study of a pianist preparing a musical performance. *Psychology of Music*, **17**, 95–109.

Miller, G. A. (1956). The magic number seven, plus or minus two: some limits on our capacity for information processing. *Psychological Review*, **63**, 81–93.

O'Neill, S. A. and Boulton, M. J. (1996). Boys' and girls' preference for musical instruments: a function of gender? *Psychology of Music*, **24**, 171–83.

Palmer, C. (1989). Mapping musical thought to musical performance. *Journal of Experimental Psychology: Human Perception and Performance*, **15**, 331–46.

Papoušek, H. (1996). Musicality and infancy: biological and cultural origins of precocity. In *Musical beginnings: origins and development of musical competence* (ed. I. Deliège and J. A. Sloboda). Oxford University Press, Oxford.

Pinchot Kastner, M. and Crowder, R. G. (1990). Perception of the major/minor distinction: IV. Emotional connotations in young children. *Music Perception*, **8**, 189–202.

Radford, J. (1994). Variations on a musical theme. *The Psychologist*, **7**, 359–60.

Rosenthal, J. and Jacobson, L. (1968). *Pygmalion in the classroom*. Holt, Rinehart, and Winston, New York.

Rubin, D. C. (ed.) (1986). *Autobiographical memory*. Cambridge University Press, Cambridge.

Rutter, M. (1987). Continuities and discontinuities from infancy. In *Handbook of infant development* (2nd edn) (ed. J. D. Osofsky). Wiley-Interscience, New York.

Scheinfield, A. (1956). *The new heredity and you*. Kegan Paul, Trench and Trubner, London.

Sergeant, D. (1969). Experimental investigation of absolute pitch. *Journal of Research in Music Education*, **17**, 135–43.

Shaffer, L. H. (1984). Timing in solo and duet piano performances. *Quarterly Journal of Experimental Psychology*, **36A**, 577–95.

Sloboda, J. A. (1985). *The musical mind: the cognitive psychology of music*. Oxford University Press, Oxford.

Sloboda, J. A. (1990). Music as a language. In *Music and child development* (ed. F. Wilson and F. Roehmann). MMB Inc., St. Louis, Miss.

Sloboda, J. A. (1991). Music structure and emotional response: some empirical findings. *Psychology of Music*, **19**, 110–20.

Sloboda, J. A. and Howe, M. J. A. (1991). Biographical precursors of musical excellence: an interview study. *Psychology of Music*, **19**, 3–21.

Sloboda, J. A., Hermelin, B., and O'Connor, N. (1985). An exceptional musical memory. *Music Perception*, **3**, 155–70.

Sloboda, J. A., Davidson, J. W., Howe, M. J. A., and Moore, D. G. (1996). The role of practice in the development of expert musical performance. *British Journal of Psychology*, **87**, 287–309.

Sosniak, L. A. (1985). Learning to be a concert pianist. In *Developing talent in young people* (ed. B. S. Bloom). Ballatine, New York.

Sosniak, L. A. (1990). The tortoise, the hare, and the development of talent. In *Encouraging the development of exceptional skills and talents* (ed. M. J. A. Howe). British Psychological Society, Leicester.

Todd, N. P. (1985). A model of expressive timing in tonal music. *Music Perception*, **3**, 33–58.

Zenatti, A. (1976). Influence de quelques variables socio-culturelle sur le développment musical de l'enfant. *Psychologie Française*, **21**, 185–90.

PART V

Musicianship

11 | *The social in musical performance*

Jane W. Davidson

INTRODUCING THE SOCIAL

For all present at a live performance of a repertoire piece from the Western art music canon, the communication and reception of the musical score is the central concern, but the composition, performance, and perception of the work are dependent on a number of complex social factors. There are sociocultural rules which dictate and give value to the composition and its performance (e.g. the use of particular scale systems; a model aesthetic; the size of an ensemble; and specifically defined inter-performer, inter-audience, and performer–audience behaviours). In addition, there are moment by moment issues of coordination, cooperation, and feedback to and from co-performers and audience which occur during the performance. That is, there are overriding sociocultural factors which shape the processes and behaviours brought to the performance context, alongside more immediate factors related to direct human interaction.

The vital social aspects of performance have largely been ignored by psychological researchers. Farnsworth's pioneering text *The social psychology of music*, originally published in 1954, fails to mention either the sociocultural or interactive aspects of musical performance. In common with the dominant trend in modern cognitive psychology, most research in the psychology of music has been almost entirely 'disembodied'. Mind processes have been investigated, but humans as social agents who possess bodies as well as minds have been overlooked (Clarke and Davidson, submitted for publication).

In this chapter, an attempt will be made to detail the constituent elements of a social psychology of musical performance. Although there are many possible points of departure for such a task, the author's own training and performing experience leads to a focus on the performance of the Western art music canon. Clearly, the exploration of musics from different sociocultural traditions such as pop, non-western, folk, and jazz will produce important and slightly different perspectives, but given the limited scope of the current chapter, a focus on only one tradition will provide an initial framework which will hopefully stimulate further, more wide-ranging investigations.

SOCIOCULTURAL INFLUENCES

Historical practices

Young and Colman (1979) draw the reader's attention to the role of the past in structuring the present. In particular, they cite how by the mid-eighteenth century the gradual rejection of the Baroque functions of the continuo, the development of instrument manufacture, performance technique, and the widening social appeal of music as a form of entertainment produced an ever-increasing variety of instrumental combinations. In essence, specific cultural practices involving technological developments led composers to write for particular ensembles or individuals, and in turn these ensembles and individuals presented their music in particular ways. As a consequence of these practices, specific ensembles and musical forms have become part of the cultural expectation of what constitutes Western art music: the sonata, the concerto, and the symphony; and the corresponding emergence of the string quartet, the chamber orchestra, the symphony orchestra, the wind quintet, the piano trio, the solo singer and accompanist, and some specific solo instruments (e.g. violin, cello, piano, flute) are obvious examples.

Cook (1990) explores the history of performance practice, citing the example of the sonata. He demonstrates that in the Baroque period, composers like Corelli, Geminani, and Handel often only supplied the performer with a skeleton of the music, the ornamentation which contributes crucially to the effect of the music being provided by the performer. Cook's example demonstrates the role of shared cultural values in the construction and production of the performance: not only was the Baroque composer confident that the performer would furnish the score with ornamentation, but the Baroque performer's education and experience permitted him or her to perform the work with ornamentation appropriate to the composer's expectations.

Educationally, the development of particular 'schools' of composition and performance clearly had a huge influence on the development of styles of playing and composition. Violin teaching provides a clear example of the immense cultural impact of specific teachers. In 1782, for example, the Italian G. B. Viotti moved to Paris. In Paris, it is believed that he promoted the Stradivari violin as the most beautiful of instruments, and assisted Toute in the development and production of the modern bow. Additionally, his own playing focused on exploitation of the timbres of the G string, a strong *cantabile* line and a seamless *legato* bow change. But perhaps most importantly, he taught Baillot, Rode, and Kreutzer who went on in 1803 to write a treatise entitled *Méthode du violon*, which became the approved violin text of the Paris Conservatoire. This text was only superseded some 30 years later by Baillot's solo publication *L'art du violon*. Baillot's teaching style was developed by his former pupil, Alard, who, besides being recognized as a great teacher, published a treatise on playing. In turn, Alard became the teacher of the virtuoso performer, Sarasate. Kreutzer also had a number of 'star' pupils, and of them, Massart went on to teach the great twentieth century composer–violinist, Kreisler. So, generation after generation, it appears that Viotti's ideas on technique and aesthetic values were carried forward. The consequence was to produce a style of playing which was to become recognized as being specifically French in character.

Of course, there is a tension between the past structuring the present and the present structuring our interpretations of the past. There is an entire research area in musicology devoted to historical practices, and there is much on-going debate about authenticity and musical meaning. For example, it is known that in performance Beethoven often re-ordered or omitted movements from his own sonatas. Lawson (1995), a distinguished performer of the 'early' clarinet, takes note of such a 'fact' in his own performances of the music of Beethoven and others. However, he points out that the late twentieth century performer and audience have had a whole range of late twentieth century cultural influences shaping their views of musical form and concert behaviour. This means that the aesthetic of what constitutes a performance today is rather different to that of Beethoven's time. Therefore, compromises need to be reached as no performance of music from a different period in time can be heard and experienced as it was at the time of initial creation. Indeed, Cook (1990) suggests that nowadays we actually perceive musical form in an entirely different manner. He argues that the increasingly harmonically unstable compositions of the twentieth century have influenced our perceptual systems to such a degree that we are unable to perceive harmonic relations between movements of large-scale forms such as a classical symphony or sonata.

In summary, the perceptual experience and production of works has changed as a result of emerging cultural values and practices: there is an interaction between the past and present. Contemporary performer-researchers attempt to create performances which draw on historical information to create an impression of older practices, but there is an acknowledgement that the historically informed performance can never be truly authentic as interceding historical practices, tastes, and conventions inform the contemporary performer and audience's experience Nonetheless, the past has a strong influence on the present, and commonly accepted techniques of playing and musical forms such as the sonata, the symphony, and specific ensembles which constantly use these forms (e.g. soloist and piano accompanist, string quartets, and symphony orchestras) are legacies of the past which have become firmly established and integral to the contemporary musician's conception of music.

Sociocultural circumstances which have produced musical forms and styles have equally contributed to musical performance behaviours.

Performance etiquette

As Wilson (1994) points out, many of the behaviours which surround a musical performance are transmitted by traditional practices, and have their roots in ritual experience. Art music examples of these behaviours include: wearing a specific formal dress (e.g. dinner jacket, tail coat, evening dress); walking on to the stage and bowing to greet the audience; and, if you are a soloist with an orchestra, formally thanking the conductor and leader in front of the audience for their collaboration. This is done by shaking hands when men thank men, or by embracing if women and women, or women and men thank one another. Actual performance behaviours are equally culturally mediated. For example, during the performance of a concerto, the soloist will sit or stand relatively still when he or she is not actually playing, and similarly the orchestra members will not begin to talk or walk around during their moments of rest.

This social etiquette operates in two directions, as there are certain behaviours performers expect of audiences: in general terms, to wear more informal clothing than the performers, to applaud as the performers walk on stage, to sit in silence during a performance, to applaud after the performance, even to applaud vigorously to provide the performer with the cue that the performance was perceived to be so good that an encore should be played.

In other performance traditions, even within the framework of Western culture, different rules apply. In pop, jazz, and folk, for instance, performers are often seen wearing jeans and T-shirts, talking to one another, sipping drinks, or dancing around the stage. Similarly, it is acceptable for audience members to dress in exactly the same manner as the performers, sing, dance, drink, and chat, though the boundaries of these behaviours are quite clearly defined. An audience member who begins to shout as opposed to chat quietly, or a performer who shows signs of intoxication, may be removed from the performance situation.

Although performance etiquette is a broadly sociocultural issue, the most relevant explanation for it within the current context comes from work on social influence in small groups from the general field of social psychology. The pioneer of the work was Asch (1955, 1958) who explored social conformity. The basic study was simple: looking at a drawing of a standard and three comparison lines, an individual was asked to decide which of the three comparison lines was equal in length to the standard. Although the task appeared straightforward, it was undertaken in the presence of the six others who were confederates of the experimenter. Each of the seven people sat in a semicircle and in turn was asked to make their discriminations aloud, with the non-confederate being last on each occasion. Consistently, all the confederates named the same line as being identical to the comparison although it was in fact a different length. The seventh individual could see that the line was not identical but frequently gave responses to agree with the six others. Since Asch's preliminary study, similar results have been obtained using slightly different judgement tasks and drawing on different populations. The results are astounding: individuals will deny what their eyes tell them in order to conform to the majority position. Clearly, nothing quite so extreme is going on in the music performance situation, but performers and audiences are conforming to the majority position in terms of their social behaviour.

Whilst social conformity is a very powerful influence, research has shown that rejection of mainstream social influence can occur, but only if certain conditions are favourable. For instance, Maass and Clark (1983, 1984) demonstrated that minorities can move majorities towards their point of view if the minority position is consistent with the developing norms of the larger society, and if the minority group is perceived to be more confident, and occasionally, more competent than the majority. But perhaps most importantly, Maass and Clark emphasize the need for the internalization of beliefs. That is, there is not just compliance or public conformity, but rather a real change in private attitudes. Here, research dating back to Newcomb's studies of 1943 has demonstrated that *'reference'* is crucially important. That is, identification with others. It is important since it provides the basis for the regulation, sustenance, and development of behaviour and beliefs.

An illustration of Maass and Clark's findings which relates to social etiquette in musical performance involves the British string quartet, The Lindsays. This quartet of four men has been together for over 25 years, and is an extremely successful ensemble which has made many recordings of standard and contemporary repertoire, and has established an extensive international performing career. Yet, these men do not wear dinner jackets and bow ties. Rather, they wear colourful silk shirts and casual trousers. Nor do they simply acknowledge their audiences through sequences of bows and nods: they can often be seen during concerts chatting informally with their audiences, or exchanging comments to one another between pieces. The Lindsays have a resident venue in The Studio at The Crucible Theatre in Sheffield, UK. They perform in a space which places the audience all around the performers, and in very close physical proximity. Arguably, the high musical reputation of The Lindsays and the unusual venue in which they regularly perform have enabled them to move against the mainstream position on dress code and stage behaviour. Additionally, The Lindsays have a very strong local following in Sheffield, and therefore their position is not under threat: they can afford to manipulate some boundaries, knowing that they have loyal supporters. In fact, the boundaries The Lindsays are shifting fall within the larger societal movement towards increasing informality in formal social settings.

So far, it has been demonstrated that sociocultural and social norm behaviours have a profound and vital role in both the production and perception of a musical performance. Interpersonal relations are also very important.

PRESENCE OF OTHERS

Teachers and 'key' supporters

Perhaps one of the most significant social relationships in music is that between teacher and pupil. The historical impact of teachers has already been explored, but recent empirical research (cf. Chapter 10) has shown that the relationship between teacher and pupil in the music lesson is a particularly interesting social phenomenon, for unlike many other forms of learning which tend to occur in groups, in musical instrument learning the teacher and pupil most often work in one-to-one settings. This means that the personal relationship is an important factor in the learning process. In Chapter 10, it is shown that a good personal relationship (characterized by the pupils as a feeling of 'warmth') seems to be a critical variable in performer success, at least in the initial stages of learning.

McDonald (1992) has demonstrated that 'warmth' is most typically found in familial relationships where there is affection and intimacy. Therefore, it appears that successful young pupils form familial-type bonds with their teachers in the initial period of learning. These personal bonds develop over time, and the pupil also begins to recognize what may be considered the professional characteristics of the teacher (the ability to play well, teach well, etc.). It is evident that the successful learner holds both these personal and professional characteristics in high esteem. For the unsuccessful learner, this separation of personal and professional characteristics does not occur. Research by Rosenthal and Jacobsen (1968) and Blatchford *et al.* (1989) demonstrates that the teacher–pupil relationship is highly interactive, e.g. a teacher with high expectations is more likely to elicit high achievements from his/her pupils than a teacher with low expectations. This would suggest that pupils do not form opinions about their teachers' characteristics in isolation. It could be, for instance, that the child who is unsuccessful in music never has professional characteristics highlighted and demonstrated as being of value. (Further details about the nature of pupil–teacher interactions can be found in Chapter 15.)

So, it appears that in formal learning contexts, musical skill acquisition is a collaborative act between teacher and pupil. Teachers are not the only people with whom the learner interacts. Parents, siblings, peers, professional performers all, as Chapter 10 demonstrates, contribute in significant ways to motivating practice, learning, and general engagement in musical activity. Therefore, it appears that learning is a collaborative, social achievement between the learner and key others. Clearly, many technical skills and expressive values are imparted in positive music learning situations, whether they are with a teacher or more informally with friends (more details can be found in the account of performance skills made in Chapter 10), but there are many other elements of music-making besides the skill acquisition process which are shaped by interactions with others.

Social facilitation

Musicians recount euphoric, positive experiences with regard to public performance. For instance, it is known that the famous tenor, Caruso, said he could only achieve the correct mental state in order to sing his top Cs convincingly when he was in the presence of an audience. Psychological research from the nineteenth century confirms this anecdotal reporting. For instance, Triplett, in 1897, recorded that racing cyclists achieved higher times when they were racing against each other rather than when they raced against the clock. Many experiments have demonstrated the facilitating effects of co-action on human performance, although the mere presence of others is not necessarily facilitating. Cottrell's (1972) 'learned evaluation hypothesis' provides an account representative of the current belief on social facilitation. It suggests that facilitation occurs only when other people are positively appraised. If the other people are negatively appraised, the effects on performance can be quite destructive. This cognitive appraisal of co-performers or audiences can have direct effects on levels of physiological arousal. Increased heart-rate, with associated increase in oxygen supplies, and the sharpening of the visual system can all enhance musical performance as breathing and attention can be heightened. This is often referred to as optimal arousal. However, when the appraisal is negative, arousal levels can increase so dramatically that palpitations, body tremors, breathlessness, visual disturbances, and sweatiness result which can severely impair performance. Alternatively, arousal levels may not increase at all, so that physiological arousal does not occur and the performance can be lethargic.

The task itself has an impact on performance. If the task is well-learned, and the other people are appraised to be moderately evaluative, the performer's response is most likely to be enhancement of the performance. If, however, the task is novel or under-learned, the performer's dominant response is likely to be impairment (Hinde 1987).

In musical performance contexts, the debilitating impact of negative audience appraisal is commonly discussed (see Chapter 12), although the fact that audiences can elicit positive effects is often overlooked. Conversely, it is recognized that trusted co-performers can help to reduce anxiety levels —'a trouble shared is a trouble halved'—but, the negative influences of co-performers are often forgotten. The essence of social facilitation theory is that 'others' have the potential to elicit positive and negative responses, depending upon how they are appraised. But, in addition to the critical variable of appraisal, it appears that the number of audience members or co-performers can have a direct impact on arousal levels: fewer people typically elicit less arousal.

As this chapter unfurls, it is increasingly apparent that many social factors contribute to the performance. Although the section above has dealt explicitly with performance contexts, it is equally possible to see how social facilitation will operate in music lessons, and in the home when the developing musician is practising in front of family members. Strongly related to the facilitation effects is the role individuals play when in the presence of others. In musical contexts, these roles are strongly related to group function.

Group function

Earlier in the chapter it was established that a variety of sociocultural factors determine the emergence of different performance groups (soloist and accompanist, piano trio, the chamber orchestra, etc.). For the purposes of contrast, only two groups will be considered here: the string quartet and the symphony orchestra.

The string quartet

In general social psychological research, Douglas (1993) showed that in order for any group to function, the members need to have a sense of 'affiliation'. That is, there needs to be a connection or association between individuals. In string quartets, it is obvious that the players have a common connection to the musical score, and this suggests that at one level there is a cohesive group. Certainly, all four instrumentalists contribute similar musical elements to the performance, and all use essentially comparable instrumental techniques. It is well known that string quartets can function extremely well, with ensembles like The Lindsays (mentioned earlier in the chapter) working together for longer than 25 years on a day-to-day basis. However, as Young and Colman (1979) point out, interdependence is necessary in order for a coherent musical whole to be produced, and it seems that such closeness depends on trust and respect of each individual's boundaries. In these terms, it is possible to see a huge problem facing string quartets: namely, that musical interpretation is highly personal and differences in taste can often seem so individualized that conflicts of opinion are bound to give rise to disagreement.

How can four individuals function as one unit? Research by Murningham and Conlon (1991) on successful and failing British string quartets showed that in successful groups, although there were personal differences of opinion, recognition and negotiation of the need for compromise appeared to permit players to overcome conflict. Instead, for instance, of continuing a conflictual discussion, the quartet members often adopted a time-out strategy, with individuals leaving the discussion until another time. In fact, there was rather more emphasis on making music than talking, whereas in the unsuccessful quartets, discussion would often overtake the music-making.

Also, it was apparent that the successful quartet members had well established rules including what could and what could not be discussed; and if conflict did not disappear, one interpretation of a musical work was presented in one performance, and another interpretation in another. The result was that inevitably, on the basis of the experience of the performance, one interpretation was eventually selected. The successful quartets with established ground rules, Murningham and Conlon hypothesized, were able to perceive conflict as being a positive and healthy part of their working process. For the unsuccessful quartets, conflict was perceived as being highly destructive.

Leadership was another key issue which had a direct impact on successful group function. Murningham and Conlon found that, in the majority of cases, the first violinists were the leaders of the quartets in both administrative and performance decision-making capacities. In the most successful quartets, the first violinists tended to be both directive and democratic, flexibly using these strategies as they perceived them to be relevant to a particular situation. In the unsuccessful groups, leaders would often feign a democratic approach to the other group members, but ultimately, would control decision-making. These strategies are directly reflective of the general research literature on leadership which suggest that leaders need to acknowledge individual needs within a group by allowing each member the opportunity to express his or her ideas, yet to be unambiguous and assertive in their instructions to the group members (Wilke and Van Knippenberg 1988).

Within the string quartet, Murningham and Conlon (1991) discovered that the individual member of the quartet who needed to be regarded with the utmost respect in order to secure good group function was the second violinist. This was partially because the violin scoring in quartet writing leaves the second violinist in a continually supporting role: for the second violinist to perceive him or herself as an equal musical contributor to the group, it is necessary for the other quartet members to demonstrate that they value the opinions and playing of their second violinist. Indeed, in the successful groups, Murningham and Conlon discovered that the second violinists were often highly complimented by the other group members, and were generally contented in their positions. In the unsuccessful groups, there was generally far less understanding or concern for the second violinist's position. In summary, it appears that particular roles and styles of inter-action are required in order for a string quartet to function successfully.

The orchestra

A small number of studies have examined orchestras as social units (cf. Faulkner 1973; Atik 1992, 1994, 1995; and Allmendinger *et al.* 1994). Research findings reveal that in order to create a sense of ensemble, group members need to be able to meet the challenges of the tasks (that is, they need to be capable and skilled); individual activity needs to be directed towards achieving group goals; and the leader's role must be perceived as being facilitative (Forsyth 1983). Since between 50–100 people make up an orches-tra, with section leaders and a conductor, it is evident that complex and subtle interactions are required in order that these three key elements of ensemble functioning can be successfully achieved.

One would assume that meeting the challenges of the task should be the least of the problems facing a professional orchestra in which players are selected for their high levels of musical skill. However, as Allmendinger *et al.* (1994) discovered, recognition of an individual's performance skills is a vital part of motivating an individual towards feeling part of the group. Therefore, contented orchestral members tend to be those who feel that they are valued, and more importantly, have sufficient time to prepare their repertoire, as well as to sustain and develop their playing technique.

The orchestra is divided into sections, each section having a leader. This leader, like any, needs to be both directive and democratic. For instance, in string sections, the leader usually indicates the bow markings. However, the leader needs to be open to the possibility of accepting alternative markings from other violinists so that, pragmatically, the best possible result can be achieved and the individual making the alternative suggestion feels that he or she is contributing to the section. The possibility for every in-dividual to be heard seems vital for empowerment and motivational reasons (Allmendinger *et al.* 1994). As Brown (1986) reveals, a careful balance between individual needs and group needs is required. This balance needs to be placed within a rule-based context. Indeed, rather like the boundaries on the second violinist in the quartet, there needs to be some acceptance of the role an individual has within a group.

The respect for, and understanding of, membership roles are highly per-tinent issues in whole orchestra contexts when a conductor—the person who occupies the top of the group hierarchy and acts as the overall coordinator of timing and expression—is present. In the rehearsal context, the conductor usually refers comments to the members of a section as a whole. Specific issues emerging from such comments are often dealt with by the section leader. Therefore, a clear hierarchy is in operation. If someone from the back desk of the second violins suddenly were to express a highly personal agenda in front of the whole orchestra, the other players and the conductor would perceive the expression as inappropriate to the context, and even an abuse of position.

Of course, these issues are complex. There is one notorious section of film footage in which Leonard Bernstein, conducting a rehearsal, gets into a head-to-head conflict with a trumpeter. In front of the whole orchestra, the trumpeter is asked to repeat a section Bernstein feels is inaccurate. After several repetitions, Bernstein's annoyance is extreme—he shouts at the player—and the player, who is obviously humiliated by the potential weakness in his own playing and infuriated by Bernstein's manner, shouts back in retaliation. There is deadlock. The trumpeter exerts his independence because he has not been treated with civility, and so his position within the hierarchy of the group and the boundaries of it is broken. Self-preservation becomes more important than group function.

Conductors frequently join orchestras for no more than a couple of rehearsals and a single performance. This means that conductors continually face situations in which they must legitimize their position of authority. Atik (1994) notes that two processes are critical to the successful legitimation of the conductor's position: a phase in which trust and respect between the orchestral members and conductor are tested, and the negotiation of a mutually acceptable set of expectations. In the case of Leonard Bernstein and the trumpeter, it appears that neither of these processes were successfully achieved. Atik emphasizes that mutual efforts in conductor and orchestral member interactions are required, and although he acknowledges that some conductors are rather more charismatic or inspirational than others, he notes that a flexible conducting style seems crucial to the creation of an orchestral whole. Like the quartet, it appears that for the orchestra there is a number of distinctive dynamic factors which facilitate orchestral group function.

The audience

Audiences, although largely comprised of individuals coming together for a single performance and therefore having no former knowledge of one another, also function as a group. Although there is no existing research on music audiences, work on crowd behaviour shows that there is a tendency for unified behaviour to emerge (Diener 1979; Zimbardo 1970). The state of psychological de-individuation which seems to occur can lead to both pro- and anti-social behaviour. A recent example is the rioting which broke out in Los Angeles when police were cleared of having assaulted Rodney King, though video footage shown on national TV had shown the police brutally assaulting King.

In Western art music performances, generally speaking, the audience group function seems to be one which confines itself to absolute social conformity. As Cook (1990) points out, group disapproval is directed at audience members who, for example, applaud at the end of a movement of a concerto, rather than waiting until the end of the work. However, on rare occasions, audiences can become unruly. Consider, for example, the famous rioting which occurred during the first performance of Stravinsky's *Rite of Spring*. In this case, it seems that the audience were presented with music that was beyond their cultural expectation and understanding of art music.

Effective communication

Research by Yarbrough (1975), Davidson (1993, 1994, 1995) and Durrant (1994) demonstrates that within musical performance contexts there are distinctive verbal and non-verbal skills which enable the communication and coordination of musical ideas.

Performers

Good verbal and non-verbal communications between co-performers during the rehearsal period are essential in order to produce an agreed style of interpretation. In actual performance, communications are equally important, although in this context, non-verbal communications dominate, as the players are unable to stop and discuss matters. There is a substantive literature which demonstrates that expert musicians rehearse and consolidate their ideas to such a high degree that in the performance situation very similar overall timing profiles occur, even when performances may be months apart (e.g. Shaffer 1984). However, some features of the musical score can be more or less emphasized depending on moment-by-moment and quite spontaneous modifications to the interpretation (Sloboda 1985). So, it appears that rehearsals are occasions to learn the score and plan the coordination of timing, as well as to establish general expressive features of the music. In the live performance situation, the variations which occur spontaneously are critically dependent on the co-performers being able to detect and act immediately upon one another's ideas. In performance from a score, these spontaneous variations tend to be connected with the interpretative features of the music, but where the performance is memorized, slips may occur, during which co-performers may have to make moment-by-moment adjustments to accommodate the loss of memory.

Murningham and Conlon's (1991) research demonstrated that string quartets used discussion during rehearsals, but as was noted above, the most successful quartets tended not to speak, but rather picked up information from one another when playing. Investigating small group ensembles,

Clayton (1985) discovered that physical proximity has a crucial role to play in the coordination of the music, visual and aural cues being of paramount importance. Indeed, when performers could not see one another, their performances were less coordinated in terms of both timing and dynamics. Yarbrough (1975) has shown that co-performer interactions are successful when there are high levels of eye contact and use of facial expressions, particularly expressions of approval and disapproval. This suggests that mutual encouragement and support are of importance in the performance context. Where a conductor is present, Durrant (1994) notes that an ineffective conductor is one who most frequently attempts to communicate his or her intention through discussion, whereas the successful conductor uses far more body movement than speech to communicate her or his ideas.

Body movements both accompany language and occur independently of it. Ekman and Friesen (1969) identify four specific categories: adaptors, regulators, illustrators, and emblems. The first of these are not speech-related and are concerned with self-stimulation, e.g. nose-picking, scratching, etc. Regulators are movements which systematize the back and forth nature of speaking and listening in conversations. For instance, a hand movement can be used to interrupt someone's speech, whilst the cessation of hand movements can cue speech closure and therefore indicate that another person can take over the role of talker. Illustrators punctuate speech and trace ideas, e.g. making a cradling gesture when talking about an infant. Emblems are non-verbal symbols with direct speech translators, e.g. a 'thumbs up' symbolizing a positive or good response.

Conducting in musical contexts clearly uses illustrators and emblems. Illustrators are often self-explanatory gestures of emphasis; for example, a hand turned upward with open palm and fingers is moved in an exaggerated shaking movement to indicate force and power. Emblems vary enormously in conducting, however: some are frequently used in everyday speech and body movement whilst others are far more abstract. Therefore, a conductor may need to introduce some emblems over a period of time for the meaning to become apparent. In a comprehensive survey of conductor practices, Durrant (1994) notes that the best rehearsals are often concerned with getting participants to develop their sensitivities to the conductor's movements. In educational research, Decker and Kirk (1988) have categorized and then specified movements conductors should use in terms of effectiveness, and Davidson (1991) has shown that movement repertoires are used for specific expressive ends. It appears that in music performance there is a complex, non-verbal 'vocabulary' which permits the transference of much information between co-performers. Emblems and illustrators are used between all types of co-performers, not just conductors and followers. For example, the downward nod of the cellist in a quartet may signify that the phrase beings 'now'.

Besides communicating information about the coordination of timing, expressive ideas (e.g. playing louder here, or softer there), and personal support (e.g. an emblem signifying 'yes, that's great') between co-performers, recent research by Davidson (1993, 1994, 1995) has shown that specific movements reveal much about the performer's expressive interpretation of the musical structure. For example, in a performance of one of Beethoven's bagatelles for piano, a pianist used highly distinctive head-shaking movements consistently whenever he played a cadence, and a wiggle movement of the upper torso as he played ornaments. These movements were found to be absolutely integral to the production of the music. Indeed, when pianists in a specifically controlled situation (learning a piece of a two octave range which did not require any shifts in body position from the normal upright sitting position) were prevented from moving their torsos during sight-reading, learning, and performance, the final performances were far less musically expressive than those where the performers had been allowed to use their torsos freely (Davidson and Dawson 1995). Davidson (1993) has shown that these specific gestures are of salience to onlookers. For co-performers this may mean that physical expressions of musical structure provide a means of understanding and sharing musical intentions. But Davidson's research focused specifically on audience perceptions, and demonstrated that performers' movements were important to the audience's perception of the music.

The audience

Davidson (1991) asked individual observers of a video recording of solo pianists to identify whenever they saw a moment within each performance that was of expressive salience, that is, in which the movements provided specific information. It was discovered that there were many specific moments which: (i) had specific movement forms (expressive gestures); and (ii) were of structural importance (phrase boundaries, phrase peaks, left-hand rests, etc.). Therefore, it appears that the body movements of the performers inform the audience about their musical intention. But perhaps most significantly, Davidson (1995) discovered that when a performer gave three performances of the same piece of music, each with a different expressive intention (to play with an exaggerated, understated, or normal manner), the differences could be clearly detected from the performer's movements alone.

Of course, there is a substantive literature (cf. Sloboda 1983; Clark 1989) which shows that experienced listeners are able to detect many subtle expressive changes in timing and dynamics, and thus perceive the performer's intention from musical sound alone. However, Davidson (1995) discovered that while it was possible for experienced musicians to discriminate between three different performance interpretations from sound only, non-musicians relied almost entirely on visual information for their judgements of the performer's intentions. This suggests that in a live or video performance viewing, audiences can enhance their understanding of a musical performance by observing the performer's movements. However, in an aural recording, unless listeners are highly skilled, some of the performance intention may be lost.

Delalande (1990) explores the link between audience perception and the performer's use of his or her body in an interesting consideration of the performing career of the pianist, Glenn Gould. Gould's professional career fell into two distinct phases: an early period during which he gave concert tours as well as making sound recordings, and a later period when all his music-making was constrained to the recording studio. Both live and studio settings can be regarded as essentially social contexts, for even in the studio recording, there is an intended general listening audience, and there are always a number of technicians and sound engineers present during the studio sessions. However, in Gould's case video footage from both phases of his career reveal such differences in the use of the body that it must be assumed that the presence of a live audience had some role in shaping the types of movements used. Delalande discovered that in live performances, Gould's movements had a degree of unpredictability, but great fluency. In the recording studio, the movements were far more repetitive and fixed. It is feasible that in the earlier performances, Gould was using movements which had a direct communicative intention for the audience: literally demonstrating his ideas to the audience. In the latter performances, Gould was not perhaps so directly motivated to communicate socially with the audience, only to express the musical structure. This is only one possible interpretation of Gould's performance, but nevertheless raises interesting issues about the critical role the performer–audience interaction has in shaping the performance.

Of course, to come full circle and reconsider the role of historical influences on the performance, it is evident that bodily communication is just as subject to sociocultural influences as is the interpretation of musical style, as the writings of Schumann and Glinka (in Morgenstern 1956) and Gellrich (1991) attest. Schumann describes a performance given by Liszt:

Within a few seconds tenderness, boldness, exquisiteness, wildness succeed one another; the instrument glows and flashes under the master's hands ... he must be heard and seen; for if Liszt played behind a screen, a great deal of poetry would be lost (excerpt from R. Schumann, *On music and musicians*, quoted by Morgenstern 1956, p. 155).

Here the effectiveness of the non-verbal communication is apparent. However, as Glinka (from O. Fouque's *Glinka, d'après ses mémoires et sa correspondances*, and quoted by Morgenstern 1956, p. 129) revealed by referring to Liszt as an 'exaggerator of nuance', even in the nineteenth century, Liszt's performances did not suit everyone's taste. Gellrich (1991) casts further light on this issue by suggesting that all musicians use gestures which to some extent have been learned by watching others (teachers, performers, etc.), and which are certainly influenced by the dominant cultural aesthetic. This might mean that a performance given by Liszt today would employ bodily gestures completely inappropriate to late twentieth century tastes.

Communication is a two-way process; performers are just as likely to pick up information from the audience as audiences are likely to pick up information from the performer. Not only do general behaviours like applause provide the performer with feedback about their performance, but moment-by-moment, smiles, frowns, laughs, coughs, etc. can all have an effect on the performer (Wilson 1994).

SUMMARIZING THE ROLE OF THE SOCIAL IN MUSICAL PERFORMANCE

This chapter has focused on a number of social factors which seem to be crucial to the construction and execution of a musical performance. The areas explored are by no means comprehensive, as inevitably there will be gaps in any piece of writing attempting to define a topic. However, it is hoped that the ideas explored here will provide a grounding for further study of this vital aspect of music which has been sadly neglected. Figure 11.1 shows a model which attempts to encapsulate the social influences which act on the performance of music. The various levels of social influence and interaction can be traced in the concluding section of this chapter, which is a description of an excerpt from a performance given by the author.

With heartbeat pounding in my ears, I step onto a vast stage of over 300 performers. The audience applauds generously. I follow the chamber orchestra conductor, tenor, and baritone soloists, and am pursued by the conductor of the main orchestra and chorus, and the chorus master of the cathedral choristers. As we all reach centre stage, a tightly packed line is formed, and taking the lead from a pre-planned discussion, the tenor directs us in a near synchronous bow. As my head dips, I see my family sitting in the auditorium where I had asked them to be, about 10 rows back. As my head rises, I notice several friends. One person stands out in particular, a singer, who gives me a 'thumbs up'. I smile in response. As my eyes dart across the sea of faces, I notice one friend on the very back row craning his neck to see over the 600 heads in front of him. I think: I wonder what is he going to make of Britten's War Requiem? Bow completed, I turn and stride to my seat among the first violins. As I reach my chair, the leader and her companion at the first desk beam at me. I smile in

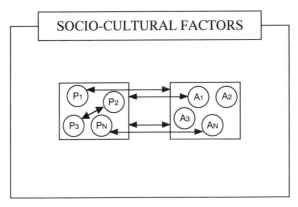

Fig 11.1 A model showing the social elements of musical performance. Embedded within the overriding sociocultural factors (historical music practices and social etiquette) are the moment-by-moment interactions between performer (P1–PN) and audience (A1–AN), inter-performer (P1–P2–P3 etc.), and inter-audience (A1–A2–A3 etc.). Note that these interactions occur at individual (A1–P1), group, and a combination of individual and group levels.

response, and raise my eyebrows in a shrug to intimate: 'here goes!' The leader is shaking her fingers, suggesting that the tips are cold. Mid shake, she points to the floor, indicating where a glass of water has been left for me. As I sit, I snatch up the glass and take a nervous swig. I peer across the vast expanse of cellos and double basses to my left, over to the chamber orchestra hoping for a glimpse of my singer colleagues, but they have vanished from view. The chamber orchestra conductor, at his podium, seems to be smiling at each of his players in turn. The applause ceases. I look to the main conductor who is less than four feet in front of me. He is adjusting his music: full score and vocal score are precariously balanced next to one another. I look down onto my lap and thumb through the score to my entry. I look intently at the first interval of my solo; inwardly, sing this rising fifth several times. I wonder how Britten asked Galina Vishnevskaya to prepare the part. I recall how she sang these lines on the original recording, and I quickly play through Heather Harper's version in my mind. After several seconds, the audience is completely silent, and I look up to see the conductor raise his baton. There is a momentary pause, and then a sweeping gesture of his arms, head, and eyes seems to embrace all 300 performers. A decisive downward stroke of the baton cuts the hush of the audience, heralding the low menace of the opening orchestral figure.

During the first 20 minutes of the piece as I await my entry I follow the score, attempting to focus on different musical nuances and inflections. Simultaneously, I notice my heart-rate slow and I focus on the conductor's breathing pattern, and notice the sweat dripping from his forehead. Occasionally, I glimpse at my two violinist friends and see their bodies gently sway during sections when they are playing, and notice their stillness and focus during sections where they are counting and waiting for their entries. With the performance underway, I cannot easily turn to look at the other soloists or the chorus without drawing audience attention to me, but I can hear them rise, sing, and sit. I realize that I did not see the chorus as I came on stage—how could I have missed 200 faces? I can see the front row of the audience very clearly: one person is following the score; another has his eyes closed, with face turned towards the ceiling; and a third person sits with a handkerchief clasped to her nose and mouth, and frequently stifles her coughs and sneezes. The 20 minutes melt away. Having been fairly calm through the opening of the work, my heart really starts racing as the baritone and chamber orchestra perform *Bugles Sang*. I sip my water and think to myself: 'Well, you cannot get out of this now, so you had better give of your best!' The baritone finishes, and I stand to sing. The main conductor keeps his head down fixed to the score. I keep my eyes fixed on him. He raises his arms and eyes to the orchestra and me and brings us in together on the rising fifth. After the first phrase, I have a bar's rest, so I use the opportunity to follow my singing teacher's advice to take a deep breath at this point, so I consciously feel my back expand, and keep my shoulders low and relaxed. Having established my contact with the conductor and orchestra, it is my intention to deliver the second phrase directly to the audience. I do this by tilting my body slightly forwards and by looking into the auditorium at my strategically placed family. By the time I sing the octave leaping A in the fifth phrase, I feel full of energy and buoyancy. I can hear my voice soaring over the chorus and orchestra. I can see the audience, and know that each person is listening to me. I sense concentrated energy exuding from everyone in the hall. This is a thrilling few minutes. As I finish the section, the conductor gives me a generous wink, and I sink into my seat. My heart is still racing, but with joy, not anxiety.

REFERENCES

Allmendinger, J., Hackman, J. R., and Lehman, E. V. (1994). *Life and work in symphony orchestras: an interim report of research findings*. Report No. 7, Cross-National Study of Symphony Orchestras, pp. 95–107.

Asch, S. E. (1955). Opinions and social pressures. *Scientific American*, **193**, 31–5.

Asch, S. E. (1958). Effects of groups pressure upon modification and distortion of judgements. In *Readings in psychology* (ed. E. E. Maccoby, T. M. Newcomb, and E. L. Hartley). Holt, Rinehart, and Winston, New York.

Atik, Y. (1992). *The conductor and the orchestra: A study in leadership, culture, and authority*. Unpublished masters dissertation. University of Manchester Institute of Science and Technology.

Atik, Y. (1994). The conductor and the orchestra: interactive aspects of the leadership process. *Leadership and Organization Development Journal*, **13**, 22–8.

Atik, Y. (1995). People factors in the performing arts. *Performing Arts Medicine News*, **3**, 7–12.

Blatchford, P., Burke, J., Farquhar, C., Plewis, I., and Tizard, B. (1989). Teacher expectations in infant school: associations with attainment and progress, curriculum coverage and classroom interaction. *British Journal of Educational Psychology*, **59**, 19–30.

Brown, R. (1986). *Social psychology*. Free Press, New York.

Clarke, E. F. (1989). The perception of expressive timing in music. *Psychological Research*, **51**, 2–9.

Clarke, E. F. and Davidson, J. W. (submitted for publication). *The body in music as mediator between knowledge and action*.

Clayton, A. M. H. (1985). *Coordination between players in musical performance*. Unpublished doctoral dissertation, University of Edinburgh.

Cook, N. (1990). *Music, imagination, and culture*. Oxford University Press, Oxford.

Cottrell, N. B. (1972). Social facilitation. In *Experimental social psychology* (ed. C. G. McClintock). Holt, Rinehart, and Winston, New York.

Davidson, J. W. (1991). *The perception of expressive movement in music performance*. Unpublished doctoral dissertation. City University, London.

Davidson, J. W. (1993). Visual perception of performance manner in the movements of solo musicians. *Psychology of Music*, **21**, 103–13.

Davidson, J. W. (1994). What type of information is conveyed in the body movements of solo musician performers? *Journal of Human Movement Studies*, **6**, 279–301.

Davidson, J. W. (1995). What does the visual information contained in music performances offer the observer? Some preliminary thoughts. In *The music machine: psychophysiology and psychopathology of the sense of music* (ed. R. Steinberg). Springer Verlag, Berlin.

Davidson, J. W. and Dawson, J. C. (1995). *The development of expression in body movement during learning in piano performance*. Paper presented at Society for Music Perception and Cognition Conference, University of California, Berkeley.

Decker, H. and Kirk, C. (1988). *Choral conducting: focus on communication*. Prentice Hall, New Jersey.

Delalande, F. (1990). *Human movement and the interpretation of music*. Paper presented at the Second International Colloquium on the Psychology of Music, Ravello, Italy.

Diener, E. (1979). Deindividuation, self-awareness, and disinhibition. *Journal of Personality and Social Psychology*, **37**, 1160–71.

Douglas, T. A. (1993). *Theory of groupwork practice*. Macmillan, London.

Durrant, C. (1994). Towards an effective communication: a case for structured teaching of conducting. *British Journal of Music Education*, **11**, 56–76.

Ekman, P. and Friesen, W. V. (1969). The repertoire of non-verbal behaviour: categories, origins, usage, and coding. *Semiotica*, **1**, 49–98.

Farnsworth, P. R. (1954). The social psychology of music. Iowa State University Press, Ames, Iowa.

Faulkner, R. R. (1973). Orchestra interaction: some features of communication and authority in an artistic organization. *The Sociological Quarterly*, **14**, 147–57.

Forsyth, D. (1983). *An introduction to group dynamics*. Brooks/Cole, California.

Gellrich, M. (1991). Concentration and tension. *British Journal of Music Education*, **8**, 167–79.

Hinde, R. A. (1987). *Individuals, relationships, and culture*. Cambridge University Press, Cambridge.

Lawson, C. J. (1995). *The Cambridge companion to the clarinet*. Cambridge University Press, Cambridge.

Maass, A. and Clark, R. D. (1983). Internalization versus compliance: Differential processes underlying minority influence and conformity. *European Journal of Social Psychology*, **13**, 45–55.

Maass, A. and Clark, R. D. (1984). Hidden impact of minorities: fifteen years of minority influence research. *Psychological Bulletin*, **95**, 428–50.

McDonald, K. (1992). Warmth as a developmental construct: an evolutionary analysis. *Child Development*, **63**, 753–73.

Morgenstern, S. (1956). *Composers on music*. Faber and Faber, London.

Murningham, J. K. and Conlon, D. E. (1991). The dynamics of intense work groups: a study of British string quartets. *Administrative Science Quarterly*, June, 165–86.

Rosenthal, R. and Jacobson, L. (1968). *Pygmalion in the classroom*. Holt, Rinehart, and Winston, New York.

Shaffer, L. H. (1984). Timing in solo and duet piano performances. *Quarterly Journal of Experimental Psychology*, **36**(A), 577–95.

Sloboda, J. A. (1983). The communication of musical metre in piano performance. *Quarterly Journal of Experimental Psychology*, **35**(A), 377–96.

Sloboda, J. A. (1985). *The musical mind*. Oxford University Press, Oxford.

Yarbrough, C. (1975). Effect of magnitude of conductor behaviour on students in mixed choruses. *Journal of Research in Music Education*, **23**, 134–46.

Young, V. M. and Colman, A. M. (1979). Some psychological processes in string quartets. *Psychology of Music*, **7**, 12–16.

Wilke, H. and van Knippenberg, A. (1988). Group performance. In: *Introduction to social psychology* (ed. R. Brown). Basil Blackwell, Oxford.

Wilson, G. D. (1994). *Psychology for performing artists*. Jessica Kingsley, London.

Zimbardo, P. G. (1970). The human choice: Individuation, reason, and order versus deindividuation, impulse, and chaos. In W. J. Arnold and D. Levine (eds.) *Nebraska symposium on motivation*, Vol. 16. University of Nebraska Press, Lincoln.

12 | *Performance anxiety*

Glenn D. Wilson

Performance anxiety, popularly known as 'stage fright', is the exaggerated and sometimes incapacitating fear of performing in public. It is not restricted to the inexperienced amateur but has been known to afflict some of the most famous performers in history, including Laurence Olivier, Richard Burton, David Niven, and Sergei Rachmaninov (Aaron 1986). There may be differences in the reasons: with the beginning performer, stage fright is likely to be connected with shyness and uncertainty about one's ability (or even the recognition at some level of consciousness or unconsciousness that one is not really talented enough for the job at hand). With the established professional it may take the form of 'burn-out' similar to that experienced by sports stars like Björn Borg—the feeling that once on a pedestal there is nothing left but to be knocked off it again, and that only a disaster would be newsworthy. Some older actors also become frightened of memory loss, perhaps connected with alcoholism as well as age, and ageing instrumental players worry increasingly about tremor, just as singers are concerned about vocal steadiness.

SYMPTOMS

Whatever the precise causes, the symptoms of stage fright are much the same as those of any other phobia or fear reaction—intense activation of the sympathetic branch of the autonomic nervous system (the 'flight–fight emergency reaction'). Many of the symptoms which cause impairment to musical performance can be understood as after-effects of some adaptive bodily function (Williams and Hargreaves 1994). For example:

(1) the heart pumps harder to supply oxygen to the muscles (resulting in palpitations);
(2) the liver releases stored energy (producing a feeling of 'edginess');
(3) the lungs work harder and airways widen (breathlessness);
(4) the stomach and gut shuts down so that energy is diverted to the muscles ('butterflies' and nausea);
(5) body fluids such as saliva are redirected into the bloodstream (dry mouth and difficulty in swallowing);

(6) there is a sharpening of vision (visual disturbances, e.g. blurring);
(7) the skin sweats to cool the working muscles (sweaty palms and forehead);
(8) calcium is discharged from tense muscles ('pins and needles').

These reactions would have some degree of survival value if the task was to fight a rival or flee from a sabre-toothed tiger. Unfortunately, human pride is such a powerful motive that the fear of public humiliation or disgrace often produces the same degree of emotional panic and this may be counter-productive to a finely-tuned vocal or instrumental performance.

PREVALENCE

Wesner *et al.* (1990) distributed a questionnaire concerning experiences of performance anxiety to all students and faculties at the University of Iowa School of Music, obtaining responses from a sample of 302. Not surprisingly, auditions and solo performances were the situations rated as most anxiety-evoking. Distress due to anxiety was common within the group, 21 per cent reporting 'marked distress' and another 40 per cent reporting 'moderate distress'. 'Marked impairment' of performance due to anxiety was reported by 17 per cent of the sample and 'moderate impairment' by another 30 per cent. Of those reporting impairment, the most troublesome symptoms, in order, were: poor concentration (63 per cent), rapid heart rate (57 per cent), trembling (46 per cent), dry mouth (43 per cent), sweating (43 per cent) and shortness of breath (40 per cent). Flushing, quavering voice, nausea, and dizziness were less frequently reported symptoms. Nine per cent admitted that they often avoided performance opportunities because of anxiety and 13 per cent said that they had interrupted a performance on at least one occasion due to anxiety. Over a third felt that anxiety had at least some adverse effect on their careers and 15 per cent had sought help for an anxiety-related problem.

These figures are not untypical. A survey by the International Conference of Symphony and Opera Musicians (ICSOM) found that 24 per cent of respondents reported performance anxiety as a problem (Fishbein *et al.* 1988). Similar high levels of stage fright have been reported in smaller scale studies (Liden and Gottfries 1974, Steptoe and Fidler 1987). Marchant-Haycox and Wilson (1992) found that, in a comparative study of various groups of performing artists, the highest proportion of performance anxiety sufferers was among the musicians (47 per cent), followed by singers (38 per cent), dancers (35 per cent), and actors (33 per cent). Overall, these figures suggest that stage fright is a very common problem and that it is perhaps especially rife among musicians compared with other types of performer.

INDIVIDUAL DIFFERENCES

Since not all musicians are affected by performance anxiety, it is important to consider the personality and clinical correlates of susceptibility to this problem. Given that stage fright represents a fear of negative evaluation by other people, it is not surprising to find that of all phobias, it is most closely related to *social* phobia (Cox and Kenardy 1993; Steptoe and Fidler 1987). However, performance anxiety also connects with other forms of anxiety and so may be thought of as a component or correlate of general trait anxiety (Cox and Kenardy 1993; Hamann 1982). Since anxiety and phobic reactions generally occur more in women than men, it is also unsurprising that debilitating performance anxiety is more commonly reported by female than male musicians (Wesner *et al.* 1990).

Stage fright has been found to correlate with neuroticism and introversion in actors (Steptoe *et al.* 1995) and musicians (Steptoe and Fidler 1987). In a mixed group of performers, however, neuroticism was found to predict other stress symptoms, such as depression, migraine, and panic, rather than performance anxiety *per se*, while introversion was only related to complaints of shoulder ache (Marchant-Haycox and Wilson 1992).

The Steptoe and Fidler study divided musicians into separate groups of professionals, students, and amateurs, and this revealed some differential relationships. Professionals showed a particularly strong correlation between neuroticism and stage fright (.70) although correlations were also significant for students (.39) and amateurs (.31). For students, there was a high correlation with phobias in general (.48) and fear of social situations in particular (.51), these relationships being much lower within the other two groups. The meaning of these differences is not entirely clear, though it is possible that neuroticism is a constitutional trait that professional musicians may be saddled with for the whole of their career, whereas phobias (which predict stage fright more strongly among students) may be unlearned over time or better coped with in maturity. For professionals only, there was a reduction in stage fright with age (−.35) and experience (−.38). (Of course, the students were more homogeneous in these respects.)

SITUATIONAL FACTORS

It appears that individuals who are generally anxious (neurotic), introverted, and prone to social phobias are more likely to suffer from performance anxiety and that age and experience are less than fully protective. However, there are certain situations that are relatively stressful to performers regardless of their individual susceptibility. Clearly, anything that increases the musician's sense of exposure will raise levels of performance anxiety. This includes solo as against group performance, public performance as against practice, competitive (judged) performances against performances for plea-sure, and performance of difficult or ill-prepared works against those that are easy, familiar, or over-learned (Hamann 1982).

Abel and Larkin (1990) demonstrated the role of evaluation stress in a group of music students (eight males and 14 females) by measuring their heart-rate and blood pressure in the run-up to performance. Compared to preparation for a non-threatening performance, the anticipation of perform-ing to a jury resulted in increases in heart-rate and blood pressure (both systolic and diastolic) as well as higher levels of self-reported anxiety. Cer-tain interesting sex differences also appeared: males showed greater increases in blood pressure but females reported more anxiety feelings. Females, rather paradoxically, reported increased confidence prior to the jury, whereas males did not. The authors attribute these sex differences to gender socialization but it is equally likely that genetic/hormonal factors are responsible. In particular, the male pattern of physiological arousal would seem to prepare for an active response whereas the female reaction may be seen as more concerned with communicating the emotional distress to others.

Brotons (1994) assessed heart-rate and self-reported anxiety in 64 instru-mental and vocal music students during juried (evaluative) and non-juried conditions. Again, the presence of a jury produced increases in both heart-rate and self-reported anxiety, but there was no association between the two measures, suggesting that there may be different types of performance anxiety (e.g. physiological vs cognitive). Sex differences were not examined in this study, which is unfortunate because on the basis of Abel and Larkin's results (above) they may have partly accounted for the separation of physio-logical and self-reported anxiety.

Cox and Kenardy (1993) demonstrated an interaction between social phobia and degree of exposure in determining performance anxiety. Com-paring levels of performance anxiety in students in three situations (practice, group performance, and solo performance), they found that students high on Spielberger's *Trait Anxiety* (STAI-T) measure were more anxious in all conditions. However, when students were classified into those low and high on Turner's *Social Phobia and Anxiety Inventory* (SPAI) those high on social phobia were markedly more anxious in the solo condition. In the practice condition social phobia had no impact upon performance anxiety. Hence social phobia appears to interact more with performance conditions (specifically solo vs group performance) than does trait anxiety, which has a relatively standard effect on performing anxiety across conditions.

Work on the phenomenon of 'social facilitation' (the effect of an audience on behaviour such as work output and sporting prowess) suggests that whereas introverted and anxious individuals are likely to perform worse under scrutiny, extraverts may sometimes perform better. Graydon and Murphy (1995) found such an interaction between extraversion and audience conditions in performance on a table tennis serving task; extraverts were better than introverts when an audience was present but introverts were superior when performing alone. Assuming that something similar might apply to performing arts (e.g. juggling and piano playing) it is clear that situational and personality factors need to be considered together in predicting quality of performance. Presumably, anxious introverts are more likely to be overwhelmed by the pressure of an audience and rendered distractible, whereas extraverts are positively motivated to produce superior performance.

OPTIMAL AROUSAL

There is widespread recognition of the fact that some degree of emotional arousal is beneficial to performance, giving it a certain 'spark' that it might not otherwise have. This is why 'live' broadcasts are usually preferred over those that are pre-recorded. The knowledge that tapes can be edited is likely to reduce tension below the optimum level. It is also clear that the level of tension that is optimal for performance quality as judged by expert audiences is often so high as to be felt as uncomfortable and thought to be detrimental by performers themselves (Hamann 1982; Konijn 1991).

Equally, it is recognized that if tension becomes too great there is ultimately a deterioration of performance quality because concentration is lost, memory blocks occur, and hands or voice lose their steadiness. Hence it is widely agreed that there is an inverted-U shaped relationship between emotional arousal and performance, with low arousal producing 'dull', 'lifeless' performances and over arousal leading to detrimental stress manifestations. This corresponds to a well-known principle in psychology called the Yerkes-Dodson Law (Duffy 1962), which further states that complex tasks show deterioration at lower levels of anxiety than simple tasks.

Wilson (1994) has suggested a three-dimensional extension of the Yerkes-Dodson Law as it applies to musical performance, which integrates three major sources of stress that can very independently:

(1) the *trait anxiety* of the performer—and indeed other relevant personality traits such as introversion and social phobia;
(2) the degree of *task mastery* that has been attained, ranging from simple, well-rehearsed pieces to complex, under-prepared material;
(3) the degree of *situational stress* prevailing, i.e. environmental pressures such as public performance, audition, or competition.

Whether anxiety is beneficial or detrimental to performance depends on the interplay among these three groups of variables (Fig. 12.1).

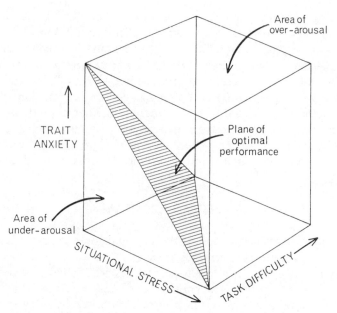

Fig 12.1 A three-dimensional extension of the Yerkes-Dodson Law, in which optimal performance is seen as a function of the interplay among personality-based proneness, task difficulty, and situational stress (Wilson 1994).

Certain practical inferences can be drawn from the model in Fig. 12.1. For example, highly anxious individuals will perform best when the work is easy and the situation relaxed, while performers low in anxiety will perform better when they are more challenged by the work and have a more exacting audience. Performers who are particularly prone to anxiety would be advised to choose easy pieces or works with which they are very familiar, at least for audition purposes or important public occasions. If the choice of work is outside the control of the performer then hard rehearsal may turn a complex, difficult work into a familiar (hence relatively easy) one. Implicit in this is the suggestion that anxious performers should consider whether their stage fright has a rational basis and is telling them something useful. Perhaps they have not rehearsed the work sufficiently and are hence justifiably afraid of mistakes and memory lapses. Perhaps they are out of their depth, insufficiently experienced or lacking the skill or talent to attempt the work in question. Stage fright may represent some form of recognition by the performer, that he or she is ill-prepared for the level of performance expected.

CATASTROPHE THEORY

Hardy and Parfitt (1991) maintain that a 'catastrophe' model is more appropriate than the Yerkes-Dodson Law in accounting for the sudden nature of the deterioration of performance with anxiety. Although they worked with athletic performance, the same arguments apply to stage fright. They argue that once performers do go over the top in arousal the downturn in performance is precipitous rather than the gradual tailing off implied by the inverted-U function. Once disaster is sensed within a high-stress, competitive situation, it is virtually impossible to restore performance even to a mediocre level. Small reductions in stress will not permit the performer to regain his or her previous position at the top of the rainbow curve. According to Hardy and Parfitt, the 'catastrophic' effect applies particularly to circumstances in which *cognitive* anxiety is high as well as somatic agitation. When cognitive anxiety is low, the curve relating performance to arousal may well follow the traditional Yerkes-Dodson pattern. This interaction is illustrated in Fig. 12.2. Certain deductions from it were tested in the context of basketball goal-shooting performance and found to hold true.

Although catastrophe theory originated as a mathematical model it does seem to fit the phenomenon of stage fright in that 'vicious circles' are possible wherein the perception of mistakes or imperfections leads to further increases of anxiety, which in turn increase the likelihood of error, and so on until performance collapses entirely. When musicians are asked what is going on in their head just prior to performance, catastrophizing self-comments (e.g. 'I think I'm going to faint' or 'I'm almost sure to make a dreadful mistake and that will ruin everything') are quite common, particularly in individuals prone to stage fright (Steptoe and Fidler 1987). If musicians high on performance anxiety are inclined to exaggerate the consequences of minor mishaps and fear complete loss of control, there is liable to be an element of self-fulfilling prophecy involved. According to Steptoe and Fidler the most healthy cognitive strategy is that labelled *realistic appraisal*, typified by self-statements such as 'I'm bound to make a few mistakes, but so does everyone' and 'The audience wants me to play well and will make allowance for any slips'. Such statements recognize the likelihood of some blemishes but maintain an optimistic overall picture.

Within Hardy and Parfitt's model (Fig. 12.2) somatic anxiety refers to bodily arousal occurring in preparation for energy expenditure (e.g. increased heart rate) whereas mental anxiety refers to worries about whether the performance will be successful and the social consequences of failure. Clearly, the latter is more likely to lead to a loss of concentration, memory lapses, and a drastic escalation of anxiety (panic). In terms of the three-dimensional model,

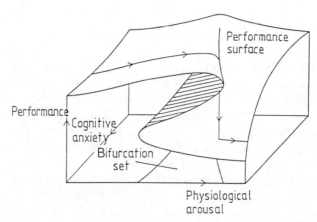

Fig 12.2 A cusp catastrophe model of the relationship between anxiety and performance. In this model, anxiety is split into two separate components, labelled 'cognitive' (referring to mental ruminations and worries) and 'physiological' (bodily manifestations of high arousal). When cognitive anxiety is low, the familiar inverted-U curve of the Yerkes-Dodson Law is observed, but when cognitive anxiety is high there is a drastic collapse of performance once the optimal peak of physiological arousal has been passed (Hardy and Parfitt 1991).

mental anxiety could derive equally from individual proneness (trait anxiety), awareness that a work is complex or under-prepared (task difficulty), or concerns about the consequences of failure (situational stress). Thus Hardy and Parfitt's model is not incompatible with an analysis based on the interaction of three stressor variables; rather it is an elaboration that makes intuitive sense and merits further research. There are no doubt various types of anxiety and arousal and those that involve rumination concerning failure and social embarrassment are more likely to impair stage performance than physical agents which affect bodily arousal, such as coffee and exercise.

THE TIMING OF ANXIETY

Salmon *et al.* (1989) stress the importance of the timing of anxiety peaks in relation to the performance. Following well-known research with parachutists, they suggest that experienced performers learn to let their arousal peak sharply just *before* the performance, whereas less experienced performers suffer anticipatory anxiety which builds over a long period of time and reaches its peak *during* performance itself. This expectation was supported by research in which music students required to play before a jury

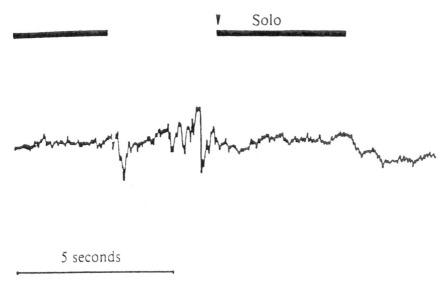

Fig 12.3 The negative shift in brain potential immediately preceding a hornist's solo during an orchestral performance (Haider and Groll-Knapp 1981).

at the end of a semester rated their anxiety at various times leading up to the performance. As expected, there was a progressive build-up of anxiety as the time of the performance approached. However, some students reached their peak of anxiety about an hour before the performance while others were more anxious during the performance itself. Comparison of these two groups revealed that those who peaked during performance were less experienced and more anxious overall than those who peaked beforehand.

As performers gain experience their emotional arousal probably changes in nature as well, with fearfulness giving way to a more adaptive focusing of attention and preparation for action. Figure 12.3 shows an EEG record obtained by telemetry from the motor cortex of an orchestral horn player in the moments just leading up to and during his solo. The graph rises (becoming electrically more negative) to reach a peak just before the solo begins. This pattern, known as 'contingent negative variation', indicates a preparation in the brain for some kind of task performance, a gathering of resources in expectation of having to exercise a skilled behaviour sequence. Performance has been shown to be superior when preceded by these negative shifts in potential (Suter 1986) so they seem to reflect a useful kind of preparation. The changes observed by Salmon *et al.* (1989) may represent not just a shift with experience in the timing of arousal, but a change from diffuse worry toward focused attention.

MANAGEMENT

It has been suggested that performance anxiety is not necessarily a bad thing. Up to a point it facilitates performance and that point is beyond the level considered disadvantageous by performers themselves. Secondly, the anxiety may be transmitting an important message to the performer concerning the wisdom of undertaking the engagement or the need for further preparation. That said, there are certain individuals who suffer destructive anxiety symptoms without good reason, and for them some kind of treatment is necessary.

Drugs

Some performers attempt self-medication with anxiety-reducing drugs such as alcohol, Valium or cannabis. 'Anxiolytic' drugs operate in emotional brain centres such as the amygdala of the limbic system and reduce both the acquisition and expression of conditioned emotional responses. These drugs may get musicians through a performance, but they have side-effects that are detrimental in the long run. Because they are inclined to be general cerebral depressants, impeding all brain processes simultaneously, the 'fine edge' of performance is lost. Furthermore, these drugs diminish judgement and induce a degree of mild euphoria, so the performers themselves are apt to believe they are doing well. Hence they acquire the superstitious habit of doping themselves up with drink or somesuch tranquillizer before each performance. The more they drink the better they feel about their performance, although it is usually getting worse as far as the audience is concerned. When they do try performing sober, they feel even more exposed and anxious than usual and their discomfort reinforces the belief that they are better off on drink. This sets up dependence on the drug. As time goes by, the amount of drink needed to maintain the feeling of well-being increases, performance is further diminished, and memory lapses become a progressive problem. The spiral is insidious, and unless the performer can find a way to break out of it, ultimately destructive to a musical career. Two controlled studies of the effects of anxiolytics on musical performance anxiety have been reported. One (Clark and Agras 1991) found buspirone to be largely ineffective, while the other (James and Savage 1984) found benzodiazepines to interfere with performance.

Much the same criticisms apply to the use of stimulants like amphetamine and cocaine. While they may seem to give energy, euphoria, and inspiration in the short term, they are habit-forming and ultimately destructive to general health (apart from usually being illegal). A cup of coffee may increase alertness, but even excessive amounts of caffeine cause a performer to become jittery, nervous, and suffer from insomnia.

Little information is available concerning how widespread is the use of recreational drugs among performers. Despite the reputation of pop and jazz musicians for drug abuse, Wills and Cooper (1988) report rather modest figures. In their sample, 30 per cent 'sometimes' used cannabis, but only 11 per cent admitted using cocaine, and 4 per cent amphetamines. Very few admitted even trying heroin or LSD, and alcohol consumption was roughly similar to that of the general population.

The only drugs that are prescribed with any degree of frequency for musical performance anxiety are the beta adrenergic blockers, such as nadolol, oxprenolol, and propranolol, which act specifically to inhibit the peripheral manifestations of the flight–fight emergency reaction. The theory is that beta-blockers eliminate the physical (autonomic) symptoms of anxiety that may interfere with performance (e.g. butterflies, palpitations, sweatiness, unsteady hand or voice) while leaving the head clear for optimal performance. They are also supposed to be free of the psychomotor impairment that renders anxiolytics dubious for the purpose. An American survey (Fishbein *et al.* 1988) found that 27 per cent of professional musicians were using beta-blockers under prescription (ostensibly for hypertension, since the Federal Drugs Administration has not approved their use for stage fright) while many others used them occasionally without prescription.

Despite the popularity of beta-blockers, evidence concerning their efficacy is mixed. Controlled clinical trails show that they do reduce heart-rate and tremor, but they have minimal effect on subjective anxiety and do not consistently improve the quality of musical performance as independently judged (Brantigan *et al.* 1979; Clark 1989; James *et al.* 1977; James and Savage 1984; Neftel *et al.* 1982). There is also concern about possible side-effects, including loss of sexual potency, sleep disturbance, baldness, nausea, tiredness, and blunting of affect. In asthmatic people they are particularly dangerous and they occasionally seem to precipitate heart failure. Even though these side-effects are unlikely at the low doses usually recommended for performance anxiety, they do suggest the need for caution and reinforce arguments in favour of psychological rather than medical solutions.

Behaviour therapy

Since performance anxiety may be construed as a type of social phobia, the treatment techniques used for phobias would seem appropriate. One of the most widely used techniques, *systematic desensitization*, emphasizes the need for progressive exposure to the object of fear whilst maintaining a relaxed state. Mere exposure does not seem effective in extinguishing stage fright since many musicians perform for years without getting over it (Steptoe and Fidler 1987; Wesner *et al.* 1990). While there are some studies showing that classic desensitization therapy is useful for stage fright and speech anxiety

(Appel 1976; Allen *et al.* 1989; Wardle 1975), something more than exposure (even combined with relaxation) seems needed for the seasoned musician who continues to experience performance anxiety after years in the profession.

As it appears that destructive thoughts (negative self-talk) are often involved in the mediation and escalation of performance anxiety (Lloyd-Elliott 1991; Steptoe and Fidler 1987), some form of *cognitive restructuring* would seem to be indicated. Kendrick *et al.* (1982) conducted a controlled study of the efficacy of attention training and behaviour rehearsal in the treatment of performance anxiety in a group of 53 pianists. The attention training consisted of the identification of negative and task-irrelevant thoughts during piano performance followed by training in their substitution with positive, task-oriented self-talk. Behaviour rehearsal consisted of playing repeatedly before friendly and supportive audiences. On a variety of outcome criteria, both treatment procedures were found to be effective relative to a wait-list control group. However, on some measures attentional training was superior to rehearsal. Although Kenrick *et al.* admitted that their treatments included many other elements such as verbal persuasion, modelling, instruction, performance accomplishments, group influence, and homework assignments, they nevertheless concluded that dealing with maladaptive thoughts is an important addition to behaviour therapy programmes. Noting that behaviour rehearsal produced almost as much change towards positive self-talk as attention training, they wondered whether all therapies ultimately work on this principle, and are successful to the extent that cognitions are modified.

Sweeney and Horan (1982) compared cue-controlled relaxation and cognitive restructuring, and a combination of the two, against a control condition (musical analysis training) that generated equivalent demand characteristics with 49 music students who volunteered for a musical performance anxiety reduction programme. Both methods were effective in reducing state anxiety measured by pulse rate and self-report. The relaxation procedure also reduced self-reported trait anxiety and improved musical performing competence, whereas the cognitive restructuring was effective on a behavioural anxiety index. The combined treatment, not surprisingly, showed most of the benefits of each individual procedure.

Clark and Agras (1991) compared cognitive-behavioural therapy with the anxiolytic buspirone, and a combination of the two, with 34 subjects suffering performance anxiety (including 15 full-time musicians, 10 of whom had tried propranolol and three of whom had stopped performing altogether). The cognitive-behaviour therapy consisted of identifying negative self-statements, giving homework exercises to modify them, providing coping models, relaxation training, and encouraging exposure to feared situations. Buspirone fared no better than the placebo but the cognitive-behavioural procedure yielded significant reductions in subjective anxiety, and improved quality of musical performance. This study supports that of Kendrick *et al.* (1982) in showing that cognitive-behaviour therapy is an effective treatment for musical performance anxiety. Unfortunately, it does little to clarify the essential components of the treatment cocktail.

A particular form of cognitive restructuring that may be included in therapeutic programmes is that called *stress inoculation* (Meichenbaum 1985). The idea is that developing realistic expectations is just as important as replacing negative self-statements with positive ones. Performers are therefore taught to anticipate the symptoms of anxiety that are bound to arise before important public appearances and to turn them to constructive use. Anxiety cues are acknowledged as inevitable but 'reframed' as less threatening, even desirable, reactions. For example, the performer is taught to reappraise the adrenaline effects (pounding heart, sweating, shallow breathing, etc.) as normal emotional reactions that are not conspicuous to the audience and which can contribute to a more lively, exciting musical interpretation. This method has not been evaluated with controlled trials but may turn out to be a useful adjunct to cognitive-behavioural programmes (Salmon 1991).

A cognitive strategy that may need attention because it can be seriously counter-productive is that described as *self-handicapping* (Jones and Berglas 1978). In many competitive contexts some individuals are so afraid of losing self-esteem that they 'hedge bets' by setting up excuses for failures in advance. For example, they deliberately have a late night before an exam, or drink alcohol before a musical performance so that they can say to others as well as themselves in the event of failure, 'I would have done better if it wasn't for . . .'. Of course, in so doing they increase the chances of needing an excuse. Some performers have a reputation for always offering excuses before an appearance (e.g. 'I have a sore throat at the moment'; 'I've never seen this music before'). These approximate to negative self-talk, which easily become self-fulfilling prophecies of failure. The next step in this process is to sabotage one's own performance by *actual* self-handicapping, such as failing to attend rehearsals, damaging one's instrument, or getting drunk beforehand. Susceptible individuals and their therapists should watch for signs of this and replace them with positive, optimistic strategies.

Alexander technique

Although it is not specifically directed at alleviation of performance anxiety, the Alexander technique (AT) deserves mention if only because it is so widely used by musicians for this purpose. AT derives from the writings of an Australian actor called Fred Alexander who died in London in 1955, after seeking (and apparently finding) a solution to his own problems of voice loss under stress. It is claimed to be a method of 'kinaesthetic re-education' which uses a mixture of verbal instructions and hands-on demonstration to replace bad postural habits ('misuse') with good ones. It seeks economy of effort and balance in movements so as to minimize physical (and hence mental) tensions. Watson and Valentine (1987) found that 53 per cent of a British sample of professional orchestral musicians used some form of complementary medical technique for anxiety reduction, and of these, AT was most frequently cited (43 per cent). Thus it appears to have become something of a 'craze' in Britain (though it is much less known in the US).

In one of the few rigorous studies of AT, Valentine *et al.* (1995) assigned a group of 25 musicians to an experimental condition (15 lessons in AT) or control condition (no such lessons). Measures were taken on four occasions: at audition, in class prior to treatment, in class after treatment, and at final recital. This provided a high and low stress condition before AT lessons and the same post-treatment. Measures included physiological and self-report indices of anxiety and ratings of videos of musical performance by judges who were blind to treatment assignment. The Alexander-trained group showed superiority on overall musical and technical performance, a more positive attitude to performance, reduced heart-rate variance and less self-rated anxiety. However, these benefits were largely confined to the low stress performance situation and did not transfer to the high stress (recital) condition. Furthermore, the improvements were not related to positive changes in postural habits as rated by the AT teachers, suggesting that any benefits observed resulted from some other mechanism. A probable candidate would be some kind of cognitive restructuring (e.g. distraction from anxiety cues or destructive self-talk) similar to that deliberately sought by cognitive-behaviour therapists. AT does appear to work to some extent but probably not for the reasons its proponents believe.

Hypnotherapy

Since it is possible that all treatment methods (including placebo) incorporate an element of suggestion, hypnotism may be one of the best ways to focus this effect, increasing suggestibility as well as inducing relaxed states. Stanton (1993) has described a two-session hypnotherapy procedure, combining success imagery and rational-emotive therapy, for the alleviation of musical performance anxiety. Three cases are described with apparently successful and cumulative effects.

In a more controlled follow-up study of the efficacy of hypnotherapy, Stanton (1994) paired music students according to their scores on a performance anxiety inventory and assigned one of each pair to hypnotherapy and one to a control group. Hypnotherapy consisted of two 50-minute sessions of relaxation suggestion, one week apart, which included breathing induction, visual imagery (clouds and a lake), and verbal suggestions linking these images to increased mental control. The control group met twice at the same interval for 50-minute discussion sessions. The hypnotherapy group (but not controls) showed a significant lowering of performance anxiety as measured by the inventory immediately after treatment and continued improvement six months later. Thus, hypnotherapy does seem to help performance anxiety. The next step would be to compare its effectiveness with that of the cognitive-behavioural procedures; it is a pity that Stanton used an 'inert' control rather than a credible rival procedure so that such a comparative assessment might have been made.

SUMMARY

Performance anxiety is a common problem among amateur and professional musicians alike, affecting between one quarter and a half of all performers. It is most likely to afflict individuals high in neuroticism or trait anxiety, introverts, and those prone to social phobia, and most strongly felt in exposed and evaluative situations (e.g. solo performances, auditions, and competitions). Although some degree of tension adds spark to a performance, high levels of cognitive anxiety combined with complex task demands can produce a 'catastrophic' collapse of performance in certain susceptible individuals. The most successful treatment approaches are those that combine relaxation training with anxiety inoculation (developing realistic expectations relating to autonomic symptoms) and cognitive restructuring (modifying self-talk in a positive direction). The Alexander technique and hypnotherapy have both been demonstrated to be useful, though it is likely they partake of the same principles as those used explicitly by cognitive-behaviour therapists. Beta-blockers may be a useful stop-gap but long-term dependence on drugs of any kind is best avoided.

REFERENCES

Aaron, S. (1986). *Stage fright: its role in acting*. Chicago University Press, Chicago.

Abel, J. L. and Larkin, K. T. (1990). Anticipation of performance among musicians: physiological arousal, confidence, and state anxiety. *Psychology of Music*, **18**, 171–82.

Allen, M., Hunter, J. E. and Donahue, W. A. (1989). Meta-analysis of self-report data on the effectiveness of public speaking anxiety treatment techniques. *Communication Education*, **38**, 54–76.

Appel, S. S. (1976). Modifying solo performance anxiety in adult pianists. *Journal of Music Therapy*, **13**, 2–16.

Brantigan, C., Brantigan, T., and Joseph, N. (1979). The effect of beta-blockade on stage-fright: a controlled study. *Rocky Mountain Medical Journal*, **76**, 227–33.

Brotons, M. (1994). Effect of performing conditions on music performance, anxiety, and performance quality. *Journal of Music Therapy*, **31**, 63–81.

Clark, D. B. (1989). Performance related medical and psychological disorders in instrumental musicians. *Annals of Behavioural Medicine*, **11**, 28–34.

Clark, D. B. and Agras, W. S. (1991). The assessment and treatment of performance anxiety in musicians. *American Journal of Psychiatry*, **148**, 598–605.

Cox, W. J. and Kenardy, J. (1993). Performance anxiety, social phobia, and setting effects in instrumental music students. *Journal of Anxiety Disorders*, **7**, 49–60.

Duffy, E. (1962). *Attention and behaviour*. John Wiley and Son, New York.

Fishbein, M., Middlestadt, S. E., Ottati, V., Strauss, S., and Ellis, A. (1988). Medical problems among ICSOM musicians: overview of a national survey. *Medical Problems of Performing Artists*, **3**, 1–8.

Graydon, J. and Murphy, T. (1995). The effect of personality on social facilitation whilst performing a sports related task. *Personality and Individual Differences*, **19**, 265–7.

Haider, V. M. and Groll-Knapp, E. (1981). Psychological investigation into the stress experiences of musicians in a symphony orchestra. In *Stress and Music* (ed. M. Piparek). Braumüller, Vienna.

Hamann, D. L. (1982). An assessment of anxiety in instrumental and vocal performers. *Journal of Research in Music Education*, **30**, 77–90.

Hardy, L. and Parfitt, G. (1991). A catastrophe model of anxiety and performance. *British Journal of Psychology*, **82**, 163–78.

James, I. M. and Savage, I. (1984). Beneficial effect of nadolol on anxiety-induced disturbances of performance in musicians: a comparison with diazepam and placebo. *American Heart Journal*, **4**, 1150–5.

James, I. M., Griffith, D. N. W., Pearson, R. M., and Newbury, P. (1977). Effect of oxprenolol on stage-fright in musicians. *Lancet*, **2**, 952–4.

Jones, E. E. and Berglas, S. (1978). Control of attributions about self through self-handicapping strategies: the appeal of alcohol and the role of underachievement. *Personality and Social Psychology Bulletin*, **4**, 200–6.

Kendrick, M. J., Craig, K. D., Lawson, D. M., and Davidson, P. O. (1982). Cognitive and behavioural therapy for musical performance anxiety. *Journal of Consulting and Clinical Psychology*, **50**, 353–62.

Konijn, E. A. (1991). What's on between the actor and his audience: empirical analysis of emotion processes. In *Psychology and performing arts* (ed. G. D. Wilson). Swets and Zeitlinger, Amsterdam.

Liden, S. and Gottfries, C. (1974). Beta-blocking agents in the treatment of catecholamine-induced symptoms in musicians. *Lancet*, **2**, 529.

Lloyd-Elliott, M. (1991). Witches, demons, and devils: the enemies of auditions and how performing artists make friends with these saboteurs. In *Psychology and performing arts* (ed. G. D. Wilson). Swets and Zeitliger, Amsterdam.

Marchant-Haycox, S. E. and Wilson, G. D. (1992). Personality and stress in performing artists. *Personality and Individual Differences*, **13**, 1061–8.

Meichenbaum, D. (1985). *Stress inoculation training*. Pergamon, New York.

Neftel, K. A., Adler, R. H., Kappeli, L., Ross, M., Dolder, M., Kaser, H. E., *et al.* (1982). Stage fright in musicians: a model illustrating the effect of beta-blockers. *Psychosomatic Medicine*, **44**, 461–9.

Salmon, P. (1991). Stress inoculation techniques and musical performance anxiety. In *Psychology and performing artists* (ed. G. D. Wilson). Swets and Zeitlinger, Amsterdam.

Salmon, P., Schrodt, R., and Wright, J. (1989). Preperformance anxiety in novice and experienced musicians. *Medical Problems of Performing Artists*, **4**, 77–80.

Stanton, H. E. (1993). Alleviation of performance anxiety through hypnotherapy. *Psychology of Music*, **21**, 78–82.

Stanton, H. E. (1994). Reduction of performance anxiety in music students. *Australian Psychologist*, **29**, 124–7.

Steptoe, A. and Fidler, H. (1987). Stage fright in orchestral musicians: a study of cognitive and behavioural strategies in performance anxiety. *British Journal of Psychology*, **78**, 241–9.

Steptoe, A., Malik, F., Pay, C., Pearson, P., Price, C. and Win, Z. (1995). The impact of stage fright on student actors. *British Journal of Psychology*, **86**, 27–39.

Suter, S. (1986). *Health psychophysiology: mind–body interaction in wellness and illness.* Erlbaum Associates, Hillsdale, N.J.

Sweeney, G. A. and Horan, J. J. (1982). Separate and combined effects of cue-controlled relaxation and cognitive restructuring in the treatment of musical performance anxiety. *Journal of Counselling Psychology*, **29**, 486–97.

Valentine, E. R., Fitzgerald, D. F. P., Gorton, T. L., Hudson, J. A., and Symonds, E. R. C. (1995). The effect of lessons in the Alexander technique on music performance in high and low stress situations. *Psychology of Music*, **23**, 129–41.

Wardle, A. (1975). Behaviour modification by reciprocal inhibition of instrumental music performance anxiety. In *Research in music behaviour: modifying music behaviour in the classroom* (ed. C. K. Madsen., R. D. Greer, C. H. Madsen, Jr). Teachers College Press, New York.

Watson, P. and Valentine, E. (1987). The practice of complementary medicine and anxiety levels in a population of musicians. *Journal of the International Society for the Study of Tensions in Performance*, **4**, 26–30.

Wesner, R. B., Noyes, R., and Davis, T. L. (1990). The occurrence of performance anxiety among musicians. *Journal of Affective Disorders*, **18**, 177–85.

Williams, J. M. G. and Hargreaves, T. R. (1994). Neuroses: depressive and anxiety disorders. In *Companion encyclopedia of psychology*, Vol. 2 (ed. A. M. Coleman), pp. 875–96. Routledge, London.

Wills, G. and Cooper, C. L. (1988). *Pressure sensitive: popular musicians under stress.* Sage, London.

Wilson, G. D. (1994). *Psychology for performing artists: butterflies and bouquets.* Jessica Kingsley, London.

PART VI

Real world applications

13 | Clinical and therapeutic uses of music

Leslie Bunt

INTRODUCTION

The clinical practice of music therapy straddles many disciplines. Every music therapist brings to the profession a unique blend of musical and personal skills and experiences, applied practically in the service of children and adults with wide-ranging physical and mental health care needs. Effective clinical practice also requires awareness of the relevant psychological and therapeutic processes and knowledge of the appropriate medical background. Many factors therefore combine together when a music therapist works with an individual or a group: science, art, and compassion all have their part to play in constructive music therapy practice.

This chapter begins with some historical background to the emergence of music therapy. A personal definition of music therapy and summary of the wide range of its applications follow. In the light of two examples, the chapter then reviews the relationship of music therapy to well-established treatment methods, namely the medical model, psychoanalysis, behaviour therapy, and humanistic psychology. When Farnsworth (1969) included a chapter on the use of music as therapy in *The social psychology of music* he commented on a lack of scientific evidence and explanation: evaluative research has begun to redress this balance and the present chapter ends with a summary of some of the recent research carried out. This research raises many questions regarding the methods by which music therapy is described and the discipline's core relationship to music.

THE EMERGENCE OF THE MUSIC THERAPY PROFESSION

The specific discipline of music therapy is a middle to late twentieth century development. However, music was perhaps the first artform to be employed therapeutically (Fleshman and Fryrear 1981) and the use of music to alleviate illness and distress in many cultures and historical periods is demonstrated by several sources, e.g. Egyptian medical papyri, the Bible and other religious texts, Greek medical practice, creation stories, mythology, magic, and tribal medicine (see Alvin 1975; Benenzon 1981). Music in both song and dance is still used today in the healing rituals of many tribal cultures and Moreno (1988) draws connections between aspects of contemporary Western music therapy and these very ancient healing traditions.

From around the turn of this century, the relaxing and entertaining qualities of music were used in Western hospitals mainly to boost patient morale and to aid convalescence. This was on the vague assumption that it might activate metabolic functions and relieve mental stress and fatigue (Feder and Feder 1981). The early literature abounds with anecdotal and over-zealous accounts of people being reached by music when nothing else could (see case examples in Licht 1946; Podolsky 1954; Schullian and Schoen 1948). Modern music therapy began to emerge immediately after the Second World War when musicians were employed on a regular basis to help the rehabilitation of returning war veterans. The musicians wanted to understand more about the various medical and psychological backgrounds and how their music could be adapted to the various contexts; the physicians needed clearer evidence concerning the effects of intervention than that provided by the earlier anecdotal accounts. The scene was set for the formation of specific music therapy training courses. The United States led the way, with the first full academic course being taught at the University of Kansas in 1946 and the National Association of Music Therapy (NAMT) being formed in 1950. A second association, the American Association of Music Therapy (AAMT), was formed in 1971. The NAMT and AAMT currently support over 70 degree courses at all levels and offer full registration into the profession after a period of internship (Maranto 1993). There are currently over 3000 practising music therapists in the US alone.

Music therapy is now gaining increased recognition worldwide with developments in over 30 countries (see Maranto 1993). There is an active World Federation of Music Therapy that organizes international conferences and continues to develop standards in training and ethics. Also, music therapy is now recognized as a paramedical discipline by the British Department of Health. In addition to this raised profile however, it is also worth noting that countries differ in the emphasis they place on the musical versus psychological/medical skills of the therapist (see Benenzon 1981), and this leads to international variation in what precisely constitutes 'music therapy'.

WHAT IS MUSIC THERAPY?

Firstly, music therapy is not about helping people with their music in the way that a speech and language therapist is concerned with alleviating barriers to the 'normal' expression of speech and language (Michel 1976).

Nor is it about developing musical skills nor teaching people to play an instrument, although these factors may be an unintentional by-product of the therapeutic process. Therapy itself implies the concept of change and many definitions of music therapy stress the development of aims and the client–therapist relationship: therapy is communicative, social, and inter-active. If we look at definitions worldwide we see a continuum: one end emphasizes the music, whilst the other emphasizes the relationship. Each therapist's position on the continuum is influenced by training, personal philosophy, and therapeutic orientation.

In some countries psychologists, psychiatrists, and other clinicians use music as part of the therapy, what Bruscia (1987) refers to as 'music in therapy'. Examples of this are the use of music as a form of relaxation to support a more verbally-based psychotherapy, or in dentistry and surgery. Some of these uses are reviewed below in the section on 'Music in therapy'. In other countries the music itself is central, and Bruscia (1987) terms this 'music as therapy'. An example of 'music as therapy' is the Nordoff–Robbins approach (Nordoff and Robbins 1971, 1977) in which music is the central ingredient, with changes in the music often being mirrored in changes with-in the client–therapist relationship. Other examples are reviewed in the sec-tion below on 'Music as therapy'. Any definition must therefore address the music and the therapeutic objectives. Furthermore, there are responsibilities for therapists to serve clients by attending to, listening to, and being vigilant towards them. One possible definition that summarizes these strands is that:

Music therapy is the use of sounds and music within an evolving relationship between child or adult and therapist to support and encourage physical, mental, social, and emotional well-being (Bunt 1994).

AREAS OF PRACTICE

Music therapy is employed with people of all ages, both individually and in groups. It is also applied currently in a diversity of settings, e.g. special hospitals and units for people with varied learning difficulties, physical dis-abilities, neurological problems, and mental health problems; pre-school assessment centres and nurseries; special schools; day centres, hospitals, and residential homes for older people; centres for people with visual or hearing impairments; hospices; and within the prison and probation service. More recently, music therapy has been applied to stress reduction, victims of sex-ual abuse, and people living with HIV/AIDS. In Britain, the two main areas have historically concerned people with learning difficulties and adults with mental health problems. This can be illustrated by two examples of my own work (adapted from Bunt 1994, pp. 22–6, 62) which give the flavour of a therapy session and also serve as material for later illustrations.

Example 1—Individual work

A is a 2.5 year-old child with profound learning difficulties (Rett's Syndrome). We sit opposite each other and when presented with a skin-top tambour she reaches out and makes an occasional stroking movement. I reply similarly, reflecting both the musical and non-musical parameters of A's gesture (loudness, quality, duration, speed of movement, etc.). A long delay passes until her next 'sound gesture'. She looks at me with a fixed gaze. There are no vocalizations but many hand-to-mouth movements. Over the ensuing 12-week period of individual sessions she begins to play in increasing short bursts of sounds, sometimes playing two separate sounds. There is an increasing amount of activity and the events come in quicker succession. She vocalizes a range of vowel sounds and short phrases which contain discrete pitches and melodic intonation. I elaborate these in my vocal and instrumental replies. A apparently begins to make connections between a vocal sound, short rhythmic patterns, and my sounds. She also starts to use her voice outside the session, connecting gestures with vocal sounds. The nursery staff comment on the reduction of her screaming and apparent frustration.

Example 2—Group work

Eight adults attend a music therapy group on a hospital psychiatric unit's acute admissions ward. The group is introduced to a range of percussion instruments. Group members begin exploring the instruments and are invited to introduce themselves with one. I begin a steady heartbeat pulse and ask group members to play any kind of pattern on their instrument. Only some people begin immediately. The pulse changes and the music builds to a loud and fast climax. The group members then comment on its effects. One member feels embarrassed and suggests playing with eyes closed. I propose that people try to internalize the pulse. They change instruments if desired and we repeat the structure. The session becomes more interactive, with people playing short musical 'call and response' messages for each other. Many ways of playing the instruments are explored and group members comment on the emotions expressed and received via the music. I then suggest freer improvisation work. The group finds the first improvised piece rather chaotic and I suggest improvising to a given theme. For this, one group member suggests 'climbing a mountain', although others say they feel too low or lack sufficient energy to begin the climb. Another member wants to fly like a large bird above the mountain. The piece begins in relative silence and each member of the group tracks their own feelings as it progresses. These feelings are discussed subsequently, with the music acting as a release. One group member suggests a second piece—'getting back to base camp'.

Different instruments are chosen for this and the piece ends quietly and reflectively.

THE RELATIONSHIP OF MUSIC THERAPY TO OTHER TREATMENT MODELS

Many commentators still feel that the effects of music therapy can be best evaluated if the technique draws on more established psychological and therapeutic models. Indeed, Ruud (1980) points out that this is a natural process of evolution before music therapy can establish itself as a unique discipline. Four principal models have often been proposed, namely medical, psychoanalytic, behavioural, and humanistic.

Music therapy and a medical model

The early development of music therapy occurred in medically-dominated contexts, and it is consequently understandable that much emphasis was placed on the discovery of supportive physiological evidence. Connections were explored between listening to music and changes in, for example, breathing, pulse rate, body metabolism, muscle reflexes, the electrical conductivity of the body, and attention (see Arrington 1954). Indeed, A's behaviour (see Example 1) over the 12 weeks indicates a progressive increase in attention and vocal/instrumental activity. Similarly, the hospital-based group (Example 2) also became more attentive and engaged with the music, with rhythm particularly acting as an organizer and energizer. Indeed, rhythm's ability to create structure and order played a major role in the establishment of music therapy in client groups where such order appeared lacking or confused, e.g. cerebral palsy, learning disability, and psychosis. More generally, group work often elicits spontaneous feedback about feeling 'warmed up' and less fatigued at the end of a session.

However, it is notoriously difficult to separate emotional from physical aspects of such responses, with all manner of potential connections and explanations linking the two (Bunt *et al.* 1988). This becomes accentuated if we consider the physiological responses generated over a series of interactive sessions, such as in the first example above. Also, physiological responses to music may be related to ungeneralizable, personal idiosyncrasies. Indeed, early research findings were often inconsistent, particularly with regard to the effect of specific musical changes on specific (rather than general) physiological changes (see Saperston 1995). Furthermore, the early literature also focused on instantaneously occurring and short-lived effects, often using a restricted range of pre-recorded music presented on equipment of varying quality.

Nevertheless, a fortunately very rare condition called musicogenic epilepsy (see Critchley and Henson 1977) provides some powerful evidence that music does have the potential to influence fundamental physiological processes: in this condition, a specific grouping of musical parameters can trigger temporary loss of consciousness. Powerful effects of music are also apparent in the occasional example of music helping to recall patients from coma (see Gustorff's case example in Ansdell 1995). Similarly, Sacks (1991) provides case material concerning music's power to free the movements of Parkinsonian patients ('remusicking' as he beautifully describes it). Moreover, Rider (1987) is one of several American music therapists investigating the effect of music on the body's immune system and the reduction of pain, stress, and anxiety. Finally, vibroacoustic therapy is a recent development which involves playing music but crucially also a low frequency pulsed tone through a specifically adapted chair or bed containing in-built speakers: growing evidence suggests that this pitch/pulse-based therapy has striking benefits for people with, for example, profound physical disabilities, pulmonary disorder, or rheumatoid conditions (see Skille and Wigram 1995). Further evidence on the medical uses of music is presented in the section below on 'Music in therapy'.

One of the best known features of music therapy within the medical model/ physiological framework is the 'iso' principle. 'Iso', based on the Greek for 'equal', implies that the therapist attempts to match the parameters and mood of the music (in both active and receptive forms) to the mood, tempo, and loudness, etc. of the client (Altshuler 1954). In Example 1 above, I attempted to match A's tempo and behaviour patterns with the level of the sounds I presented, adapting this as A began making more sounds. Likewise, in Example 2, I identified musical common denominators to make initial contact with the group, exploring music at the start that was neither too fast nor too slow, too loud nor too soft. This helped to bring the group together, to find some early cohesion. Perhaps this is what Benenzon (1981) means by the 'group iso'. We can even extend the notion of rhythmic entrainment and sychronization to a measure of health in general, one view of 'dis-ease' being a lack of synchronization with oneself, immediate others, and the surrounding world (Capra 1983).

Music therapy and psychoanalysis

Although there is no clear psychodynamic meaning of music (Noy 1966–7), some therapists have related processes in music therapy to psychoanalytical theory. Apparently Freud did not derive much pleasure from music, being unable to discover any rational explanation for how it affected him. He related creativity to processes of sublimation, regression, compensation, fantasy, and escape, although later analysts criticized this. Storr (1989) for one has questioned why any artistic creation need stand for anything other than itself. Similarly, Jung was interested in music and is reported to have commented on how it could reach deep archetypal material. He recommended that music should be part of every analysis (Hitchcock 1987).

Many music therapists have turned to the work of the later psychoanalysts such as Winnicott (1971). One fundamental aspect of Winnicott's theory concerns how the child gradually develops a distinction between self and other, i.e. 'me' and 'not me', with several therapists employing music to facilitate this distinction. In Example 1 above, the tambour can be viewed as, at first, a prolongation of the child's body; a part of the child's sense of self (me) that can be contacted by looking and touching during active play. As the child begins to interact with the therapist, the instrument acquires some of its own unique properties, resisting the child's actions and becoming 'not me'. Over time, the instruments or even the music itself can take on this socalled 'transitional' role, filling the psychological gap between therapist and child and highlighting aspects of shared understanding.

Aspects of Example 2 above can also be viewed within a psychoanalytic framework. It is apparent that the non-verbal nature of the interactions appealed to the group: an instrument will not retaliate and cannot be hurt. It can contain all manner of projected feelings, even those very uncomfortable and destructive ones that are difficult to verbalize. Members of the group were able to gain insights about their feelings after initial exploration within a musical context. The group provided a safe, contained space for such exploration, eventually becoming very cohesive. The second example also shows how an instrument can take on a symbolic meaning as when one member of the group chose a bird-like swooping sound to symbolize the screeching and whooping of a giant bird at the top of the mountain. Many features of this example can be linked to the curative factors outlined by Yalom (1985) as basic to any kind of group psychotherapy.

Stern (e.g. 1985) is another clinician to have inspired music therapists. One central feature of his work concerns how communication is really a process of 'affect attunement': two communicators must understand each other's underlying emotional state and cone this has been achieved, communication may occur through several modalities. Consider an example of two adolescents walking along the street. One has his hands in his pockets and kicks a stone that he comes across. His friend asks him whether he is worried about impending exams and the first boy replies by shrugging his shoulders. Such a process of affect attunement between two individuals can also be applied to music therapy. A child's overt behaviour can be taken to indicate his/her emotional state. This behaviour may then be answered by the therapist in a way that partially imitates but also extends that communication, so as to indicate an understanding of what the child was attempting to express. For example, a child may play a drum at a quick tempo which is taken by the therapist to indicate a feeling of excitement: the therapist then plays the drum (or responds via another modality such as the voice) at a similar tempo but also loudly. Turn-taking between the child and therapist may then ensue. In essence, Stern's notion of 'affect attunement' can be translated as 'tuning in to the child' (Bunt 1994): it is a means of sharing the space and time that exists when people make music together. Pavlicevic (1995) has also discussed the relevance of Stern's work to music therapy. She argues that 'in music therapy emotional creativity is sounded through the musical act: music and emotion are fused, so to speak' (p. 52).

In light of this interest in psychoanalytical approaches, Priestley (1995) has developed exploratory or analytical music therapy where close connections are made between the musical and verbal parts of the session. In individual work a patient is encouraged to talk through the area to be explored in the traditional analytical way, before moving into improvised music-making. The music is then recorded and played back with the therapist acting as a catalyst in exploring the links between this music and the verbal part of the session. John (1992) similarly challenged the profession to develop towards a form of music psychotherapy. Other therapists, however, believe that music lies a long way, perhaps the farthest away, from the world of verbal analysis and the search for semantic meaning. Ansdell (1995), for example, emphasizes the central position of music within music therapy. He proposes continued reference to the musical content without the need for verbal elaboration. It is interesting that a similar debate is occurring within the art therapy profession, with some art therapists emphasizing the art, others already labelling their work as art psychotherapy.

Music therapy and behaviour therapy

In partial response to psychoanalytic theory, music therapy pioneers in the US during the 1960s and 1970s called for an objective and scientific approach, regarding music therapy as a science of behaviour (Madsen *et al* 1968). In light of this, there has been extensive use of techniques borrowed from behaviour therapy. This draws on the well-known operant condition-ing paradigm and emphasizes how certain activities can be shaped and encouraged (or reinforced) by rewarding the actor so that the action and the reward become associated. A substantial body of research has studied the effects of offering musical activities, particularly listening to music, as a reward for specific behaviours. Such techniques have produced significant improvements in both short and long-term objectives, e.g. the use of music listening to develop attention, reading, or numeracy skills (see, for example, Miller *et al*. 1974; Roskam 1979); or to reduce aggressive, stereotyped, hyper-active, or maladaptive behaviours (see, for example, Jorgenson 1974; Lathom 1964; Scott 1970; Steele 1968).

In many ways the very act of playing an instrument during therapy has intrinsic reward and we could use the behaviour therapist's terminology to describe the two examples above. A's initial gestures were positively and immediately reinforced since the therapist responded encouragingly by matching the girl's music. She began to make associations between a gesture and responses from both the instrument and the adult. Reinforcement caused learning about the stuff of relationships—listening, watching, vocalizing, cause and effect, turn-taking, and all the subtleties of reciprocal interaction. It is also possible to apply a behavioural perspective to the group therapy session described in Example 2. Clearly the group experienced the music as a mainly rewarding experience, being motivated by the sounds of the instruments to continue playing. Through this continual reward, they began to associate the way they approached the instruments (and the session itself) with aspects of their own difficulties by, for example, relating their musical achievements to the possibility of achievement in other aspects of their lives.

There are many often rather nebulous factors to consider during any period of music therapy, and behavioural research helped reduce these to a few quantifiable variables which incorporated baseline measures, e.g. scores on standardized tests of reading ability: this made it possible to gather empirical evidence on the benefits of musical rewards versus no rewards on specific therapeutic outcomes. However, despite such advantages, behavioural approaches have been criticized for ignoring central themes within music therapy such as the role of unconscious processes and the treatment of causes rather than merely symptoms. A further criticism is that behavioural perspectives examine only measurable external objectives (e.g. performance on tests) rather than more subjective emotional benefits (e.g. feelings of well-being). Nevertheless, such criticisms are perhaps harsh since the research aimed to address only the narrow issue of reward and subsequent behaviour and it promoted the scientific validity of music therapy, particularly in the US.

Music therapy and humanistic psychology

Therapists with more humanistic and eclectic approaches argue that psychoanalytical research into deep-rooted influences is too problematic and that the behaviourist's examination of small 'bits' of behaviour is too narrow (Ruud 1980). Instead they concentrate on working within the present moment, emphasizing development of the person's whole potential through musical interactions and evolving therapeutic relationships. There is concern for individual differences, freedom of choice, personal intentions, and feelings of self-worth. Links are made with such established methods as Rogerian client-centred counselling, which emphasizes empathy, acceptance, and genuineness (Rogers 1969); Gestalt therapy (Perls *et al.* 1973), which emphasizes treating the whole person; and the notion of 'peak experiences' (Maslow 1970). Connections are also being made with more transpersonal therapies, e.g. psychosynthesis (see Assagioli 1965). Elements of Example 1 above provide a useful illustration of a humanistic approach. The therapy focuses on the here and now in an attempt to communicate with the child, and in the process of this placed value on her music. There was also an attempt to empathize with and understand the child. Similarly, in Example 2, the group members were encouraged to express themselves by saying what they thought specific aspects of the music meant and also by being able to choose the type of music they wanted to create.

The underlying emphasis on growth, relationships, and self-actualization may account for the growing number of humanistic music therapists, since these themes are central to most arts therapists' philosophy. Indeed, Wilber (1979) notes that whilst psychoanalysis has helped to untangle the various levels of the unconscious, there is much still to be discovered, at least in the West, by exploring the highest levels of super-consciousness. Music and other arts might contribute greatly to this, although we should not ignore the link between music and more unconscious processes.

SOME EFFECTS OF INTERVENTION

An earlier section described how the therapeutic uses of music might be divided into two types. In the case of music in therapy, the music itself is often an adjunct to other interventions, with the goal of promoting, for example, pain relief following surgery. In the case of music as therapy, the music is the main treatment provided as a means of improving the client's condition, and as such occupies a more central position in the intervention. The most obvious question concerning these two approaches is whether they have a beneficial influence on patients, and this section describes some of the outcomes resulting from music in therapy and music as therapy.

Music in therapy

Music has been used most frequently in therapy by the medical and dental professions. A large number of empirical studies have now been carried out and these indicate several areas where music can have positive effects on patients undergoing treatment for a variety of conditions. Standley (1995) has recently reviewed the literature on the medical/dental uses of music and the coverage here draws heavily on her conclusions. She employed a statistical procedure termed a meta-analysis which allowed her to measure the 'effect size' that music had in the studies reviewed. Although the underlying

Table 13.1 Examples of medical/dental variables influenced by music (adapted from Standley 1995).

Variable	Effect size	Variable	Effect size
Podiatric pain	>3.28	Length of labour during childbirth	0.99
Paediatric respiration	3.15	Perceived satisfaction	0.98
Pulse (dental patients)	3.00	Abortion—associated pain	0.96
Use of analgesia (dental patients)	2.49	Helplessness (dental patients)	0.94
EMG	2.38	Walking speed (stroke patients)	0.94
Blood pressure (dental patients)	2.25	Relaxation (open heart surgery)	0.88
Distraction (haemodialysis)	2.08	EMG of spasticity	0.85
Observed paediatric anxiety	1.97	Exhalation strength	0.83
Grasp strength (stroke patients)	1.94	Blood pressure—surgical	0.82
Cortisol—surgical recovery	1.80	Neonate crying	0.72
Perceived anxiety (cardiac patients)	1.77	Neonate weight gain	0.71
Headache pain intensity	1.76	Contentment (cancer patients)	0.67
Pain—debridement of burns	1.52	Cervical dilation time	0.52
Post-operative pain	1.49	Physical comfort	0.51
Obstetrical relaxation	1.32	Emesis intensity (chemotherapy)	0.47
Intracranial pressure	1.21	Sleep (open heart surgery)	0.42

mathematics can be rather daunting, all that needs to be stated here is that the larger the effect size obtained, so the stronger the influence that music had on patients. By this process, Standley investigated the effect of music on 129 dependent variables and found that its effect was positive for all but four. Some examples of the variables influenced by music and the size of the effects are given in Table 13.1 (see Ammon 1968; Bob 1962; Bonny 1983; Budzynski *et al.* 1970; Chetta 1981; Cofranesco 1985; Curtis 1986; Frank 1985; Gfeller *et al.* 1988; Goloff 1981; Locsin 1981; Monsey 1960; Oyama *et al.* 1983; Scartelli 1982; Schuster 1985; Shapiro and Cohen 1983; Staum 1983; Tanioka *et al.* 1985). These show the diversity of medical/dental conditions that can be influenced positively by music.

Standley concludes that several generalizations can be made on the basis of these studies. For example, the benefits of music are greater for women than for men, and for children and adolescents than for adults or infants. Self-reports by patients indicate less of an effect of music than do behavioural observations or physiological measures, and pre-recorded music is less effective than music played by a trained music therapist who adapts this in line with patient needs. The effects of music vary widely according to the diagnosis in question but are greatest for dental patients and those suffering chronic pain (e.g. migraine headaches). With regard to specific dependent measures, music has its greatest impact on respiratory rate; EMG; and amount of analgesic medication. The smallest effects are for the length of labour in childbirth; the amount of anaesthesia required by patients; the number of days spent in hospital; and measures of neonate behaviour such as movement, crying, and weight gain (although music was beneficial even in these cases).

Standley's analysis also allowed the derivation of seven typical techniques by which music is employed in medical/dental contexts and the remainder of this section is given over to a brief review of these (see above references for specific examples). The first technique, 'passive music listening', can be used either in isolation or in conjunction with anaesthesia, analgesia, suggestion, relaxation techniques, or imagery. Music serves as an analgesic, anxiolytic, or sedative and is used to reduce pain, anxiety, or stress so that patients require fewer drugs to achieve these goals. Such music is used in a variety of contexts such as surgery (particularly for local anaesthesia); kidney dialysis; burn patients; cancer patients; and neonatal care. Within this approach, the music begins prior to the pain/fear-inducing stimulus and it is suggested that it will relieve pain, anxiety, etc. The patient's favourite music is played via earphones (to mask outside noises) or a speaker pillow, with the patient controlling as many aspects of the music (e.g. loudness) as possible. Overt signs of reduced pain or stress are reinforced.

The 'active music participation' technique uses music to focus attention on physical activities (e.g. childbirth) and/or to structure exercise. It may have several objectives such as the reduction of pain through physical movement; increased joint motility; increased duration, strength, or coordination of motor abilities; or increased capacity and strength of respiration. As might be expected, music is used in these contexts for the treatment of patients with a variety of muscular problems such as chronic pain; respiratory deficiencies; gait disturbances; or those suffering from a stroke, burns, orthopaedic difficulties, cerebral palsy, or paralysis. The typical method is to select specific exercises appropriate to the diagnosis, before evaluating the patient's baseline capacity for these tasks. A musical style is then selected which will facilitate the desired movements (e.g. disco music for forceful movements, or waltz music for more fluid movements). The therapist then models and teaches the exercise to the patient and adapts the music as the patient progresses: the patient is taught to focus on relevant musical elements (e.g. the beat) as a part of this. The therapist then reinforces the patient's progress towards improved physical capabilities.

In an approach that is clearly linked to the above definition of music therapy, the 'music and counselling' technique uses music to initiate and enhance relationships between the therapist, patient, and family. The general aims are to reduce the stress, trauma, and fear associated with major illnesses suffered by the self or significant others; to help the acceptance of death, disability, or scarring; or to enhance interpersonal interactions and treatment decisions at times of distress. The content of the music is used to initiate and maintain counselling interactions by offering opportunities/ prompts for pleasure, reminiscence, verbalization, closeness, etc. The therapist reinforces statements which accept the patient's current condition and those which are free of blame, bitterness, or guilt.

A fourth technique involves 'music and developmental or educational objectives', in which the music is used to reward or structure learning with, for example, children hospitalized for long periods. More specifically, when used as a reward *per se*, music reinforces attentiveness to educational tasks or learning itself by typically constituting reward for the achievement of a pre-determined goal and growing independence. Alternately, the therapist can provide music as a structure for presenting academic information; as a framework for teaching family members the importance of children achieving developmental milestones; or as a means of shaping more general educational objectives.

In the 'music and stimulation' technique, music is employed to provide auditory stimulation. The technique aims to increase overt responses to stimuli perceived through all modalities, such that the music is often combined with other sources of stimulation (e.g. stroking, moving visual stimuli, pleasant scents) and is most frequently employed with comatose or brain damaged patients, stroke victims, or premature neonates. The patient's preferred music is played through a speaker pillow, the movement of which can bring about further stimulation. Once an overt behavioural or a physiological response is made, the therapist uses behavioural techniques to establish stimulus–response links between the stimulation and activity by the patient. Over time, the therapist aims to pair the stimulus with a verbal command so that the patient responds to the human voice. A second use of the technique is to reduce depression/anxiety due to sensory deprivation in necessarily unchallenging or isolated environments. In this context, music is employed with people recovering from serious burns, organ transplants, or contagious diseases. The patient's preferred music is combined with a variety of other activities such as looking at slides, reminiscing about the memories associated with certain smells, or touching different types of surface (e.g. fur, sandpaper). The therapist reinforces pleasure responses and imaginative thinking.

A sixth technique, 'music and biofeedback', uses music to reinforce or structure increased awareness, self-control, and monitoring of the patient's internal physiological state. The approach is used with patients whose physical disorders are primarily attributable to controllable, internal physiological functions, for example, to lower blood pressure and heart rate in coronary patients; to increase blood flow in patients with circulatory problems; or to teach epileptics and migraine headache sufferers how to relax in response to stress. The patient's preferred music is played through headphones, and may be used to enhance his/her ability to relax, or as reinforcement for achieving desired physiological states such as a low heart rate. The therapist helps the patient to transfer these skills to everyday situations where music can be heard, such as home, work, or the car.

The final technique, 'music and group activity', is perhaps most closely related to the music as therapy approach considered in the following section. Music is used to structure pleasurable and positive interpersonal inter-actions with the aims of reducing depression/anxiety due to social isolation, and increasing feelings of well-being. It has been employed particularly with groups of patients experiencing long-term hospitalization. The approach uses music that corresponds with the patients' conditions (e.g. quieter activi-ties for the seriously ill) and combines listening with participation in musical activities.The emphasis is very much on music as fun, with live (sometimes solo) performances involving patients, visitors, and medical personnel. The sessions often end with relaxation/guided imagery to music in order to reduce discomfort and prepare the patients for rest.

As is clear from the above, the use of music in therapy is rooted firmly in the more empirically-oriented medical and behavioural models, and as such might be criticized for neglecting the diversity of techniques and approaches that are available to the music therapist. Nevertheless, the strong emphasis on quantifiable patient improvement brought about by well-established physiological and psychological mechanisms should also help to make music therapy more acceptable to the medical profession. This in turn should increase acceptance (and funding) of a second type of intervention, music as therapy, where music is central to the treatment of people whose problems may have a more psychological than physiological basis.

Music as therapy

Given the diversity of techniques and client populations, it is impossible here to enter into a detailed discussion on the effectiveness of music as therapy. However, a series of projects based within the Department of Music at The City University, London, illustrate some of the potential benefits when music is used as the therapy with a diverse range of clients. The early work at The City University was influenced by several ethologists (e.g. Hinde 1976; Richer 1979) who argued that every new discipline requires extensive periods of direct observation, with the development of clear non-inferential descriptions, i.e. an 'apprenticeship' allowing methodological refinement and hypothesis-generation. Such work seems very appropriate for a profession moving through its adolescence into early adulthood.

Odell (1995) devised time-based measures relating, for example, to eye direction, time spent using the materials, and verbalizing, and showed that, when sustained over time, music therapy sessions significantly increased elderly mentally ill clients' levels of 'engagement' within these measures. Oldfield and Adams (1995) investigated the efficacy of music therapy in accomplishing a set of individualized objectives when working with adults with profound learning difficulties. Objectives included: levels of active participation, holding on to objects, or relaxing body parts. Extensive video analysis of some of the behaviours of four adults indicated improvements as a result of music therapy as compared to play activities. My work with children with special needs (Bunt 1994) also used time-based measures and video analysis to examine changes over time in, for example, vocalizations; looking behaviour; imitation and initiation of ideas; level of adult support and direction; and turn-taking. Music therapy positively influenced all these as compared to no music therapy or playing with a well-known adult.

More recently, another researcher at The City University, Hoskyns (1995) has employed Kelly's Theory of Personal Constructs in pre- and post-music therapy evaluations of individual offender clients. The results showed correlations between an active–passive dimension, for example, and the therapist's more subjective case observations. Lee (1995, 1996) has contributed a qualitative element to this body of research by examining the musical processes leading to therapeutic outcomes. His work with clients living with HIV/AIDS has developed ways of analysing what clients and therapists view as 'significant moments' in musical improvisations. Lee has collated powerful verbal evidence from the clients themselves that is used side-by-side with the musical analysis and verbal transcripts from other listeners. Integration of various approaches is also a feature of Rogers's (1992) research on music therapy in the area of sexual abuse. As with Lee's work, this research is at the cutting-edge of attempts to understand what is going on in the music when the music is used as the therapy.

More generally, recent developments in the psychology of music are beginning to focus on the musical issues that many music therapists consider truly important. In particular, music psychology is considering the complex cognitive processes which underlie our music listening and playing. Knowledge of such processes allows music therapists to consider chosen aspects of the music and pursue them in depth. By working together with psychologists, music therapists may begin to discover more about people's musical behaviour. In music therapy there is a vast range of behaviours to observe. We can begin to look at the whole or chosen aspects of the whole and consider them in more detail. Indeed, perhaps now is the time to bring many of these different research approaches together to discover a methodological framework from within the discipline of music therapy. Ansdell (1996), for one, is reviewing the current terminologies used to describe music therapy in moving towards his notion of a 'discourse of music therapy'. Qualitative research clearly is becoming more dominant within international music therapy research (Aigen 1995) but several interesting issues may arise at the boundary points between this and quantitative analysis. Can there be more synthesis of existing methods?

CONCLUDING POINTS

Music is very adaptable and can be used to meet the differing needs of the children and adults who attend music therapy. This contributes to the enormous challenge faced by music therapists. Music can clearly influence clients in medical, psychoanalytic, behavioural, and more general humanistic terms, with two important implications. First, such a diverse panoply of riches calls for celebration and not rigid confinement to any one particular approach or methodological school. Second, it would be foolhardy to pretend that one approach alone provided a complete explanation of the therapeutic process. Instead, music crosses many boundaries, e.g. mind–body, physical–spiritual, conscious–unconscious. A more accurate explanation of the therapeutic process needs to account for all these influences, such that a more integrated approach might be not only desirable but also necessary to the further development of music therapy. Such work will be undoubtedly difficult but may be crucial for the development of music therapy out of its adolescence and into the 21st century.

AUTHOR'S NOTE

Some of the material from this chapter has previously appeared in Bunt, L. (1995). Muziektherapie. In *Muziekpsychologie* (ed. F. Evers, M. Jansma, P. Mak, and B. de Vries). Van Gorcum, Assen. The author is grateful to Adrian North for preparation of the Music in therapy section.

REFERENCES

Aigen, K. (1995). Principles of qualitative research. In *Music therapy research: quantitative and qualitative perspectives* (ed. B. Wheeler). Barcelona, Philadelphia.

Altshuler, I. (1954). The past, present, and future of music therapy. In *Music therapy* (ed. E. Podolsky). Philosophical Library, New York.

Alvin, J. (1975). *Music therapy.* John Clare Books, London.

Ammon, K. (1968). *The effects of music on children in respiratory distress.* American Nurses Association Clinical Session, pp. 127–33.

Ansdell, G. (1995). *Music for life: aspects of creative music therapy with adult clients.* Jessica Kingsley, London.

Ansdell, G. (1996). Talking about music therapy. A dilemma and a qualitative experiment. *British Journal of Music Therapy*, **10**, 4–16.

Arrington, G. (1954). Music in medicine. In *Music therapy* (ed. E. Podolsky). Philosophical Library, New York.

Assagioli, R. (1965). *Psychosynthesis*. Crucible, Wellingborough.

Benenzon, R. O. (1981). *Music therapy manual*. Charles C. Thomas, Springfield, Illinois.

Bob, S. R. (1962). Audioanalgesia in paediatric practice: a preliminary study. *Journal of the American Podiatry Association*, **52**, 503–4.

Bonny, H. L. (1983). Music listening for intensive coronary care units: a pilot project. *Music therapy*, **3**, 4–16.

Bruscia, K. (1987). *Improvisation models of music therapy*. Charles C. Thomas, Springfield, Illinois.

Budzynski, T., Soyva, J., and Adler, C. (1970). Feedback-induced muscle relaxation: application to tension headache. *Behaviour Therapy and Experimental Psychiatry*, **1**, 205–11.

Bunt, L. (1994). *Music therapy: an art beyond words*. Routledge, London.

Bunt, L., Clarke, E., Cross, I., and Hoskyns, S. (1988). A discussion on the relationship between psychology of music and music therapy. *Psychology of Music*, **16**, 62–71.

Capra, F. (1983). *The turning point*. Fontana, London.

Chetta, H. D. (1981). The effect of music and desensitization on pre-operative anxiety in children. *Journal of Music Therapy*, **18**, 74–87.

Cofranesco, E. M. (1985). The effect of music therapy on hand grasp strength and functional task performance in stroke patients. *Journal of Music Therapy*, **22**, 125–49.

Critchley, M. and Henson, R. (1977). *Music and the brain*. Heinemann, London.

Curtis, S. L. (1986). The effect of music on pain relief and relaxation of the terminally ill. *Journal of Music Therapy*, **23**, 10–24.

Farnsworth, P. (1969). *The social psychology of music*. Iowa University Press, Ames, Iowa.

Feder, E. and Feder, B. (1981). *The 'expressive' arts therapies: art, music and dance as psychotherapy*. Prentice-Hall, New Jersey.

Fleshman, B. and Fryrear, J. L. (1981). *The arts in therapy*. Nelson-Hall, Chicago.

Frank, J. (1985). The effects of music therapy and guided visual imagery on chemotherapy induced nausea and vomiting. *Oncology Nursing Forum*, **12**, 47–52.

Gfeller, K., Logan, H., and Walker, J. (1988). The effect of auditory distraction and suggestion on tolerance for dental restorations in adolescents and young adults. *Journal of Music Therapy*, **27**, 13–23.

Goloff, M. S. (1981). The responses of hospitalized medical patients to music therapy. *Music Therapy*, **1**, 51–6.

Hinde, R. (1976). On describing relationships. *Journal of Child Psychology and Psychiatry*, **17**, 1–19.

Hitchcock, D. (1987). The influence of Jung's psychology on the therapeutic use of music. *Journal of British Music Therapy*, **1**, 17–21.

Hoskyns, S. (1995). Observing offenders: the use of simple rating scales to assess changes in activity during group music therapy. In *Art and music therapy and research* (ed. A. Gilroy and C. Lee). Routledge, London.

John, D. (1992). Towards music psychotherapy. *Journal of British Music Therapy*, **6**, 10–12.

Jorgensen, H. (1974). The contingent use of music activity to modify behaviours which interfere with learning. *Journal of Music Therapy*, **11**, 41–6.

Lathom, W. (1964). Music therapy as a means of changing the adaptive behaviour level of retarded children. *Journal of Music Therapy*, **1**, 132–4.

Lee, C. (1995). The analysis of therapeutic music. In *Art and music therapy and research* (ed. A. Gilroy and C. Lee). Routledge, London.

Lee, C. (1996). *Music at the edge: the musical experiences of a musician with AIDS*. Routledge, London.

Licht, S. (1946). *Music in medicine*. New England Conservatory of Music, Boston, Mass.

Locsin, R. (1981). The effect of music on the pain of selected post-operative patients. *Journal of Advanced Nursing*, **6**, 19–25.

Madsen, C., Cotter, V., and Madsen, C. (1968). A behavioural approach to music therapy. *Journal of Music Therapy*, **5**, 69–71.

Maranto, C. (1993). *Music therapy: international perspectives*. Jeffrey Books, Pennsylvania.

Maslow, A. (1970). *Motivation and personality*. Harper and Row, New York.

Michel, D. E. (1976). *Music therapy–an introduction to therapy and special education through music*. Charles C. Thomas, Springfield, Illinois.

Miller, D. M., Dorow, L. G., and Greer, R. D. (1974). The contingent use of art for improving arithmetic scores. *Journal of Music Therapy*, **11**, 57–64.

Monsey, H. L. (1960). Preliminary report of the clinical efficacy of audioanalgesia. *Journal of California State Dental Association*, **36**, 432–7.

Moreno, J. (1988). The music therapist: creative arts therapist and contemporary shaman. *The Arts in Psychotherapy*, **15**, 271–80.

Nordoff, P. and Robbins, C. (1971). *Therapy in music for handicapped children*. Gollancz, London.

Nordoff, P. and Robbins, C. (1977). *Creative music therapy*. John Day, New York.

Noy, P. (1966/67). The psychodynamic meaning of music. *Journal of Music Therapy*, 3–4.

Odell, H. (1995). Approaches to music therapy in psychiatry with specific emphasis upon a research project with the elderly mentally ill. In *The art and science of music therapy: a handbook* (ed. T. Wigram, B. Saperston, and R. West). Harwood Academic Publishers/Gordon and Breach Science Publishers, Langhorne.

Oldfield, A. and Adams, M. (1995). The effects of music therapy on a group of adults with profound learning difficulties. In *Art and music therapy and research* (ed. A. Gilroy and C. Lee). Routledge, London.

Oyama, T., Hatano, K., Sato, Y., Kudo, M., Spintge, R., and Droh, R. (1983). Endocrine effect of anxiolytic music in dental patients. In *Angst, schmerz, musik in der anasthesie* (ed. R. Droh and R. Spintge). Editiones Roche, Basel.

Pavlicevic, M. (1995). Music and emotion: aspects of music therapy research. In *Art and music therapy and research* (ed. A. Gilroy and C. Lee). Routledge, London.

Perls, F. S., Hefferline, R., and Goodman, P. (1973). *Gestalt therapy—excitement and growth in the human personality*. Penguin, Harmondsworth.

Podolsky, E. (1954). *Music therapy*. Philosophical Library, New York.

Priestley, M. (1995). *Essays in analytical music therapy*. Barcelona, Philadelphia.

Richer, J. (1979). Human ethology and mental handicap. In *Ethology and nonverbal communication in mental health* (ed. S. Corson). Pergamon, Oxford.

Rider, M. (1987). Treating chronic disease and pain with music-mediated imagery. *The Arts in Psychotherapy*, **14**, 113–20.

Rogers, C. (1969). *On becoming a person: a therapist's view of psychotherapy.* Constable, London.

Rogers, P. (1992). Issues in working with sexually abused clients in music therapy. *Journal of British Music Therapy,* **6**, 5–15.

Roskam, K. (1979). Music therapy as an aid for increasing auditory awareness and improving reading skill. *Journal of Music Therapy,* **16**, 31–42.

Ruud, E. (1980). *Music therapy and its relationship to current treatment theories.* Magnamusic-Baton, St. Louis, Missouri.

Sacks, O. (1991). *Awakenings.* Pan, London.

Saperston, B. (1995). The effect of consistent tempi and physiologically interactive tempi on heart rate and EMG responses. In *The art and science of music therapy: a handbook* (ed. T. Wigram, B. Saperston, and R. West). Harwood Academic Publishers/Gordon and Breach Science Publishers, Langhorne.

Scartelli, J. P. (1982). The effect of sedative music on electromyographic biofeedback assisted relaxation training of spastic cerebral palsied adults. *Journal of Music Therapy,* **19**, 210–18.

Schuster, B. L. (1985). The effect of music on blood pressure fluctuations in adult hemodialysis patients. *Journal of Music Therapy,* **22**, 146–53.

Scott, T. J. (1970). The use of music to reduce hyperactivity in children. *American Journal of Ortho-psychiatry,* **40**, 677–80.

Shapiro, A. G. and Cohen, H. (1983). Auxiliary pain relief during suction curettage. In *Angst, schmerz, musik in der anasthesie* (ed. R. Droh and R. Spintge). Editiones Roche, Basel.

Shullian, D. M. and Schoen, D. (1948). *Music and medicine.* Henry Schuman, New York.

Skille, O. and Wigram, T. (1995). The effects of music, vocalization and vibration on brain and muscle tissue: studies in vibroacoustic therapy. In *The art and science of music therapy: a handbook* (ed. T. Wigram, B. Saperston, and R. West). Harwood Academic Publishers/Gordon and Breach Science Publishers, Langhorne.

Standley, J. (1995). Music as a therapeutic intervention in medical and dental treatment: research and clinical applications. In *The art and science of music therapy: a handbook* (ed. T. Wigram, B. Saperston, and R. West). Harwood Academic Publishers/Gordon and Breach Science Publishers, Langhorne.

Staum, M. J. (1983). Music and rhythmic stimuli in the rehabilitation of gait disorders. *Journal of Music Therapy,* **20**, 69–87.

Steele, A. L. (1968). Programmed use of music to alter uncooperative problem behaviour. *Journal of Music Therapy,* **5**, 131–9.

Stern, D. (1985). *The interpersonal world of the infant: a view from psychoanalysis and developmental psychology.* Basic Books, New York.

Storr, A. (1989). *Psychoanalysis and creativity in Churchill's black dog, and other phenomena of the human mind.* Collins-Fontana, Glasgow.

Tanioka, F., Takazawa, T., Kamata, S., Kudo, M., Matsuki, A., and Oyama, T. (1985). Hormonal effect of anxiolytic music in patients during surgical operations under epidural anaesthesia. In *Music in medicine* (ed. R. Spintge and R. Droh). Editiones Roche, Basel.

Wilber, K. (1979). *No boundary.* Shambhala, Boston, Mass.

Winnicott, D. W. (1971). *Playing and reality.* Tavistock, London.

Yalom, I. (1985). *The theory and practice of group psychotherapy.* Basic Books, London.

14 | *Music and consumer behaviour*

Adrian C. North and David J. Hargreaves

The commercial and industrial uses of music (see Bruner 1990; Gardner 1985*a*) account for billions of dollars worldwide, involved with such diverse activities as honouring royalty payments for using music in TV advertisements, installing music systems in shops, or promoting new pop music records and CDs. Given the frequency with which people are exposed to music on the radio or in shops or television advertisements, it is possible to argue that such commercial uses constitute one of the principal sources of our everyday exposure to music in the Western world. This remains the case despite the existence of pressure groups such as Pipedown in the UK, and arguments that commercial uses of music may have negative effects (e.g. Englis and Pennell 1994), be less appropriate than silence (Olsen 1994), and at times constitute noise pollution (cf. Hopkins 1994).

What links all these commercial uses is their concern with how music can lead to profit, for example by enhancing advertising effectiveness, by influencing customers' in-store behaviour, or by attracting people to a commercial radio station. In these contexts, music typically ceases to be an aesthetic object as such, and is instead a marketing tool or at best a product for consumption. This chapter looks at these issues in the context of television advertisements and shops, and also the music industry itself. Psychological studies have made a major contribution to the understanding of these areas, although given the inter-disciplinary nature of the field (see Holbrook 1987), we have also drawn upon other approaches such as consumer research and sociology in order to provide a broader perspective

ADVERTISING

Music might play many different and complementary roles in advertising, such as attracting attention, implicitly or explicitly carrying the message, creating emotional states, or acting as a mnemonic cue (Hecker 1984). This potential utility seems to be reflected by the frequency with which it is employed by advertisers. For example, Stewart and Furse (1986) report that music was present in 42 per cent of the 1000 television commercials they considered, and Stewart and Koslow (1989) report a similar frequency in a different large sample of advertisements. Furthermore, Appelbaum and Halliburton (1993) report that this figure increases to 89.3 per cent when considering advertisements screened internationally, and indicate that music is typically the predominant element in these advertisements. Whilst this clearly suggests the importance of music in television commercials, research has only recently begun to ask why this should be so. The main explanations advanced so far are based on three key concepts, namely classical conditioning, involvement, and more recently the notion of musical 'fit'.

Attitude towards the ad and classical conditioning

Interest in music increased dramatically in the early 1980s as a result of a series of studies focusing on the concept of 'attitude towards the ad' (or Aad). The more traditional approach to advertising before this had adopted the 'attitude towards the brand' approach. This concerned how advertisements could influence consumer *beliefs* and attitudes regarding the favourable consequences of consuming the brand in question, and emphasized product attributes and benefits. However, this approach was challenged by studies showing that the affective consequences of being exposed to a television advertisement were themselves important mediators of consumer behaviour.

Mitchell and Olson (1981) presented subjects with advertisements for facial tissues and found that differences in attitudes towards the tissues could not be wholly accounted for by differences in product attribute beliefs (e.g. softness, absorbency) elicited by the advertisements: subjects' affective responses to the advertisements (e.g. like–dislike, good–bad) also had a significant influence on their disposition towards the product. Similarly, Moore and Hutchinson (1983) found that following exposure to print advertisements, subjects were more likely to consider products associated with advertisements that produced positive rather than negative affective responses. Several other studies have shown that Aad mediates the relationship between advertising and consumer behaviour (see review by Brown and Stayman 1992). Consequently, the Aad approach emphasizes that advertising should leave the consumer with a positive feeling about the product: advertisement music may bring about such feelings, and the most frequently investigated possible mechanism for this has been the well-known classical conditioning paradigm.

In practical terms, classical conditioning implies that pairing a product (conditioned stimulus) with a liked piece of music (unconditioned stimulus) should produce an association between the two, and therefore liking for the product (a conditioned response). Gorn (1982) demonstrated this mechanism in perhaps the best known study of music in marketing contexts. Subjects were shown a slide of either a light blue or beige coloured pen in the presence of music that was either liked (taken from the film 'Grease') or disliked (classical Indian music). As a supposed token of thanks for participating, subjects could choose one of the two types of pen from boxes located at opposite sides of the room, and 79 per cent of subjects chose the pen associated with liked music. This suggests that liked music is effective in advertisements because it conditions preference for a product associated with it. Similar findings are reported by Bierley *et al.* (1985) who showed that preference ratings for stimuli that predicted pleasant music were greater than for those that predicted unpleasant music. Similarly, Tom (1995) found that music could condition preference even when subjects were not attending to the stimuli (i.e. the state in which we are perhaps more typically exposed to advertising). The classical conditioning hypothesis has also been borne out by several non-musical marketing studies (see, for example, McSweeney and Bierley 1984; Shimp *et al.* 1991).

Despite its apparent acceptance by many authors in the marketing literature, the classical conditioning hypothesis has attracted a considerable number of criticisms. The least serious of these has concerned several occasions where music has failed to classically condition responses to products. For example, Pitt and Abratt (1988) employed a methodology virtually identical to Gorn's, but with different products to be conditioned—red and blue condoms. The resulting absence of conditioning effects suggests that the process may not operate for products which are 'very personal, controversial, and anything but boring' (p. 136). Also, Allen and Madden (1985) failed to replicate Gorn's findings when humorous stories replaced music as the unconditioned stimulus presented concurrent with the pens, suggesting that conditioning may not be a universal advertising process. Similarly, Alpert and Alpert (1989) found that the mood associated with different greeting cards could not be conditioned by pairing them with happy and sad music. Other authors have argued that the influence of affective responses to advertising music might be underspecified by global terms such as 'liking' (Holbrook and Batra 1987; Chapter 5, this volume), and perhaps also overemphasized by the use of still rather than moving pictures in research (Dunbar 1990).

Two other studies further question the utility of the classical conditioning approach. First, Kellaris and Cox (1989) argue that findings which support this approach may have resulted from demand artefacts: they found that subjects' pen selection choices were influenced by merely imagining that they heard liked or disliked music associated with the pens, which suggests that conditioning effects may be the result of subjects' expectations about their likely behaviour rather than music *per se*. Kellaris and Cox also showed that the specific nature of the cover story given to subjects may be important. Second, Middlestadt *et al.* (1994) questioned the extent to which conditioning studies really investigated the effects of advertisement music on only *affective* responses as such. Their study found that music made different aspects of the apple juice advertised to subjects more or less salient, i.e. it influenced *beliefs* as well as affect. For example, 23 per cent of subjects who saw the commercial with music noted 'drinking a natural drink' as one of the benefits of the juice, whereas this figure fell to 4 per cent in a no music condition. The most prudent conclusion to draw at the moment is that the debate over classical conditioning continues (cf. Darley and Lim 1993; Shimp *et al.* 1993).

Elaboration likelihood, involvement, and 'fit'

Whilst the classical conditioning approach may not provide a comprehensive explanation of musical effects in advertising, it has made a clear contribution to the more detailed Elaboration Likelihood Model. Gorn (1982) conducted a second experiment to test the generality of conditioning effects, and the main difference between this and his first experiment described above was that half of the subjects were not told they would receive a pen until they were asked actually to choose between the two pen colours, whereas the remaining subjects were told at the beginning of the study that they would receive a pen for having participated. The former group tended to choose the pen advertised with liked music, whereas the latter group tended to choose the pen that was advertised with information emphasizing that it did not smudge: in other words, musical conditioning seemed to operate when subjects had no reason to evaluate the advertised brand, whereas product information seemed to be more important when they were motivated to process brand-relevant information.

Findings such as these can be explained in terms of the Elaboration Likelihood Model (or ELM—Petty and Cacioppo 1981; Petty *et al.* 1983). The ELM states that there are two routes to persuasion, central and peripheral. In the central route, attitudes are formed by careful consideration of information relevant to the attitude object (e.g. does this pen smudge?). In the peripheral route, attitudes are formed without active thinking about the object and its attributes, but rather by *associating* the object with positive or negative cues, such as liked or disliked music: in other words, by some form of conditioning mechanism. Persuasion occurs via the central route when elaboration likelihood is high, i.e. the person has the *motivation, opportunity, and ability* to process (or elaborate on) information about the product. This has been termed 'high involvement' with the advertisement. Persuasion occurs via the peripheral route when people are in a state of 'low involvement' with the advertisement, and do not have the motivation, opportunity, or ability to elaborate on the information they have regarding the attitude object: conditioning may influence such processing because lower motivation, opportunity, or ability to process the advertisement may invoke simpler cues and heuristics in the process of attitude formation. Consequently, advertising cues such as liked music should be more important in persuasion when the viewer is unwilling or unable to evaluate overt commercial messages concerning the advertised brand. This might be why music is used so much in advertising, since most viewers may pay little attention to advertisements, and as such should be in a state of low involvement. Similarly, we might expect to see music used more in advertisements for products that have no obvious advantages over their competitors: in such a situation it would be pointless for advertisers to attempt to argue that their product has better attributes, and thus invoke central route evaluative processes.

Several studies have investigated the ELM with non-musical peripheral cues such as pictures (e.g. Miniard *et al.* 1991; Mitchell 1986; Stuart *et al.* 1987), source expertise (e.g. Ratneshwar and Chaiken 1991; Yalch and Elmore-Yalch 1984), and the celebrity status of a product endorser (e.g. Petty *et al.* 1983; Sanbonmatsu and Kardes 1988), although Park and Young (1986) also supported the predictions of the ELM in hair shampoo advertisements employing music. One group of subjects was asked to try to learn about the effectiveness of the shampoo. This meant that they would be highly involved with the advertisement, and would be expected to process the information in the commercial (i.e. central route). Subjects in another group were asked to imagine that they had no need to buy shampoo, and this would be expected to bring about a low level of involvement, or an unwillingness to process the information about the product. Consistent with the ELM, music had a positive effect for low-involvement subjects leading to, for example, better brand attitudes than those subjects in a no music condition. In contrast, music had a distracting effect for subjects in the high-involvement group, leading to lower brand attitudes than for those in a no music condition. (See also Thorson *et al.* (1991) on involvement and music in political commercials.)

Bitner and Obermiller (1985) note several areas where the ELM requires further development, such as whether peripheral or central processing give rise to the most enduring attitudes, and whether these two routes are independent (see also Gardner 1985b). On a more positive note however, MacInnis *et al.* (1991) have discussed how advertising cues might increase consumers' involvement with an advertisement, and therefore perhaps its retention (e.g. Craik and Lockhart 1972): they propose several specific means by which this could be achieved, and it is a simple task to see how music could serve for such means. For example, *motivation* to process the advertisement could be enhanced by increasing attention to it, e.g. by playing loud music, whereas *opportunity* to process the information could be influenced by reducing the advertisement's cognitive load, e.g. by playing slow rather than fast music. MacInnis *et al.* recommend that *ability* to process the advertisement can be enhanced by cues which access relevant knowledge structures, and this leads to the idea of musical 'fit'.

The ELM states that affect-evoking music should have a distracting effect for high-involvement consumers who are trying to process information about the product. However, MacInnis and Park (1991) argued that music may positively influence these high-involvement consumers if it 'fits' the advertisement, or corresponds with 'consumers' subjective perceptions of the music's relevance or appropriateness to the central ad message' (p. 162). In essence, music that fits the advertisement should be effective for high-involvement consumers because it primes relevant beliefs about the product, e.g. sophisticated classical music in an advertisement for perfume. As such the music works not by influencing affect towards the advertisement, but rather by conveying and activating relevant *information*, and this contrasts with the affect-based classical conditioning approach described above. Indeed, the effects of musical fit should be more beneficial for high- than for low-involvement consumers, since appropriate music focuses attention on the message: low-involvement consumers, by definition, are less motivated to process the product in terms of the accompanying music. MacInnis and Park (1991) provided some initial support for this argument in a study of shampoo commercials using 'You Make Me Feel Like a Natural Woman' as appropriate music: musical fit positively influenced the response of high-involvement consumers, and therefore seemed to be priming relevant knowledge. Kellaris *et al.* (1993) obtained similar results in 'radio advertisements' when instrumental rather than lyrical properties were used to promote music-message congruence.

The notion of 'fit' might explain why Stout and Leckenby (1990) found that advertisements were perceived more positively (e.g. 'right for me') and as more informative when they contained music associated readily with the advertised brand (see also Blair and Hatala 1992), and why Hall *et al.* (1986) found that viewers preferred pop music videos in which the visual and lyrical content were matched. In a similar vein, Brannon and Brock (1994) propose a link between persuasion and 'the extent to which messages resonate . . . with the schemas assigned to attitude objects' (p. 169). MacInnis and Park's findings also correspond with Scott's (1990) view that previous research has tended to overlook 'the communicative meaning that a musical piece may have' (p. 225), and 'precludes consumers' ability to judge and understand various styles and melodies as appropriate and communicative, in particular message contexts, exclusive of personal taste' (p. 226; see also Dunbar 1990). Indeed, a great deal of research indicates that responses to music are directly related to their cultural and contextual meaningfulness (e.g. Dowling and Harwood 1986; Merriam 1964; Meyer 1967; Zuckerkandl 1956; Chapter 5, this volume). In short, music may be effective in commercials because it communicates meaning/information as well as affect.

To conclude this section, music can influence responses to the advertisements in which it is employed. This might be the result of a conditioning process whereby response to the music generalizes to the product. Such a process may be more effective when consumers lack the motivation, opportunity, or ability to process information in the advertisement. However, musical meaning may also prime specific beliefs about the product, and this deserves further research attention.

SHOPS

The role of music in inducing affect has also been investigated by research on music in shops and stores. Kotler (1973–74) is usually acknowledged to have introduced the concept of store atmospherics: 'the effort to design buying environments to produce specific emotional effects in the buyer that enhance his purchase probability' (p. 50; see also Markin *et al.* 1976). The approach focuses on various atmospheric/environmental variables such as lighting, crowding, layout, or even scent (Gulas and Bloch 1995), although a few studies have also begun to investigate the role of music. These seem warranted given research showing that store managers' use of music was not guided by any empirical investigation (Burleson 1979). Other studies have shown that affect towards a store and store image are related to patronage frequency and money spent (Darden *et al.* 1983; Golden and Zimmer 1986); store choice (Bawa *et al.* 1989; Malhotra 1983; Nevin and Houston 1980; Stanley and Sewall 1976); and brand loyalty, promotion sensitivity, price sensitivity, and response to new brands (Bawa *et al.* 1989): since in-store music might mediate affect towards the store and store image, these findings suggest that a more detailed understanding of in-store music may lead to positive marketing effects.

Customer activity

Several studies have shown that the arousing qualities of in-store music can mediate the tempo of consumer behaviour. The first and perhaps most theoretically-oriented of these was carried out by Smith and Curnow (1966). They tested the 'arousal hypothesis' that a certain noise level will increase activity by playing loud and soft music in a supermarket. Customers in the loud music condition spent less time on average in the supermarket (17.64 minutes) than those in the soft music condition (18.53). Arousing music made customers shop more quickly. Similarly, Milliman (1982) played slow (<73 bpm) and fast (>93 bpm) music in a supermarket, and measured the time it took customers to move between two points in the store. Customers were slower under the slow (127.53 seconds) than the fast (108.93 seconds) tempo conditions, but perhaps because of this also spent more in the former condition ($16 740.23 and $12 112.85 respectively).

A follow-up study in a restaurant (Milliman 1986) confirmed these results since slow music led to longer meal times, and more drinks being bought. These results were supported by Roballey *et al.* (1985), who found that fast music in a university staff cafeteria led to more bites per minute than slow music (means = 4.40 and 3.83 respectively); and McElrea and Standing (1992) who found that fast music in a bar led to faster drinking than did slow music. In conjunction, these studies indicate that as in-store music becomes more arousing, so consumers act more quickly, but as a consequence of this perhaps spend less money: maybe store managers must balance the desire to increase sales volume through unarousing music with the additional sales produced by increasing the flow of customers brought about by arousing music.

Purchasing and affiliation

Several studies suggest that affective responses to music may also mediate purchasing and affiliative behaviour. Areni and Kim (1993) applied MacInnis and Park's idea of 'fit' (see above) to shopping behaviour by playing classical music (high fit) and Top 40 music (low fit) in a wine cellar: although the two types of music did not influence the number of bottles of wine sold, classical music led to customers buying more expensive wine that did Top 40 music. Similarly, Alpert and Alpert (1990) found that sad music led to higher purchase intentions for greetings cards than did happy music, and they speculate that this was because sad music was more appropriate for the cards. Although far from conclusive, these studies could be seen as initial evidence that the idea of musical 'fit' extends into the domain of in-store music, so that music primes the selection of certain goods.

The three remaining studies of affect and in-store music draw on Mehrabian and Russell's (1974) model of environmental psychology. In light of subsequent developments, the model can be summarized as stating that people respond to environments along two principal dimensions, namely pleasure and arousal. As an environment becomes more pleasurable so people are likely to demonstrate 'approach behaviours' towards it, such as a greater willingness to return or affiliate with others. The arousal-evoking qualities of the environment act so as to amplify the effects of pleasure. This has obvious relevance to in-store music which could make the environment more pleasurable, but also influence the extent to which it is arousing through qualities such as musical tempo, volume, or complexity, etc. (see Berlyne 1971; North and Hargreaves, in press, *a*). Also, two formal (although non-musical) tests of the Mehrabian and Russell model have shown that the pleasure and arousal evoked by commercial environments can predict consumer behaviour (Donovan and Rossiter 1982; Donovan *et al.* 1994).

Dube *et al.* (1995) manipulated the musical background of a video simulation of a bank, and found independent and interactive effects of musically-induced pleasure and arousal on consumers' desire to affiliate with bank employees. Higher desire to affiliate was generally associated with higher degrees of pleasure and arousal. Similarly, Baker *et al.* (1992) considered the joint effects of two ambient cues (music and lighting) and two social cues (the number and friendliness of employees) on respondents' pleasure, arousal, and willingness to buy in a video simulation of a card and gift shop. In the 'low social' condition (i.e. one employee who ignored the subject), quiet background music and soft lighting led to greater pleasure and willingness to buy from the store than foreground music and brighter lighting. Finally, North and Hargreaves (1996*a*) found that disliked music in a cafeteria was more noticeable to diners than affectively-neutral music: furthermore, North and Hargreaves (1996*b*) found that liking for the music in this cafeteria was related positively to liking for the cafeteria; willingness to return; the extent to which diners were willing to affiliate with others (see also Fried and Berkowitz 1979); and the number of people actually coming to the environmental source of the music, namely a stall offering leaflets. The latter finding suggests that music may be able to attract consumers to a given commercial setting, and this effect was predictable partly on the basis of how arousing the music was. This pattern of findings seems to support the prediction of the Mehrabian and Russell model that musically-induced pleasure leads to affiliation and general approach behaviours towards commercial environments (although the role of arousal in this is less clear however, and perhaps awaits further research).

Waiting time

Another reason for the commercial use of music is the belief that it can influence consumers' responses to being kept waiting (e.g. in queues), and several recent studies have shown a relationship between music, waiting, and consumer behaviour. For example, Ramos (1993) found that manipulating the musical style played to on-hold callers to a telephone advisory service influenced the number that hung up before their call was answered. Similarly, Stratton (1992) asked subjects who were supposedly waiting for the start of an experiment to wait alone or in groups whose members either did or did not talk to one another. Non-talking groups who waited to musical accompaniment found the period less stressful than non-talking groups without music. The non-talking groups without music gave higher time duration estimates than other groups. Yalch and Spangenberg (1990) also found that background music led to under-25 year-old clothes shoppers reporting having spent more unplanned time in-store, whereas older subjects showed the same effect when foreground music was played.

Why should music have such an influence on time perceptions? Wansink (1992) proposed what might appear to be the intuitively obvious line of argument that consumers should be expected to underestimate time durations when they hear liked music. However, Kellaris has shown the opposite; in effect, times does *not* fly when you're having fun, and he explained this in terms of research on cognitive psychology. First, the 'Pollyana principle' (e.g. Matlin 1989) states that pleasant information is processed and recalled more effectively. Second, time perception is positively related to the number of events that are processed within the given period (e.g. Levin and Zackay 1989; Ornstein 1969). Kellaris and Mantel (1994) used these two lines of research to explain their finding that disliked music led to shorter time estimations than liked music: they suggest that less information was encoded and retrieved when disliked (i.e. unpleasant) music was played, and this reduction in processing led to shorter time estimates. Interestingly, the effect was only found for females (see also Kellaris and Altsech 1992), but this too corresponds with research showing that males estimate the kind of short durations employed by Kellaris more accurately, and that females are more prone to underestimating time intervals (see, for example, Krishnan and Saxena 1984; Rammsayer and Lustnauer 1989).

Kellaris and Kent (1992) related these effects to structural musical properties by demonstrating that perceived duration was longest for subjects exposed to major mode (i.e. affectively positive) music, and shortest for subjects exposed to minor mode (i.e. affectively negative) music. Similarly, Kellaris and Altsech (1992) (see also Kellaris *et al.*, in press) found that for females at least, loud music led to longer time estimates than soft music, and this corresponds with the earlier argument that time estimation is positively related to the amount of information processed during that period: several authors (e.g. Konečni 1982) have suggested that arousing (e.g. loud) music seems to require more processing than unarousing (e.g. soft) music.

In a study which perhaps possesses greater ecological validity, Chebat *et al.* (1993) investigated the effects of musical tempo on the perceived duration of a video-simulated bank queue. Musical tempo did not directly affect perceived time spent in the queue. However, in a slow music condition, the degree of visual stimulation (e.g. camera movement, more customers) and mood were positively related to time perception. Although these effects were explained in terms of a different theoretical model (including elements of the Mehrabian and Russell framework) to that proposed by Kellaris, the positive effects of mood on time estimation do seem to be consistent with Kellaris' hypothesis that 'time doesn't fly when you're having fun'.

Part of the appeal of Kellaris' findings is their counter-intuitive nature, and they certainly deserve further research. In the meantime, they seem to have some provocative implications. First, retailers could perhaps use music to decrease the perception of elapsed time in queues etc. by playing disliked or slow music. They could also perhaps play liked or fast music to increase perceived time when, for example, trying to quicken the turnover of tables in a busy restaurant (Kellaris and Altsech 1992). Kellaris' findings also contrast with those discussed above which show that liked music leads to liking for commercial environments: there may be a trade-off between using liked music to evoke liking for the environment and thus perhaps increase spending, and using disliked music to decrease the perception of elapsed time.

In concluding this section, we should note one study which suggests that music may have a more global effect on in-store behaviour. Zullow (1991) determined the top 40 selling songs in the USA for each year between 1955 and 1989, and rated their lyrics in terms of 'pessimistic rumination' (i.e. depressive content). Variations in pessimistic rumination predicted the US government's principal measure of consumer optimism, and this in turn predicted gross national product with a one to two-year time lead, such that changes in the song lyrics *preceded* changes in the economy. This suggests that pop music lyrics can predict recession via reduced consumer optimism. Moreover, Zullow concludes by noting that the very high levels of pessimistic rumination at the time of writing predicted an American recession in the early 1990s! The possible commercial implications of such effects do not require further comment.

THE MUSIC INDUSTRY

We have concentrated so far on how music is applied in different commercial situations; but perhaps the most obvious commercial use of music is in the music industry itself, which makes money by recording, promoting, performing, broadcasting, and selling music. We mentioned in Chapter 1 that the technological revolution has greatly increased people's access to music, and several studies have reflected the rise of pop music radio, music television, and record buying. Perhaps the most dramatic of these was carried out by Stack and Gundlach (1992) who demonstrated that the frequency with which country music was played on the radio was directly related to the suicide rate of urban whites (and this was independent of divorce, geographical variation, poverty, and gun ownership). Many other studies have focused on comparatively mundane manifestations of music's increased accessibility through the mass media.

Pop music radio and television

In Chapter 5 we discussed how the plugging of records on the radio can mediate their popularity. In this context, Rothenbuhler and McCourt (1992; see also Rothenbuhler 1985) have provided a fascinating account of the factors associated with the selection of records for radio airplay. The main theme in this is the absolute dominance of commercial interests: the primary concern underlying record selection is to attract listeners to the advertisement breaks, which are the means by which the stations make money. The music is little more than a means of delivering an audience to advertisers, and several processes of record selection are geared towards this aim.

Even before reaching a radio station, each song has passed through a series of filters (e.g. record companies) that select only music with probable mass commercial appeal. Once at the radio station, songs are deliberately not selected if they even *might* cause listeners to switch channels and fail to hear the advertisements. The principal means of achieving this is the selection of only those songs that fit the station's 'format' (e.g. Top 40, Adult-Orientated Rock; see Hirsch 1969): by playing music of a certain specific type, the station attracts and holds a reasonably homogenous group of listeners which can be delivered to advertisers. The main sources of information about which particular songs to play within the general format are industry-based, for example, other radio stations, record promoters/consultants, and trade newspapers, rather than listener requests. Furthermore, the homogeneity of musical output that this leads to is exacerbated by the use of a 'playlist'—a small number of specific songs which receive heavy airplay because of their likely appeal to the target audience.

The conservatism of the process is best exemplified by the phenomenon of the 'consensus cut' in which the stations (often under guidance from record promoters) tend to follow each other by playing the same track from an album to avoid 'looking stupid' (Rothenbuhler 1985, p. 219). It would be interesting to see if the same processes applied to non-pop formats (e.g. classical music radio), and to the UK's largest pop music station, Radio 1, which is run by the *publicly-funded* BBC. In the meantime, findings such as these certainly provide a broader perspective to conventional psychological research on musical preference, and it would be interesting to determine whether the musical factors considered by psychologists (e.g. complexity, typicality; see Chapter 5) are related to the frequency with which a record receives radio airplay.

Although founded as recently as 1 August 1981, Music Television (MTV) and similar television channels (e.g. VH-1 and CMT) have been subject to a surprisingly large amount of analysis by both academics and social commentators (see review by Sherman and Etling 1991). Several authors have considered similarities between its goals and those of commercial music radio, such as attracting specific audiences for advertising purposes, and keeping these viewers watching until the next advertising break (see, for example, Denisoff 1985; Levy 1983; Sherman and Etling 1991; Wolfe 1983). Content analyses of pop music videos suggest that they are produced to achieve these aims by promoting instant gratification (Kaplan 1987; Pittman

1985; Levy 1983) through quick editing (Fry and Fry 1987), and images that are often 'violent, male-orientated, and with sexual content' (Sherman and Dominick 1986, p. 92). Indeed, there has been considerable concern over the portrayal of women and the effect of this on girls' socialization (Brown and Campbell 1985; Brown *et al.* 1986), since females tend to be portrayed as less active and worthy of attention (Brown and Campbell 1986); subservient (Vincent *et al.* 1987); 'vampiric dominatrixes' (McKenna 1983); and generally as 'the comic book fantasies of adolescent males' (Gehr 1983, p. 40), although this position might have changed somewhat in the late 1990s. It is also worth noting here that there is little evidence that viewers imitate the messages of pop music videos (e.g. Greenfield *et al.* 1987; Thornton and Voigt 1984; Walker 1987).

Music as product

Record retailing is probably the most overtly commercial use of music, with people paying to own a copy of their favourite pieces. The USA Department of Commerce reported in 1992 that 'the dollar value of manufacturers' shipments of pre-recorded music was $7.54 bn, up 14.62 per cent from 1989' (pp. 31–3; see also Frith 1992). Despite this, record buying has been largely neglected by social scientists, and there are no identifiable programmes of research. However, some individual studies have provided fascinating evidence on several aspects of music purchasing.

Lacher (1989) noted that the consumption of music differs from that of other products in that we have many opportunities to sample music before buying (e.g. through the radio), rarely buy the same music twice, and consume the music repeatedly although it has little utilitarian value. This suggests that the purchasing of recorded music may require specialized theoretical explanations. In the light of this, Lacher and Mizerski (1994) proposed a model of music consumption in which 'sensorial', 'imaginal', 'emotional', and 'analytical' responses to music all contributed towards three constructs that may hypothetically influence the recorded music purchase decision, namely overall affective response, experiential response (e.g. being 'swept up' into the experience of the music), and the need to re-experience the music. Their research suggested that these three constructs were all related to music purchase intentions, although the need to re-experience the music was the strongest predictor of such intentions.

Meenaghan and Turnbull (1981) employed a variety of archival measures (e.g. radio airplay, record sales) to present data illustrating the typical 'product life cycle' of successful pop singles. The central feature of this was that successful records moved through five stages in a typically 16 week-long period between their release and final abandonment by the music industry. In stage one ('pre-release'), songs and artists were selected for their likely market performance. Stage two ('buzz-creation') was short, occurring just before and during release, and was characterized by promotion by the record company in an attempt to persuade TV and radio stations that the song was not a risk. Stage three ('pre-threshold') occurred between release and entry into the charts, and was characterized by the media deciding whether to feature the song: such exposure was a crucial determinant of record sales, and typically *preceded* them. Stage four ('commercial life', or the time spent on the chart) was approximately 11 weeks long. During the early weeks of this stage, radio airplay was the most important determinant of sales, and was used as a guide to which songs should receive TV exposure. If a song reached the Top 20 it tended to receive television coverage, and this then became more closely associated with sales than radio airplay, with the latter declining in importance as this stage progressed. Stage five ('final decline') corresponded with falling sales, and was very short. Sales were often negligible within only three weeks of a song leaving the chart, although the speed of this decline tended to correspond with that of the earlier sales increase. This model, in conjunction with Rothenbuhler's research on commercial radio, suggests quite strongly that the music industry *determines* rather than reflects the popularity of particular songs, with commercial, industry-based factors determining which songs are released, broadcast, and ultimately purchased (see also Anderson *et al.* 1980; Peterson and Berger 1975; and Chapter 5 on radio plugging).

Two other studies have taken a similar archival approach in examining data from the pop music record charts. Dixon (1982) considered how variables taken from the Billboard Top 200 chart could predict the waxing and waning in popularity of 234 LPs. Records generally entered the charts at low positions, and this entry position was a strong (and often the best) predictor of how high they climbed; how long they sustained their peak popularity; how long they remained on the chart after peaking; whether they went 'gold'; and whether there were other records by the same artist currently on the charts. However, records took roughly the same amount of time to achieve their peak position irrespective of chart entry position. Entry and peak chart position were enhanced by prior hit singles from the LPs, although singles taken from the LPs after their release did not have a similar effect. Third week chart position was the best predictor of peak chart position.

North and Hargreaves (1996c) considered 200 successful pop music artists from between 1955 and 1994 in terms of their chart performance; ratings of their eminence by subjects aged between 9 and 78 years; and the amount of space they received in pop music encyclopaedias. Artists who had been successful more recently tended to be rated as more eminent by subjects (a 'reverence for the recent' effect), but received less space in music encyclopaedias than older artists ('reverence for the past'). Those artists rated as eminent by subjects tended to have released the most singles, consistent with research showing that the probability of success in a field is directly related to productivity (see, for example, Dennis 1966; Lehman 1953; Simonton 1984). The rated eminence of older artists was also more closely related to record sales and the duration of their chart careers than was the eminence of recent artists, and LP sales were more closely related to the artists' rated eminence than were singles sales. Finally, although statistically significant, there was only a moderate correlation between the artists' performance on the UK and USA charts.

The studies in this section provide some indications that the popularity of musicians and their recordings follow predictable patterns that should be of considerable interest to consumer researchers and music psychologists. They also suggest that archival sources such as record sales and pop music charts may provide valuable data since they represent a rigorous, frequent (i.e. weekly), and large (i.e. nationwide) measure of musical consumption that is accessible to academic researchers (see, for example, Hesbacher *et al.* 1978). Record buying is perhaps the ultimate behavioural measure of musical preference, involving the purchaser's time, effort, and money. Given these advantages, record charts should be an extremely useful source of future data for psychomusicological and consumer research, despite the commercial distortions imposed upon them by the music industry.

CONCLUSION

This literature clearly indicates the extent to which music is related to, and may influence, commercial processes. However, the many commercial uses to which music is put, and the amount of money spent on these, far outweigh the extent to which empirical research has provided clear guidance for commercial practitioners. Although the number of studies has grown over the past two decades, there is still a clear need for research that replicates earlier investigations (Hubbard 1994); that refines and extends the tentative empirical models described above; and that investigates severely neglected areas such as the effect of music on employees (see Oldham *et al.* 1995; Radocy and Boyle 1988). We also look forward to the continued growth of three trends, namely the use of archival data; more sophisticated measures of response to music than the 'like–dislike' distinctions employed until recently; and investigations of the concept of 'fit' and appropriateness (which correspond with recent research in experimental aesthetics—see Chapter 5). More generally, research on the commercial uses of music should have important implications for consumer research, music psychology, and commercial practice: the field is under-investigated at present, and the practical and theoretical potential of further research seems readily apparent.

REFERENCES

Allen, C. T. and Madden, T. J. (1985). A closer look at classical conditioning. *Journal of Consumer Research*, **12**, 301–15.

Alpert, J. I. and Alpert, M. I. (1989). Background music as an influence in consumer mood and advertising responses. *Advances in Consumer Research*, **16**, 485–91.

Alpert, J. I. and Alpert, M. I. (1990). Music influences on mood and purchase intentions. *Psychology and Marketing*, **7**, 109–33.

Anderson B., Hesbacher, P., Etzkorn, K. P., and Denisoff, R. S. (1980). Hit record trends, 1940–1977. *Journal of Communication*, **30**, 31–43.

Appelbaum, V. and Halliburton, C. (1993). How to develop international advertising campaigns that work: the example of the European food and beverage sector. *International Journal of Advertising*, **12**, 223–41.

Areni, C. S. and Kim, D. (1993). The influence of background music on shopping behavior: classical versus top-forty music in a wine store. *Advances in Consumer Research*, **20**, 336–40.

Baker, J., Levy, M., and Grewal, D. (1992). An experimental approach to making retail store environmental decisions. *Journal of Retailing*, **68**, 445–60.

Bawa, K., Landwehr, J. T., and Krishna, A. (1989). Consumer response to retailers' marketing environments: an analysis of coffee purchase data. *Journal of Retailing*, **65**, 471–95.

Berlyne, D. E. (1971). *Aesthetics and psychobiology*. Appleton-Century-Crofts, New York.

Bierley, C., McSweeney, F. K., and Vannieuwkerk, R. (1985). Classical conditioning of preferences for stimuli. *Journal of Consumer Research*, **12**, 316–23.

Bitner, M. J. and Obermiller, C. (1985). The elaboration likelihood model: limitations and extensions in marketing. *Advances in Consumer Research*, **12**, 420–5.

Blair, M. E. and Hatala, M. N. (1992). The use of rap music in children's advertising. *Advances in Consumer Research*, **19**, 719–24.

Brannon, L. A. and Brock, T. C. (1994). Test of schema correspondence theory of persuasion: effects of matching an appeal to actual, ideal, and product 'selves'. In *Attention, attitude, and affect in responses to advertising* (ed. E. M. Clark, T. C. Brock, and D. W. Stewart). Lawrence Erlbaum Associates, Hillsdale, New Jersey.

Brown, J. D. and Campbell, K. (1986). Race and gender in music videos: the same beat but a different drummer. *Journal of Communication*, **36**, 1–15.

Brown, S. P. and Stayman, D. M. (1992). Antecedents and consequences of attitude toward the ad: a meta-analysis. *Journal of Consumer Research*, **19**, 34–51.

Brown, J. D., Campbell, K., and Fischer, L. (1986). American adolescents and music videos: why do they watch? *Gazette*, **37**, 19–32.

Bruner, G. C. (1990). Music, mood, and marketing. *Journal of Marketing*, **54**, 94–104.

Burleson, G. L. (1979). *Retailer and consumer attitudes towards background music*. Unpublished manuscript, Department of Business Administration, University of Texas at El Paso.

Chebat, J-C., Gelinas-Chebat, C., and Filiatrault, P. (1993). Interactive effects of musical and visual cues on time perception: an application to waiting lines in banks. *Perceptual and Motor Skills*, **77**, 995–1020.

Craik, F. and Lockhart, R. (1972). Levels of processing. *Journal of Verbal Learning and Verbal Behaviour*, **11**, 671–84.

Darden, W. R., Erdem, O., and Darden, D. K. (1983). A comparison and test of three causal models of patronage intentions. In *Patronage behavior and retail management* (ed. W. R. Darden and R. F. Lusch). North-Holland, New York.

Darley, W. K. and Lim, J-S. (1993). Assessing demand artefacts in consumer research: an alternative perspective. *Journal of Consumer Research*, **20**, 489–95.

Denisoff, R. S. (1985). Music videos and the rock press. *Popular Music and Society*, **10**, 59–61.

Dennis, W. (1996). Creative productivity between the ages of 20 and 80 years. *Journal of Gerontology*, **21**, 1–8.

Dixon, R. D. (1982). LP chart careers: indices and predictors of ascent and descent in popularity. *Popular Music and Society*, **8**, 19–43 .

Donovan, R. J. and Rossiter, J. R. (1982). Store atmosphere: an environmental psychology approach. *Journal of Retailing*, **58**, 34–57.

Donovan, R. J., Rossiter, J. R., Marcoolyn, G., and Nesdale, A. (1994). Store atmosphere and purchasing behavior. *Journal of Retailing*, **70**, 283–94.

Dowling, W. J. and Harwood, D. L. (1986). *Music cognition*. Academic Press, New York.

Dube, L., Chebat, J-C., and Morin, S. (1995). The effects of background music on consumers' desire to affiliate in buyer–seller interactions. *Psychology and Marketing*, **12**, 305–19.

Dunbar, D. S. (1990). Music, and advertising. *International Journal of Advertising*, **9**, 197–203.

Englis, B. G. and Pennell, G. E. (1994). 'This note's for you . . .': negative effects of the commercial use of popular music. *Advances in Consumer Research*, **21**, 97.

Fried, R. and Berkowitz, L. (1979). Music hath charms . . . and can influence helpfulness. *Journal of Applied Social Psychology*, **9**, 199–208.

Frith, S. (1992). The industrialization of popular music. In *Popular music and communication* (2nd edn) (ed. J. Lull). Sage, London.

Fry, D. L. and Fry, V. H. (1987). Some structural characteristics of music television videos. *The Southern Speech Communication Journal*, **52**, 151–64.

Gardner, M. P. (1985a). Mood states and consumer behavior: a critical review. *Journal of Consumer Research*, **12**, 281–300.

Gardner, M. P. (1985b). Does attitude toward the ad affect brand attitude under a brand evaluation set? *Journal of Marketing Research*, **22**, 192–8.

Gehr, R. (1983). The MTV aesthetic. *Film Comment*, **19**, 37, 39, 40.

Golden, L. L. and Zimmer, M. R. (1986). Relationships between affect, patronage frequency, and amount of money spent with a comment on affect scaling and measurement. *Advances in Consumer Research*, **13**, 53–7.

Gorn, G. J. (1982). The effect of music in advertising on choice behavior: a classical conditioning approach. *Journal of Marketing*, **46**, 94–101.

Greenfield, P. M., Bruzzone, L., Koyamatsu, K., Satuloff, W., Nixon, K., Brodie, M. A. et al. (1987). What is rock music doing to the minds of our youth? A first experimental look at the effects of rock music lyrics and music videos. *Journal of Early Adolescence*, **7**, 315–29.

Gulas, C. S. and Bloch, P. H. (1995). Right under our noses: ambient scent and consumer responses. *Journal of Business and Psychology*, **10**, 87–98.

Hall, J. L., Miller C., and Hanson, J. (1986). Music television: a perceptual study of two age groups. *Popular Music and Society*, **10**, 17–28.

Hecker, S. (1984). Music for advertising effect. *Psychology and Marketing*, **1**, 3–8.

Hesbacher, P., Downing, R., and Berger, D. G. (1978). Sound recording popularity charts: a useful tool for music research. II. Some recommendations for change. *Popular Music and Society*, **6**, 86–99.

Hirsch, P. (1969). *The structure of the popular music industry*. Survey Research Center, University of Michigan, Ann Arbor.

Holbrook, M. B. (1987). What is consumer research? *Journal of Consumer Research*, **14**, 128–32.

Holbrook, M. B. and Batra, R. (1987). Assessing the role of emotions as mediators of consumer responses to advertising. *Journal of Consumer Research*, **14**, 404–20.

Hopkins, J. (1994). Orchestrating an indoor city: ambient noise inside a mega-hall. *Environment and Behavior*, **26**, 785–812.

Hubbard, R. (1994). The dangers of generalising from published marketing studies. *Journal of the Market Research Society*, **36**, 257–60.

Kaplan, E. A. (1987). *Rocking around the clock*. Methuen, New York.

Kellaris, J. J. and Altsech, M. B. (1992). The experience of time as a function of musical loudness and gender of listener. *Advances in Consumer Research*, **19**, 725–9.

Kellaris, J. J. and Cox, A. D. (1989). The effects of background music in advertising: a reassessment. *Journal of Consumer Research*, **16**, 113—18.

Kellaris, J. J., Cox, A. D., and Cox, D. (1993). The effect of background music on ad processing: a contingency explanation. *Journal of Marketing*, **57**, 114–25.

Kellaris, J. J. and Kent, R. J. (1992). The influence of music on consumers' temporal perceptions: does time fly when you're having fun? *Journal of Consumer Psychology*, **1**, 365–76.

Kellaris, J. J. and Mantel, S. P. (1994). The influence of mood and gender on consumers' time perceptions. *Advances in Consumer Research*, **21**, 514–18.

Kellaris, J. J., Mantel, S. P., and Altsech, M. B. (in press). Decibels, disposition, and duration: the impact of musical loudness and internal states on time perceptions. *Advances in Consumer Research*.

Konečni, V. J. (1982). Social interaction and musical preference. In *The psychology of music* (ed. D. Deutsch). Academic Press, New York.

Kotler, P. (1973–74). Atmospherics as a marketing tool. *Journal of Retailing*, **49**, 48–64.

Krishnan, L. and Saxena, N. K. (1984). Perceived time: its relationship with locus of control, filled versus unfilled time intervals, and perceiver's sex. *The Journal of General Psychology*, **110**, 275–81.

Lacher, K. T. (1989). Hedonic consumption: music as a product. *Advances in Consumer Research*, **16**, 367–73.

Lacher, K. T. and Mizerski, R. (1994). An exploratory study of the responses and relationships involved in the evaluation of, and in the intention to purchase new rock music. *Journal of Consumer Research*, **21**, 366–80.

Lehman, H. C. (1953). *Age and achievement*. Princeton University Press, Princeton, New Jersey.

Levin, I. and Zackay, D. (ed.) (1989). *Time and human cognition*. Elsevier Science, North-Holland.

Levy, S. (1983). How MTV sells out rock & roll. *Rolling Stone* (December), 30, 33, 34, 37, 74, 76, 78, 79.

McElrea, H. and Standing, L. (1992). Fast music causes fast drinking. *Perceptual and Motor Skills*, **75**, 362.

MacInnis, D. J. and Park, C. W. (1991). The differential role of characteristics of music on high- and low-involvement consumers' processing of ads. *Journal of Consumer Research*, **18**, 161–73.

MacInnis, D. J., Moorman, C., and Jaworski, B. J. (1991). Enhancing and measuring consumers' motivation, opportunity, and ability to process brand information from ads. *Journal of Marketing*, **55**, 32-53.

McKenna, K. (1983). Videos—low in art, high in sex and sell. *Los Angeles Times Calendar* (August), 66.

McSweeney, F. K. and Bierley, C. (1984). Recent developments in classical conditioning. *Journal of Consumer Research*, **11**, 619–31.

Malhotra, N. K. (1983). A threshold model of store choice. *Journal of Retailing*, **59**, 3–21.

Markin, R. J., Lillis, C. M., and Narayana, C. L. (1976). Social-psychological signific-ance of store space. *Journal of Retailing*, **52**, 43–54.

Matlin, M. W. (1989). *Cognition*. Holt, Rinehart, and Winston, Chicago.

Meenaghan, A. and Turnbull, P. W. (1981). The application of product life cycle theory to popular record marketing. *European Journal of Marketing*, **15**, 1–50.

Mehrabian, A. and Russell, J. A. (1974). *An approach to environmental psychology*. MIT Press, Cambridge, Mass.

Merriam, A. P. (1964). *The anthropology of music*. Northwestern University Press, Evanston, Illinois.

Meyer, L. B. (1967). *Music, the arts, and ideas*. University of Chicago Press, Chicago.

Middlestadt, S. E., Fishbein, M., and Chan, D. K-S. (1994). The effect of music on brand attitudes: affect- or belief-based change? In *Attention, attitude, and affect in response to advertising* (ed. E. M. Clark, T. C. Brook, and D. W. Stewart). Lawrence Erlbaum Associates, Hillsdale, New Jersey.

Milliman, R. E. (1982). Using background music to affect the behavior of supermarket shoppers. *Journal of Marketing*, **46**, 86–91.

Milliman, R. E. (1986). The influence of background music on the behavior of restaurant patrons. *Journal of Consumer Research*, **13**, 286–9.

Miniard, P. W., Bhatla, S., Lord, K. R., Dickson, P. R., and Unnava, H. R. (1991). Picture-based persuasion processes and the moderating role of involvement. *Journal of Consumer Research*, **18**, 92–107.

Mitchell, A. A. (1986). The effect of verbal and visual components of advertisements on brand attitudes and attitude toward the advertisement. *Journal of Consumer Research*, **13**, 12–24.

Mitchell, A. A. and Olson, J. C. (1981). Are product attribute beliefs the only mediator of advertising effects on brand attitude? *Journal of Marketing Research*, **18**, 318–32.

Moore, D. L. and Hutchinson, J. W. (1983). The effects of ad affect on advertising effectiveness. *Advances in Consumer Research*, **10**, 526–31.

Nevin, J. R. and Houston, M. (1980). Images as a component of attractiveness to intra-urban shopping areas. *Journal of Retailing*, **56**, 77–93.

North, A. C. and Hargreaves, D. J. (1996a). Responses to music in a dining area. *Journal of Applied Social Psychology*, **26**, 491–501.

North, A. C. and Hargreaves, D. J. (1996*b*). The effects of music on responses to a dining area. *Journal of Environmental Psychology*, **16**, 55–64.

North, A. C. and Hargreaves, D. J. (1996*c*). Eminence in pop music. *Popular Music and Society*, **20**, 41–46.

North, A. C. and Hargreaves, D. J. (in press, *a*). Liking, arousal potential, and the emotions expressed by music. *Scandinavian Journal of Psychology*.

Oldham, G. R., Cummings, A., Mischel, L. J., Schmidtke, J. M., and Zhou, J. (1995). Listen while you work? Quasi experimental relations between personal-stereo headset use and employee work responses. *Journal of Applied Psychology*, **80**, 547–64.

Olsen, G. D. (1994). The sounds of silence: functions and use of silence in television advertising. *Journal of Advertising Research*, **34**, 89–95.

Ornstein, R. E. (1969). *On the experience of time*. Penguin, New York.

Park, C. W. and Young, S. M. (1986). Consumer response to television commercials: the impact of involvement and background music on brand attitude formation. *Journal of Marketing Research*, **23**, 11–24.

Peterson, R. A. and Berger, D. G. (1975). Cycles in symbol production: the case of popular music. *American Sociological Review*, **40**, 158–73.

Petty, R. E. and Cacioppo, J. T. (1981). *Attitudes and persuasion: classic and contemporary approaches*. William C. Brown, Dubuque, Iowa.

Petty, R. E., Cacioppo, J. T., and Schumann, D. T. (1983). Central and peripheral routes to advertising effectiveness: the moderating effect of involvement. *Journal of Consumer Research*, **10**, 135–46.

Pitt, L. F. and Abratt, R. (1988). Music in advertisements for unmentionable products—a classical conditioning experiment. *International Journal of Advertising*, **7**, 130–7.

Pittman, R. (1985). MTV's lesson: we want what we want when we want immediately. *Ad-week* (May), 34, 36.

Radocy, R. E. and Boyle, J. D. (1988). *Psychological foundations of musical behavior*. Charles C Thomas, Springfield, Illinois.

Ramos, L. V. (1993). The effects of on-hold telephone music on the number of premature disconnections to a statewide protective services abuse hot line. *Journal of Music Therapy*, **30**, 119–29.

Rammsayer, T. and Lustnauer, S. (1989). Sex differences in time perception. *Perceptual and Motor Skills*, **68**, 195–8.

Ratneshwar, S. and Chaiken, S. (1991). Comprehension's role in persuasion: the case of its moderating effect on the persuasive impact of source cues. *Journal of Consumer Research*, **18**, 52-62.

Roballey, T. C., McGreevy, C., Rongo, R. R., Schwantes, M. L., Steger, P. J., Wininger, M. A., and Gardner, E. B. (1985). The effect of music on eating behavior. *Bulletin of the Psychonomic Society*, **23**, 221–2.

Rothenbuhler, E. W. (1985). Programming decision-making in popular music radio. *Communication Research*, **12**, 209–32.

Rothenbuhler, E. W. and McCourt, T. (1992). Commercial radio and popular music: processes of selection and factors of influence. In *Popular music and communication* (2nd edn) (ed. J. Lull). Sage, London.

Sanbonmatsu, D. M. and Kardes, F. R. (1988). The effects of physiological arousal on information processing and persuasion. *Journal of Consumer Research*, **15**, 379–85.

Scott, L. M. (1990). Understanding jingles and needledrop: a rhetorical approach to music in advertising. *Journal of Consumer Research*, **17**, 223–36.

Sherman, B. L. and Dominick, J. R. (1986). Violence and sex in music videos: TV and rock 'n' roll. *Journal of Communication*, **36**, 79–93.

Sherman, B. L. and Etling, L. W. (1991). Perceiving and processing Music Television. In *Responding to the screen: reception and reaction processes* (ed. J. Bryant and D. Zillmann). Lawrence Erlbaum Associates, Hillsdale, New Jersey.

Shimp, T. A., Hyatt, E. M., and Snyder, D. J. (1993). A critique of Darley and Lim's 'alternative perspective'. *Journal of Consumer Research*, **20**, 496–501.

Shimp, T. A., Stuart, E. W., and Engle, R. W. (1991). A program of classical conditioning experiments testing variations in the conditioned stimulus and context. *Journal of Consumer Research*, **18**, 1–12.

Simonton, D. K. (1984). *Genius, creativity and leadership*. Harvard University Press, Cambridge, Mass.

Smith, P. C. and Curnow, R. (1966). 'Arousal hypothesis' and the effects of music on purchasing behavior. *Journal of Applied Psychology*, **50**, 255–6.

Stack, S. and Gundlach, J. (1992). The effect of country music on suicide. *Social Forces*, **71**, 211–18.

Stanley, R. and Sewall, M. (1976). Image inputs to a probabilistic model: predicting retail potential. *Journal of Marketing*, **39**, 48–53.

Stewart, D. W. and Furse, D. H. (1986). *Effective television advertising: a study of 1000 commercials*. Lexington Books, Lexington, Massachusetts.

Stewart, D. W. and Koslow, S. (1989). Executional factors and advertising effectiveness: a replication. *Journal of Advertising*, **18**, 21–32.

Stout, P. A. and Leckenby, J. D. (1988). Let the music play: music as a non-verbal element in television commercials. In *Non-verbal communication in advertising* (ed. S. Hecker and D. W. Stewart). Lexington Books, Lexington, Massachusetts.

Stuart, E. W., Shimp, T. A., and Engle, R. W. (1987). Classical conditioning of consumer attitudes: four experiments in an advertising context. *Journal of Consumer Research*, **14**, 334–49.

Stratton, V. (1992). Influence of music and socializing on perceived stress while waiting. *Perceptual and Motor Skills*, **75**, 334.

Thornton, W. and Voigt, L. (1984). Television and delinquency: a neglected dimension of social control. *Youth and Society*, **15**, 445–68.

Thorson, E., Christ, W. G., and Caywood, C. (1991). Effects of issue-image strategies, attack and support appeals, music, and visual content in political commercials. *Journal of Broadcasting and Electronic Media*, **35**, 465–86.

Tom, G. (1995). Classical conditioning of unattended stimuli. *Psychology and Marketing*, **12**, 79–87.

US Department of Commerce (1992). *US industrial outlook*. Government Printing Office, Washington, DC.

Vincent, R. C., Davis, D. K., and Boruszkowski, L. A. (1987). Sexism on MTV: the portrayal of women in rock videos. *Journalism Quarterly*, **64**, 750–5.

Walker, J. R. (1987). How viewing of MTV relates to exposure to other media violence. *Journalism Quarterly*, **64**, 756–62.

Wansink, B. (1992). Listen to the music: its impact on affect, perceived time passage, and applause. *Advances in Consumer Research*, **19**, 715–18.

Wolfe, A. S. (1983). Rock on cable: on MTV: music television, the first video music channel. *Popular Music and Society*, **9**, 41–50.

Yalch, R. and Spangenberg, E. (1990). Effects of store music on shopping behavior. *Journal of Consumer Marketing*, **7**, 55–63.

Yalch, R. F. and Elmore-Yalch, R. (1984). The effect of numbers on the route to persuasion. *Journal of Consumer Research*, **11**, 522–7.

Zuckerkandl, V. (1956). *Sound and symbol: music and the external world* (trans. W. R. Trask). Pantheon, New York.

Zullow, H. M. (1991). Pessimistic rumination in popular songs and news magazines predict economic recession via decreased consumer optimism and spending. *Journal of Economic Psychology*, **12**, 501–26.

15 | *The social psychology of music education*

Bengt Olsson

INTRODUCTION

Music education takes place within interpersonal and institutional settings, and research in social psychology should be able to contribute to a better understanding of these settings. Social psychology emphasizes the interaction between the social world and the individual, and so a social psychologist's view of music education is likely to focus on the influence that teachers and learners have upon each other's behaviour and attitudes. A number of social psychological factors affect what teachers are able to accomplish and what students might achieve in music education.

This chapter discusses several social psychological theories in relation to music education. One intriguing initial question is why music education research has neglected interpersonal and institutional settings (Bar-Tal and Saxe 1978; Lindgren 1978). A social psychology of music education could alleviate this neglect by considering the processes of teaching and learning, and how the contexts in which these occur give rise to particular social constructions of reality in both teachers and pupils. Despite this potential, it seems that social psychologists have paid little attention to such problems, and the contribution from research in educational psychology is much more evident (Lindgren 1978).

In anthropology, the concept of culture has been viewed as not consisting of behaviours, or even patterns of behaviours, but rather as shared information or knowledge encoded in systems of symbols (Geertz 1973). However, this definition may be inadequate for any attempt to describe the social psychology of music education: the treatment of cultural meaning as purely representational in character is criticized by D'Andrade (1984), and the 'argument is advanced that meaning systems have directive and evocative as well as representational functions' (p. 89). This means that when discussing concepts like 'educational institutions', for example, it is crucial that researchers attempt to validate the *effects* of these on people's behaviour: as we will see later, Roberts' (1993) research on Canadian music education students describes the institution in terms of the 'nature of an insider community', and shows that music education students' 'situational reality' is not only based on their everyday interactions with one another, but also on outsiders' perceptions of the students.

Research on music teaching and learning might therefore deal with social psychological concepts such as attitudes and preferences, motivations, teacher expectations, attributional styles, competencies, identities, and institutions. These concepts will be used in this chapter to explain some key issues in music education, as well as in teacher training. The chapter is divided into three main sections. The first section discusses students' attitudes, preferences, and motivation, and considers how students' responses to music are part of a broader school context. The second section focuses on the teacher's perspective on music education, discussing research on teacher competence; the modification of students' behaviour; and the role of the teacher in the classroom. Finally, research on teacher training is discussed in terms of how the role of 'music teacher' develops through interaction with peers and tutors.

STUDENTS' PREFERENCES AND MOTIVATION

Musical preferences

How do teachers help students to acquire meaning from different musical forms? A common belief among music teachers is that their primary objective is to teach their students to 'love' music, but several issues lie behind this simple question. One of the main contexts for musical development is the school, and Finnäs' (1989) review of research on preference modification draws attention to those variables that have been studied in experimental research which can also be manipulated in a teaching situation. Many of the studies show that it is possible to modify an individual's musical preferences, although not all attempts are successful. Musical preferences are influenced by individual variables such as age, gender, and sociocultural background, as well as by specific characteristics of the music, and the listening situation. Finnäs outlines the following main categories:

(1) factors related to the music itself, particularly those concerning musical complexity and repeated listening;
(2) factors related to various aspects of the teaching methods employed, where the main focus is on how the music is introduced to pupils;
(3) factors related to the individuals being influenced, in particular their sex, personality, musical background, and status as listener or performer;
(4) factors related to the teacher, i.e. personality and musical background, and the relation between these and the pupils' musical culture.

In addition to those variables covered by Finnäs' review, several other features of students' musical taste have been investigated. Sink's (1992) review suggests that research from the 1960s and 1970s largely focused on how instruction could influence musical preferences. However, he suggests that subsequently 'major studies of the 1980s described sociocultural reasons for adolescent music preferences, . . . and relationships among music attitude and achievement variables' (p. 606). A good deal of this research has focused on classical music and has adopted experimental settings that encourage analytic or concentrated listening. In a similar vein, research on gender and youth culture is considering the relationship between intrinsic aspects of the music and students' sociocultural background in determining musical preferences (Roe 1984; Fornäs et al. 1994). Research also suggests that spontaneous experiences of music often include motor and kinaesthetic elements, and given this, it is perhaps surprising that nobody has yet investigated if and how musical preferences are affected by dancing or other forms of spontaneous movement to music (Finnäs 1989).

Students' gender is another variable which has received a great deal of attention in this context, with several studies in Sweden during the last decade (Bjurström 1993; Bjurström and Wennhall 1991; Folkestad and Lindström 1995; Fornäs et al. 1994; Roe 1984). In an investigation carried out in 1990 (Bjurström and Wennhall 1991), 94 per cent of interviewees between 16–25 years of age described themselves as 'very' or 'fairly interested' in music. Approximately 20 per cent of both boys and girls actively played an instrument, but their musical preferences varied. Boys mainly played music of various rock genres with particular interest in heavy metal and punk, in accordance with their listening preferences. Girls were active in choirs and in playing traditional instruments like the piano or the flute, and showed a preference for rock ballads and mainstream music. There was also a clear gender difference in the form of instrumental learning; whereas 71 per cent of the girls took lessons in music schools or privately, only 32 per cent of the boys did so. Instead, the majority of boys (59 per cent) learned to play their instruments on their own or with the help of peers, without participating in any form of organized music training.

These results were supplemented by a further study on pupils aged between 16–19 years in the upper secondary level of the Swedish *Gymnasium* (Bjurström 1993). As in the earlier study, the pupils' musical preferences were most reliably predicted by gender, but their selection of optional study courses also played an important role. These option courses are clearly related to the pupils' career aspirations, and are based on pupils' identification with the status of their proposed career and the cultural preferences associated with this (Roe 1984). Furthermore, the proposed 'social destinations' which are reflected in pupils' option courses might in turn be related to aspects of their general social background. In short, pupils' attitudes towards school, and their intended 'social destination' might constitute a specific means of considering the impact of children's social background on their musical preferences. This approach could be taken by future research on preferences for institutionalized cultural forms like classical music, opera, visual art, and literature.

Such findings emphasize the need for a broader perspective in research on modifying pupils' preferences (Bjurström 1993; Hargreaves 1986). This broader perspective should include the effects of conformity/group pressure; the social functions served by holding particular musical preferences; and a consideration of pupils' socio-economic status and general social background (see Chapters 4, 9, and 8 respectively). For example, there may be a gulf between the teacher's preference for music within the classical repertoire and the pupil's interest in rock music: this potential 'cultural clash' is sometimes explained in terms of conformity and group pressure, with individual pupils adopting their friends' tastes rather than those recommended by the teacher. Similarly, aesthetic reactions to music are partly determined by their social functions, such as commitment to, or disengagement from, school: that is, pupils may use preferences for particular pieces or musical styles as a means of rebelling against, or ingratiating themselves with, music teachers (e.g. punk rock and classical music respectively). Finally, pupils' socio-economic background can provide a useful guide as to how particular musical subcultures will evolve and reflect the values of their members. For example, Gans (1967, 1974) described how particular 'taste publics' have certain sociodemographic traits (e.g. income, religious affiliations), which lead them to prefer some types of cultural content to others (see also Murdock and Phelps 1973). This provides only a partial explanation of why pupils choose certain music or certain cultural activities however, as the rest of this chapter makes clear.

Attributional explanations of success and failure

Motivation in learning music involves more than merely preferences. Abeles *et al.* (1984) mention self-image, conformity, expectations and roles, feelings of competence, cooperation, and creativity as other important aspects of the social psychological foundations of music education. We concentrate here on explaining feelings of competence in terms of attributions of success and failure, and attribution theory provides one approach to this (see review by Thomas 1992). Research in this area involves assessing the attributions students make, that is, the reasons they give to explain why a person does well or poorly in music. In contrast to research on personal traits, in which certain individual characteristics are stressed, the main focus is on the relationships between individuals or between individuals and norms.

It is assumed that the way music education students approach a task will be influenced by whatever factors they attribute to be the causes of success or failure in its completion. In light of this, Asmus (1986) investigated 'the hypothesis . . . that the way persons perceive their own causes of success and failure affects their perceptions of the causes of success and failure in others' (p. 71). The study was based on Weiner's (1974) attribution theory which involves four major causal categories, namely *ability, task difficulty, effort, and luck*. Two of these—ability and effort—are classified as internal, i.e. originating in the person. The other two, the attributions of luck and difficulty, are classified as external because they are assumed to be caused by events outside the individual's control. Moreover, the attributions of ability and task difficulty are classified as stable (i.e. unlikely to change), whereas the attributions of effort and luck are classified as unstable (i.e. changeable). Asmus found that causal attributions in these categories differed between over-achievers and under-achievers: over-achievers felt greater pride in their success than under-achievers, who attributed their failure to a lack of ability and who consequently had low persistence since they saw goals as unattainable. Furthermore, over-achievers prefer tasks of medium difficulty whereas under-achievers prefer either extremely difficult or extremely easy tasks.

Differences in causal attributions have also been associated with various subject characteristics such as gender, self-esteem, and sociocultural status (Bar-Tal 1978). In Asmus' (1986) study, different attribution response patterns were revealed when music education students ascribed success and failure to others rather than to themselves. In general, it seems that students attribute success and failure to others 'as attributable to the internal–unstable category of effort', while their own success and failure was attributed to 'the external–stable category of task difficulty' (p. 81). In his conclusions, Asmus focuses on the need for further research to determine the relationship between music educators' attributional perceptions and those of their students. The teacher in general expects the student to persist until success has been achieved, and then to be proud of the success. Unfortunately, an under-achieving individual may have the opposite tendencies.

THE TEACHER'S PERSPECTIVE

Organizational explanations

My own study of an experimental music education programme during the 1970s (Olsson 1993) emphasized the concept of the 'institution'. In an educational sense, 'institution' involves both a material aspect (i.e. the premises, administrative organization, and economic resources) as well as the normative rules in the curriculum: these include informal, implicit rules regarding attitudes to music and music teaching, and are based on the relations between teachers as well as between teachers and students. Informal, implicit rules constitute the basis for social influence and control, and may indeed be more powerful determinants of behaviour than formal rules. For example, there may be a formal rule that pupils should attend music classes punctually, although this is typically overridden by an informal rule, agreed upon by the teacher and between the pupils, that it is permissible to arrive five minutes late. Berger and Luckmann (1967) stress this informal aspect of control in the institution, and the effect it has on normative standards of musical behaviour and performance.

From the perspective of social psychology, the norms and values within a social context are powerful factors underlying learning processes and the definition of student goals. The 'specialist' versus 'generalist' distinction in music education illustrates this. In the former tradition, talented pupils are given expert tuition, largely on traditional orchestral instruments, and typically reach high levels of achievement within the classical tradition. 'Generalist' music education is based on the premise that music can be performed, composed, and appreciated by all pupils at all levels, such that conventional instrumental skills are not a necessary prerequisite for successful participation. Consequently, the specialist–generalist distinction has different learning outcomes as a result of prevailing norms and values.

Another important aspect of norms and values concerns authority roles. In music educational organizations these roles are played by the teachers. Cady (1992) has listed eight key terms in role analysis, of which 'the actor', 'the role', and 'the position' are particularly useful in clarifying the social psychological significance of music teachers. 'The actor' is the occupant of a prescribed position in a school; 'the role' implies 'the expectations for behaviours by the occupant of a prescribed position in a school system', including those expectations held by the individual who occupies that prescribed position; and 'the position' means the 'actor's location in a social structure' (p. 65). Actors, position, roles, norms, and values form the framework of the teaching process, and their operation is of central interest in the social psychology of music education. In particular, it is possible that these concepts are mediated by the notion of *competence*.

Competence is perhaps the most important feature in defining the relationships between teachers and students (Gardner 1984; Hargreaves 1996; Stefani 1987). Furthermore, it is clearly a multi-faceted concept which can be treated as a matter of skills; of how competence is attributed to another person; of how competencies are achieved through imitation and modelling; or of how competence is valued and experienced in a certain context. Research on different kinds of competencies has been broadened by the consideration of social influence and of norms and values. Verrastro and Leglar (1992) stressed the importance of 'delineating the personal and professional characteristics, or competencies, of a good teacher' (p. 680). In other words, 'competence' should be defined in terms of the normative features of the role that a good teacher must play. One obvious consequence of this is that observable competencies must be identified, and several methods have been used to do this, such as consensual validation by experts.

Taebel and Coker (1980) provide some further evidence on what constitutes normative standards of teacher competence. They developed a preliminary list of competences based on systematic observation of classroom inter-action, and investigated the correlation between teacher competence and pupils' achievements and attitudes. Three competences were emphasized: '(1) the teacher relates his or her lesson objectives to student interests and needs; (2) the student initiates verbal interaction with the teacher; and (3) the student gives correct responses to substantive questions by the teacher' (p. 260). The first competence was the only one that correlated significantly with pupils' achievements and attitudes.

Behaviour modification

Teaching strategies involve modifying pupils' behaviour by several means, principally non-verbal modelling, and vocabulary choice and usage. In stating that such effects can occur it is perhaps worth noting the distinction made by some authors between 'acculturation' and 'training' (Hargreaves 1986; Sloboda 1985). This distinction refers to the environment in which learning takes place, and to the degree to which prescribed aims and object-ives are involved in the learning. Acculturation is spontaneous learning which occurs without conscious effort or direction. Training, on the other hand, is conscious learning, mostly involving a teacher and more or less clearly identified objectives. Whilst musical skills may develop through acculturation and/or training, the verbal and non-verbal behaviour modification techniques discussed here operate strictly on the level of the latter.

Music teachers use language to reward effort, to praise, or to disapprove student behaviours, and this has the obvious effect of shaping the latter. Madsen and Duke (1987) report that music teachers tend to use disapproval more frequently than approval, even though the use of positive reinforce-ment is considered to be more effective in shaping behaviour than is neg-ative reinforcement. Furthermore, although teachers' use of vocabulary centres on the approval/disapproval of pupils, its more general role is emphasized by research on verbal strategies. Tait's (1992) review of the literature indicates that although music teachers talk for significant periods of time, the amount of time spent talking does not always relate directly to the degree of student learning: instead teachers' vocabulary seems to be rather general and non-specific when approving/rewarding students' musical behaviour, and does not always directly reflect specific aspects of it. In other words, students are not always told specifically what they are doing correctly, and this obviously makes it harder for them to know which aspects of their progress are satisfactory. An improvement in the ability to specify those student behaviours which are positive and should be repeated would obviously increase the effectiveness of teachers' verbal feedback (Madsen and Duke 1987).

An alternative to verbal means of behaviour modification is non-verbal modelling (see reviews by Dickey 1992; Tait 1992). In an educational context, this involves the teacher demonstrating desirable behaviours, methods, or techniques, and rewarding the observer for adapting his/her behaviour in line with these. This approach to learning is perhaps most commonly associated with Bandura's (1986) theory of social cognition which states that 'children learn not simply through imitation *per se*, but through complex cognitive processing of the observed behaviors' (Tait 1992, p. 528). Thus, modelling might greatly affect the quality of music teaching and learning and could serve many functions. There are three major areas of modelling in music education, namely *musical* modelling, in which the teacher's performance provides a complete notion of what is desired from the student; *aural* modelling, in which the teacher employs vocalization (e.g. humming) to convey particular meanings or points of emphasis within the music; and *physical* modelling, which involves facial expressions, physical gestures, or formal conducting.

Sang (1987) describes four skills necessary for effective non-verbal modelling: 'The first skill is a teacher's ability to demonstrate basic musical performance behaviours . . . such as tone quality or articulation . . . The second skill is the demonstration of the more subtle aspects of musical performance . . . such as phrasing or vibrato. Third, and closely related to the first two skills, is a teacher's ability to demonstrate a variety of musically-related performance behaviors such as posture, playing position, or embouchure. Finally, a teacher should be able to demonstrate a wide variety of brief melodic and rhythmic sequences on an instrument by ear and also provide a musically correct model' (pp. 3–4).

There seems to be considerable potential for the use of modelling skills in both teaching and conducting, and it has long been advocated by educational reformers such as Pestalozzi, Suzuki, and Kodály. Indeed, this potential is not only limited to teaching and conducting in schools. 'Aural modelling has always been a natural and intrinsic part of jazz, where body language reinforces felt accents, syncopations, phrase beginnings and endings, climaxes, cadence points, dramatic gestures, and dynamic growth and decay' (Tait 1992, p. 529). Professional conductors make considerable use of aural modelling in their rehearsal procedures as well. Indeed, Sang (1987) and Dickey (1992) have argued that modelling is a more effective strategy than verbal description for teaching musical performance, but this raises further issues from the social psychological point of view: for example, how does the interaction between teacher and pupil influence the outcomes of the skills, and how important is the setting (e.g. classroom environment) in which the skills are performed? More generally, the research reported here highlights the need for a better understanding of the factors which govern the exchanges taking place between teachers and pupils.

The teacher's role

Research in primary classrooms views them as places where teachers and pupils bargain with each other to obtain conditions which, as far as possible, satisfy their mutual needs. There is a flow of interaction between teachers and pupils, and between pupils themselves, as well as a need for cooperation to achieve good work and behaviour. Thus, the bargaining between all persons involved in the classroom is based on how well the individuals fulfil their roles. Another way of describing the situation is to look at the different 'risks' involved in the interaction. Hargreaves *et al.* (1989) refer to some observational studies of primary classroom practices (Doyle 1979, 1986; Galton 1987) in discussing how bargaining is related to the ambiguity inherent in many tasks which teachers set in the classroom. 'The more ambiguous the task the higher the risk of failure for pupils and the greater the pupils' attempts to get the teacher to make the task safe either by giving hints about the situation (guided discovery) or by reducing its complexity' (Hargreaves *et al.* 1989, p. 149). The pupils' understanding of the teacher's intention may well be related to their need to comprehend the given task, and so another important teacher competence concerns their ability sometimes to remove risk and ambiguity from the teaching process.

But different teacher roles may be appropriate for different subjects, and in the arts there exists a prevailing ideology that the teacher's role is mainly that of 'facilitator'. This is because the tasks which arts pupils are set tend to be much more open-ended than those prescribed by other subjects. Contrary to the authoritarian teacher role, the facilitator's role involves 'supervision' and 'being a good model' (Olsson 1993), and behind this ideology lies the notion of the 'hidden curriculum', i.e. the existence of implicit rules and values not fully articulated by the teacher. The view of the teacher as facilitator is particularly prominent in the assessment of creative works in the classroom. In the DELTA (Development of Learning and Teaching in the Arts) project (Hargreaves 1989; Hargreaves and Galton 1992), teachers' 'working theories' of their pupils' aesthetic learning were investigated. One very clear finding which emerged from this study was that when teachers were given the opportunity to clarify their ideas and the ambiguities in the language they used to describe children's work, there was substantial agreement about the quality of different pieces of work from different pupils. Also, these assessments seemed to be made in terms of a single evaluative dimension which could be tentatively described as 'positive–negative'. Secondly, and paradoxically, the more explicitly the teachers defined the end product of the work they had initiated, the more rigorous they seemed to be in assessing the quality of the work. Thus, the 'teachers were inclined to give more credit for original ideas which emerged from spontaneous creations than for competent pieces of work which were more constrained, and in which the teacher expectations were more explicit' (Hargreaves and Galton 1992, p. 38).

Hargreaves (1996) proposes a conceptual model of teaching methods in music education which encapsulates many of the issues in this section. The model comprises two orthogonal dimensions, namely 'specialist–generalist' and 'control–autonomy'. The 'control–autonomy' distinction refers 'to the teacher's implicit and explicit structuring of the lesson in terms of day-to-day planning and presentation; the degree to which the content, techniques, and media to be used are specified in advance; and the availability and variety of resources' (p. 149). As described earlier, the 'generalist–specialist' distinction refers to the tradition of the musically-trained specialist music teacher, as distinct from the generalist who has a broad background in various subject areas, only one of which is music. The model associates different pedagogical approaches with each of the four quadrants that result from these orthogonal dimensions. For example, 'It is easy to locate traditional conservatory-based training within the 'specialist–control' quadrant since typical 'classical' conservatory training requires a great deal of detailed, high-level study of a relatively circumscribed repertoire of composed music' (p. 149). Hargreaves argues that music educators such as Paynter (e.g. 1992), Schafer (1965), or Orff (e.g. Orff and Keetman 1958) can be identified with the 'specialist–autonomy' quadrant since they are located within 'serious' specialist institutions, but favour allowing pupils a great deal of creative control. Within the 'generalist–control' quadrant, it is possible to identify a good deal of British teaching of younger pupils: techniques such as group singing take place 'within a fairly constrained framework of conventional tonal music' (p. 150). The 'generalist–autonomy' quadrant is perhaps hardest to describe given its broad, open-ended nature, although Hargreaves suggests that suitable examples may be provided by the aleatory techniques of composers such as John Cage, or the 'scratch orchestra' experiments of Cornelius Cardew: these do not rely on conventional instrumental techniques or a specified repertoire. Although the scheme is still approximate and provisional, it may be able to provide a link between research on teachers' methodologies, training backgrounds, values, and styles.

RESEARCH ON TEACHER TRAINING

Teacher identity

One theoretical approach to research on teacher training is that of 'symbolic interactionism' (Blumer 1969; Roberts 1993) which addresses how individuals assign roles to themselves and others. Theories within this approach address the nature of 'referent others' and the ongoing validity of self-identity, dealing with how people act out roles and develop appropriate codes of behaviour. These codes of behaviour provide frameworks through which people interpret the actions of others, and also select their own 'strategies' or plans of action. For example, music students' behaviour might be interpreted in light of the knowledge that they are aspiring musicians, and perceive themselves as such.

Roberts (1993) has investigated the interaction between Canadian music education students in terms of 'role identities'. How is a role identity as a music teacher achieved, and in what kind of context does this identification take place? Parents, friends, and previous instrumental tutors have given the students support in the work which culminates in their acceptance at the teacher training departments, and this obviously confers a certain identity upon the students. However, once they are accepted for music education courses, they have to reformulate this identity since, according to Roberts, identification with the role of 'musician'/'music teacher' involves a continuous negotiation between the student and the others with whom they come into contact during their course.

It seems that the training institutions assume that the competence of a music teacher in schools requires a high standard of musical skills and knowledge. Consequently, students not only view themselves as musicians, but also wish to be seen as such by others. It is a matter of self-identification, and Roberts describes how the students come to view themselves as musicians by identifying with important normative reference persons and groups. One such important normative reference person is the expert tutor or 'applied instructor': 'Thus the students see the interaction with their applied instructor as very significant in terms of attracting a legitimate claim on the label "musician" and they uniformly report that they "work *for* the applied instructor". This provides an arena where their claim on a "musician" identity can be publicly recognized or legitimated' (Roberts 1993, p. 67). The 'applied instructor' is seen as the person most able to supply support for the student's claim to be a musician. If students perceive that their claims are denied, they may try to get another teacher.

A typical normative reference group is the instrumental group to which the student belongs. Students are usually banded together into like-instrument groups which provide a certain form of limited mutual support.

However, these groups also help their members to develop various 'strategies in pursuit of a negotiated identity'(Roberts 1993). For example, there is competition for the limited number of places in the groups, and to attract status the instrumentalists must compete with one another for the same opportunities. They do this by criticizing others' performances in an attempt to impress their peers, and when performing themselves, they try to stress their own role as a musician.

Group processes also provide a less direct means of conferring identity since music education students perceive themselves as being confined to a close-knit community (Cohen 1985; Olsson 1993). Within this, the students consult their peers and tutors more regularly than do students following other courses (as a result of, for example, having to perform together), and this high level of contact within the group strengthens the identity of individual member as 'musicians'/'music teachers'. Furthermore, people from outside the music education department appear to bolster that identity by labelling the students as 'musicians'. In summary, these studies indicate that the socially constructed concept of the music education student as 'a musician' is validated in the context of many different activities.

The Sämus project

The Sämus project (Olsson 1993), a study of teacher training carried out in the 1970s, demonstrated the importance of a strong identity as 'musician' in guiding educational practice. In this study, new genres, e.g. rock, jazz, and folk music, were introduced into the curriculum. In the objectives of the training programmes there was a strong emphasis on pluralism and creativity. That is, the students were expected to learn to play all kinds of music as well as gaining basic skills in improvisation and composing, and the new genres provided an obvious opportunity for this. However, the open and non-directive framework of the programme was treated in a very traditional way by the participants. The teachers interviewed largely reported that their own teacher training was based on the classical repertoire, and gave them a strong identity as a 'musician'. Seemingly as a consequence of this, the participants in the study based their work within the new genres on the same criteria of aesthetic value as classical music (Olsson 1993, p. 230). The participants' identity as 'musicians' was stronger than the teacher training objectives.

One basic means of achieving a musician's identity seemed to be the typically individualized approach by which instrumental tuition was given to one student at a time during the lesson. The students themselves preferred this kind of tuition for *all* musical styles in spite of the possibilities in the curriculum for alternative approaches, according to the kind of music being taught. One might expect that they would prefer to be taught, for example, rock music by alternative group-based methods, since most popular music involves group-based norms and modes of behaviour which are incompatible with those of the traditional conservatory or university department of music. By emphasizing the individual aspects of tuition in jazz, rock, and folk music skills, and by neglecting their collective and social implications, some types of new musical material were treated in a traditional way, thus enhancing the students' identity as 'musicians'. This demonstrates that the power of institutional practice and individual student identity can effectively rule out methods of tuition which may be much more appropriate for certain genres and styles of performance: pre-existing traditions may be a stronger influence on educational practice than the curriculum itself (see also Brändström and Wiklund 1995).

CONCLUSION

This review of social psychological research on music education has taken a broad perspective. Schools are complex *social* environments in which teaching, learning, and other interactions take place. Perhaps the most important question raised by these studies concerns what kinds of research can be considered to be integral to the social psychology of music education. Some of the studies reviewed here may better be thought of as representing 'social psychology *for* music education', i.e an attempt to use social psychological principles in explaining educational problems:

The basic assumption of this approach is that social behavior that occurs in the classroom can be explained by a set of 'basic' social-psychological principles that do not depend on the context in which the behavior occurs; that is, wherever human beings are, they perceive; have attitudes, motivations, and beliefs or values; and associate in groups. The perspective of social psychology is simply imposed on education. (Bar-Tal and Saxe 1978, p. xii)

This seems to imply that a more sophisticated and specialized form of social psychology might be relevant to music education, and its application is long overdue: music educational problems provide specific and complex issues which should also be of interest to social psychologists. Furthermore, a multidisciplinary approach is clearly desirable, since research in music sociology, music anthropology, and music psychology, as well as aesthetic philosophies of music, can broaden the analytic tools of social psychological research on music education. In short, the social psychology of music education will undoubtedly develop further, and this chapter has demonstrated some of the ways in which research might progress and assist those working in educational contexts.

REFERENCES

Abeles, H., Hoffer, C., and Klotman, R. (1984). *Foundations of music education.* Schirmer Books, New York.

Asmus, E. (1986). Achievement motivation characteristics of music education and music therapy students as identified by attribution theory. *Bulletin of the Council for Research in Music Education,* **86**, 71–85.

Bandura, A. (1986). *Social foundations of thought and action: A social cognitive theory.* Prentice Hall, Englewood Cliffs.

Bar-Tal, D. (1978). Social outcomes of the schooling process and their taxonomy. In *Social psychology of education: Theory and research* (ed. D. Bar-Tal and L. Saxe). Hemisphere Publishing Company, London.

Bar-Tal, D. and Saxe, L. (ed.) (1979). *Social psychology of education: Theory and research.* Hemisphere Publishing Company, London.

Berger, P. and Luckmann, T. (1967). *The social construction of reality: A treatise in the sociology of knowledge.* Allen Lane, London.

Bjurström, E. (1993). *Spelar rocken någon roll? Kulturell reproduktion och ungdomars musiksmak.* Statens Ungdomsråd, Ungdomsrådets utredningar 2, Stockholm.

Bjurström E. and Wennhall J. (1991). Ungdomar och musik, i *Årsbok om ungdom 1991.* Statens Ungdomsråd, Stockholm.

Blumer, H. (1969). *Symbolic interactionism: Perspectives and methods.* Prentice-Hall, Englewood Cliffs, NJ.

Brändström, S. and Wiklund, C. (1995).*Två musikpedagogiska fält. En studie om kommunal musikskola och musiklärarutbildning.* Pedagogiska institutionen, Umeå Universitet, Diss. Umeå.

Cady, H. L. (1992). Sources of theory for research in school music. In *Handbook of research on music teaching and learning* (ed. R. Colwell). Schirmer Books, New York.

Cohen, A. P. (1985). *The symbolic construction of community.* Ellis Horwood Limited Publishers, Chichester.

D'Andrade, R. (1984). Cultural meaning systems. In *Culture theory: Essays on mind, self, and emotion* (ed. R. A. Shweder and R. A. Le Vine). Cambridge University Press, New York.

Dickey, R. (1992). A review of research on modeling in music teaching and learning. *Bulletin of the Council for Research in Music Education,* **113**, 27–40.

Doyle, W. (1979). Classrooms tasks and student abilities. In *Research on teaching: Concepts, findings and implications* (ed. P. Petersen and H. Walberg). McCutchan, Berkeley, California.

Doyle, W. (1986). Classroom organisation and management. In *Handbook of research on teaching* (3rd edn) (ed. M. C. Wittrock). Macmillan, New York.

Finnäs, L. (1989). How can musical preferences be modified? A research review. *Bulletin of the Council for Research in Music Education,* **102**, 1–58.

Folkestad, G. and Lindström, B. (1995). *Gender and experience and attitudes towards computers and technology.* Department of Education and Educational Research, Göteborg University.

Fornäs, J., Boèthius, U., Forsman, M., Ganetz, H., and Reimer, B. (ed.) (1994). *Ungdomskultur i Sverige.* Brutus Östings Bokförlag Symposion AB, Stockholm/Stehag.

Galton, M. (1987). An ORACLE chronicle: a decade of classroom research. *Teaching and Teacher Education,* **3**, 299–313.

Gans, H. J. (1967). Popular culture in America: Social problem in a mass society or social asset in a pluralist society? In *Social problems: a modern approach* (ed. H.S. Becker). Wiley, London.

Gans, H. J. (1974). *Popular culture and high culture.* Basic Books, New York.

Gardner, H. (1984). The development of competence in culturally defined domains. A preliminary framework. In *Culture theory: Essays on mind, self, and emotion* (ed. R. A. Shweder and R. A. Le Vine). Cambridge University Press, New York.

Geertz, C. (1973). *The interpretation of culture.* Basic Books, New York.

Hargreaves, D. J. (1986). *The developmental psychology of music.* Cambridge University Press, Cambridge.

Hargreaves, D. J. (ed.) (1989). *Children and the arts.* Open University Press, Milton Keynes.

Hargreaves, D. J. (1996). The development of artistic and musical competence. In *Musical beginnings: The origins and development of musical competence* (ed. I. deLiege and J. A. Sloboda). Oxford University Press, Oxford.

Hargreaves, D. J. and Galton M. (1992). Aesthetic learning: psychological theory and educational practice. In *N.S.S.E. yearbook on the arts in education* (ed. B. Reimer and R. A. Smith). N.S.S.E., Chicago.

Hargreaves, D. J., Galton, M., and Robinson, S. (1989). Developmental psychology and arts education. In *Children and the arts* (ed. D. J. Hargreaves). Open University Press, Milton Keynes.

Lindgren, H. (1978). Historical perspectives on social psychology of education. In *Social psychology of education: theory and research* (ed. D. Bar-Tal and L. Saxe). Hemisphere Publishing Company, London.

Madsen, C. and Duke, R. (1987). The effect of teacher training on the ability to recognize the need for giving approval for appropriate student behavior. *Bulletin of the Council for Research in Music Education,* **91**, 103–9.

Murdock, G. and Phelps, G. (1973). *Mass media and the secondary school.* Schools Council/Macmillan, London.

Olsson, B. (1993). *Sämus—musikutbildning i kulturpolitikens tjänst? En studie om en musikutbildning på 1970–talet.* Göteborgs Universitet, Musikhögskolan, Diss. Göteborg.

Orff, C. and Keetman, G. (1958). *Orff-Schulwerk music for children* (trans. M. Murray). Schott, London.

Paynter, J. (1992). *Sound and structure.* Cambridge University Press, Cambridge.

Roberts, B. (1993). *I, musician. Towards a model of identity construction and maintenance by music education students as musicians.* Memorial University of Newfoundland.

Roe, K. (1984). *Youth and music in Sweden: Results from a longitudinal study of teenagers' media use.* Mediapanel, report no 32. Lunds Universitet, Sociologiska Institutionen, Lund.

Sang, R. (1987). A study of the relationship between instrumental music teachers' modelling skills and pupil performance behaviors. *Bulletin of the Council for Research in Music Education,* **91**, 155–9.

Schafer, M. R. (1965). *The composer in the classroom.* BMI, Toronto.

Sink, P. (1992). Research on teaching junior high and middle school general music. In *Handbook of research on music teaching and learning* (ed. R. Colwell). Schirmer Books, New York.

Sloboda, J. A. (1985). *The musical mind: The cognitive psychology of music*. Oxford University Press, Oxford.

Stefani, G. (1987). A theory of musical competence. *Semiotica*, **66**, 7–22.

Taebel, D. and Coker, J. (1980. Teaching effectiveness in elementary classroom music: relationships among competency measures, pupil product measures, and certain attribute variables. *Journal of Research in Music Education*, **28**, 250–64.

Tait, M. (1992). Teaching strategies and styles. In *Handbook of research on music teaching and learning* (ed. R. Colwell). Schirmer Books, New York.

Thomas, N. (1992). Motivation. In *Handbook of research on music teaching and learning* (ed. R. Colwell). Schirmer Books, New York.

Verrastro, R. and Leglar, M. (1992). Music teacher education. In *Handbook of research on music teaching and learning* (ed. R. Colwell). Schirmer Books, New York.

Weiner, B. (1974). *Achievement motivation and attribution theory*. General Learning Press, Morristown, NJ.

Name index

Subject index

ability, *see* skill
adolescence 71–3, 161–87
advertising 268–74
aesthetic response, *see* preference
anxiety 33–5, 229–45
applied music psychology 249–305
appropriateness
  in commercial settings 271–75
  and preference 94–7
aptitude, *see* skill
arousal
  and consumer activity 274–5
  and performance 215–16, 233–6
  and personality 27–9
  and preference 75–8, 84–103
attribution theory 293–4
audiences 215–16, 219–20, 222–4

behaviour modification
  in education 296–8
  in music therapy 256–7
  in performance anxiety 239–41

children 40–1, 52–9, 188–203, 291–99;
  see also adolescence
complexity, *see* experimental aesthetics
composers/composition 13–14,
  107–22
conditioning 78–80, 269–71
consumer behaviour 11, 78–80, 132,
  268–89
court music 136–7

delinquency 39–40, 175–83

early research 8–14
education 11–12, 40–1, 150–1, 290–305
eminence 8–11, 113–16, 281–2
emotion, *see* preference
environmental psychology 93–9,
  275–6
ethnic factors 14, 123–40, 147–8
experimental aesthetics 75–8, 84–99,
  107, 111
extraversion 27–9

familiarity 87–90
functions of music, *see* uses of music

gender 35–7, 46–63, 147, 202, 232, 292

historiometry 107–22

identity 39–40, 171–5, 300–2
individual differences, *see* personality, *and*
    preference, demographic influences
institutional influences
  in education 294–7
  in the music industry 87–8, 163–4,
    278–80
instruments 51–7
introversion 27–9

lifestyle, *see* subcultures

massification, *see* taste publics
medicine, *see* therapy
mood, *see* prefrence
MTV, *see* television, music television
music industry, the 87–8, 163–4, 278–80
music psychology 3–5
musical ability, *see* skill

peers 68–73, 115, 152, 171–5, 200, 214–24,
  300–2
performance 13–14, 25–37, 195–7, 209–45
performance anxiety 229–45
personality 25–45, 175–9, 231; *see also*
    gender
practice 192–5; *see also* skill
preference 8–11, 37–40, 68–73, 84–103,
  110–16, 135, 141–58, 161–87, 291–2

radio 87–8, 152–4, 278–80; *see also*
    television
rebellion, *see* delinquency
record buying 87–8, 161, 280–2
religious music 137

The social psychology of
music